In this path-breaking and commanding text, Glynos and Howarth call for and set out a distinctive approach to a reconstruction of social science. Established and emergent traditions of enquiry – naturalism and hermeneutics – are carefully reviewed and critiqued as a vehicle for elaborating the first systematic and sustained application of poststructuralist insights to a critical analysis of the nature of explanation and method. This is an important, challenging book for researchers across the social sciences, including the fields of management and business. It also has wider relevance for anyone who uses social scientific data, or is curious about how a 'science' of the social might be possible.

Hugh Willmott
Professor in Organizational Studies,
University of Cardiff, UK

This edifying book is a tremendous accomplishment, offering a fresh look at both epistemology (what counts as knowledge) and ontology (our underlying presuppositions about the way the world goes round). But more than that, this book raises poststructuralist discourse theory to a new level of intellectual prestige. The raw material for a coherent poststructuralist discourse theory has been available for some time. And now, thanks to David Howarth and Jason Glynos, the wide ranging poststructuralist literature has been deployed to redescribe social science research as problematization and articulation – a context-sensitive research protocol that challenges positivism's universalizing causal laws, which have inappropriately colonized the social sciences. This is careful yet imaginative scholarship, worthy of widespread attention across the social sciences.

Hugh T. Miller
Professor of Public Administration
Florida Atlantic University, USA

This is one of those exceedingly rare books which is both philosophically astute as well as of considerable practical use. It breaks new, creative ground concerning age-old issues in political theory and the philosophy of the social sciences. At the same time, it offers to the political analyst valuable heuristic strategies for engaging in critical empirical inquiry.

Henk Wagenaar
Professor of Public Policy
University of Leiden, Amsterdam

Beginning with a much-needed critique of scientism and the current state of affairs in the social and political sciences, Glynos and Howarth develop an original, sophisticated and rigorous account of discourse theory. Using the guiding idea of 'logics of critical explanation', Glynos and Howarth propose nothing less than a new ontology for social and political theory. This is excellent work that should be debated and discussed in the years to come.

Simon Critchley
Professor of Philosophy
New School for Social Research, USA

Logics of Critical Explanation in Social and Political Theory

The Social Science Wars have precipitated a renewed interest in the character, purpose and methods of social science. Positivists and naturalists are criticized by interpretivists and critical theorists, while quantitative researchers are challenged by those who favour qualitative and ethnographic techniques. In turn, mainstream social scientists have responded with a vigorous defence and restatement of their commitments.

Logics of Critical Explanation in Social and Political Theory proposes a novel approach to practising social and political analysis based on the role of logics. The authors articulate a distinctive perspective on social science explanation that avoids the problems of scientism and subjectivism by steering a careful course between law-like explanations and thick descriptions. Drawing upon hermeneutics, poststructuralism, psychoanalysis, and post-analytical philosophy, this new approach offers a particular set of logics – social, political, and fantasmatic – with which to construct critical explanations of practices and regimes.

While the first part of the book critically engages with law-like, interpretivist and causal approaches to critical explanation, the second part elaborates an alternative grammar of concepts informed by an ontological stance rooted in poststructuralist theory. In developing this approach, a number of empirical cases are included to illustrate its basic concepts and logics, ranging from the apartheid regime in South Africa to recent changes in higher education.

The book will be a valuable tool for scholars and researchers in a variety of related fields of study in the social sciences, especially the disciplines of political science and political theory, international relations, social theory, cultural studies, anthropology and philosophy.

Jason Glynos is a Lecturer in Political Theory in the Department of Government at the University of Essex, UK. He is also Director of the Masters Programme in Ideology and Discourse Analysis at the University of Essex.

David Howarth is a Senior Lecturer in Political Theory in the Department of Government at the University of Essex, UK. He is also Co-Director of the Centre for Theoretical Studies and Director of the Masters Programme in Political Theory at the University of Essex.

Routledge Innovations in Political Theory

1 **A Radical Green Political Theory**
Alan Carter

2 **Rational Woman**
A feminist critique of dualism
Raia Prokhovnik

3 **Rethinking State Theory**
Mark J. Smith

4 **Gramsci and Contemporary Politics**
Beyond pessimism of the intellect
Anne Showstack Sassoon

5 **Post-Ecologist Politics**
Social theory and the abdication of the ecologist paradigm
Ingolfur Blühdorn

6 **Ecological Relations**
Susan Board

7 **The Political Theory of Global Citizenship**
April Carter

8 **Democracy and National Pluralism**
Edited by Ferran Requejo

9 **Civil Society and Democratic Theory**
Alternative voices
Gideon Baker

10 **Ethics and Politics in Contemporary Theory**
Between critical theory and post-marxism
Mark Devenney

11 **Citizenship and Identity**
Towards a new republic
John Schwarzmantel

12 **Multiculturalism, Identity and Rights**
Edited by Bruce Haddock and Peter Sutch

13 **Political Theory of Global Justice**
A cosmopolitan case for the World State
Luis Cabrera

14 **Democracy, Nationalism and Multiculturalism**
Edited by Ramón Maiz and Ferrán Requejo

15 **Political Reconciliation**
Andrew Schaap

16 National Cultural
   Autonomy and
   Its Contemporary Critics
   Edited by Ephraim Nimni

17 Power and Politics in
   Poststructuralist Thought
   New theories of the political
   Saul Newman

18 Capabilities Equality
   Basic issues and problems
   Edited by Alexander Kaufman

19 Morality and Nationalism
   Catherine Frost

20 Principles and Political
   Order
   The challenge of diversity
   *Edited by Bruce Haddock,
   Peri Roberts and Peter Sutch*

21 European Integration and the
   Nationalities Question
   *Edited by John McGarry and
   Michael Keating*

22 Deliberation, Social Choice
   and Absolutist Democracy
   David van Mill

23 Sexual Justice/Cultural
   Justice
   Critical perspectives in political
   theory and practice
   *Edited by Barbara Arneil,
   Monique Deveaux, Rita Dhamoon
   and Avigail Eisenberg*

24 The International Political
   Thought of Carl Schmitt
   Terror, liberal war and
   the crisis of global order
   *Edited by Louiza Odysseos and
   Fabio Petito*

25 In Defense of Human Rights
   A non-religious grounding in a
   pluralistic world
   Ari Kohen

26 Logics of Critical Explanation
   in Social and Political Theory
   Jason Glynos and David Howarth

Logics of Critical Explanation in Social and Political Theory

Jason Glynos and David Howarth

Routledge
Taylor & Francis Group

LONDON AND NEW YORK

First published 2007
by Routledge
2 Park Square, Milton Park, Abingdon, Oxon OX14 4RN

Simultaneously published in the USA and Canada
by Routledge
270 Madison Ave, New York, NY 10016

*Routledge is an imprint of the Taylor & Francis Group,
an informa business*

Transferred to Digital Printing 2007

© 2007 Jason Glynos and David Howarth

Typeset in Garamond by
Newgen Imaging Systems (P) Ltd, Chennai, India

British Library Cataloguing in Publication Data
A catalogue record for this book is available
from the British Library

Library of Congress Cataloging in Publication Data
A catalog record for this book has been requested

ISBN10: 0–415–40428–2 (hbk)
ISBN10: 0–203–93475–X (ebk)
ISBN10: 0–415–46212–6 (pbk)

ISBN13: 978–0–415–40428–0 (hbk)
ISBN13: 978–0–203–93475–3 (ebk)
ISBN13: 978–0–415–46212–9 (pbk)

Contents

Acknowledgements   xi

Introduction   1

1   Retroduction   18

2   Contextualized self-interpretations   49

3   Causal mechanisms   83

4   Ontology   103

5   Logics   133

6   Articulation   165

    Conclusion   209

    Notes   216
    Bibliography   237
    Index   253

Acknowledgements

As Michel Foucault often noted, writing a book is best practised as an intellectual adventure, whose final destination and ultimate outcome can never be guaranteed. It involves intellectual collaboration, a fair bit of financial and emotional support, not to mention the good graces of *Fortuna*. In all these respects, this book is no exception.

First, and foremost, it is the result of an intense intellectual collaboration between the two authors, an intensity that was noted with some curiosity, and perhaps not a little amusement, by administrators and staff in the Literature and Film Studies Department at the University of Essex, whose reading room we often colonized when trying to render our often inchoate thoughts a little more coherent. The arguments that have emerged from this collaboration reflect our ongoing engagement with different theoretical traditions, as well as different approaches and methods in social science and political analysis, which we have been teaching, researching, and discussing since our appointment to the Department of Government several years ago.

In particular, our ideas have been powerfully shaped by our respective encounters in the Ideology and Discourse Analysis (IDA) Programme in the Department of Government, also known as the Essex School in Discourse Theory. The IDA programme was established by Ernesto Laclau shortly after the publication of *Hegemony and Socialist Strategy* in 1985 (Laclau and Mouffe, 1985). Ernesto has been a constant source of inspiration and support for the ideas and arguments developed in this book. In equal fashion, the ideas put forward here also bear the strong imprint of other core members of this research programme, especially Aletta Norval and Yannis Stavrakakis. In this context, we should also mention Lasse Thomassen and Jacob Torfing, from whom we received much encouragement for our project, and who also read several drafts of individual chapters and even versions of entire manuscripts.

Many of those in the programme with whom we have discussed the issues explored in this book, and from whom we have profited, are now academics teaching and researching in universities and institutes across the globe. We have benefited from their input partly as a result of the recently established Ideology and Discourse Analysis World Network (IDA World), whose aim is to facilitate the exchange of ideas on the topic of IDA through the internet, as well as through conferences and annual workshops. In this context, we have benefited from the feedback of Sebastian Barros, Mercedes Barros, Mark Devenney, Torben Dyrberg, Alex Groppo, Alan Hansen, Juan-Pablo Lichtmeyer, Oliver Marchart, Emilia Palonen, Carlos Pessoa, Anna Schrober, Rei Shigeno, and Rosa Nidia Buenfil.

Earlier drafts also enjoyed the discerning gaze of members of the political theory group at Essex over the course of the last few years. These include Sheldon Leader, Albert Weale, and Richard Bellamy. Others here at Essex and far beyond have also offered us helpful feedback in the context of numerous conferences, workshops, and summer schools around the world, including Steven Griggs, Sean Nixon, Mike Roper, Eva Sorenson, Tamara Metze, Margo van den Brink, Peter Kitchenman, and Todd Bridgman. Their comments have been most useful in helping us to express our arguments in a clearer fashion.

Three institutions in particular have provided the main arenas for many of the collaborations and encounters mentioned thus far: the Doctoral Research Programme in IDA, the Centre for Theoretical Studies, and the Department of Government, all at the University of Essex. The flourishing Doctoral Research Programme has provided an outstanding context within which to discuss theoretical, methodological, and empirical research. Our book has drawn inspiration from, and has been motivated in part by, our individual and collective interactions with our Masters and PhD students over the last five years or so, too numerous to name in person, but no less important for that. But our book was also discussed in detail over many PhD seminars during the course of the last academic year, each chapter benefiting considerably from this public exposure and perceptive critique. These encounters embodied for us genuine collective research at its best, helping us to shape our thoughts into a more robust final product. Our special thanks in this regard go to those who attended this seminar series, comprising both IDA PhD students and visiting PhD students: Pete Bloom, Ryan Brading, Carl Cederstrom, Sam Dallyn, Erdem Damar, Peter Edwards, Jonathan Dean, Laura Glanc, Steve Gormley, Jenny Gunnarsson-Payne, Cengiz Gunes, Sarah Hartley, Christos Iliadis, Leonidas Karakatsanis, Stefan Milizer, David Payne, Isis Sanchez, and Wei Yan Chang.

In our experience, the University of Essex has always been at the centre of passionate intellectual engagement and discussion, and the Centre for Theoretical Studies has added its not inconsiderable weight and resource to this flourishing intellectual environment. Not only has it served to connect different sorts of critical theorizing within the university, but it has also enabled us to witness and participate in some of the leading intellectual debates and conversations in the contemporary human and social sciences, many of which have shaped the writing of this book. In this regard, Slavoj Žižek's long association with the Centre and the IDA programme has been a source of much intellectual nourishment. Of equal import, from our point of view, have been the debates between poststructuralists and post-Marxists on the one hand, and critical realists on the other. In addition, as graduate students and lecturers, we have been fortunate to attend lectures and mini-courses by the likes of Bill Connolly, Jacques Derrida, Hubert Dreyfus, Stephen Mulhall, James Tully, Rudi Visker, and Hugh Willmott, and traces of their work will no doubt be discerned in our book.

The Department of Government at the University of Essex continues to provide a demanding and rigorous institutional context in which to converse and debate politics and political analysis. In addition to those we have already mentioned, we are grateful to David Sanders and Carole Parmenter for their supportive stewardship of the department. We are also grateful for the constant encouragement and friendly criticism of our colleagues John Bartle and Joe Foweraker, as well as Todd Landman, who engaged us in debates about method from a very early stage. Finally, the Essex Discourse Theory Summer School, which is hosted by the Department of Government, has provided us with the opportunity to develop some of the ideas presented in this book. In particular, we would like to thank Elinor Scarborough and Eric Tanenbaum for encouraging this approach to social and political analysis in the Summer School as a whole, as well as the many students who participated in these courses and seminars for their interesting questions and views.

Lastly, but certainly not least, we would like to thank Jackie Pells for her efficient and cheerful administrative support in helping us to complete this manuscript. In this regard, too, we would like to thank Heidi Bagtazo, Harriet Brinton, and Amelia McLaurin at Routledge for their patience, expertise, and goodwill in overseeing the publication of this book. Thanks finally to the anonymous reviewers of our original manuscript.

It is clear that our book is deeply indebted to the many people who have inspired and critically engaged with us, as well as to the University of Essex, which has provided much more than one would expect from a campus university in the northeast Essex countryside. But, of course, the real debt is to our families, who have supported us through thick and thin. We thus dedicate this book to our families: Anita, Michael, Byron, Jes, Jordan, Carter, Moe, Ivan, Eric, and Lorraine; and Aletta and James.

Colchester, 9 March 2007

Introduction

> In the final analysis we are not confronted with exclusive choices: *either* empirical theory *or* interpretative theory *or* critical theory. Rather, there is an internal dialectic in the restructuring of social and political theory. When we work through any of these moments, we discover how the others are implicated. An adequate social and political theory must be *empirical*, *interpretative*, and *critical*.
>
> (Bernstein 1976: 235)

More than thirty years has now passed since Richard Bernstein wrote these concluding words to *The Restructuring of Social and Political Theory*. Having criticized the then – and still – dominant view that social and political theorists ought to distinguish and then choose between explanation, interpretation and critique, he optimistically advocates their dialectical integration for any theoretical approach worth its salt. In the meantime, the contours of our intellectual landscapes in the social sciences, not to mention the political and cultural landscapes, have changed considerably. The fashionable interest in Marxism, linguistic philosophy, existentialism, and the Frankfurt school of critical theory, has given way to discussions about postmodernism, critical realism, interpretivism, poststructuralism, deconstruction, post-colonialism, and so forth.

But one thing *has* remained constant during this period, and that is the extraordinary resilience of positivism in social and political studies, whose protagonists desire a fully-fledged scientific study of politics and society.[1] Indeed, though one may point to important challenges facing this onward march of 'positive theory', its overall trajectory and momentum appear difficult to check. For instance, while the emergence of the 'perestroika movement' in political science,[2] coupled with a renewed interest in various interpretive approaches, are welcome interventions in the field of political analysis, it is important to ensure that they represent more than just a momentary backlash that would only confirm the marginalization of critical and interpretive approaches.

An underlying assumption of this book is that unless this unilateral forward march is checked, Bernstein's hope for an integrated social and political theory, which does not have to choose between explanation, interpretation and critique, will remain an empty dream. For this reason, we seek to *reactivate* a crisis in the social sciences. Here, we allude to Edmund Husserl's diagnosis of 'a crisis of the European sciences' in the 1930s, in which the founder of transcendental phenomenology felt his entire intellectual project threatened by a growing philosophical naiveté that was crystallized either in an unreflective objectivism and narrow-minded positivism, or a relapse into forms of irrationalism and subjectivism (see Husserl 1965: 179–85).

Talk of a crisis in the social sciences, especially in the fields of social and political analysis, is perhaps an exaggeration, or even a cliché. Nevertheless, the demands for greater methodological pluralism emanating from certain quarters of the American Political Science Association, renewed debates about the character and purpose of social and political analysis in Britain and the rest of Europe, the growth of new or revamped approaches to social science research (e.g. feminism, discourse analysis, psychoanalysis, critical realism, hermeneutics, critical theory, deconstruction, and so forth), together with criticisms about the inadequacies of the social sciences in elucidating and explaining, let alone predicting, important changes in our rapidly changing world, attest to a growing unease about the methods, purposes and ideals of social science.[3]

Scientism and beyond

One way to conceptualize this emergent disquiet is to highlight the increasing *scientism* of the dominant approaches and methods of social and political theory. To use Habermas's prescient formulation, this disquiet is focused on the widespread 'conviction that we can no longer understand science as *one* form of knowledge, but rather must identify knowledge with science' (Habermas 1978: 4). For us, the chief problem with this underlying disposition in social and political analysis is the pre-dominance of an elusive and unattainable ideal: a science of politics and society – at least one modelled on a particular conception of natural science. This ideal, which stretches back at least to Hobbes, has not only proved difficult to realize in the form of laws and reliable empirical generalizations (whether causal or correlational), but it has skewed the overall purposes of the social sciences, separating positive science from questions of critique and evaluation.

The dream of those who want a science of politics in the modern period comprises, among other things, the discovery of a set of laws or robust empirical generalizations that approximate those found in the natural sciences, which would allow political scientists, as well as policymakers, administrators and practitioners, to explain and predict relevant political events and practices. Michel's 'iron law of oligarchy' and 'Duverger's law' lent early hope to the belief that the behaviour of political parties, voters, groups and policy-makers, not to mention the effects of electoral systems and other political institutions on political activity, could all be drawn under the sway of a purely positive theory. Over the course of the twentieth century this dream has had many incarnations, beginning with the development of political science in the United States at the start of the century, followed by the behaviouralist and post-behaviouralist revolutions of the post-war period, and the growth of formal approaches, principally in the guise of rational choice and game-theoretical accounts of political science.[4] Each, however, has been predicated on laying the solid foundation of a positive science and thus ending philosophical debate about the contested status of social and political science.

What is problematic with this vision is not just an empirical deficiency that centres on the paucity of actual laws or weaknesses in predictive capabilities, but also the way in which this vision is underscored by an ontological deficiency that raises profound doubts about the very desirability of positive theory. To develop this claim, we focus initially on the problem of prediction and its constitutive connection to the law-like model of social science explanation. Of course, the notion of prediction has acquired numerous connotations. Often it is linked to the task of forecasting events and processes, whether they are elections or economic cycles. At other times, it is equated with the making of 'informed conjectures' about the possible trends or outcomes of social and political processes. In order to clarify the way we propose to use the concept of prediction in our book, we can appeal to Derek Sayer's helpful distinction between prognosis and prediction. While *prognosis* refers to 'the likely course of future events which, although well-grounded in our analysis of the conditions and mechanisms underpinning present phenomena, cannot be generated out of this analysis by simple deduction', *prediction* is understood as 'a deduction of what will necessarily follow if (1) certain laws, L1 ... n, themselves deducible from the theory, T, obtain, and (2) requisite antecedent conditions, C1 ... n, are satisfied' (Sayer 1983: 139). In our book we focus mainly on the way prediction in this latter sense is deployed in relation to processes of theory-formation and theory-testing, and thus in relation to the explanatory capacity of scientific theories.

It is therefore clear that a key motivating factor of our book concerns the spectre of scientism, especially its current positivist incarnation, which is evident in the paradigmatic status accorded to causal laws. But naturally our general dissatisfaction with the causal law paradigm also leads us to consider the alternatives. In fact, two leading responses to the inadequacies of the law-like model are considered: those that stress the role of contextualized self-interpretations and those that emphasize the role of causal mechanisms. With the term 'contextualized self-interpretation' we gather together a set of hermeneutical theories which explicitly and directly question the compatibility of the natural and social sciences, and which offer an alternative ontological framework in which to embed their accounts of the social and political worlds. In this approach, thick descriptions of individual and collective meanings, beliefs, and traditions are opposed to the search for law-like explanations of social phenomena.

But the critiques of the causal law paradigm are not confined to hermeneutical positions. On the contrary, those who favour the use of causal mechanisms to explain social phenomena are also sceptical of any attempt to make causal laws and prediction constitutive of social science explanation.[5] Thus, in Elster's words, the use of mechanisms can sometimes help us to 'explain without being able to predict, and sometimes predict without being able to explain'. But while many scientific theories enable us to do both, this is the 'exception rather than the rule' in the social sciences (Elster 1989: 8). This view has been more strongly expressed by critical realists like Roy Bhaskar, who feel that 'the appraisal and development of theories in the social sciences *cannot be predictive* and so must be *exclusively explanatory*' (Bhaskar 1998: 21).

These two sorts of critique of the causal law paradigm are helpful in exposing difficulties in the dominant paradigm, but they are not themselves without difficulty. Advocates of causal mechanisms err on the side of abstracting mechanisms from the historical contexts in which they function, thus reifying them in a way that constrains their contingency and militates against their full contextualization. In this approach, the universalism of the causal law ideal still exerts a powerful attraction. Proponents of contextualized self-interpretations, by contrast, run the risk of simply extolling the virtues of historical context and concrete particularity, thus precluding the development of critical explanations that can somehow transcend the particularity of a given situation, both in terms of accounting for practices and in providing an immanent critical vantage-point for their evaluation and political engagement.

In sum, the dilemmas that arise from our initial problematization of the dominant approaches to social and political analysis can be expressed in the form of two questions. Can we develop an approach that respects the self-interpretations of social actors, while not reducing explanations to their subjective viewpoints alone? Is it possible to have a type of explanation that admits of a certain generality, provides the space for critique, and yet respects the specificity of the case under investigation? In responding to these perennial questions, which we do in the affirmative, it is necessary to develop an approach to explanation that satisfies certain valid insights of hermeneutics and naturalism, but which does not retreat back to a purely subsumptive or ideographic account of social and political phenomena. For this purpose, we develop the notion of logics, counter-posing them not simply to causal laws but also to causal mechanisms and contextualized self-interpretations. In so doing, we draw upon the poststructuralist tradition of thought in a way that addresses the diremptions brought about by the positivist hegemony in contemporary social science. Even so, it is worth noting that some of the problems we seek to address in this book reside closer to home: that is to say, in the very tradition from which we speak.

Two dilemmas of poststructuralist discourse theory

Over the last twenty years or so, proponents of poststructuralism have made important advances in developing an alternative ontological standpoint with which to critically explain a range of phenomena. More specifically, in the field of social and political analysis, they have begun to furnish the theoretical means to conceptualize the character and transformation of social structures, and to clarify the relationship between social structures, political agency and power. They have also endeavoured to provide the conceptual resources with which to explore the political constitution and dissolution of social identities, while striving to account for the dynamics of human subjectivity. And finally they have sought to move us beyond the simple critique and deconstruction of texts, practices and institutions to offer an alternative conception of ethics for the critical evaluation of political and moral norms and structures.

Discourse theorists working within the poststructuralist tradition of thought – and this book is firmly situated within this subset of poststructuralist theory – focus their attention on the reproduction and transformation of hegemonic orders and practices.[6] They develop the theoretical means to account for the ways in which subjects are gripped by certain ideologies or discourses (even if the latter are not necessarily in their interests, or indeed consistent with their beliefs), while also seeking to account for the different ways in which dominant orders are contested by counter-hegemonic or other resistance projects, where the latter involve the construction of new identities. Of central importance in this regard is an insistence on 'the primacy of politics' to explain and critically engage with a range of social phenomena. In short, discourse theorists have developed – and are continuing to develop and refine – the conceptual grammars with which to account for the way certain political projects or social practices remain or become hegemonic.[7]

In more concrete terms, empirical research has been conducted across a broad range of connected areas. The sheer range and diversity of these studies in widely varying historical and geographical contexts cannot be enumerated here. Confining ourselves to the fields of social and political theory, we note how there have been path-breaking studies of the relationships between states, as well as the latter's interaction with a range of other social actors and forces operating on the international stage.[8] Research has also focussed on the investigation of social and political struggles within states and organizations at different levels of governance, not to mention the exploration of marginal-ized identities, protest movements and the dynamics of public policy making and implementation at a national and local level in a range of historical contexts.[9] Attention has also been paid to the uneven logics of globalization, as well as to the role of the media in shaping discourses, language, and identities.[10]

Nevertheless, despite these theoretical and empirical advances, there are many who remain strongly critical or deeply sceptical about this tradition of research. From the outset, theorists such as W.G. Runciman doubted the very existence of structuralism, never mind the more exotic discourse of post-structuralism, while as early as 1987 Anthony Giddens boldly declared both to be 'dead traditions of thought', even though many of the more significant poststructuralist contributions to social and political theory had yet to be made (Giddens 1987: 195; Runciman 1970).[11] Indeed, it is common for Marxists, positivists, critical realists and interpretivists, who agree about precious little else, to forge a common front in dismissing the pretensions of structuralists and poststructuralists as protagonists of a fashionable form of linguistic idealism that is committed to nothing more than the 'free play of signifiers' (Dreyfus and Rabinow 1982: 125).

However, even some who identify themselves as poststructuralist discourse theorists, or are at least strongly sympathetic to its basic assumptions and concepts, have raised important queries about the approach. Two such criticisms – that we shall name the *methodological* and *normative deficits* respectively – are especially pertinent to the arguments put forward in this book. We need therefore to say a few words about the way we understand these terms; the precise import of the allegations that have been made; and how we propose to respond to these concerns.

The charge of a methodological deficit is raised in Jacob Torfing's appraisal of the current state of discourse theory, where he suggests among other things that discourse theorists '*must critically reflect upon the questions of method and research strategy*' (Torfing 2005: 25). Here, however, it is important to stress that the notion of a methodological deficit that underlies this challenge, as well as the tasks it engenders, must be construed in the widest possible sense of the term. To put it more precisely, following in the spirit of Marx, Weber and Durkheim, while questions of method ought not to neglect the problems that arise from the collection, analysis and status of empirical data, they most definitely ought to focus on the *full* range of theoretical issues that arise in the social sciences from the activities of describing, explaining, evaluating and criticizing.

The upshot of this from our point of view is that methodological questions necessarily touch upon the ontological and epistemological dimensions of any social inquiry, as well as the specific techniques of data gathering and analysis pertinent to a particular concrete case. This means that our response to this methodological challenge must take up the full range of philosophical and theoretical issues it necessarily implies. Indeed, as there are very few texts in the poststructuralist tradition that tackle the question of method and the nature of explanation in a sustained and philosophical way, we see our book as helping to fill this gap.

If allegations of a methodological deficit question the ability of poststructuralist discourse theory to explain and interpret, then the notion of a normative deficit touches upon the issue of critique. This is neatly captured by Simon Critchley's assessment of Ernesto Laclau's theory of hegemony, in which he questions the capacity of poststructuralist discourse theory to evaluate and transcend the existing order of things in the name of something new. As he puts it

> If the theory of hegemony is simply the description of a positively existing state of affairs, then one risks emptying it of any critical function, that is, of leaving open any space between things as they are and things as they

may otherwise be. If the theory of hegemony is the description of a factual state of affairs, then it risks identification and complicity with the dislocatory logic of contemporary capitalist societies ... The problem with Laclau's discourse is that he makes noises of both sorts, both descriptive and normative, without sufficiently clarifying what it is that he is doing. This is what I mean by suggesting that there is the risk of a kind of normative deficit in the theory of hegemony.

(Critchley 2004: 117)

Critchley's critical comments epitomize a number of concerns raised about the normative orientation and content of poststructuralism in general, and discourse theory in particular.[12] To express it more fully, if claims of a methodological deficit raise questions about the explanatory capacity of poststructuralist theory, then allegations of a normative deficit highlight difficulties about the critical and reconstructive capacity of poststructuralist theory. In short, does poststructuralism – and discourse theory in particular – embody a new form of descriptivism or theoreticism? Again, our book develops a set of middle-range categories that enable us to locate more precisely the place and role of normative and ethical critique in poststructuralist discourse theory.

In general, in responding to the methodological and critical challenges outlined, it is important to stress that we avoid a number of possible though ultimately unsatisfactory solutions. On the one hand, we resist the temptation to offer a 'method' or 'technique-driven' solution to the alleged methodological deficits, as this would blind us to the fact that any set of methods or techniques is always relative to, and thus grounded upon, a particular ontological stance (even if the latter is only implicitly evident in a series of research practices or instruments).

On the other hand, we reject solutions that would involve a retreat into a type of relativism or subjectivism where 'anything goes', because this response would place no methodological constraint on the production and assessment of putative explanations and critical evaluations. On the contrary, the whole point of our book is to develop an ontological stance and a grammar of concepts, together with a particular research ethos, which makes it possible to construct and furnish answers to empirical problems that can withstand charges of methodological arbitrariness, historical particularism, and idealism. Indeed, in seeking to render our views on method more explicit, we hope to provide the means to evaluate our approach and the studies it informs.

Finally, we reject the option of developing a comprehensive normative framework, whether it takes the form of setting out the underlying principles of social justice that ought to shape the basic structure of our institutional arrangements, or whether it is predicated on articulating the fundamental communicative and procedural pre-conditions for reaching a rational consensus about common moral and political norms. As thinkers such as Connolly, Derrida and Foucault have rightly insisted, the lure of elaborating a fully-fledged normative schema with which to evaluate and prescribe policies and practices runs the risk of failing to engage with the singular instances of power, domination and oppression that require careful empirical analysis, ethical critique and political intervention. And yet we hope to show where and how normative and ethical considerations can and ought to be brought to bear in conducting concrete empirical research.

Logics of critical explanation

As is evident from the title of our book, our response to the challenges levelled at positivism, hermeneutics, naturalism, and poststructuralism is to elaborate an approach to social and political analysis that is captured by the expression 'logics of critical explanation'.[13] By *logics* of critical explanation, we refer to three senses of the term, each of which helps to flesh out our approach in more detail. In descending order of generality, the notion first picks out the ways in which processes of theory construction and explanation are understood, involving very general considerations about problem construction, the selection of theoretical concepts, modes of reasoning in the sciences, whether inductive, deductive or retroductive, and so on. Second, the concept refers to a particular approach or 'style of reasoning' in the social sciences (Hacking 1985), comprising the grammar of assumptions and concepts that informs a particular approach to the social world: a way of formulating problems, addressing them, and then evaluating the answers that have been produced. For example, in developing our own approach we focus on positivist, hermeneutical, critical realist, and poststructuralist styles of theorizing. Finally, the concept is understood in a more substantive sense to constitute the basic unit of explanation of our approach; logics in this sense contrast with laws, self-interpretations, and mechanisms. Working within the field of poststructuralism, our central aim in this regard is to construct an explanatory logic, together with the grammar of concepts and assumptions that serve as its conditions of possibility, and to articulate a typology of basic logics – social, political and fantasmatic – which can serve to characterize, explain and criticize social phenomena.

The terms *critical* and *explanation* in 'logics of critical explanation' are more often than not separated out in contemporary and modern conceptions of philosophy and (social) science. Kant's critical project drew a sharp line between theoretical and practical reason – between the domains of knowledge and morality – and positivists have widened the division between questions of fact and explanation on the one hand, and questions of critique and normative evaluation on the other, by emphasizing the value neutrality of social scientific inquiry. Weber also championed the cause of a 'value-free' social theory, though for him this meant the 'intrinsically simple demand that the investigator and teacher should keep unconditionally separate the establishment of empirical facts... and his own practical evaluations' of them (Weber 1949: 11). Weber thus distinguishes between the 'value-relevance' of the social sciences, in which he accepts that 'judgements of interest' are implicated in the choice of a particular research object, and the necessary 'value-freedom' of the social scientist with respect to the way she conducts her research and the way she uses the results of her research. He thus rejects the belief that researchers should employ their theories and explanations to support a specific political practice, project or ideology (Hesse 1978: 9). At the heart of this more nuanced conception of the relationship between values and social science is Weber's wish to exclude partisanship and overt political bias in the production and dissemination of knowledge, though it stems in equal measure from his commitment to naturalism in the sciences, and his ambivalent attitude toward law-like and causal explanations in the natural sciences (Hesse 1978: 9–10).[14]

There have been a number of stern rebukes to these dominant understandings. For example, the first generation of Critical Theorists took their target to be the complicities and partialities of 'traditional theory', which they traced back to Descartes and the origins of modern philosophy, though it was especially evident in the hegemony of nineteenth and twentieth century positivism. Traditional theory in its various guises takes natural science and especially mathematics to be its paradigm, thereby privileging deductive and inductive reasoning, coupled with the desire to provide an as complete and systematic picture of the world external to thought. However, in his 'Traditional and Critical Theory', Max Horkheimer stresses the way in which the purveyors of traditional theory are submerged in particular social worlds and practices, which they then serve to buttress by presenting the generation, character and use of scientific knowledge as neutral and objective (Horkheimer 1972: 190). Thus, what is overlooked is how its conception of knowledge is integrally connected to the solving of problems *within* taken for granted structures, especially the dominant forms of economic production.

Critical theory, by contrast, is conceived as a dialectical and engaged practice that seeks to provide the means to challenge historically malleable structures of domination and oppression in the name of a universal human emancipation. Theoretical reasoning in this sense is a reflective rather than purely technical and problem solving exercise that is concerned to highlight and intensify the contradictions of a particular order, while simultaneously proposing alternatives:

> [T]he critical theory of society is, in its totality, the unfolding of a single existential judgment. To put it in broad terms, the theory says that the basic form of the historically given commodity economy on which modern history rests contains in itself the internal and external tensions of the modern era; it generates these tensions over and over again in an increasingly heightened form; and after a period of progress, development of human powers, and emancipation for the individual, after an enormous extension of human control over nature, it finally hinders further development and drives humanity into a new barbarism.
>
> (Horkheimer 1972: 227)

In his passionate critique of traditional theory, however, the early Horkheimer relied upon a somewhat simplistic social theory, largely derived from the Marxist tradition. He also remained committed to the power of universal reason – though not in its purely Kantian manifestation since this was seen to be too individualistic and disengaged – to expose the mismatch between Enlightenment ideals and the 'actually existing' social practices and institutions of modern capitalist societies.

Famously, however, perhaps notoriously, in the *Dialectic of Enlightenment*, which Horkheimer co-authored with Theodor Adorno, this critique of traditional theory and positivism mutated into a totalizing rage against reason and the Enlightenment project itself (Bernstein 1991; Habermas 1987). In this *volte-face*, Adorno and Horkheimer narrate the way in which the Enlightenment ideals of rational demystification and disenchantment revert back to a new form of ideological myth, thus ensuring the victory of an instrumental reason that is complicit with the emerging 'administered society' (Adorno and Horkheimer 1973).

Also, in another strange twist, the second generation of critical theorists, led mainly by Habermas, inverted this movement once again. In his early work, Habermas launched an epistemological critique of science, especially in its positivist incarnation, by showing the intrinsic connections between certain sorts of knowledge and various forms of human interest (Habermas 1978). But this was followed by a growing endorsement of the resources of universal reason, now understood in communicative terms, to provide the means for rationally agreed moral norms, so long as the appropriate procedures and conditions could be secured. In this later conception, critique was linked to a largely normative project that centred on the defence of universal rights and procedures, as embodied in the modern liberal-democratic constitutional state (Habermas 1996).

In the spirit of critical theory, though in a very different style, Roy Bhaskar's critical realism contests and re-inscribes the dominant distinctions and oppositions. In his challenge both to positivists, who oppose fact and value, and theoreticists, who split abstract theory and social practice, he develops a practice of 'explanatory critique' in the human sciences that is explicitly orientated towards 'human emancipation' (Bhaskar 1989: 102, 186). Indeed, in his words, a suitably conceived and constructed social science makes the connection between certain sorts of explanatory theory and the practices of critique and evaluation 'mandatory' (Bhaskar 1989: 101, 105). Thus, while Bhaskar does not posit an absolute identity between explanation and critique, he argues that if certain theories (such as those informed by the philosophy of critical realism) can identify false (that is, ideological) beliefs by providing causal explanations of the sources of those beliefs, then we can and must move immediately to a negative evaluation of the source of false beliefs, as well as a positive evaluation of social action aimed at the latter's challenge and removal (Bhaskar 1989: 101–5). In short, well-founded explanatory theory has intrinsic implications for critique and thus for human emancipation.

However, while we accept Bhaskar's attempt to articulate the practices of explanation and critique in the development of a critical human science, we take issue with the substance of his social theory, and we question the particular ontological and epistemological framework within which it is located. For our approach is predicated on the articulation of an alternative social ontology that stresses the *radical contingency* and *structural incompleteness* of all systems of social relations. In so doing, we draw heavily on what in Lacanian theory is conceptualized as the disruptive presence of 'the real' in any symbolic order, that is, a presence that marks the impossibility of any putative fullness of being, whether at the level of structures, subjects or discourses (Lacan 1978: 167; 1991a: 66; 2006: 324). Moreover, the effect of our ontological framework is not only to destabilize the conditions upon which the standard models of social science are grounded, but also to provide the conditions for developing an alternative approach to social and political analysis that *inter alia* concedes a central role to subjectivity (as distinct from subjectivism) in characterizing, explaining and criticizing practices and regimes.

The centrality of this ontological starting-point requires us to say a little more by way of its justification. Following Bhaskar and others, we begin by assuming that any legitimate approach to social and political analysis requires at least some ontological assumptions and commitments (see Connolly 2006; Hay 2006). But the commitment to ontology can mean different things. For some, the articulation of an ontological framework consists in providing a kind of 'furniture of the world' that sets out the sorts of things, and their respective properties, which we encounter in engaging with objects and other subjects. However, in our view the importance of ontology is not just about *what* sorts of things exist, but *that* they exist and *how* they exist. Indeed, of capital importance in this regard is the fact that objects and subjects are marked by an 'essential instability' that problematizes a simple listing of their necessary intrinsic properties and causal capacities. Therefore, of greater import for us is their contingency, historicity and precariousness. Indeed, in terms of political analysis, this perspective enables us to highlight the *constructed* and *political* character of social objectivity, and then to articulate a connected series of concepts and logics that can help us to analyse social relations and processes, while remaining faithful to our ontological commitments.

Argument and structure of the book

Working within this ontological framework, our overall argument is composed of five inter-related elements: problematization, retroductive explanation, logics, articulation and critique. Leaning on Foucault, we begin with the idea of a problem-driven approach to social and political analysis. This involves constructing theoretical and empirical objects of investigation, in which the latter arise from pressing practical concerns of the present. Second, we develop the idea of retroductive reasoning, which for us provides the grounds for an appropriate *form* of explanation in the social sciences. Third, we introduce our concept of a logic, which is developed in opposition to contextualized self-interpretations and causal mechanisms, and we elaborate three kinds of logic that are linked together in a particular empirical context to explain a problematized phenomenon.

This provides us with the appropriate *content* of a prospective explanation. It is clear, however, that any putative *explanans* will comprise a plurality of logics in a historically specific and complex set of social circumstances. This means, fourth, that it is necessary to *articulate* these various types of logic together in order to explain a constructed *explanandum*. Finally, but importantly, the work of critique and evaluation in our approach does not precede – or follow after – the practices of problematization, characterization, and explanation. Instead, the task of social criticism is internally connected to them. This involves the construction of a distinctive conception of ethics and normative evaluation, in which the former is related to the radical contingency of social relations, and the latter to historically specific relations of domination and oppression.

The basic logic of our argument is reflected in the overall structure of the book. In Chapter 1, we borrow from Aristotle, Peirce and Hanson to propose the explicit adoption of retroductive reasoning as the paradigm for understanding the task of explanation in the social sciences. Retroduction is thus opposed to the predominance of induction and deduction. We locate this retroductive conception of explanation within an overarching logic of investigation comprising the moments of *problematization, retroductive explanation, persuasion* and *intervention*. In developing this argument, we first explore how retroductive reasoning has been invoked to make sense of the practice of *natural* science. Following Norwood Hanson, we show how retroduction can be used to construct scientific theories by the process of *positing* hypotheses designed to render recalcitrant phenomena more intelligible. However, in the natural sciences explanation and testing are still construed in deductive-nomological and hypothetico-deductive terms, and prediction is granted a constitutive role. Indeed, this view makes possible a sharp distinction between the contexts of discovery and justification (Popper 1980; Reichenbach 1938).

But things change when we move from the natural to the social sciences, mainly because the deductive form of (exhaustive and predictive) testing and explanation is problematized by our insistence upon the contextual particularity of a putative explanation, as well as the latter's always presupposed, contestable framework of concepts and assumptions. Instead, we propose different and more capacious criteria to justify and evaluate our explanations, whose effect is to undermine positivism's absolute separation between the contexts of discovery and justification. In this view, the elements of problematization, retroductive explanation, and persuasion are related, though analytically distinguishable, parts of an interconnected whole. And this means that retroductive reasoning can no longer be confined to the context of discovery. Indeed, if explanation and testing cease to be linked in an essential way to deduction and prediction, then the practice of explanation can be seen to intrude into the context of discovery. In short, then, the *form* of explanation in social science ought to be understood in retroductive and not deductive (or inductive) terms.

We then explore three possible contenders for filling out the *content* of our explanatory form: contextualized self-interpretations, causal mechanisms, and logics. Advocates of each of these contenders *claim* to – indeed for us *must* – share two key insights. First, they accept the view that a social science explanation must pass through and take seriously the self-interpretations of the actors engaged in the practice under study. This is the 'minimal' hermeneutical insight that all three contenders take on board, thus distinguishing them from the positivist view, which is content to rely upon what Charles Taylor calls 'brute data identifications' (Taylor 1985a: 28). The three contenders also share a second insight: social science explanations are not reducible to the self-interpretations of the social actors under study. In other words, in explaining social and political phenomena, we can not rely *exclusively* on what people say, or on their self-understandings, even though these views must be taken into account in any legitimate social explanation. The question then becomes one of fleshing out this 'beyond' of self-interpretations.

Focussing on the work of Peter Winch, Charles Taylor, and Mark Bevir & Rod Rhodes, the aim of Chapter 2 is to explore the *hermeneutical* account of the social sciences, which makes *contextualized self-interpretations* the basic unit of explanation. After initially demonstrating a convergence in the hermeneutical critique of positivism and naturalism, we interrogate the explanatory and critical capacity of hermeneutics more generally. Our claim here is that while hermeneuticists highlight a number of deficiencies in the causal law paradigm, they replace the latter's subsumptive universalism with a descriptive and normative particularism. This is problematic in our view because their respective ontological frameworks fail to provide a satisfactory set of concepts to characterize and explain social phenomena, but also because their approach leads either to a diminishing of our critical capacity, which is evident in Winch's relativistic tendencies, or indeed to its precise opposite: an overbearing normativism that results in a largely *external* critique of social practices, generally predicated on a strong notion of rationality. The latter tendency is evident in the writings of Taylor, as well as Bevir and Rhodes.

In Chapter 3, we explore the *naturalist* response to the failings of the law-like model. Here our focus is on those who have substituted the role of causal mechanisms for causal laws as the basic component of a legitimate social science explanation. We concentrate mainly on the work of Jon Elster, not simply because he is an exemplary advocate of the social mechanisms approach, but also because his work shares important affinities with other thinkers who seek to move beyond the causal law paradigm. For example, Bhaskar's naturalism appeals explicitly to the role of causal mechanisms in explaining social phenomena, while the recent writings of Ian Shapiro, Bob Jessop, and Colin Hay also make use of a critical realist conception of mechanisms and causal powers to develop an alternative account of social science explanation.

But though Elster's work mounts a powerful critique of the causal law paradigm, especially the unrealistic demand to make the testing of predictions a decisive criterion of explanation, we argue that the mechanisms approach suffers in turn from a residual positivism that problematizes its distinctiveness vis-à-vis the causal law approach. We do this by showing how the ideal of a causal law continues to exert a powerful influence on Elster's worldview, arguing that this in turn leads to two problematic features of his approach. These are what we term his psychologism and – perhaps somewhat counter-intuitively – his idealism. In sum, we suggest that Elster does not so much advance us through and beyond hermeneutics as return us to the positivism of the causal law model. Moreover, we suggest that many aspects of our argument are equally applicable to theorists such as Bhaskar, Shapiro and Hay.

Chapter 4 unfolds our alternative ontological framework for developing a different approach to critical explanation in the social sciences. Influenced principally by Heidegger, Lacan, and Laclau & Mouffe, but also drawing on Foucault, Wittgenstein, and Derrida, we put forward an 'ontology of lack', which is a negative ontology premised on the radical contingency of social relations.[15] Stated simply, we take this axiom to imply that any system or structure of social relations is constitutively incomplete or lacking for a subject. Consider in this regard Ernesto Laclau's claim that every social identity is always-already dislocated (Laclau 1990: 39). On the one hand, we take this to be a strictly ontological understanding of dislocation, in which each and every symbolic order is penetrated by an impossibility that has to be filled or covered-over for it to constitute itself. The category of dislocation can also be understood, however, in more ontical terms: moments in which the subject's mode of being is disrupted by an *experience* that cannot be symbolized within and by the pre-existing means of discursive representation. From this perspective, practices are governed by a dialectic defined by incomplete structures on the one hand, and the collective acts of subjective identification that sustain or change those incomplete structures on the other.[16]

Our fundamental ontological premise is then used to redescribe social relations by stipulating different *dimensions* of social reality. The *social* dimension captures those situations in which the radical contingency of social relations has not been registered in the mode of public contestation, whereas the *political* dimension refers to those situations in which subjects responding to dislocatory events re-activate the contingent foundations of a practice by publicly contesting and defending the norms of that practice. On the other hand, the *ideological* and *ethical* dimensions of social reality capture the way subjects are either complicit in concealing the radical contingency of social relations (the ideological), or are attentive to its constitutive character (the ethical).

In articulating this basic ontological standpoint, we take our principal objects of investigation to be *practices* or *regimes of practices*, where our aim is to critically explain their transformation, stabilization, and maintenance. Drawing on Heidegger, we claim that such an inquiry will always have an ontical and an ontological impulse. Given the background ontological framework laid out in Chapter 4, the following chapter introduces and formalizes the category of a logic, which constitutes our basic unit of critical explanation. In general terms, our conception of logic refers to the purposes, rules and ontological presuppositions that render a practice or regime possible and intelligible. An understanding of the logic of a practice aims, therefore, not just to describe or characterize it, but also to capture the various conditions that make that practice 'work' or 'tick'.

More concretely, in the realm of social science explanation, we delineate three kinds of logic – social, political and fantasmatic – that speak to different dimensions of social reality. Closely associated with the social dimension, *social logics* enable us to characterize practices in a particular social domain (for example the practice of modularization within universities), or an entire regime of practices (for instance Thatcherism, apartheid, or the audit regime). *Political logics* provide the means to explore the conditions of possibility and vulnerability of social practices and regimes by focusing on the latter's *contestation* and *institution*. Here we invoke Laclau and Mouffe's logics of equivalence and difference to investigate the way in which the traces of radical contingency associated with the original institution of practices and regimes can in certain circumstances be reactivated by subjects, thus enabling them to construct new meanings, practices and identities. Finally, if political logics are most closely associated with the political dimension of social relations, *fantasmatic logics* are closely linked to the ideological dimension. In this regard, the logic of fantasy, which is predicated on the Lacanian category of enjoyment (*jouissance*), shows how subjects are rendered complicit in concealing or covering over the radical contingency of social relations. However, insofar as fantasmatic logics are subverted we also have a means of accounting for conditions under which the ethical dimension of social reality can be foregrounded.

Since the social, political, ideological and ethical dimensions of social reality are always to some degree present in any particular practice or regime, each of the three logics has a role to play in articulating a complete explanatory account. This means that our overriding aim in Chapter 5 is to establish the distinctive features and status of each of these logics by relating them to our overall social ontology. At the same time, we are able to distinguish our approach from those that appeal to contextualized self-interpretations and causal mechanisms. While in our view logics are subject-dependent, in the sense that our explanations require a passage through a subject's contextualized self-interpretation (the hermeneutical constraint), they also require something that transcends them. However, as we argue in Chapter 3, this 'something more' is not adequately addressed by theorists such as Elster, Bhaskar and Shapiro. We seek instead to develop this 'something more' in a way that remains more faithful to the hermeneutical insight.

While much of our discussion in Chapters 4 and 5 focuses on the explanation of problematized social phenomena, we also stress that our approach carries important *critical* implications. In particular, we argue that political and fantasmatic logics not only provide the means to explain the emergence and reproduction of practices and regimes, but they also highlight the contingency of the latter's institution and grip. Political and fantasmatic logics thus furnish the means for the ethical critique and normative evaluation of practices and regimes. In rendering these ideas more explicit, we draw upon William Connolly's notion of *ontopolitical* interpretation (Connolly 1995) to show how different logics are linked together as part of an *ethicopolitical* practice of critical explanation. The theme of critique in social science explanation is returned to in Chapter 6, where we emphasize both the normative and ethical aspects of this practice.

However, the main thrust of Chapter 6 is to address a number of methodological and epistemological issues that are raised, but not fully addressed, in previous chapters. These include questions pertaining to the epistemological and methodological status of case studies within our approach; the role of comparative research in deepening, modifying and 'testing' our critical explanations; the conceptualization of the relationship between theoretical categories and empirical analysis, especially the way in which different theoretical and empirical elements come together to form an explanatory narrative; as well as the implications of our approach for the way we should understand hypothesis-generation, validation, generalisation and theory-building.

We respond to these questions by condensing many of the issues of social science explanation into what we call the *problem of subsumption*. The latter denotes an understanding of the relationship between concepts and objects as external to each other, in which objects are gathered under concepts without the object or the concept undergoing any modification during the process of subsumption. But in critical opposition to subsumption, we develop the concept and practice of *articulation* in order to characterize the way we ought to understand both social science research practice and many aspects of the general logic of critical explanation. A major part of this discussion centres on our preferred understanding of the role of case studies, comparative research and generalization in the social sciences. We also connect our concept of articulation to the practice of judgement, as it is understood by thinkers such as Kant and Wittgenstein, showing how this conceptual linkage enables us to address issues concerning the application of abstract theoretical concepts and logics to empirical objects, or how to incorporate into our approach theoretical concepts and empirical generalizations derived from other traditions of thought.

In discussing these epistemological and methodological issues, we illustrate our approach by problematizing the recent reforms and changing practices of the UK's higher education system, which involve the introduction, sedimentation, and maintenance of a new audit regime. Though this by no means constitutes a case study, we do spend some time outlining the background context to this regime so as to better illustrate the overall contours of our approach. What in other words would the relevant social, political, and fantasmatic logics look like or imply in such a case? Drawing on this discussion, we also highlight the implications of our 'method' of articulatory practice for issues of critique. More specifically, with reference to our study of the higher education audit regime, we introduce the notion of counter-logics to flesh out our conception of critical explanation. Further, by developing themes introduced in Chapters 4 and 5, we show how our account of logics enables us to situate and relate the tasks of ethical *and* normative critique in poststructuralist discourse theory. But before we can develop these implications we need to begin by setting out the general form of critical explanation in social and political analysis.

1   Retroduction

The ultimate goal of a positive science is the development of a 'theory' or 'hypothesis' that yields valid and meaningful (i.e., not truistic) predictions about phenomena not yet observed.

(Friedman 1953: 7)

We have reason to wonder if human activity will ever lend itself to fundamental analysis by truly scientific methods – whether there is a mystery about man that makes his actions largely unpredictable.

(Duverger 1972: 6)

Faith in mathematical and statistical methods in the social sciences is surprisingly tenacious in the face of repeated failures to meet positivist ideals of explanation and prediction.[1] This chapter makes the case for a post-positivist paradigm of explanation by contesting the causal law paradigm, which privileges prediction as a constitutive element of the explanatory process. Of course, this aim is not new (see Steinmetz 2005). Nevertheless, in view of the tenacity of the positivist impulse in social science to survive in different guises, we need to continue to explore new ways of challenging and engaging with it, as well as new ways of conceptualizing alternatives. As Stephen White points out in the context of political studies, '[a]lmost all political theorists and scientists affirm some notion of a post-positivist model of inquiry. But when pushed to explain exactly what is meant by that, both at the theoretical-philosophical level, as well as at the level of concrete research, most of us become relatively inarticulate quite quickly' (White in Topper *et al.* 2006: 734).

In responding to White's challenge, our book sets out to recast the perennial debates between positivism and its 'others' from a poststructuralist point of view. In this chapter we claim that the default tendency to rely on deductive (and inductive) reasoning, the hypothetico-deductive method of scientific investigation, and the covering-law model of explanation, is a product of the hegemonic grip of a particular, though admittedly powerful, conception of the natural sciences – what we call the causal law paradigm.[2] Our main critical argument is that it is problematic to model social processes on natural processes in this way – whether as universal laws, causal generalizations, or robust empirical correlations – because it leads to rather narrow conceptions of testing and explanation, in which the element of prediction is elevated at the expense of contextual and ontological factors. In short, our target is the law-*like* conception of explanation and testing that the causal law paradigm elevates to the status of an ideal.

As against inductive and deductive modes of reasoning, we argue more positively that retroductive reasoning provides us with a general *form* or *logic* of explanation in the social sciences. Although Aristotle has been credited with its original identification, retroduction has been insightfully developed and applied in the philosophy of science by Charles Sanders Peirce, Norwood Hanson, Roy Bhaskar and others. However, while we draw upon these scholars, it is only by being sensitive to the distinctive ontologies underpinning the natural and social worlds that we can fully reap the potential of retroduction for the social sciences. In so doing, we rework the sharp distinction drawn in positivist images of social science practice between what we call, following Reichenbach, the 'context of discovery' and the 'context of justification' (Reichenbach 1938). Despite Reichenbach's staunch defence of induction as a means of distinguishing science from non-science, it is widely accepted that Popper's appeal to falsificationism as an alternative criterion of demarcation also relied on this distinction (Popper 1980). And though the reworking of this distinction has been a staple of the history and philosophy of science ever since its introduction,[3] we do so in order to challenge the positivist conception of causal explanation in the social sciences in a particular way.[4] More specifically, we challenge the compartmentalizing tendencies of positivist social science investigation – a logic of scientific discovery followed by exhaustive empirical testing and explanation – and propose instead one overarching logic of investigation comprising three interlocking moments: the *problematization* of empirical phenomena; the *retroductive explanation* of these phenomena; and the *persuasion* of – and *intervention* into – the relevant community and practices of scholars and lay-actors.

These ideas are developed in three steps. First, we introduce the concept of retroduction as it has been invoked in the philosophy of natural science. Although in our view retroductive reasoning is present in all forms of scientific practice, we follow Norwood Hanson in suggesting that it is either left implicit in the practices of scientists and/or confined to a particular realm of scientific activity, namely, the activity of conceiving and proposing hypotheses (Hanson 1961: 71). Second, we show how retroduction can and should be made relevant to social science practice and explanation. This involves indicating the way it has already been discussed in the philosophy of social science by theorists such as Bhaskar and Derek Sayer, as well as developing our own argument about how its relation to social science practice and explanation should be understood. Our argument specifies the way in which the ontological shift from the natural to the social world results in our abandoning the positivist understanding of the distinction between the contexts of discovery and justification. In a third step, we explore the consequences of this insight for thinking about practices of theory construction and critical explanation in the human sciences.

The problem of prediction in social science

One reason to be sceptical about transforming prediction into a constitutive feature of social science explanation might be the dramatic failures of social scientists to anticipate major economic and political events, whether the South East Asian financial crisis of 1997, the fall of the Berlin wall in 1989, or the relatively peaceful and stable transition from Apartheid to democracy in South Africa. Of course, objections can be raised against this position. For instance even the natural sciences are often unable to predict many individual phenomena (such as weather events) with satisfactory precision. And yet the question still remains as to whether it is plausible or desirable to hold up prediction as a constitutive feature of social science explanation. From this perspective, it appears that social scientists do not fare well, even in their very own (positivist) terms, whether in economics or political science (see Tetlock 2005). As some scholars have put it, again in relation to the study of politics, 'the program of identifying simple general laws concerning political structures and processes has so far yielded meagre results', its strength lying 'in its identification of empirical regularities to be explained, not in its provision or verification of explanations' (Tilly and Goodin 2006: 20).[5]

The privileging of prediction is often justified by the need to have a good basis upon which to retain or reject a model. 'If two different models produce different predictions then we know they are competing. But if we are not sure what the predictions are from two models we do not even know if they are competing. They might [even] be the same model' (Dowding 2001: 93). And Rebecca Morton is cited approvingly in this context: 'Empirical analysis that never builds towards an explicit set of assumptions and predictions about the real world is no better than pure description' (Morton 1999: 44).

But in hypostatizing prediction in this way, social scientists run the risk of prejudging, and thus severely restricting the scope and nature of social science research, in the style of 'if a hammer is all you've got, then sooner or later everything starts to look like a nail'. As Ian Shapiro points out,

> making a fetish of prediction can undermine problem-driven research via wag-the-dog scenarios in which we elect to study phenomena because they seem to admit the possibility of prediction rather than because we have independent reasons for thinking it worthwhile to study them. This is what I mean by method-drivenness...In principle it sounds right to say 'let's test the model against the data'. In reality, there are few uncontroversial data sets in political science.
>
> (Shapiro 2002: 609)[6]

In our view, the tendency to hypostatize prediction reflects the desire among social scientists to imitate the ideals of what they take to be modern natural science, especially physics, as well as to adopt the ontological commitments that sustain these ideals.[7] As Dowding puts it, '[t]he interpretations we privilege in the end are the ones that provide the best predictions *in precisely the same manner* as our interpretations of the patterns we ascribe to the physical world' (Dowding 2004: 140; emphasis added). This view reflects the dominance of the hypothetico-deductive method of science, and its associated conception of causal explanation, which is taken as a kind of formalization of natural science practice. It is to the basic features of this method and its particular style of reasoning that we now turn.

As Hubert Dreyfus has argued, this model of natural science is regarded by many as the crowning glory in the development of 'ideal theory', and it can be traced back to Socrates and Plato through to Descartes and Kant in the modern period (Dreyfus 1986: 11). It consists of six essential characteristics: *explicitness* (a theory must be fully spelled out, and not based on intuition and interpretation); *universality* (a theory should hold true for all places at all times); *abstractedness* (a theory must not refer to particular examples); *discreteness* (a theory must be stated in terms of context-free elements that are not reducible to human interests, traditions, institutions, and so forth); and *systematicity* (a theory must be a whole in the sense that decontextualized elements – attributes, features, factors, etc – are related to each other by rules or laws) (Dreyfus 1986: 12). Finally, it was left to the modern natural sciences – the theories propounded by Copernicus, Galileo, Kepler, Newton, and so forth – to add the sixth characteristic, namely, *predictive power and exhaustiveness*. In this regard, theory must provide a complete description of the domain investigated, that is, it must specify all types of changes affecting the domain, as well as specifying their effects. Importantly, as Dreyfus puts it, 'this completeness permits precise prediction' (Dreyfus 1986: 12).

This idealized model of science, which of course does not have to be realized to function as an ideal, is usually instantiated in the hypothetico-deductive method and the corresponding 'covering law' or 'deductive-nomological' model of explanation. In both, the idea of prediction is allotted a constitutive role *vis-à-vis* theory-building and explanation. Simplifying Popper's classic formulation of the hypothetico-deductive method, the potential falsifiability of a proposed hypothesis – its capacity to be disproved by observed facts – serves as a demarcation criterion for a scientific statement. Theories are corroborated or falsified by deducing empirical statements or predictions, and then testing these against observational evidence.[8] Deduction, therefore, assumes a prominent role within the context of *justification*, that is, with respect to the testing, verification, falsification, formalization, and presentation of theories.[9]

The allied task of *explaining* facts, following Carl Hempel's widely accepted account, is 'deductive-nomological' in form, in which an *explanandum* is deduced from a set of premises that includes a universal law. More precisely, laws comprise law-like statements from which, given an appropriate set of initial conditions, the fact that has to be explained can be logically derived (Elster 1983a: 26). And importantly, from our point of view, it is here that the boundary between explanation and prediction tends to blur. This is because *explanation and prediction are linked together in a deductive framework*, their difference amounting only to a difference in temporal perspective: 'Explaining x is predicting x after it has actually happened . . . Predicting x is explaining it before it has actually happened' (Hanson 1972: 41). Or, to put it in Popper's terms, 'the use of a theory for the purposes of *predicting* some event is just another aspect of its use for the purpose of *explaining* such an event' (Popper 1966: 262–3).

To use Hempel's stylised example, if we wish to employ the deductive-nomological model to explain the fact that our car radiator iced up on a cold night, we require a set of initial conditions – the liquid in our car radiator was water; the radiator did not leak; and the temperature fell below zero degrees Celsius – coupled with a law-like statement to the effect that water freezes at zero degrees Celsius. When these elements are combined they generate a particular account (*explanans*) which explains deductively the event or fact (*explanandum*). In addition, explanation enables us to predict future (or retrodict past) occurrences, so that we can take precautions and insert anti-freeze in our radiator during the winter (Hempel 1965: 232).

More formally, the deductive-nomological model can be expressed in the following way:

1 Law or theories
2 Initial conditions

3 Event or fact explained and/or predicted

And the above example can be displayed as in Table 1.

The deductive-nomological model of explanation and prediction can also be used to express 'Duverger's law' (Duverger 1959) – the claim that under certain conditions the simple majority electoral system favours the two-party system – one of the few 'laws' that have been confidently asserted by political scientists (see Connolly 1981: 9–18). Stated simply, it can take the form of Table 2.

It is clear from Table 2 that Duverger's law enables political scientists to explain the relationships between certain sorts of electoral and party systems, as well as to predict future relationships – or retrodict past relationships – thus making the practice of institutional design more reflective and efficient.

Table 1 The deductive-nomological model: a natural science illustration

Explanans	Law	Water freezes at 0 degrees
	Initial conditions	Liquid in car is water; the radiator did not leak; temp falls below 0 degrees
Explanandum	Event/process	Therefore radiator freezes

Table 2 The deductive-nomological model: a social science illustration

Explanans	Law	The simple majority electoral system favours the two-party system
	Initial conditions	Legalization of party organizations; secret ballot; inclusion of party affiliation on ballots; diffusion of ethnic/class membership across electoral districts; etc.
Explanandum	Event/process	Therefore x party system is two-party

We shall return to Duverger's law later in the chapter. For now, it suffices to note that the structure of subsuming an event under law-like statements parallels the role of prediction in the hypothetico-deductive model. In other words, the *explanandum* is explained by facts which, had they been known in advance, would have allowed us to predict it (Lessnoff 1974: 22). The grip of the hypothetico-deductive and deductive-nomological pictures of science, coupled with the obvious success of the natural sciences, explains why it appears natural for many social scientists to link prediction and explanation so rigidly. However, these claims only appear natural if one accepts the unity of method in the sciences – and the hypothetico-deductive method more precisely – while remaining unperturbed by the failures and anomalies of the positivist project in the social sciences.

Of course, these observations do not by themselves invalidate positivism. Even the most dramatic failures of prediction cannot conclusively falsify the central tenets of positivism.[10] Indeed, far from falsifying its research programme, these failures can serve to demonstrate that social scientists are not positivist enough, and that they should embrace the spread of more sophisticated mathematical and quantitative techniques *tout court*. Construed as empirical deficiencies, the failure of positivism is thus understood in epistemological terms, leaving intact the ideals and ontological assumptions borrowed from the natural sciences.[11]

But equally, this does not mean that the questioning of predictive capacity as an essential component of explanation ought to imply an ontological structure that is intrinsically undetermined or infinitely malleable – a pure flux of random events and processes. After all, as has been repeatedly shown in the domain of complex adaptive systems and chaos theory, phenomena can be both fully determined *and* unpredictable (Schroeder 1991: 167; see also Prigogine 1996 and Stengers 1997). The key is to locate the right level at which invariance is operative in the world, and to ask how best to characterize it. As far as the social world is concerned, we argue that though this invariance may be historically specific, it is a structure or pattern shaped in significant ways by the (ontological) fact that we are 'meaning-producing' or 'self-interpreting' animals (see Taylor 1985a: Ch. 2). In this chapter, then, we draw initially and minimally upon hermeneutical thinking to question the law-like model of explanation and prediction in the social sciences, leaving it until Chapter 2 to explore this tradition more fully and to engage with it more critically. However, before we explore this 'minimal' hermeneutical program, we wish to consider at least one productive affinity between social science and natural science, which will be crucial to our later argument.

Retroduction and the philosophy of science

Following Reichenbach and Popper, we have shown how explanation in the natural sciences is closely associated with what we take to be the context of *justification*, suggesting there are at least some reasons, though by no means conclusive ones, for being sceptical about importing natural science conceptions of testing, prediction, and explanation into the social sciences. In this section, we are more optimistic about drawing out some parallels between the two sciences, which centre on a distinct form of reasoning pertaining to the context of *discovery* in the natural sciences. This form of reasoning has been called retroduction or abduction. Given certain facts or anomalies (conclusions) retroductive reasoning describes the way plausible hypotheses are produced (our search for premises). It is *prima facie* appealing from a social science perspective because it designates a backward-looking modal form of inference with which many social scientists are very familiar. For example, it is not unusual for social scientists to take the resounding hegemonic success of Thatcherism as the given anomaly, and then to proceed backwards to furnish an account of how and why this was so (Gamble 1994; Hall 1988).

Norwood Hanson is one of a number of philosophers of science who has suggested that this form of reasoning best captures the nature, practice, and development of natural science, especially the practice of theory-construction. He invokes retroductive reasoning to suggest that Kepler, for example, 'did not *begin* with the hypothesis that Mars's orbit was elliptical and *then* deduce statements confirmed by Brahe's observations. These latter observations were given, and they set the problem – they were Johannes Kepler's starting point' (Hanson 1961: 72). After a detailed account of the way Kepler arrived at his 'ellipse hypothesis' Hanson concludes that Kepler

> wrote *De Motibus Stellae Martis* in order to set out his reasons for suggesting the ellipse. These were not deductive reasons; he was working from *explicanda* to *explicans*. But neither were they inductive – not, at least, in any form advocated by the empiricists, statisticians and probability theorists who have written on induction.
>
> (Hanson 1961: 85)

As Hanson notes, alongside inductive and deductive types of inference, Aristotle lists a third – translated by Peirce as 'abductive' or 'retroductive' reasoning – which consists 'in studying facts and devising a theory to explain them' (Peirce 1934: 145).

In more formal terms, Peirce offers the following definitions of these three forms of reasoning. He begins with *deduction*, which

> is that mode of reasoning which examines the state of things asserted in the premises, forms a diagram [whether geometric, algebraic, or otherwise] of that state of things, perceives in the parts of that diagram relations not explicitly mentioned in the premises, satisfies itself by mental experiments upon the diagram that these relations would always subsist, or at least would do so in a certain proportion of cases, and concludes their necessary, or probable, truth.
>
> (Peirce 1960: 28)

Induction, by contrast,

> is that mode of reasoning which adopts a conclusion as approximate, because it results from a method of inference which must generally lead to the truth in the long run. For example, a ship enters port laden with coffee. I go aboard and sample the coffee ... I conclude by induction that the whole cargo has approximately the same value per bean as the hundred beans of my sample.
>
> (Peirce 1960: 28)

Retroduction, finally,

> is the provisional adoption of a hypothesis ... For example, all the operations of chemistry fail to decompose hydrogen, lithium, glucinum, boron, carbon, nitrogen, oxygen, fluorine, sodium ... We provisionally suppose these bodies to be simple; for if not, similar experimentation will detect their compound nature, if it can be detected at all.
>
> (Peirce 1960: 29)[12]

The conceptual irreducibility of retroduction, and thus its integrity, is important for Hanson because it provides the key to a better account of the practice of theory-building in the natural sciences (Hanson 1961). Not only does it furnish a corrective to the way scientists understand their own practice, but it also supplies a corrective to the way scientific practices are understood by philosophers and historians of science. 'Physicists rarely find laws by enumerating and summarising observables', argues Hanson, nor do they 'start from hypotheses'; instead, 'they start from data' (Hanson 1961: 70). Indeed, as he puts it, the 'struggle for intelligibility (pattern, organization) in natural philosophy has never been portrayed in inductive or H-D [hypothetico-deductive] accounts' (Hanson 1961: 87).

Retroduction is at one with induction in suggesting that the vector of reasoning points from the data to the laws. However, as Hanson insists, inductive and deductive reasoning cannot *originate* any theories or laws whatever. From an inductive point of view, this is because theories are simply summarized projections of these data, while from a deductive perspective they are derived from a law or an axiom. Retroduction by contrast moves from data to hypothesis to laws.[13] In short, though more open-ended than deduction and induction, retroductive reasoning is still a legitimate type of inference. While deductive reasoning purports to *prove* what is the case, and inductive reasoning purports to *approximate* what is the case, retroductive reasoning *conjectures* what is the case (Peirce in Hanson 1961: 85). As Peirce puts it, retroduction is a 'logical inference, asserting its conclusion only problematically, or conjecturally, it is true, but nevertheless having a perfectly definite logical form' (Peirce in Hanson 1961: 86).

Hanson is all too aware of the temptation to dismiss retroduction on account of its apparent unwieldiness, abandoning it to the unfathomable whims of circumstance. From this point of view, at least induction has the decency to attempt to give some non-arbitrary content to the discovery process. But Hanson vigorously disputes the allegation that the generation of hypotheses is

> so often affected by intuition, insight, hunches, or other imponderables as biographers or scientists suggest. Disciples of the Hypothetico-Deductive account often dismiss the dawning of a hypothesis as being of psychological interest only, or else claim it to be the province solely of genius and not of logic. They are wrong ... To form the idea of acceleration or of universal gravitation does require genius: nothing less than a Galileo or a Newton. But that cannot mean that the reflexions leading to these ideas are unreasonable or a-reasonable. Here resides the continuity in physical explanation from the earliest to the present times.
>
> (Hanson 1961: 72; see also Hanson 1972: 66–7)

Indeed, the single most important criterion for admitting a hypothesis, however tentatively, is that it *accounts* for the phenomenon or problem at stake. In this sense, retroductive reasoning takes a three-fold form. To begin with, a surprising, anomalous, or wondrous phenomenon is observed (P). This phenomenon 'would be explicable as a matter of course' if a hypothesis (H) were true, and so there is good reason to think that H is true (Hanson 1961: 86). In other words, the hypothesis is not inferred until its content is already present in the explanation of P. This contrasts with inductive accounts that 'expect H to emerge from repetitions of P' and with H-D [hypothetico-deductive] accounts which 'make P emerge from some unaccounted-for creation of H as a "higher-level hypothesis"' (Hanson 1961: 86).[14]

It is important to stress that although Peirce and Hanson see no conceptually necessary connection between a phenomenon (P) and a hypothesis (H), this does not mean that there are no 'clear criteria governing what count as acceptable putative explanans, whether or not we choose to dignify its retroductive inference with the tag of "logical" ' (Sayer 1983: 116–17). Some defenders of retroduction, for example, posit criteria such as exhaustiveness, independence and consistency. In this view, it follows that a potential hypothesis must 'account for the phenomena posing the difficulty', 'cannot itself rest on the features in P which it is required to explain', and the component propositions of an *explanans* must not contradict one another (Sayer 1983: 117).

Despite the above use of retroductive reasoning, its utility in helping us to generate a new model of explanation in social and political analysis is potentially limited for two inter-related reasons. A first difficulty concerns its apparent restriction to the process of theory-construction. Or to put it in other terms, whereas retroduction is linked to the context of discovery – the *generation* or *positing* of hypotheses – explanation is usually tied to the context of justification, that is, the *testing* and *acceptance* of hypotheses by means of deduction, prediction, and experiment. As we are interested in connecting retroductive reasoning to questions of explanation, and thus the domain of justification, we need to show how we can extend the scope of retroduction's relevance to the context of justification. Secondly, the use of retroductive reasoning by philosophers such as Hanson and Peirce is confined principally to the task of acquiring a better understanding of natural science practice. As we wish to show the relevance of this logic for social analysis, we need to consider the potential difficulties and conceptual requirements of its being extended beyond the natural sciences. It is to these tasks that we now turn.

Retroduction and social science explanation

There are at least two ways in which our discussion of retroduction can be connected to issues in the philosophy of *social* science. One way is to consider the role of retroduction in the process of social science theory construction. After all, Hanson invokes retroduction with a very precise aim: 'to understand the dynamics of "theory construction" in the natural sciences' (Hanson 1972: 63).[15] But the other way to connect retroduction and social science, which is directly relevant to the aim of this chapter, is through the category of *explanation*. In the main, Hanson implies that retroduction (and *hypothetical* explanations) is tied to the context of discovery while explanation proper is linked more closely to the context of justification. This is because a 'proper' explanation in the natural sciences presupposes that a retroductively inferred hypothesis has already been accepted as part of its theory. However, using insights initially gleaned from a minimal hermeneutical ontology of social practices, we will argue that the form of reasoning involved in positing a hypothesis and the form of reasoning involved in accepting a hypothesis cannot be differentiated so starkly in a social science context.

In order to justify this claim, we need to rework Peirce's and Hanson's arguments, first, because they are not directly concerned with the social sciences and, second, because of the peculiar circumstances of the social sciences. With respect to the latter, there are the general doubts we have already expressed about the role of prediction and the empirical testing of theories in the social sciences. And if there are question marks about the empirical testing of predictions in the social sciences, then legitimate queries ought also to be raised about the privileging of nomological explanation *per se*. These issues alone give cause for concern in conceptualizing the boundary between discovery and justification, as well as the tasks of explaining and predicting in the social sciences, and the complex relationships between such tasks.

In justifying the central role we wish to confer upon retroductive reasoning, we start by noting that members of the critical realist school of social science have already invoked retroductive reasoning. For example, Derek Sayer discerns a 'method of retroduction' at the heart of Marx's later theorizing, which he opposes to accounts of Marx's method put forward by the Hegelian and Althusserian schools (Sayer 1983, 1987). Whereas Althusser, for example, allegedly starts from simple theoretical abstractions such as the commodity, from which he generates more concrete and historical categories, Sayer claims that Marx had no special insight into the social reality he sought to elucidate. In other words, instead of conceding abstractions such as the 'commodity' or 'money' a privileged, almost mystical, epistemological status, Sayer argues that 'Marx's historical categories [such as the "capitalist mode of production"] . . . are generated neither from "simple abstractions" in general [such as the "commodity"], nor from transhistorical categories in particular [such as "production in general"]. They are emphatically a posteriori constructs, arrived at precisely by abstraction from the "real and concrete". Marx had no mysteriously privileged starting point' (Sayer 1983: 102). Instead, Marx's method follows a logic of hypothesis formation in which he posits certain mechanisms, together with the conditions and essential social relations on which these mechanisms depend, which *if they did exist* would account for the phenomenal forms under investigation (Sayer 1983: 135).

In a similar vein, Roy Bhaskar and his followers have drawn upon retroductive reasoning to develop a naturalist philosophy of social science (Bhaskar 1975, 1998). In developing his critical realist philosophy, Bhaskar begins with a Kantian question: what are the conditions of possibility for science? His answer is that the practices of science – conducting experiments, making observations, and so forth – presuppose a realist ontology. That is to say, for science to be an intelligible activity it must necessarily and universally assume that the world is populated by real things and structures, whose properties and causal mechanisms can be discovered and characterized (Outhwaite 1987: 31). Indeed, it must further be assumed that these properties and mechanisms persist in the 'open systems' beyond the closed experimental situation, where the hypothesized causal chains can be isolated from potentially contaminating influences (Bhaskar 1975: 91).

This transcendental account of science seeks to capture the depth and richness of the object world by proposing a three-fold stratification: the *real*, which is made up of the inherent properties of, and causal mechanisms linking, objects; the *actual*, which consists of events; and the *empirical*, which is made up of our experiences of such events (Stones 1996: 28–32). For Bhaskar, the passage between each of these discrete levels is contingent. Thus, events can occur without being experienced by a subject and, crucially, multiple causal mechanisms and tendencies can occur, yet counteract one another, such that no actual event takes place.

Bhaskar explicitly construes the transcendental arguments he employs to establish these claims as a species of retroductive reasoning (Bhaskar 1998: 50). This form of reasoning is also used in explaining concrete phenomena (events, patterns, and so forth). Such explanations presuppose the discovery of underlying causal or generative mechanisms that *account* for the flux of empirical data we encounter in the world, such that the logic of explanation is based on the *contingent* interaction of *necessary* causal mechanisms. Moreover, ascertaining the existence and nature of a mechanism consists in 'the building of a model . . . of a mechanism, which *if* it were to exist and act in the postulated way would account for the phenomenon in question' (Bhaskar 1998: 12). This leads to a conception of natural science as a 'continuous dialectical movement' consisting of three inter-related steps. Scientists begin by identifying a phenomenon (or range of phenomena) to be investigated, before constructing hypotheses and empirically testing the purported explanations. This allows them to identify the generative mechanisms at work, which then become new phenomena to be explained, and the dialectical process begins again (Bhaskar 1998: 12).

With respect to the social world, Bhaskar asks a similarly Kantian question about the conditions under which a social science is possible: *'what properties do societies and people possess that might make them possible objects of knowledge for us?'* (Bhaskar 1998: 13). Here his answer is that 'an ontology of structures' (Bhaskar 1998: 20), rather than the individual acts of human agents, or rule-governed behaviour, constitutes the true object of social science (Bhaskar 1998: 20). Moreover, in the social sciences, the logic of discovery and explanation is modified because of the ontological complexity of its object, even if both the natural and social worlds share the same three-fold, ontological stratification comprising the empirical, the actual, and the real. According to Bhaskar, social structures – unlike natural structures – do not exist independently of the activities they govern,[16] nor are they simply external to the agents' conceptions of what they are doing.

Finally, as the social sciences are inherently 'open systems', in the sense that they are not amenable to natural science's familiar 'closed' experimental set-ups that can be controlled for potentially spurious factors, they are not suitable for the kind of empirical testing employed in the natural sciences. This means that the social sciences are not oriented towards explanations qualified by a battery of predictive tests successfully completed. In short, while Bhaskar posits the existence of causal mechanisms and trends in the social sciences (Bhaskar 1998: 21), he opposes the presumption that such trends and mechanisms are reducible to empirical regularities, and he challenges the belief that such mechanisms can be confirmed within the confines of 'closed systems' (*à la* natural science). Thus, as Bhaskar puts it, 'the appraisal and development of theories in the social sciences *cannot be predictive* and so must be *exclusively explanatory*' (Bhaskar 1998: 21).

Critical realists therefore reject the 'epistemic fallacy' associated with empiricism and positivism, which reduces the investigation of the world to our knowledge claims about it. In this view, the philosophy of science and social science is confined to the kinds of statement we can make about objects or events – whether or not they are true or false, analytical or synthetic, and so forth. In equal measure, Bhaskar and his school are concerned with the way the world has to be in order for knowledge claims and experience to be possible at all. More precisely, their insistence that the world is composed of *real objects* with specific properties and generative mechanisms, which are presupposed in our actions and experiences at the phenomenological level, and which make possible our knowledge of the world, constitutes a welcome turn to ontology in the social sciences.

However, this particular understanding of the ontological is restricted to an elaboration of the sorts of objects and mechanisms that make up the (social) world. By contrast, as we will see in Chapter 4, ontology for us is not reducible to an inventory of the kinds of things in the world. In our view, we cannot sever beings from the relational contexts in which they appear, and from the particular interpretations that constitute their meaning. In Bhaskar's account of structure and agency, he clearly privileges the role of structures as a set of constraints on human action, which define for them the potential range of outcomes and strategies. But there is a danger of paying short shrift to the necessary and complex connection between the empirical and ontological levels of analysis, that is, the realm of lived experience and action, on the one hand, and the underlying structures and modes of being, on the other hand, that make the former possible.

Towards a retroductive conception of social science explanation

Despite these difficulties, critical realists are correct to accord a prominent role to retroductive reasoning in both the transcendental production of ontological categories, and in the generation of concrete explanations of empirical phenomena. Indeed, they make a crucial contribution to the development of retroductive reasoning in the social sciences by questioning the rigid separation between the original intuitions and practices that produce theories and laws on the one hand (context of discovery), and their demonstration and acceptance on the other (context of justification). Of course, while the picture of natural science implied by the invocation of the discovery/ justification distinction may be at odds with recent history and philosophy of natural and social science, its importance for us lies in the fact that it is a picture that is still alive and well in the contemporary practice of (positivist) social science. It is for this reason that we think it still necessary to explore different languages with which to critically interrogate the positivist understanding of this distinction between the two contexts.

In this environment, what is usually called the context of discovery involves all those activities that result in the positing of a hypothesis H (either in the form of inductively inferred laws, or in the form of laws that have been derived from axioms), and which therefore contribute to the development of theoretical tools with which to explain a phenomenon X. The context of justification, on the other hand, draws a boundary around those activities that result in the acceptance of a hypothesis H, which usually takes the form of theorems or empirical predictions that are deductively inferred, tested, and then used to explain X. As Popper expresses it in one of his formulations,

> the act of conceiving or inventing a theory, seems to me neither to call for logical analysis nor to be susceptible of it. The question how it happens that a new idea occurs to a man ... may be of great interest to empirical psychology; but it is irrelevant to the logical analysis of scientific knowledge. This latter is concerned not with questions of fact ... but only with questions of justification or validity ... Its questions are of the following kind. Can a statement be justified? And if so, how? Is it testable? Is it logically dependent on certain other statements? Or does it perhaps contradict them? ...
>
> Accordingly I shall distinguish sharply between the process of conceiving a new idea, and the methods and results of examining it logically.
>
> (Popper 1980: 31)

The separation between these two domains of practice in the natural sciences might be deemed plausible because it appears that the form of reasoning involved in *positing* a hypothesis is central to the first context, but unimportant to the logic of *accepting* them in the second context. In trying to determine the structure of benzene, for example, Kekule's dream of a snake chasing its own tail may have constituted sufficient reason for him to posit the closed hexagonal structure hypothesis (cf. Weisberg 1993). However, the form of reasoning involved in accepting this hypothesis is clearly distinct from the way in which it was generated. Thus, in the natural sciences it is possible to devise a test that controls for spurious conditions, enabling the scientist to isolate those features of the structure that may *demonstrate* its hexagonal nature.

Of course, critical realists are not opposed to the separation of these two contexts in accounting for the logic of discovery and explanation in the natural sciences, where there is a legitimate role for the testing of predictions through sophisticated falsificationism for instance. However, in the social sciences they are keen to blur this sharp distinction (see also Elster 1983a: 237, note 1). This arises out of their scepticism about the constitutive link between explanation and prediction in social science, and because the social world is an open system that is not susceptible to 'closed' experimental observation and analysis. The sheer complexity of the social world, with its 'multiplicity of interacting tendencies', appears to lead them to relax the strong criterion of testing predictions in order to judge the worth of a putative explanation (Outhwaite 1987: 57).

Instead they argue that the conditions for a good explanation are satisfied if the postulated mechanism is capable of explaining the phenomenon investigated; that there are good reasons for believing in the existence of the mechanism; and that it is not possible to think of any equally plausible alternatives. And in a situation of competing explanations that satisfy these criteria, critical realists accept that the guidelines for choosing between them will be 'necessarily vague', as 'there seem to be no general grounds for rational preference' (Outhwaite 1987: 58–9). Indeed, this vagueness informs their ethos of conducting research in the social sciences, for they include injunctions such as not being 'afraid of theoretical abstraction'; being aware of the wider context within which explanations must be fitted; and accepting that a priori theoretical concepts (such as social structure) have a role to play in evaluating social theories. However, critical realists do value simplicity as a means of choosing between rival theories, mainly because they 'maximise the chances of further intertheoretical debate within the sciences concerned', thus opening up rather than closing down discussion (Outhwaite 1987: 59). Indeed, critical realists put in a plea for social science research to be as open-ended and dialogical as possible (Bhaskar 1989: 178–9).

The critical realist intervention is helpful because it goes some way towards suggesting why retroductive reasoning is central to how we should think about social science explanation. Nevertheless, there are two qualifications we need to make. First, while we are in agreement with the formal aspect of retroductive reasoning, we are sceptical about the precise way the form of their retroductive *explanans* is given content. More specifically, the content critical realists opt for – causal mechanisms – flows directly out of their ontological commitments, which also provides them with the 'rational framework' that guides the above-mentioned open-ended dialogue. Bhaskar's naturalist claim is that we can and should think of the social sciences 'in exactly the same sense, though not in exactly the same way, as the natural ones' (Bhaskar 1998: 159), but that, because the social world is much more complex and open, there are far too many processes and causal interactions with which to cope. This, of course, helps account for the difficulties of prediction in the social sciences, and may even provide grounds for better predictions in the future. However, the critical realist position – 'ontologically bold but epistemologically cautious' as one commentator puts it (Outhwaite 1987: 53) – restricts the scope of contingency to the multiple interactive possibilities among the plurality of generative mechanisms, which in turn points to a residual positivism (see also Topper 2005: 145). In our account, however, contingency goes 'all the way down' so to speak. It is not just the complexity of the interactions between various mechanisms that concerns us, but the intrinsic contingency of the mechanistic structures themselves – a point we shall return to in Chapter 3, where we will critically engage with Elster's work on causal mechanisms.

The second qualification we wish to make in relation to the critical realist intervention concerns the precise logic of the argument linking explanation, retroduction, and the blurring of the boundary between contexts of discovery and justification. Though Bhaskar's discussion is suggestive, especially his appeal to the distinction between transitivity and intransitivity, which we have not discussed here, the overall logic of the argument remains indeterminate (Bhaskar 1998: 21–2, 47; see also Laclau and Bhaskar 1998: 10, 13). We wish therefore to develop our own version of this argument now, highlighting how this furnishes us with a post-positivist conception of social science explanation.[17]

Positivism to post-positivism

In moving from a positivist to a post-positivist picture of social science, the impact on the status and scope of retroduction can be schematized as in Figure 1. This figure sets out our minimal retroductive *form* of explanation, showing the movement from a positivist to a post-positivist picture of social science. *In nuce*, adapting Peirce and Hanson to suit our purposes, our logic of

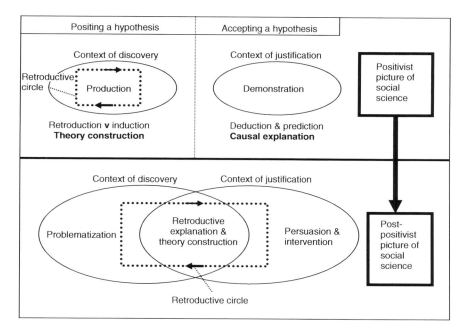

Figure 1 Two pictures of social science.

explanation begins with something we encounter in the present – an anomalous phenomenon that needs to be rendered intelligible for example – which calls for thought and theorization. This active process of problematization involves the constitution of a problem – or an *explanandum* to use more traditional terms – which invariably results in the transformation of our initial perceptions and understandings. Work is then started on furnishing an explanation that can render the recalcitrant phenomenon more intelligible. This process is understood in terms of the logic of retroductive explanation and theory construction, which involves a to-and-fro movement between the phenomena investigated and the various explanations that are proffered. In this way, an initially chaotic set of concepts, logics, empirical data, self-interpretations, and so on, at varying levels of abstraction, are welded together, so as to produce an account which, if it removes our initial confusion, can constitute a legitimate candidate for truth or falsity.

Our *justification* of the explanation proffered is complex, for it involves a set of criteria that are *internal* to the process of constructing an explanation or narrative, as well as the related practices of persuading others of its accept-ability by engaging in a series of theoretical and practical interventions. Importantly, however, the *criteria* which are internal to the process of justifying a putative *explanans* are not construed in the same way as those informing the positivist paradigm. The latter involve subjecting statements to a series of exhaustive predictive tests against all available data to determine their truth or falsity, and/or statistical significance.

But though our criteria are not as hard and universal as those put forward by positivists, they can still be publicly stated, and they do provide normative guidance, which applies across a range of empirical investigations. For example, we can ask whether an explanation best fits the problem under investigation in the sense that it renders it intelligible, and whether it is more illuminating than rival interpretations. In general, our criteria comprise standards of credibility and consistency, evidentiary support, exhaustiveness, and so on. But the way these criteria are understood cannot short-circuit the process of interpretation. In fact, a central problem with the positivist picture of social science concerns its assumption that it is possible to avoid debates about ontology. And we suspect that the desire to by-pass interpretations arises because positivists are either all too aware that interpretations rely upon contestable ontological presuppositions and thus bracket them, or they remain oblivious of this dependence and are content to conduct normal science.

In this regard, we consider it crucial that any putative explanation must take seriously the self-interpretations and meanings of the actors investigated (the minimal hermeneutic requirement). However, the precise way in which we *interpret* subjects' self-interpretations and incorporate them into our explanations will depend upon the ontological presuppositions informing the particular approach. This is why an explanation is not reducible to the self-interpretations of subjects, either in terms of its generation or in terms of is acceptance. For example, a hermeneuticist may seek to tie her interpretations of the subjects' self-interpretations as closely as possible to the context of the concrete practice in which they are embedded, while a critical realist may seek to base her interpretations on one or more set of mechanisms whose contingent interaction accounts for the constitutively open and complex character of the social world. But, as we shall argue in the course of this book, our poststructuralist approach connects interpretations to a set of logics predicated on a more radical notion of contingency.

As a result of this complex mediating movement between problematization, interpretation, and ontological projection – which we capture with the idea of a retroductive circle – an explanation is constructed and presented for critical scrutiny. This picture contrasts sharply with the positivist picture of social science, and we can bring out this contrast by outlining the movement (depicted in Figure 1) from a positivist to a post-positivist picture of social science practice in six steps.

The *first* step of our argument simply reiterates the positivist understanding of social science testing and explanation as *deductive* in form. Starting with a hypothesis, positivist social science proceeds to *deduce* implications, which insofar as they accurately predict or retrodict empirical phenomena can be said to have *explained* the phenomena. The resultant laws and empirical generalizations can then be used to explain related empirical phenomena. This conforms to the deductive-nomological model of explanation, wherein particular phenomena are deemed to have been explained when they are *subsumed* under a universal causal law. For example, we might explain why a particular country has a two party system by invoking Duverger's Law which states that '*the simple-majority single-ballot system favours the two party system*' (Duverger 1959: 217). Here a particular case is explained by subsuming it under the universal law.

In the *second* place, we claim that positivism's deductive form of explanation and validation makes possible the drawing of a stark boundary between the contexts of discovery and justification. Popper puts this in the following terms:

> [I]t is irrelevant from the point of view of science whether we have obtained our theories by jumping to unwarranted conclusions or merely by stumbling over them (that is, by 'intuition'), or else by some inductive procedure. The question, 'How did you first *find* your theory?' relates, as it were, to an entirely private matter, as opposed to the question, 'How did you *test* your theory?' which alone is scientifically relevant.
>
> (Popper 1961: 135)

And though there are clear tensions in his work on this point,[18] here at least Popper goes on to say that this 'is not only true for the natural but also for the social sciences' (Popper 1961: 135). In sum, a positivist conception of testing and explanation is committed to the ideal that a hypothesis is detachable from the context of its discovery, enabling efforts to be directed primarily at the context of its justification.[19]

Subscribing to the distinction between contexts of discovery and justification means that the hypothesis (the model, causal law, etc.) and its predictions are of central importance to a positive social science. The model stands or falls on the basis of its deduced predictions/explanations. As Dowding puts it, for example, without a good descriptive history of British agricultural policy there is little chance of coming up with a hypothesis about why Britain adopted the agricultural policy it did over the post-war period (Dowding 2001: 91). But the problem with a purely historical account 'is that it cannot *demonstrate* that it has provided all the answers' (Dowding 2001: 90; emphasis added), because such a history cannot tell us whether all the relevant causal factors have been accounted for, or which causal factors are the most important. This is why social scientists need to specify models with which to produce 'definite predictions' *qua* deduced or 'logical implications' that take us beyond the context of discovery (Dowding 2001: 92).[20]

The *third* part of our argument is that the deductive form of validation and explanation does not hold for the social sciences. There are several reasons to be sceptical about the use of deduction in sustaining the distinction between the contexts of discovery and justification. In the main, however, they concern the centrality of self-interpretations in the social world; the relevance of context in attributing sense and significance to data against which hypotheses are tested; as well as the contestability of the ontological presuppositions necessarily brought to bear when self-interpretations and data are subjected to interpretation. In other words, we suggest that one reason to be sceptical in this regard has to do with the fact that hypotheses concerning the social world are 'logically tied' (Winch 1990: 89) to the reasons and self-interpretations of agents (the hermeneutical insight). And the reflexive nature of the objects that are studied in the social sciences implies that our interpretation of the contextual factors become constitutive of the posited hypothesis. In other words, the situational features comprising the content and condition of the hypothesis do a lot of explanatory work. In this view, our interpretations as analysts of the contextualized reasons and self-interpretations carry a large share of the explanatory burden, thereby diminishing the prospect and significance of the deductive form of testing and explanation.

An illustration from the work of James Farr can exemplify this kind of argument (Farr 1987). His discussion of Duverger's law, in particular, reinforces the claim that the deductive-nomological model of explanation is inappropriate in social science, either as a guiding ideal, or as a means to understand social science practice. In so doing Farr emphasizes the minimal hermeneutical requirement for explanation and understanding in political science by highlighting the political analyst's explicit or implicit concern with the actors' language and meanings (Farr 1987: 51). In this view, a well-founded political analysis can claim to understand and explain an action if it can be shown 'to have been "adequate to the situation *as the agent saw it*"' (Farr 1987: 52; emphasis added). Of course, how far we go in deferring to the self-interpretations of the actors in generating or accepting a proto-explanation will be a function of the specific ontology (e.g. hermeneutical, critical realist, poststructuralist) underpinning one's approach. What is essential here is that the minimal hermeneutical insight be taken seriously, in the sense that our explanations ought to be properly contextualized in relation to the self-interpretations of subjects themselves. With this proviso in mind, then, we can turn to Farr's discussion of Duverger's law.

Duverger's law, it will be recalled, states that 'the simple-majority single-ballot system favours the two party system' (Duverger 1959: 217). Farr points to familiar technical difficulties 'about prediction and the support of counterfactual conditionals' (Farr 1987: 57), as well as the long list of exceptions which continues to grow, even as adherents to the covering-law model try to accommodate them with ever-more complex refinements (see also Riker 1982 and Benoit 2006). But even '*if* there were *no* exceptions', asks Farr, 'why...would majority (or plurality) electoral systems bring about two-party systems?' (Farr 1987: 58). Here is Duverger's answer: 'In cases where there are three parties operating under the simple-majority single-ballot system the electors soon realize that their votes are wasted if they continue to give them to the third party: whence their natural tendency to transfer their vote to the less evil of its two adversaries in order to prevent the success of the greater evil' (Duverger 1959: 226; cited in Farr 1987: 58). Thus the situation is very different in a system of proportional representation, or when voters interpret the meaning of their votes in a different way. For example, some voters may not vote for purely instrumental reasons, but because of their ideological commitments, or because they see the act of voting as 'the moral exercise of civic duty'. Hence, 'the judgment of rationality, in these various situations, depends on the meaning of the situation as the voters see it. Upon this hangs much of our explanations of the nature of the party system' (Farr 1987: 59). Indeed, the fragile nature of these 'laws' is driven home by noting how political analysts' explanations can change the very object of their study – what has been described in terms of the 'feedback effect' (Jervis 1997) or the 'looping effect' (Hacking 1995). As Farr correctly notes, this means that 'it is possible to change the so-called "laws" of political life, however hard they seem' (Farr 1987: 60–1).[21]

By appealing to examples where political scientists purport to have established laws or 'strong probabilistic tendencies' – Duverger's law or Roberto Michels's 'iron law of oligarchy' – Farr argues that they actually offer quite exemplary, though mis-described, context-dependent analyses.[22] As Farr puts it, Duverger's and Michel's contributions lie not so much in discovering laws, but 'in providing a *situational analysis* which lies behind the political tendency glossed in generalised form as a "law"' (Farr 1987: 59; emphasis added), thereby providing an explanation of specific instances of the laws themselves.[23] Thus it is the *situational* elements that appear to carry the lion's share of the burden of explanation, not the purported psychological or other laws (Farr 1987: 60). Moreover, it is the complexity and variability of those situational elements that renders a strong notion of testing, as well as the deductive form of explanation, problematic.

We can now make explicit the implications of the third step in our argument. That is to say, in rejecting the deductive form of testing and explanation in social science, we also reject the stark separation between the contexts of discovery and justification. This makes it possible for us to re-interpret this distinction heuristically rather than epistemologically. Moreover, in rejecting the role attributed to deductive reasoning we do not conclude that there are no criteria with which to judge the acceptance or otherwise of an explanatory hypothesis. It only follows that these criteria are not narrowly construed in hypothetico-deductive terms.

We capture these thoughts in a *fourth* step, by suggesting that it is possible to distinguish analytically between three dialectical moments in social science practice: the moment of *problematization*, the moment of *retroductive explanation and theory construction*, and the moment of *persuasion and intervention*. More specifically, we argue that our rejection of the stark boundary between the contexts of discovery and justification transforms their meanings and signif-icance, thus generating a *post-positivist* picture of social science practice.[24]

Consider, for instance, what happens to our understanding of the context of justification as we move from a positivist to a post-positivist picture of social science practice. A positivist understanding of the context of justification includes a narrow conception of testing and explanation. In this view, a posited hypothesis is deemed valid if and only if it enables one to deduce falsifiable predictions. Moreover, a hypothesis is accepted as a valid explanation only if its predictions are confirmed, or at least not falsified. Thus from the point of view of positivism, it makes sense to distinguish between a *hypothesis* on the one hand, and a valid *explanation* on the other hand. It adopts a hard conception of testing, whose aim is to *demonstrate* the validity of a hypothesis, thus relegating the process of hypothesis *production* to a secondary role.

By contrast, a post-positivist understanding of the context of justification includes a much more capacious conception of 'testing' and thus explanation. In this view, an account is accepted as a valid explanation only if it produces insights and greater illumination according to criteria which can be publicly articulated, criteria concerning evidence, consistency, exhaustiveness, and so on. (Of course, we accept that such criteria are themselves subject to interpretation and contestation, since they presuppose a set of ontological commitments that cannot be resolved by appealing to ontologically neutral epistemological tests.) A post-positivist conception of testing is therefore elastic (as opposed to hard) and involves theoretical and critical *interventions*, as well as practices of *persuasion*, in relation to both the agents being studied and the relevant scholarly community. Crucially, however, the persuasive aspect of justification extends to the task of convincing the relevant audience about the way the problem was characterized (or re-characterized) in positing the proto-explanation at the outset, *pointing us back to the context of discovery*.

In this view, then, one 'test' of a proto-explanation is the evaluation of publicly available accounts of specific phenomena by a tribunal of critical scholars. And while this tribunal's acceptance does not determine the validity of a proto-explanation in any simple or straightforward way, these dialogical and discursive practices are surely central in determining what is to *count* as 'a candidate for truth and falsity' (to use Foucault's phrase). Another perhaps more challenging tribunal consists of the relevant practitioners who act on the insights and explanations offered by empirical and historical research. Combining these would involve – *pace* James Tully – viewing social and political analysis as 'not only an interpretive political philosophy [held accountable by the tribunal of scholars] but also a specific genre of critique or critical attitude towards ways of being governed in the present – an attitude of testing and possible transformation' (Tully 2002: 534). More specifically, as Tully goes on to say,

> the experiments of the participants in negotiating, implementing, and reviewing concrete changes in practice provide a pragmatic, concrete *test* of the studies and their limitations. By studying the unanticipated blockages, difficulties, and new problems that arise in the cycle of practices of freedom – of negotiations, implementation, and review – political philosophers can detect the limitations and faults of their initial account, make improvements, and exercise again, on the basis of the new problems, this *permanent critical ethos of testing* the practices in which we are governed.
>
> (Tully 2002: 551; emphasis added)[25]

In our *fifth* step, we claim that post-positivism's more capacious understanding of testing and explanation conforms to the retroductive form of reasoning, usually associated with the positing of a hypothesis. Positing a hypothesis, we recall, involves retroductive reasoning (the pragmatist insight), which is distinct from both inductive and deductive reasoning, because its criterion of validity depends on whether the posited hypothesis *accounts* for a problematized phenomenon by rendering it intelligible (Hanson 1961: 86). This means that the processes of hypothesis generation and explanation merge into one retroductive form, as there is no single or a priori specifiable criterion that can determine by virtue of its content (e.g. its capacity to withstand falsifiable predictions) whether a hypothesis explains a problematized phenomenon. All this is simply to say that the judgement of whether a hypothesis furnishes us with a valid explanation cannot be settled by declaring in advance that only one criterion decides whether a hypothesis is true or not, thus attempting to 'get behind' or 'short-circuit' the practice of interpretation. The retroductive *circle*, once confined to the context of discovery, is now much more expansive, spanning and unifying all three of our dialectical moments: problematization, retroductive explanation, and persuasion and intervention. And the latter will necessarily involve the use of various rhetorical and argumentative strategies in the endeavour to convince sceptics of an explanation's validity and pertinence.

On this account, the problem, the theory and its ontological presuppositions, as well as the positing and accepting of proto-explanations, all find themselves articulated in an ongoing dialectic. Not unlike Rawls's method of 'reflective equilibrium' they undergo constant reformulations during the process of generating a plausible and convincing explanation (Rawls 1971: 48–52; 1996: 28) – a process which in principle remains open, and which does not necessarily exhibit any convergence on a definitive and singular right answer. Persuasion and intervention thus engage us at the *ontological, political,* and *ethical levels,* since there is no neutral way to engage in processes of problematization and explanation: there is no independent yardstick beyond our interpretations which would allow us to leave them behind, and focus instead on the 'procedures' or 'methods and techniques' of science to determine the right answer.[26]

Finally, it is worth noting that we use the term 'retroductive circle' because it both resonates with, and keeps a certain distance from, the more familiar notion of the 'hermeneutic circle'. By retroductive circle we aim to capture the necessary 'to-and-fro' movement of retroductive reasoning that can extend to the practice of persuading a wider community of scholars and practitioners that they *should* accept our explanations.[27] This is because the moment of persuasion has both an instrumental aspect to it, in which the aim is to convince others that our explanation is right, and a constitutive aspect to it, in which it can cause us to revise our presuppositions and thus explanation. Thus, the practices of persuasion cannot – except heuristically – stand outside our retroductive circle; indeed, they can often furnish new insights and phenomena that lead to the revision of our retroductively inferred explanations.

From a positivist point of view, the relevant audience or tribunal is called upon to adjudicate on test findings, not to dispute historical, ontological, political, and ethical presuppositions that are linked to the formulation of the problem and hypothesis in the first place. In other words, critical engagement takes place (and ought to take place) primarily at the *epistemological and methodological levels.* While positivist social scientists will disagree about whether findings verify or falsify predictions, thus restricting the scope of the retroductive circle to the self-contained context of discovery (and not that of the context of justification), post-positivists are caught in an expansive retroductive circle, where disagreement is about the meaning and significance of findings, as well as the characterizations and origins of the problems and proto-explanations themselves. The latter are ineliminably historical, ontological, political, and ethical.

For our *sixth* and final point we suggest that the *form* of retroductive explanation can accommodate different *contents*: contextualized self-interpretations, causal mechanisms, and logics. Retroductive explanation is opposed only to deductive explanation when it is conceived in terms of a *universal subsumption.* And by universal subsumption we denote that mode of explanation that aspires to maximize the context-free status of causal laws (by discovering or approximating 'natural laws of society') or empirical generalizations (by transforming them into 'probabilistic generalizations of society', whether causal or correlational).

Therefore, *retroductive* explanations at the level of content can accommodate any entities, so long as they do *not* entail universal subsumption. For instance, they can be descriptive and normative in character, where one seeks to critically explain by *contextualizing* the *self-interpretations* of agents (to be discussed in Chapter 2); 'non-universally subsumptive' in character, where instead of subsuming them under context-free laws or empirical generalizations one furnishes post-facto explanations by subsuming the actions of agents under *causal mechanisms* that hover closer to the context (to be discussed in Chapter 3); or articulatory in character, where one seeks to critically explain by linking together *different types of logic* which have a context-dependent empirical dimension, as well as explicit ontological and ethical dimensions (to be discussed in Chapters 4, 5, and 6). We will argue that although the practice of articulation requires the intervention of the analyst (e.g. to connect theoretical categories to concrete empirical contexts), this is understood in a way that does not simply demote extreme universalism in the name of an extreme particularism.

This last step allows us to make explicit three usages of the term retroduction in this chapter: a positivist, a post-positivist, and a poststructuralist use. While the positivist outlook keeps separate the contexts of discovery and justification, situating retroduction firmly within the former, post-positivists regard the boundary between the contexts of discovery and justification as porous. While a positivist understanding of retroduction is compatible with a deductive form of explanation which entails universal subsumption, a post-positivist understanding of retroduction is compatible with a range of explanatory modes (description, general subsumption, articulation) and contents (contextualized self-interpretations, causal mechanisms, and logics). However, though situated within the post-positivist camp, broadly conceived, a poststructuralist discourse theory seeks to understand retroduction specifically as part of an overall practice of articulation and the ontology this presupposes.

Theory construction and critical explanation in the social sciences

We are now in a position to reconstruct two connected ways in which retroduction can be invoked to better understand and engage in social science practice. On the one hand, retroductive reasoning is evident in practices in which the dimension of theory construction is dominant. On the other hand, it is evident in practices whose primary aim is to explain and understand particular phenomena that are problematized from the perspective of a particular theory or paradigm. We examine each of these practices by elaborating two exemplary instances of retroductive reasoning and explanation in the social sciences. The first focuses on an explicit and distinctive post-Marxist approach to political analysis developed by Ernesto Laclau and Chantal Mouffe, which not only allows us to demonstrate a retroductive logic of theory construction, but also enables us to introduce in brief some of the ontological presuppositions of our approach to critical explanation. The second concentrates on Michel Foucault's efforts to explain aspects of the 'history of sexuality' by proposing the distinctive and critical logics of disciplinary power and bio-power.

The emergence of post-Marxist theory can be traced back to a series of empirical and political anomalies which surfaced during the 1970s and 1980s. These 'astonishing' or 'surprising' phenomena, which resisted description and explanation within the existing Marxist schemas, were eventually crystallized into a theoretical crisis of the Marxist paradigm. They included the failure of the working class to constitute itself as a universal agent of emancipation; the growth of non-class social movements and political struggles which did not conform to the orthodox Marxist schemas; the intransigence of capitalist social relations that continued to flourish despite predicted crises and prophecies of imminent collapse; the growing complexity and autonomization of social relations; the failure of Left-wing political parties both in opposition and in government in the 'advanced capitalist countries' to construct viable socialist regimes; the growth of the New Right and neo-liberalism; and so forth (see Boggs 1986). In short, the growing number and intensity of these anomalies culminated in a fully-fledged, 'organic' crisis of the Marxist paradigm.

Following their initial efforts to repair the existing, crisis-ridden paradigm in the 1970s, Laclau and Mouffe's responses since the 1980s have involved, first, a deconstruction of the essentialism and class reductionism of Marxist theory and, second, the development of an alternative ontological grounding of Marxist categories by drawing on a range of new theoretical resources.[28] The latter include Saussure's structural linguistics, Derridean deconstruction, Lacanian psychoanalysis, and post-analytical philosophy, which have been employed to elaborate a post-Marxist approach to political analysis that is predicated on a new theory of hegemony. And of central importance in this new ontological framework are the concepts of social antagonism and dislocation, both of which are premised on the radical contingency of social relations, and a constitutive negativity that cannot be reabsorbed into any objectivistic account of social reality.

For now, we need only consider their intervention from a retroductive point of view. To begin, in keeping with the approach we have outlined, it is important to stress the way in which Laclau and Mouffe sought to construct the *problem* they encountered in terms of a 'crisis of Marxism', which had then to be resolved in a particular way. Equally, it is notable that while the dimension of theory-construction is the main point of their intervention, these theoretical efforts were conditioned by a set of strategic problems confronting Left-wing politics in the 1970s and 1980s. But it is also clear that this strategic task, which was addressed to particular constituencies, and which arose from political debates that were embodied in a particular set of self-interpretations, was closely connected to the task of critical explanation. This is because the elaboration of their new assumptions and concepts was linked to the pinpointing of failures in existing explanatory schemas, and involved the articulation of theoretical resources that were designed to overcome such explanatory and normative difficulties.

In sum, Laclau and Mouffe proposed a new theoretical grammar that was rooted in a particular ontological standpoint, which they used to render intelligible a series of recalcitrant empirical phenomena and strategic dilemmas confronting a particular intellectual tradition. In so doing, the logic of their approach partakes of a retroductive form of reasoning. But why should we accept their new theoretical grammar? What are the criteria for its acceptance? It is clear that in developing their new approach Laclau and Mouffe did not rely upon the standard positivist model of testing a set of falsifiable hypotheses against all empirical evidence so as to demonstrate their validity. As against positivism, with its rigid separation of discovery and testing, the answer as to why we could or should accept their intervention depends, first, upon a range of criteria, which are internal to the production of their theoretical approach itself and, second, upon a nexus of persuasive practices, and theoretical and strategic interventions, which are designed to convince a range of relevant communities of both their validity and strategic importance.

The internal criteria we can mobilize to evaluate their theoretical solution comprise the degree to which the new approach is able to render intelligible the anomalous phenomena that arose within the existing paradigms in a way that was more plausible than rival attempts to resolve the crisis of Marxism; the consistency of its ontological presuppositions and theoretical claims; the fecundity of the research programme in identifying and addressing new possibilities of theoretical endeavour and empirical research; and the cogency and effectiveness of the critiques developed in its name, coupled with the new ethical and political possibilities the new approach makes possible. In all these respects, it is our view that Laclau and Mouffe's approach does indeed constitute a valid project of theory construction, which successfully addresses many of the anomalies they confronted, thus disclosing new possibilities for research and intervention. In fact, this book can be read as an attempt to make good this claim.

But of equal importance in this regard are their ongoing endeavours to persuade a range of relevant communities and subjects, both academic and political, of the validity and productivity of their theoretical approach and its political implications. And by 'relevant communities and subjects' we mean those social and political theorists that are or have been asked to endorse or reject the new approach, supplying reasons and arguments for their judgements, as well as those social actors that are or have been directly affected by the arguments, critical explanations, and normative consequences brought forth by the new approach. The intense and sometimes vociferous debates spawned by Laclau and Mouffe's various theoretical interventions attest to this process of persuasion and intervention (see Sim 1998, 2000; Smith 1998; Torfing 1999). Moreover, while this requirement is not entirely absent in the natural sciences – Kuhn has insisted on the role of persuasion and rhetoric in convincing a scientific community of the power of a new paradigm (Kuhn 1970) – it is of overriding importance in the social sciences, mainly because predictive demonstration is all but absent. In short, this means that the practices of problematization, retroductive explanation or accounting, and persuasion and intervention, are best viewed as related moments in an overarching retroductive circle. But it also means that the explanatory and critical dimensions are always present in a social science inquiry, even when theory construction appears to be the chief ambition of the social analyst and theoretician.

We now turn to the way retroductive reasoning can critically explain a range of more concrete social phenomena or practices. Here we discuss the first volume of Foucault's *History of Sexuality*, and the lectures entitled *Society Must Be Defended*, which, taken together, furnish us with an exemplary case of a retroductive form of explanation in the social sciences (Foucault 1979, 2003). Foucault begins his 'history of the present' by identifying an anomalous or 'wondrous' aspect of discourses about sexuality. The astonishment provoked is not because of the repression of sexuality in the modern/post-modern period – what he labels 'the repressive hypothesis' – but the *vehement insistence* that we *are* repressed, and that we need to liberate ourselves from the prohibitions erected around it by 'defying established power', thus uncovering the real truth about ourselves and ushering in a period of sexual 'bliss' and 'manifold pleasures' (Foucault 1979: 6–7). Foucault's problematization leads not so much to an enquiry into the origins and character of sexual repression, but rather to the passionate and resentful drive of modern human beings to claim that they are repressed: 'By what spiral did we come to affirm that sex is negated? What led us to show, ostentatiously, that sex is something we hide, to say it is something we silence?' (Foucault 1979: 8–9).

Foucault transforms this series of questions into a new object of investigation, which is not a first order inquiry into sexual morality or ethics – what sexual practices ought to be permitted or endorsed? What regulations and prohibitions are justified? – but rather an attempt to *account* for the discourses of sexuality by locating them in a wider set of social relations over time. 'What is at issue', he argues, 'is the over-all "discursive fact," the way in which sex is "put into discourse"' (Foucault 1979: 11). In pursuing this research object, Foucault's method is genealogical, as he seeks to bypass and then reinterpret the repressive hypothesis by 'putting it back within a general economy of discourses of sex in modern societies since the seventeenth century' (Foucault 1979: 11). And the proto-explanation that is developed and narrated through this genealogical inquiry is that from the late sixteenth century the construction of sex as an object of discourse has not been repressed or constrained, but 'has been subjected to a mechanism of increasing incitement' (Foucault 1979: 12). Instead of restrictive 'techniques of power exercised over sex' he describes a process of 'dissemination and implantation of polymorphous sexualities', as well as a 'will to knowledge' that 'has persisted in constituting . . . a science of sexuality' (Foucault 1979: 12–13).

Foucault then elaborates his proto-explanation by constructing a narrative of events and practices 'that serve as guidelines for research' (Foucault 1979: 13). He focuses on two poles of development – 'an explosion of numerous and diverse techniques for achieving the subjugation of bodies and the control of populations' – which emerged in the seventeenth and eighteenth centuries to organize the power over life (Foucault 1979: 139–40). Foucault calls the first pole of development *disciplinary power*. This is 'centred on the body as a machine: its disciplining, the optimization of its capabilities, the extortion of its forces, the parallel increase of its usefulness and its docility, its integration into systems of efficient and economic controls' (Foucault 1979: 139). By contrast, the development of *bio-power* targets the 'species body', 'the body imbued with the mechanics of life and serving as the basis of the biological processes: propagation, births and mortality, the level of health, life expectancy and longevity, with all the conditions that can cause these to vary' (Foucault 1979: 139).

More precisely, what Foucault deems 'nothing less than the entry of life into history' during the eighteenth century in some Western countries brought a range of new phenomena pertaining to the production and reproduction of the human species into the emergent orders of modern knowledge and power, and thus into the domain of political practice and technique:

> Western man was gradually learning what it meant to be a living species in a living world, to have a body, conditions of existence, probabilities of life, an individual and collective welfare, forces that could be modified, and a space in which they could be distributed in an optimal manner.
>
> (Foucault 1979: 142)

It is against this historical background of the growing concern with life in general that Foucault locates the significance of sex as a social and political phenomenon. Sex becomes a nodal point linking together the twin trajectories of disciplining the body and regulating populations: 'Sex was a means of access both to the life of the body and the life of the species', and 'it was employed as a standard for the disciplines and as a basis for regulations' (Foucault 1979: 146). With respect to the first axis, sex was linked to the disciplining of the body: 'the harnessing, intensification, and distribution of forces, the adjustment and economy of energies' (Foucault 1979: 145). Along the other axis, 'it was applied to the regulation of populations, through all the far-reaching effects of its activity' (Foucault 1979: 145).

In sum, the concern with sex articulated an uneasiness with the body and the population as a whole,

> giving rise to infinitesimal surveillances, permanent controls, extremely meticulous orderings of space, indeterminate medical or psychological examinations, to an entire micro-power concerned with the body. But it gave rise as well to comprehensive measures, statistical assessments, and interventions aimed at the entire social body or at groups taken as a whole.
>
> (Foucault 1979: 145–6)

In the words of Dreyfus and Rabinow, Foucault argues that the discourse on sexuality 'emerged as a central component in a strategy of power which successfully linked both the individual and the population into the spread of bio-power' (Dreyfus and Rabinow 1982: 168). Expressed in our retroductive terms, Foucault articulates the logic of disciplinary power with the logic of bio-power, positing them as a proto-explanation of the initially surprising symptoms and recalcitrant phenomena that provoked his inquiry in the first place. In so doing, Foucault is able to redescribe phenomena such as 'the repressive hypothesis', or the character and function of 'confessional technologies' that incite us to speak about sex, in a way that renders them intelligible, while also transforming their meaning and significance. More formally, he problematizes a set of phenomena in the present by critically engaging with dominant readings or interpretations both in academic and popular discourses, before furnishing us with an alternative explanation.[29] He then seeks to persuade us through the presentation of his alternative historical account, because it offers a better explanation and elucidation of the phenomena under investigation.

But Foucault's genealogical account not only renders phenomena more perspicuous, it also furnishes the possibility of diagnosing and criticizing phenomena in the present – the widespread belief that sex is repressed, or that we need somehow to speak truth against power, or that we need to penetrate to the deep underlying meanings of surface phenomena – that are complicit with the very system they supposedly oppose. In this view, our acceptance and affirmation of the repressive hypothesis – that we have a sexually repressed nature whose freeing requires that we put ourselves in the care of experts – actually betrays the operation of a new kind of power and control. We might think we are well on the way to liberation by throwing off the restrictive prohibitions and taboos of sexuality, but we are actually fleeing headlong into a more controlling and exacting regime of power, which is defined by the logics of disciplinary power and bio-power.

In this way, we can redescribe Foucault's account as a form of retroductive explanation. Nevertheless, the dimension of theory construction should not be elided simply because the revision of 'core' ontological assumptions is not explicitly fore-grounded. For a start, even though Foucault problematizes the existing accounts of the problem, this logic of problematization always relies upon certain ontological presuppositions regarding the nature of discursive practices, for instance, or upon normative predispositions in favour of the underdog or the marginalized.

This is important if only because the process of 'applying' theoretical categories such as 'discourse' or 'logics' to concrete objects does not come off without remainder. In a manner analogous to Wittgenstein's analysis of 'applying a rule', an application should not be seen in terms of subsuming instances under a general rule. Instead, in our terms (to be discussed in detail in Chapter 6), such an application ought to be understood as part of a general practice of *articulation*, in which the sense and meaning of explanatory categories grow organically and contingently in the very process of their application. For instance, the process of gathering together a set of practices and regimes of practice, and then characterizing them in terms of logics of disciplinary power and bio-power, is a process that is not reducible to sub-suming these practices under a category, even as it contributes to the aim of explanation. Rather it involves a practice of articulation which contributes to our very understanding of *logic*, including the more specific logics of *disciplinary power* and *bio-power*. There is no reason why this cannot be extended from the 'empirical periphery' to the 'ontological core' of one's theoretical edifice, thus showing how even a basic concept such as discourse can acquire new determinations in the process of its application. As with the earlier example, though in an inverse manner, Foucault's retroductive practice of articulation involves a dimension of theory construction, even while the dimension of critical explanation appears at the forefront of his investigation.

Conclusion

Against the background of a widespread commitment to inductive or deductive reasoning, this chapter drew inspiration from Peirce and Hanson to introduce the concept of retroduction and to elucidate the general logic of explanation in the social sciences. We suggested that the ontological shift accompanying the move from the natural sciences to the social sciences had an important implication. It enabled us to see how explanation in social science is closely tied to the context of discovery, thereby making retroduction central to it.

While Peirce and Hanson may not completely discount the role of retroductive reasoning in processes of explanation in the natural sciences, we suggest that in the social sciences retroductive reasoning virtually exhausts the process of explaining. Explanation in this domain involves the furnishing of a putative *explanans*, whose justification is related to an ability to make intelligible the *explanandum* under investigation. In this model, the *explanandum* consists of problematized social phenomena that are always to some degree mediated by existing theoretical structures *and* by the discursive practices investigated. This is a result both of the ontological preconditions for *any* scientific practice and of the distinctive circumstances pertaining to the social sciences. In our conception, the latter is marked, though not exhausted, by what Giddens (referring to the work of Winch amongst others) calls a 'double hermeneutic' (Giddens 1996: 75–6), or what Foucault calls the 'transcendental-empirical doublet', both of which highlight the peculiar role that human subjectivity plays in social science explanation (see also Howarth 2004; Topper 2005: 76).

After describing how critical realist social science embraces retroduction as a form of reasoning essential to the activity of hypothesis formation and explanation, we then explored how a minimal hermeneutical social ontology could help us to move decisively away from a positivist picture of social science explanation to a post-positivist one. In this regard, we found James Farr's critical examination of the way laws are used by social scientists an illuminating way to explain empirical phenomena. Indeed, though our own poststructuralist ontology differs from his hermeneutical social ontology, Farr's intervention has served our purposes here in helping us to problematize positivism's detachability thesis, and then to nudge us in the direction of thinking about explanation in non-universally subsumptive terms. Finally, to illustrate the role of *retroductive reasoning* in social science explanation, we examined practices foregrounding the theory construction dimension, as well as practices foregrounding the explanatory dimension.[30] In the following chapters we shall explore specific hermeneutical, naturalist and poststructuralist approaches, whose mode of explanation does not conform to universal subsumption or deduction. Subscribing rather to a retroductive form of explanation, their explanatory concepts consist of contextualized self-interpretations, causal mechanisms and logics respectively.

2 Contextualized self-interpretations

The influence of Coleridge, like that of Bentham, extends far beyond those who share in the peculiarities of his religious or philosophical creed. He has been the great awakener in this country of the spirit of philosophy, within the bounds of traditional opinions. He has been, almost as truly as Bentham, 'the great questioner of things established', for a questioner needs not necessarily be an enemy. By Bentham, beyond all others, men have been led to ask themselves, in regard to any ancient or received opinion, *Is it true?* and by Coleridge, *What is the meaning?* The one took his stand *outside* the received opinion, and surveyed it as an entire stranger to it: the other looked at it *from within*, and endeavoured to see it with the eyes of a believer in it; to discover by what apparent facts it was at first suggested, and by what appearances it has ever since been rendered continually credible – has seemed, to a succession of persons, to be a faithful interpretation of their experience. Bentham judged a proposition true or false as it accorded or not with the result of his own inquiries; and did not search very curiously into what might be meant by the proposition, when it obviously did not mean what he thought true. With Coleridge, on the contrary, the very fact that any doctrine had been believed by thoughtful men, and received by whole nations and generations of mankind, was part of the problem to be solved, was one of the phenomena to be accounted for.

(Mill 1987: 177–8; emphasis added)[1]

Our introduction and first chapter began the process of problematizing the desire for law-like explanations in the human and social sciences. As we noted, there are a number of possible challenges to this picture of inquiry, ranging from purely ideographic and descriptive approaches to those that stress statistical probabilities and causal mechanisms. In this chapter, we examine self-styled hermeneutical opponents of the causal law model that focus on understanding the meanings of human actions and practices in particular contexts. A common element of these accounts is a critique of the naturalistic ideal of causal explanation, including the pre-eminence accorded to the role of prediction as the key criterion for discriminating among competing explanatory hypotheses. Equally important, as John Stuart Mill makes clear in his comparison of Bentham and Coleridge, is the adoption of a perspective that seeks 'from within' to make intelligible the meanings and reasons social agents give for their actions and practices. This approach contrasts with the objectivistic stance of the positivist mainstream, which adopts a stance 'outside' the social and political phenomena it seeks to explain. Expressed more positively, those within the hermeneutical tradition focus on the practice of interpreting the self-interpretations of social actors in particular historical contexts. Contextualised self-interpretations thus become the key component of the hermeneutical *explanans*.

There has been a proliferation of interpretive approaches in the social and political sciences, including developments in the history of ideas; the study of political culture and institutions; analyses of public policy; the exploration of international relations; not to mention the analysis of political ideologies, discourses and media representations.[2] But as with most traditions of thought hermeneutics has a complex genealogy. Some trace it back to the collapse of the medieval cosmos, and the growing dislocation between human beings on the one hand, and a divinely sanctioned universe on the other, which prompted the emergence of 'comprehensive endeavours at biblical exegesis or scriptural "hermeneutics" during the Renaissance and the Reformation' (Dallmayr and McCarthy 1977: 2). In its more modern manifestations, hermeneutics is associated with the writings of Wilhelm Dilthey (himself drawing heavily on the teachings of the romanticist philosopher and theologian Friederich Schleiermacher), Martin Heidegger and Hans-Georg Gadamer, as well as more recent thinkers such as Paul Ricoeur, Charles Taylor and Hubert Dreyfus, who have explicitly sought to develop and extend their predecessors' writings into the fields of the human and social sciences. The centrality of contextualised self-interpretations is also evident amongst key philosophers and thinkers who adopt analytical and post-analytical styles of reasoning. It is strikingly evident, for example, in the writings of Isaiah Berlin, after he 'left philosophy for the field of the history of ideas' in the 1940s (Berlin 1978: viii), as well as Peter Winch, Stuart Hampshire and more recently Donald Davidson.

This chapter evaluates the hermeneutical challenge to the law-like model by asking to what degree it can furnish us with an adequate logic of critical explanation. This involves an interrogation of the hermeneutical model from both an explanatory and a critical point of view. This interrogation can be unfolded in two related ways. On the one hand, what are the substantive merits of the hermeneutical alternative in terms of explaining the social and political world? On the other, can the focus on interpreting self-interpretations provide legitimate grounds for critique, and if so what form does this take? In seeking to address these questions, we examine three related bodies of work – the work of Peter Winch, Charles Taylor, Mark Bevir and Rod Rhodes – in order to prepare the ground for our alternative account of critical explanation. Of course they draw on different though related theoretical sources and the precise articulations of their approaches vary.[3] Nevertheless, we think there is a striking convergence in their views about the nature and role of self-interpretations in social science explanation generally, and their critique of the causal law paradigm in social science more specifically. Some material differences do emerge, however, when it comes to examining the specific resources available in each of their approaches for generating the tools necessary for developing a convincing logic of explanation. There are parts of the chapter, therefore, where we treat them together, and parts where we deal with them separately.

In this chapter, then, we argue that while hermeneuticists raise powerful critiques of the law-like model of explanation, their alternative approach runs the risk of reducing explanation to the contextualised self-interpretations of social actors. Although they offer important theoretical and conceptual resources, they are ultimately insufficient to elaborate a convincing logic of critical explanation. We also raise issues about the ontological groundings of different hermeneutical positions, seeking to show how these positions need to be supplemented. While critical explanation requires an engagement with – and a passage through – the contextualized self-interpretations of social actors, it is not sufficient to stop there if our aim is to develop conceptual tools with which to construct convincing explanations which have an equally convincing critical bite.

Self-interpretations and the critique of positivism

Winch, Taylor, and Bevir & Rhodes all privilege the role of language and meaning in mediating the experiences of actors. Drawing inspiration from Weber and Wittgenstein, Winch argues that a form of life consists of 'meaningful behaviour', and takes actions which are performed for a reason as his paradigm of meaningfulnesss (Winch 1990: 45). Taylor draws on Heidegger and Gadamer to emphasise the centrality of meaning and inter-pretation in social science, claiming that man is a 'self-defining' and 'self-interpreting' animal, whose changes in self-definition go hand-in-hand with the changes in what he is, and how he is to be understood (Taylor 1985b: 55). The more complex the available language within which actors construct their experiences – the more refined the moral contrasts in their semantic field for example – the richer the articulations and the 'strong evaluations' that are made possible by it. Indeed, because the different webs of meaning that shape such interpretations are often 'incommensurable' in history, each 'will be glossed in terms of practices, institutions, ideas in each society which have nothing corresponding to them in the other' (Taylor 1985b: 55). Finally, Bevir and Rhodes stress that individuals do not have 'pure experiences', but 'always construct their identities, interests and beliefs in part through their particular theories' (Bevir 2005: 14). Analysts ought thus to focus on the 'reasons people have for doing what they do' (Bevir 2005: 14). Drawing explicitly on Taylor's hermeneutical model, this is because 'the beliefs of individuals' have a constitutive relationship to actions and practices, such that the latter cannot be understood properly 'except by recovering the beliefs that animate them' (Bevir and Rhodes 2005: 172–4).[4]

In order to clarify what is at stake from a hermeneutical perspective, consider Winch's discussion of the practice of voting. He takes a person, N, who votes for a particular political party and then provides a reason for his or her decision. The central point here is that any explanation of this action by an observer, O, 'rests on the fact that the concepts which appear in [the explanation] must be grasped not merely by O and his hearers, but also *by N himself*' (Winch 1990: 46). Nonetheless, Winch's notion of meaningfulness extends beyond actions performed for a reason to include those that are performed without an explicitly formulated reason, or even those actions which are not easily explicable either by an observer or the actor, because they are the result of unconscious motivations, for example, or because they are actions 'for which the agent has no "reason" or "motive" at all' (Winch 1990: 48).

Winch clarifies the idea by considering the limit case of a voter, N, who votes without deliberation and without being able to furnish a reason for his or her action. A particular political party is voted for because the family has always done so. Even here, however, Winch argues that 'although N does not act . . . for any reason, his act still has a definite sense' (Winch 1990: 49). This is because the voter is not just making a mark on a piece of paper, but *'casting a vote'*, and the particular action only has meaning as an instance of the latter practice (Winch 1990: 49). Winch captures this extended notion of meaningfulness with the idea of applying a rule. An act is meaningful for the actor and the observer if it complies with a shared set of rules or conventions, which only make sense in particular forms of life.[5] As he puts it, 'all behaviour which is meaningful (therefore all specifically human behaviour) is *ipso facto* rule-governed' (Winch 1990: 52). And this account follows from Winch's interpretation of the later Wittgenstein's conception of rule-following.

Winch uses his definition of meaningful behaviour as 'rule-governed', and the concept of a form of life, to draw a sharp distinction between the natural and social sciences. This argument is grounded on his claim that, unlike the natural sciences, the objects of study in the social sciences are not empirical or statistical uniformities between observable objects – whether physical things or human dispositions – which are understood as 'external' to human forms of life, and for which empirical generalizations and ultimately laws can be furnished, but are *meaningful* human activities, which are closely associated with notions like 'motive', 'intention' and 'acting for a reason'. Because the latter differ in kind from the former, human actions and practices presuppose a 'scheme of concepts', which is 'logically incompatible with the kinds of explanation offered in the natural sciences' (Winch 1990: 72; see also 94).

Similarly, Taylor explicitly suggests that the most important reason for the incoherence of the causal law paradigm in social science, including the failures of prediction, is the ontological world-view it presupposes.[6] He argues that at the root of empiricist or rationalist epistemologies, as well as mainstream behaviourist accounts of the natural and social sciences, is a positivism that treats everything, including human beings, as 'an object amongst others' (Taylor 1985a: 47). He thus contests this underlying picture of human beings in the world by claiming that 'our interpretation of ourselves and our experience is constitutive of what we are, and therefore cannot be considered as merely a view on reality, separable from reality, nor as an epiphenomenon, which can be bypassed in our understanding of reality' (Taylor 1985a: 47; see also Bevir 2005: 12–14).

Having noted this, it is important to stress that while hermeneuticists problematize the concept of scientific prediction in the social sciences this does not necessarily exclude the practice of prediction as such. On the contrary, as Winch puts it, if an observer (*O*) 'wants to predict how *N* is going to act he must familiarize himself with the concepts in terms of which *N* is viewing the situation; having done this he may, from his knowledge of N's character, be able to predict with great confidence what decision *N* is going to take' (Winch 1990: 91). Nevertheless, and this is crucial to Winch's argument, 'the notions which *O* uses to make his predictions are nonetheless compatible with N's taking a different decision from that predicted for him', and from this it 'does not necessarily follow that *O* has made a mistake in his calculations; for the whole point about a decision is that a given set of "calculations" may lead to any one of a set of different outcomes' (Winch 1990: 91). In short, Winch's argument weakens and relativizes our understanding of prediction alongside our changed understanding of social inquiry (see also Bevir and Rhodes 2005: 181; 2006: 103).

On a more positive note, Winch develops a fruitful contrast between the ways we understand the institutions and ways of life that confer meaning to the activities of natural scientists on the one hand, and the ways we confer meaning to the activities of social scientists on the other. In general, the understanding of an individual scientific investigator ought to take account of two sets of relations: her relation to the phenomena investigated, and her relation to her fellow-scientists (Winch 1990: 84). In fact, the latter is conceded greater importance in Winch's account because it is only by acquiring the rules governing the conduct of science – understanding the problems and procedures of a science, learning the criteria according to which judgements of identity are made, and so forth – that scientific practice is possible at all (Winch 1990: 86).

Of course this picture becomes more complex when we turn to the social sciences, for in the latter the very object of study is meaningful behaviour and it too must be surrounded with the appropriate rules in order for it to be identified and understood. In Winch's words:

> The concepts and criteria according to which the sociologist judges that, in two situations, the same thing has happened, or the same action performed, must be understood *in relation to the rules governing sociological investigation*. But here we run against a difficulty: for whereas in the case of the natural scientist we have only to deal with one set of rules, namely those governing the scientist's investigation itself, here *what the sociologist is studying*, as well as his study of it, is a human activity and is therefore

carried on according to rules. And it is these rules, rather than those which govern the sociologist's investigation, which specify what is to count as 'doing the same kind of thing' in relation to that kind of activity.

(Winch 1990: 86–7)

In other words, both the subject and object of research consists of meaningful behaviour, and it is at the *intersection* of their respective systems of rules that we can begin to understand and explain the activity under investigation. To clarify this point he draws an analogy between a social theorist and an engineer. The student of society should not be compared with an engineer studying the workings of a machine. Instead, as he puts it, it is better to compare the sociologist to an apprentice engineer who is studying what the practice of engineering is all about. The social theorist's 'understanding of social phenomena is more like the engineer's understanding of his colleague's activities than it is like the engineer's understanding of the mechanical systems which he studies' (Winch 1990: 88).

This point is reinforced by Taylor's critique of positivism. Whereas in his view the natural sciences study decontextualised and essentially meaningless objects – 'brute data identifications' as Taylor puts it – the human sciences are concerned with 'self-interpreting beings', whose changing self-interpretations are the object of study in this domain, and whose changing interpretations partly constitute and disrupt the meanings of the objects studied in it (Taylor 1985b: 28).

The consequences of this view for understanding and conducting social science are quite profound. Consider, for instance, Taylor's putative explanation of the challenge posed by radical movements in the 1960s and 1970s to the dominant structures and practices of advanced capitalist societies (Taylor 1985b: 48–50). Taylor argues that mainstream American political scientists at the time tended to understand the meaning of politics in instrumental terms. And by focusing largely on the adjudication of individual preferences, the expression of opinions in surveys, or the casting of votes in elections – all of which were integral components of 'the civilization of work and bargaining' – they assumed a conception of what counts as political activity. But this conception of politics differed radically from that held by groups such as 'the counter-culture' or 'the students' movement' who were actually contesting the taken-for-granted role of instrumental rationality in shaping and constituting the dominant values and meanings of American society, including the values and meanings informing the hegemonic practice of political science itself (Taylor 1985b: 49). In other words, while the definition of politics used in mainstream political science made possible theories based on opinions polls and electoral behaviour, which were grounded on and indeed shaped political preferences, this represented just one possible and contested interpretation of the political domain that was subject to change and possible reinterpretation. The point of Taylor's example is to draw attention to the fact that interpretation both on the part of the researchers, as well as the groups they study, is involved in determining what is to count as political facts in any particular situation. For Taylor this is emphatically not the case in the natural sciences, in which the latter's objects are not – and in principle cannot be – self-interpreting (cf. Dreyfus 1986: 5).

In sum, then, the hermeneutical critique of positivist approaches to social and political analysis proceeds from the affirmation that our interpretation of reality is *constitutive* of reality, not merely a view *on* reality which can be 'bracketed'. In other words, hermeneuticists accord language and meaning a privileged role, insofar as they necessarily mediate all experience. The move from the study of nature to the study of society thus requires that we take into account this insight by noting how in the latter case both the subject *and* the object of research consist in meaningful behaviour. The central point is that interpretation 'goes all the way down': interpretation cannot somehow be by-passed in the establishment of facts and correlations, because the interpretations of both researcher and researched are essential in determining what is to *count* as a fact.

Contextualised self-interpretations: epistemological and methodological aspects

Having examined the hermeneutical critique of positivism, and the positing of an alternative ontological framework, we need to examine hermeneuticists' alternative methods and putative explanations. For instance, if one part of Taylor's programme draws attention to the fact that human beings are self-interpreting animals, another focuses more precisely on the way in which these interpretations themselves demand interpretation. Given the ontological presuppositions that underpin the social world for hermeneuticists, what are the implications for using self-interpretations in trying to understand or explain a social or political problem? We need in other words to describe the conditions for interpreting self-interpretations.

Beginning with Taylor, any legitimate 'interpretive social science requires that we master the agent's self-descriptions in order to identify *explananda*', although 'it by no means requires that we couch our *explanantia* in the same language'. Instead, the interpretive approach 'generally demands that we go beyond' the self-interpretations of actors themselves (Taylor 1985b: 117). And, as we shall see, the same is true for Bevir and Rhodes, as well as Winch (Winch 1990: 89). Now in seeking to 'go beyond' the agent's point of view Taylor borrows from Gadamer's idea of a 'fusion of horizons' to develop 'a language of perspicuous contrast' that can provide the means for explanatory and critical analysis (Taylor 1985b: 125). It is in this respect that Taylor could be said to overcome problems associated with the 'incorrigibility thesis' – the simple adoption of the agent's point of view – 'since in many cases actors are confused, misinterpreted, have contradictory purposes, and their language may reflect this' (Taylor 1985b: 117). Just 'recovering' actors' self-descriptions may not only 'cast no light at all on what was going on', but it may even inhibit our explanation of social practices, and place a bar on our critical evaluation of them (Taylor 1985b: 117). Taylor's strategy here is to focus on the different background practices that inform the beliefs of those agents who inhabit distinct forms of life in order to make as good a sense as possible out of those actors' beliefs and actions. In short, the self-interpretation of agents must be contextualized.

The goal of social science in Taylor's approach is thus to move from a subject's 'proto-interpretation' of a practice – the pre-theoretical understanding of its actions, which is always informed 'by the language in which the agent lives [out] these meanings' (Taylor 1985b: 27) – to a more coherent and reflective understanding of the practice (Smith 2002: 123). The social scientist is thus charged with the task of improving upon the 'readings of meanings' embodied in the practices under investigation. Expressed more formally, Taylor's method of perspicuous contrast involves an effort 'to make sense of an object of study', whether it be 'a text, or a text-analogue', which in certain ways is 'confused, incomplete, cloudy, seemingly contradictory', where the 'interpretation aims to bring to light an underlying coherence or sense' (Taylor 1985b: 15). The objects of a hermeneutical science – texts or text-analogues – can be decomposed into three basic elements: they must be 'describable in terms of sense and nonsense, coherence and its absence'; they 'must admit of a distinction between meaning and its expression'; and they are 'for or by a subject' (Taylor 1985b: 17–18).

An important criterion for determining the success in moving from the proto-interpretation of a particular agent to a more considered and fully-fledged interpretation is the degree to which one 'makes clear the meaning originally present in a confused, fragmentary, cloudy form' (Taylor 1985b: 17). Nevertheless, in interpreting an object of this sort, Taylor insists that there is no point external to the situation which is being interpreted that provides a vantage-point from which to explain the meaning of a human action, text or institution in an objectivist fashion. There are no 'brute data' or 'facts of the matter' that can demonstrate the validity of a particular theory or hypothesis in a way that is ontologically and normatively presuppositionless. Indeed, as we have seen, there are no descriptions and facts that stand apart from the meanings and self-interpretations of human actors, and the latter characterizations presuppose particular cultures and 'import vocabularies' (Taylor 1985a: 45–76).[7]

To illustrate this process of generating an interpretation of a practice by means of perspicuous contrast consider how one can characterize the feeling of 'outrage', which often constitutes a powerful motivating force causing agents to engage in political activity, whether it be joining a social movement, engaging in protest, or committing an act of political violence or terrorism. Outrage is a powerful emotion we experience inside, as it were, and it may provide us with an opportunity to rethink our self-understandings, as well as our motivations to act and engage in the world. Importantly, however, it is a response to a particular situation or event: the invasion of another country by one's armed forces, or the failure to intervene in another country so as to bring about an end to genocide, for example. Thus in seeking to understand such responses we need to make sense of an agent's passions and subsequent actions in relation to the situation in which they find themselves. But these emotions and passions have also to be connected to the available languages and vocabularies within which they are articulated. A language of 'perspicuous contrast' can thus be deployed by examining 'outrage' in relation to feelings of 'disgust', 'anger', 'indignation', or 'frustration', and in relation to the moods of 'despair', 'resignation' or 'futility'.

Moreover, an actor may translate her feelings of outrage into a desire for retaliation or revenge (as is the case with the famous 'tit-for-tat' strategy discussed by game theorists, for example), turning to acts of violence, sabotage, and even terrorism. It is common for political options and strategies to become narrowed in situations of extreme antagonism and polarization, as do the available languages within which these decisions are to be made. Indeed, the choices may be so simplified that actors feel that violence is the only option left for them. Crucially for Taylor's model of interpretation, in order both to explain the meaning of a particular response and to evaluate such responses in a critical fashion, it is necessary to move between the feelings and actions of the agent on the one hand, and the available vocabularies and forms of life on the other. Was an action justified or appropriate? Were other possibilities available, and why were they not pursued? What does the interpretation disclose about the available vocabularies and their criss-crossing sets of moral and evaluative contrasts?

We thus find ourselves within what Gadamer calls a 'hermeneutic circle', where we can only grasp the meaning of an actor's affect or emotion from the inside, 'by getting somehow into their way of life', if only in our imaginations (Taylor 1985b: 24). And in 'reading' an action, practice or event we need to navigate between the particular meanings interpreted and the whole way of life within which it is embedded. In so doing, we strive to render the meaning of an action and its relation to a particular situation more coherent and intelligible, thus ridding ourselves of our initial perplexity in making sense of a particular action. For Taylor, we thus deepen our understandings of an action, rendering it more perspicuous, though at no point do we rely upon a standpoint that is *external* to the hermeneutical situation itself. We are also better positioned to evaluate our objects of investigation. In short, Taylor's discriminating approach of perspicuous contrasts should enable participants and observers to interpret and evaluate their responses and actions, and possibly to reflect on other possibilities and their consequences.[8]

At times, Taylor's project deliberately foregoes a concern with explanatory questions in favour of interpreting and rendering intelligible an existing and historically particular set of actions or practices. For instance, in his discussion of the way in which language partly constitutes our emotions, he adds an important rider to the effect that '[n]othing is said about how this emotion-insight comes into being or develops' (Taylor 1985a: 71). However, this apparent absence of explanatory concepts is perhaps truer of Winch's eclectic, rule-based approach (which we discuss in more detail in the next section) than Taylor's approach. After all, Taylor does suggest a set of explanatory concepts when seeking to provide an alternative account of the counter-cultural movements of the 1960s and 1970s, deploying terms such as 'subjective meanings', 'inter-subjective meanings', and 'common meanings' (Taylor 1985a: 36–40). The first comprise things like beliefs and opinions which may be shared (consensus) or may not (dissensus). The latter two concepts supplement individual subjective meanings by furnishing them with their conditions of possibility, which means that inter-subjective and common meanings need not be consciously held as beliefs or opinions. In this view, inter-subjective meanings provide the 'raw materials' or the 'background content' in terms of which opinions and beliefs may be expressed and understood. They are rooted in institutions and practices, and are consequently not reducible to beliefs and opinions; on the contrary, they make the latter possible.

Like inter-subjective meanings 'common meanings' are not reducible to subjective meanings and actions. This is because common meanings are sustained only through collective acts. Moreover, inter-subjective and common meanings are closely inter-connected and inter-dependent. As Taylor puts it, '[t]here must be a powerful net of inter-subjective meanings for there to be common meanings; and the result of powerful common meanings is the development of a greater web of inter-subjective meanings' (Taylor 1985a: 39). Common meanings express a common aspiration or value, furnishing actors with direction and purpose. For example, the appeal to a francophone conception of national identity by the Quebecois in Canada is a common meaning. Equally, for Taylor, bargaining is an important common meaning which shapes North American practices, such as various practices of negotiation.[9] Thus, while inter-subjective meanings furnish actors with the raw materials for making each other intelligible, common meanings provide actors with common 'reference points' that orient and make sense out of their interactions.

In the 1970s, Taylor deployed these categories to analyse late capitalist society in a critical fashion, suggesting that a withering of the dominant cultural meanings was taking place, meanings associated with what he calls 'the civilization of work' and its associated culture of bargaining, negative freedom and individualism. He then posits a 'severe challenge to this common meaning', at least in societies such as the USA during the 1960s and 1970s. In other words, the sense of instrumental rationality associated with the common meaning of bargaining was increasingly experienced as empty, leading many to reject the inter-subjective meanings and practices of negotiation, and the terms in which this common meaning is expressed. It is in this context that Taylor situates the increasing alienation of certain sectors of the population and the growing polarization of advanced capitalist societies, as 'groups tend to grow apart and develop different languages of social reality, hence to share fewer inter-subjective meanings' (Taylor 1985b: 40).

Thus Taylor is clearly trying to develop a set of concepts that can critically explain the phenomena he is investigating. Indeed, his intuitions about a hegemonic struggle between opposed sets of meanings situated within a broader field of meaning shares affinities with our own approach. However, as we shall see in the next section, the conceptual framework and method he uses are not clearly articulated, and much additional conceptual elaboration is required for them to do convincing explanatory and critical work. Even more tellingly, Taylor does not address in a systematic fashion the relationship between his more explanatory and critical concepts on the one hand, and his overall project of interpreting self-interpretations on the other. In short, it is not clear whether Taylor advances us much beyond Winch's more eclectic and deferential 'charity in interpretation'.

What then of Bevir and Rhodes? They are also committed to the task of describing and recounting the beliefs and desires of individual actors. 'We can explore [people's] behaviour', they argue, 'by examining their webs of beliefs and how they came to hold them. When political scientists so interpret beliefs, they provide insights into the behaviour of particular individuals. They *describe* the particular sets of reasons that led the relevant individuals to act' (Bevir and Rhodes 2003: 2; see also 2003: 21–2). Here we see evidence of their strong ethnographic impulse as they endeavour to recover the meanings and beliefs of individuals, which have been documented or reported by individual social actors themselves. On the other hand, their project involves a process of *ascribing* beliefs and desires to individuals. 'We can explain events and processes', argues Bevir, 'by *ascribing* beliefs and desires to actors so as to construct a narrative that locates what we want to explain in its contingent context' (Bevir 2005: 4; see also Bevir and Rhodes 2005: 180). Indeed, Bevir and Rhodes acknowledge that such ascription requires 'a reading' or 'interpretation' that does something to the beliefs and desires in question in order to explain them. These readings and interpretations generally take the form of constructed narratives or stories.

This emphasis on what they call a 'narrative form of explanation' or the construction of narratives in political science is analogous for them to the role of theory-building and theory-testing in the natural sciences (Bevir and Rhodes 2003: 20).[10] In this conception a *fact* is 'a statement, typically about a piece of evidence, which nearly everyone in the relevant community would accept as true', and *narratives* 'explain shared facts by postulating significant relationships, connections, or similarities between them' (Bevir and Rhodes 2005: 183). The upshot of these thoughts is to problematize the evaluation of rival stories by treating facts as if 'they speak for themselves'. Instead, facts are understood as always mediated by our interpretations. In a way that is reminiscent of Taylor's device of 'perspicuous contrast', Bevir and Rhodes advocate the comparison of 'bundles of narratives' by assessing their success in relating facts to one another, highlighting similarities and differences, and exploring continuities and disjunctions (Bevir and Rhodes 2005: 184).

Keeping this qualification in mind, then, Bevir and Rhodes decide between rival narratives with reference to the criteria of accuracy, comprehensiveness and consistency, all of which are underpinned by what might be termed an ethic of 'intellectual honesty'. On the one hand, the ethic involves taking criticism seriously; a preference for established standards of evidence and reason; and a preference for 'positive speculative responses that produce new exciting stories' and 'not ones that block criticism of existing stories' (Bevir and Rhodes 2005: 184). On the other hand, the criterion of accuracy means that narratives have to be bolstered by as many clearly established facts as possible; an accurate narrative, in short, 'fits the facts supporting it closely' (Bevir and Rhodes 2005: 184). The criterion of comprehensiveness means that narratives have to correspond to the facts 'with few outstanding exceptions' (Bevir and Rhodes 2005: 184). Narratives ought also to be clear and coherent, as they must link different narrative threads together in a logical and consistent fashion. Finally, because Bevir and Rhodes 'favour positive speculative responses', they also prefer narratives that are progressive, fruitful and open. Narratives ought to be progressive in that they introduce new ideas not normally associated with existing interpretations; fruitful in the sense that the new ideas put forward in progressive narratives 'receive support from the facts' (Bevir and Rhodes 2005: 184); and open in that they encourage and engage with criticisms.

Bevir and Rhodes's ethic of intellectual honesty has much to commend it and there is little in principle with which to disagree. The more general theoretical point that emerges is that they share with Taylor and Winch the belief that we need to move beyond self-interpretations to the practice of *interpreting* self-interpretations. For example, they point out how 'interviewees can be self-serving and misleading' and that 'the validity and reliability of "facts"' thereby attained can always be disputed' (Bevir and Rhodes 2003: 193). The belief is also evident when they argue that the case for interpretivism 'should not be confused with the claim that political scientists must accept actors' own accounts of their beliefs' (Bevir and Rhodes 2005: 178). They all agree, then, that interpreting self-interpretations yields *contextualised self-interpretations* as the prime means of elucidating social and political phenomena.

Nevertheless, the work of Bevir and Rhodes is also important for us because it tends to balance philosophical reflection with much greater analytical attention to the empirical domain. They thus seek to connect general hermeneutical insights about the human and social sciences to a more systematic analysis of concrete political phenomena. For example, they have sought to apply their approach to investigate and evaluate various aspects of British politics, focusing in particular on the alleged shift from 'government' to 'governance', that is, the 'shift from government by a unitary state to governance by and through networks' (Bevir and Rhodes 2003: 6).

Of course much of their project aims to refute positivist approaches to political science, while offering an approach that offers 'interpretations of interpretations' (Bevir and Rhodes 2006: 84; see also Bevir 1999: 314). But their work is also important because it holds out the promise of moving beyond Winch and Taylor to furnish us with a richer set of concepts with which to explain social and political change beyond the self-interpretations of the actors themselves. Their concept of 'dilemma' moves us in precisely this direction.

To appreciate the significance of the concept of dilemma in explaining change, it is worth situating it first in relation to their general theoretical framework. Our reading of Bevir and Rhodes has highlighted how one can only adequately understand and explain practices and actions 'by reference to the beliefs and desires of the relevant actors', which means that an adequate study of political life involves 'the interpretation of the beliefs and desires of those we study' (Bevir and Rhodes 2003: 18). This particular account leans quite heavily on Donald Davidson's model of human action, which in turn centres on the three-fold relationship between belief, desire, and action (Davidson 1980). In this conception, the beliefs and desires of individuals shape their actions, in which case the understanding of an individual's beliefs and desires enables one to account for their actions. In line with an approach that began its life as a search for 'the logic of the history of ideas' (see Bevir 1999), it is perhaps unsurprising that Bevir and Rhodes seek to resolve their objects of study into the beliefs, desires and intentions of individual actors. However, in the social sciences we invariably endeavour to understand and explain events or phenomena such as revolutions, popular uprisings, instances of political protest, or even the voting behaviour of vast electorates or assemblies. Not only does this involve 'mass behaviour', it invariably concerns 'collective actors' such as social movements, political parties, and state institutions.

Indeed, it is notable that when confronted with the complexity and heterogeneity of beliefs and desires, Bevir and Rhodes do have recourse to aggregate concepts such as practices and institutions to explain behaviour, especially what they call the 'webs' of 'meanings and beliefs' which are 'constitutive of actions and practices' (Bevir and Rhodes 2005: 177). And these 'webs' must themselves be located against the backdrop of 'inherited traditions' and 'dilemmas', which thus enable Bevir and Rhodes to explain the beliefs, actions, and change they inspire (see Bevir 1999: 176). At both the theoretical and the practical methodological levels, there is in short a retreat to forms, concepts and metaphors – 'traditions', 'webs of belief', and 'institutions' – which share the same logical properties as ideologies, social structures, and systems. For instance, the concept of *tradition* makes possible an analysis of individuals who 'inherit' – and are thus influenced by – 'a set of beliefs that forms the background to their later reasoning', but who can nevertheless via their 'local reasoning' transform such beliefs over time (Bevir and Rhodes 2005: 176).

On the other hand, *dilemma* is an explanatory concept that helps us better account for processes of social and political *change*. It relates to circumstances in which new beliefs enter a system of meaning, 'where any new belief, merely by virtue of being adopted, poses a question of the web of beliefs into which it is inserted' (Bevir 1999: 243). Consequently, dilemmas arise all the time. In the context of natural science practice, for example, dilemmas are not just rare anomalies that prompt epochal changes to scientists' webs of belief, but they are also 'the concerns that prompt scientists to extend prevailing theories during a period of normal science, and even the trivial puzzles that lead all of us to adopt new beliefs all the time in our everyday existence' (Bevir 1999: 229). Dilemmas are deemed to occur when there is a mismatch or conflict between 'perceptions of failings' (in an existing pattern of government for example) and the existing beliefs of individuals, which 'push them to reconsider beliefs and the intellectual tradition that informs those beliefs' (Bevir and Rhodes 2006: 98). It is this interplay between traditions and dilemmas that Bevir and Rhodes use to explore the question of social change. This is because change occurs when 'situated agents respond to novel ideas or problems. It is a result of people's ability to adopt beliefs and perform actions through a reasoning that is embedded in the tradition they inherit' (Bevir and Rhodes 2005: 173). Historians and researchers for their part must 'make sense of the way people modify their web of beliefs by portraying the new beliefs as responses to dilemmas confronting the old ones' (Bevir 1999: 263).

In short, the emergence of novel ideas or problems in a particular tradition offers opportunities for individuals to reflect and act in different ways, and the resultant social practices can have the effect of altering institutions and traditions. For example, evolutionary theory may provoke a dilemma for Christians who interpret the bible literally, leading them to reject evolutionary theory or to change their beliefs (Bevir 1999: 230). Or one might try to account for changes in civil service Acts, Codes, and practices by appealing to the dilemma posed to our traditional understandings of public service ethos by new ideas about public management, open competition, efficiency, and accountability (Bevir and Rhodes 2003: 134–5).

The merit of Bevir and Rhodes' approach is that it furnishes us with a parsimonious set of categories for purposes of social and political analysis and explanation. Moreover, their work contains helpful suggestions about how to ascertain the beliefs and desires of individuals; about the overall point or purpose of seeking to do so; and about the complexity and the heterogeneity of the beliefs and desires thus identified. Consider the methodological difficulty of ascertaining the beliefs and desires of the relevant individuals. Here it is worth pointing out that Bevir and Rhodes do not by any means exclude the use of quantitative data and the employment of statistical methods to construct their narrative explanations of beliefs and social practices. This is because they see their approach as imposing constraints not so much on the *creation* of particular types of data, but rather on the *analysis* of *any* type of data. This is an important point since it is one of the key insights of hermeneutics we think is crucial to affirm in keeping the 'positivist tendency' at bay. For example, treating marriage as a variable with a clear definitional content, risks occluding the actual range and significance of the meanings and beliefs associated with it, which are subject to often spectacular variation across space and time. The suggestion is not to reject quantitative or statistical techniques which rely on the clear specification of such variables, but rather that

> human scientists should treat data in ways consistent with the philosophical analysis of their task as one of interpreting interpretations. They should treat data as evidence of the meanings or beliefs embedded in actions. They should not try to bypass meanings or beliefs by reducing them to given principles of rationality, fixed norms or social categories.
> (Bevir and Rhodes 2004: 157)

But while they are not averse to using quantitative techniques of data generation, Bevir and Rhodes clearly favour qualitative means of generating the empirical evidence they draw upon in constructing their accounts. Of particular importance in this regard is the use of ethnographic methods of analysis, whether these take the form of in-depth, semi-structured interviews of key actors, the 'thick description' of social practices and the worlds within which they are embedded, or the textual analysis of speeches and official documents (Bevir and Rhodes 2004: 158). Indeed, Bevir and Rhodes highlight ethnographic and historical 'modes of inquiry' as fundamental. The former is required for the practice of *understanding*, and involves the 'reading' of 'practices, actions, texts, interviews, and speeches' in order 'to recover other people's stories' (Bevir and Rhodes 2003: 5). The latter forms part of the logic of *explanation*, which involves locating such stories 'within their wider webs of belief, and these webs of belief against the background of traditions they modify in response to specific dilemmas' (Bevir and Rhodes 2003: 5).

Moreover, Bevir and Rhodes claim that the beliefs and desires of agents are 'radically contingent', and that 'people in any given situation can interpret that situation and their interests in many ways' (Bevir and Rhodes 2005: 171), thus pointing to the constitutive heterogeneity in people's beliefs and motivations. As Jon Elster has argued persuasively, even rational choice theory, with its economical assumptions about the instrumental rationality of individual choices and actions, encounters difficulties in moving from its particular micro-foundational context to the explanation of 'large-scale historical phenomena', such as the development of European absolutism or the stability of antebellum politics in the USA (Elster 2000: 685, 692). This heterogeneity thus furnishes Bevir and Rhodes with another reason why 'ethnography and history are the best tools respectively for recovering and explaining other people's construc-tions of what they are doing' (Bevir and Rhodes 2003: 195).

Finally, and more practically, Bevir and Rhodes's theoretical assumptions mean that in the conduct of their empirical research they must restrict their objects of analysis to a manageable set of actors (such as high-ranking civil servants or individual ministers), or focus on what they take to be representative or exemplary beliefs of the personages involved. In fact, their concrete research exhibits both strategies. Their studies of the British civil service, for instance, are restricted to a narrow set of individual actors: high-ranking civil servants or Government ministers. But even here they are compelled to select what they understand to be the exemplary or representative beliefs of these personages in order to develop their alternative explanation of changes in the civil service (Bevir and Rhodes 2003). They do, nonetheless, claim that their approach is applicable to a wide range of individual and collective political phenomena, whether to different forms of governance or various instances of political protest.

Problematizing contextualised self-interpretations: epistemological, methodological, and critical aspects

Winch, Taylor, and Bevir & Rhodes all subscribe to the view that explanation emerges out of the process of contextualising subjects' self-interpretations. For them contextualised self-interpretations constitute the central element in any putative social science explanation. However, they differ in the tools and concepts they offer us in order to generate these contextualised self-interpretations. We shall now go on to examine their views in a more critical vein, offering an argument that touches on at least three broad sets of issues.

First, in generating contextualised self-interpretations, the explanatory concepts furnished by hermeneuticists tend to produce (re)descriptions which are particularistic in character. But essential as the task of generating particular re-descriptions is from the point of view of social science understanding, the tasks of explanation and critique are of equal import. The question is how to carry out all these tasks, without sacrificing any one of them. Second, the political dimension of the process of re-description is elided in hermeneutical accounts in two senses. We note that the role of the analyst in deploying concepts such as 'inter-subjective meanings', 'dilemma', or any other concepts for that matter, in order to redescribe the context is not neutral, but we suggest that this is either not foregrounded enough, or not explored adequately as a function of its implications. And we also claim that the political dimension of the *constitution* of particular meanings, traditions, dilemmas, etc., is not emphasized sufficiently. Third, hermeneuticists either shy away from explicit critical engagement (the Winchean tendency) or adopt an overly external vantage point in this critical engagement (the Taylorian tendency). This is largely because their explanatory concepts and contextualised self-interpretations 'hover' too close to the practices they seek to elucidate (Geertz 1973: 26). There appears, therefore, to be a hesitancy in developing a richer set of explanatory and critical concepts, which we think is partly due to the ontological frameworks underpinning their respective approaches. For us, this opens up the need to engage in more detailed 'middle range' theorizing which would aim to develop key explanatory concepts in more depth by linking them to a different ontological framework, something we endeavour to do in Chapters 4 and 5. We now examine aspects of all three of these issues, starting with Winch's intervention.

Winch's challenge to the dominant self-understandings of social science, certainly since the middle of the last century, has provoked a rich set of debates involving *inter alia* Alasdair MacIntyre, I.C. Jarvie, Anthony Giddens, Alan Ryan, Martin Hollis, and James Tully, to name but a few.[11] His writings have been taken to task for their supposed idealism (in the sense that ideas are taken to be constitutive of practices rather than the other way round),[12] for their alleged assault on science and the Enlightenment project, and for their inability to engage critically with ideological forms of consciousness and systems of domination, thus implicating them in any unjust and repugnant social practices being studied.

While there is some truth in many of these charges, many miss their mark.[13] For instance, Charles Taylor imputes to Winch what he calls the 'incorrigibility thesis', where the essence of the charge is that if we take an agent's self-interpretations 'with ultimate seriousness', then we rule out of court an account which shows them up as 'wrong, confused, or deluded' (Taylor 1985b: 123). It is true that Winch's approach does move in this direction, but just as the charge of idealism (or irrationalism, subjectivism, and so forth) needs to be attentive to the more nuanced and complicated picture that Winch paints, so does our assessment of the 'incorrigibility thesis'. For, as we saw earlier, Winch does *not* accept that our understanding and explanation of an action depends exclusively on the self-interpretations which the agent articulates. Nevertheless, there are at least four problems with the Winchean position that call for further analysis. The first concerns the criteria of validation that operate in his approach; the second focuses on the paucity of the explanatory concepts generated by his framework; the third centres on his problematic reading of Wittgenstein; and the final issue concerns the lack of critical bite. A discussion of these problems will lead into an examination of the degree to which Charles Taylor and Bevir & Rhodes can be said to overcome them.

In order to illustrate the issue concerning validation criteria, consider Winch's Freudian-inspired discussion of the case of an actor, N, who does not post a letter because he 'unconsciously connected the posting of the letter with something in his life which is painful and which he wants to suppress' (Winch 1990: 47). Here Winch relies on an explanation that is not immediately available to the actor concerned because the actor's 'reason' has been repressed or suppressed by the operation of the unconscious. Winch's main qualification in this regard is that explanations of the Freudian type, whose meaningfulness are apparent only 'to the expert', are only acceptable if they are couched 'in terms of concepts which are familiar to the agent as well as to the observer' (Winch 1990: 48). Now this qualification admits of a weaker and a stronger version. The weaker version suggests that the explanation must be expressed in terms which the actor could *in principle* understand. The stronger version is phrased in terms of the actor actually *assenting* to the 'validity of the proffered explanation', in which case, as Winch notes, the latter 'is almost a condition of it being accepted as the "right" explanation' (Winch 1990: 48).

A similar ambiguity arises from Winch's discussion of the use of explanatory concepts that are external to a particular practice and its related concepts and terms. Again he insists that the 'external' concept must be 'logically tied' to the field of concepts it purportedly explains (Winch 1990: 89). Though helpful in establishing the parameters of an explanation's minimal hermeneutical requirement, as we saw in Chapter 1, the precise constraints imposed by the idea of being 'logically tied' are not entirely clear, since these too can admit of weaker and stronger versions. Consequently, the epistemological and methodological consequences of this 'tying' are also unclear.

The second and related charge against Winch is that we are offered very little by way of a theoretical schema beyond rules, with which to explain social practices and phenomena in terms not already implicit in the forms of life we are investigating. While he makes it clear that the social scientist can borrow concepts from a range of different theorists – he mentions Freud, Oakeshott, and Weber to name a few – we are never informed in precise terms *what* does the explaining, *how* various concepts and theories explain, and more substantively *why* there is social change (or absence thereof). In short, while Winch's programme furnishes us with a formal account of the conditions of meaningful social research – however useful this is on its own terms – it does not offer us adequate conceptual and theoretical *elements* with which to explain social phenomena.

A third worry has to do with Winch's reading of Wittgenstein. Although Winch draws heavily on Wittgenstein to show how rules are best seen as intertwined with the practices and customs of everyday life, some of his interpretations and appropriations run counter to crucial elements in Wittgenstein's later philosophy. The difficulty with Winch's position is his tendency for purposes of analysis to *separate* rules from social practices, whether understood as the creative use of words or the performance of certain human activities, as if practices could somehow be characterized by *subsuming* them under a particular rule or set of rules. Such subsumption enables the researcher, and of course social actors themselves, to identify and characterize practices, but it runs the risk of presenting what Wittgenstein calls a 'purified' or 'sublime' picture of signs and words, where the meanings of words and practices are fixed in a determinate way by a particular community of language-users (Wittgenstein 1967: §§89, 94; see also Mulhall 2001: 87–93).

Of course, Winch does point to what might be termed the 'overdetermination' of rules, where a *new* context overdetermines rules in the sense that their meaning or application to the new context is not given by the content of the rules (Winch 1990: 32, 92; Lyas 1999: 32). After all, Winch insists on the 'open' character of rules, which are modified in their application to new circumstances.[14] However, he does not touch upon the more important 'underdetermination thesis', which puts into question the premise that an existing context can determine the rules of a practice in the first place. In this view, the reason why rules fail to specify their meaning and application in novel contexts is not because of the *newness* of the context, but because the rules of a practice themselves are constitutively underdetermined: *no* context can fully determine their content. In other words, no rule, or regime of rules, can 'ever *in principle* be rich enough to include all the circumstances of its application' (Rosen 1983: 111). Moreover, if we take the underdetermination thesis as our premise, then the claim that rules can fully characterize a practice is either refuted or rendered trivial. The claim is disproved if it is implied that the rules, which allegedly govern or determine meanings and practices, 'must be capable of non-circular specification', as the thesis demonstrates that all rules are finite constructions, which of their own accord cannot pre-determine or stand outside their own application. By contrast, the underdetermination thesis trivializes the claim, as rules are just redefined to cover all possible applications and variations (Rosen 1983: 111).

As commentators such as Stanley Cavell and Henry Staten argue, it is clear that the more radical (underdetermination) conception of rule-following is more in keeping with the later Wittgenstein's account of rules (Cavell 1976: 48–52; Staten 1984: 79–86). This is because Wittgenstein's contextualizing strategy of re-locating rules in the different contexts in which they function, rather than viewing them as abstract essences that generate independent effects of their own, is accompanied by a 'deconstructive' impulse, which draws attention to the limits of any rule in capturing all its instantiations. He thus highlights the multiple possibilities of a rule.[15]

To put it in more concrete terms, when we encounter a moment of ambiguity in rule-following – what do I do now? – or when we seek to render an alien set of practices intelligible – why are they doing what they do? – we can only offer up our best interpretation of the situation. Crucially, however, these interpretations are not rules as such, even though rules may be the sedimented outcomes of such an interpretive process. This is because interpretations 'hang in the air' so to speak and are not rules; the latter are better understood as 'customs' or signs to which we have been trained to react in certain ways (Wittgenstein 1967: §198). From this point of view, *the key element in any explanation is not a rule or system of rules but, rather, the interpretations of self-interpretations*. And it is precisely here, then, when rules no longer guide us meaningfully, that we have the practice of interpretation which can always take the form of a contest – 'a conflict of interpretations' to use Paul Ricoeur's resonant phrase (Ricoeur 1974) – about which rules do and should structure our practices.

In short, a more radicalised version of Winch's argument, which has its roots in the later Wittgenstein, suggests that *every* application of a rule involves some sort of modification, as each instance of rule-following is different no matter how apparently insignificant that difference might be (Staten 1984: 79–86). Indeed, from this point of view, a rule is no more than the instances of its various applications at any one time, and what is deemed an acceptable 'application' is continuously susceptible to alteration and contestation. Winch seems to suggest that a community fixes the meaning of a word or practice. But if practices overflow any particular rule or convention, then the fixing of meanings and practices is better understood as a *political* operation rather than a rule-based prescriptive operation. And to the extent to which the 'war of interpretations' involves a *political* dimension, the latter raises a number of interesting possibilities for the explanation of social and political phenomena, to which we shall return in developing our own critical ontology in Chapter 4.

As to the question of critique from a Winchean point of view, this emerges most explicitly in Winch's 'application' of his approach to understand a 'primitive society' such as the Azande (Winch 1974). The key issue raised by his thought-provoking essay on this topic concerns the problem of 'how to make intelligible in our terms institutions belonging to a primitive culture, whose standards of rationality and intelligibility are apparently quite at odds with our own' (Winch 1974: 94). Put starkly, and defending a principle of 'charity in interpretation', Winch's answer is that it is possible, and indeed desirable, to translate the beliefs and practices of an 'alien culture' into one's own, without thereby reducing the other's views to the perspective informing that of the interpreter. In so doing, however, he tries to defend himself against the charge of relativism in which (to use Feyerabend's notorious expression) 'anything goes' or, to use Winch's own terms, any claim is 'at the mercy of what anyone cares to say'. He therefore affirms the view that 'men's ideas and beliefs' are 'checkable by reference to something independent' – 'some reality' as he puts it. Moreover, he does not abandon the notion of rationality, conceived in formal terms as a function of logical consistency for example (Winch 1974: 82, 81, 100). His key point is that what is to *count* as 'reality' and 'consistency' depends upon an investigation of 'the wider context of the life in which the activities in question are carried on' (Winch 1974: 100).

This attempted defence against relativism, however, suggests that Winch subscribes to a conception of reality that is closed or hermetically sealed, insulating it from practical critique. The charge here is that his view makes it difficult for the critic to gain a meaningful foothold from which to put into question the practices he or she encounters. And at times this is clearly the case, as Winch's position shares important parallels with his theory of rules, in which he argues that it is the community under study that fixes or totalises the meaning and rules of a practice. Consider in this context his description of the Azande's magic practices as a '*coherent universe* of discourse', and their '*system* of magical beliefs' as constituting 'one of the principal *foundations* of their *whole* social life' (Winch 1974: 83; emphasis added; see also Winch 1974: 90–1). But there are also moments when a more nuanced view is apparent. Responding, for example, to I.C. Jarvie's charge that his approach to understanding a society 'is a kind of conceptual empathy which imprisons you in a discourse that cannot evaluate itself', Winch argues that beliefs 'may be more or less widely current amongst the members of a society and there may be stronger or weaker tendencies to criticize and discuss such beliefs amongst those members' (Winch 1977: 209). He also claims that some societies have institutions and traditions of a predominantly critical nature, such that where they do exist 'individuals are more likely to think critically about the ideas and practices current in their society than where they do not' (Winch 1977: 209). In this context he suggests that seemingly closed forms of life such as the Azande contain a heterogeneous set of institutions and practices, of which 'an institution like that of Zande witchcraft' might be one. Thus 'Zande life contains other important elements which may develop in such a way as to make witchcraft practices lose their foothold' (Winch 1977: 213). Indeed, when discussing whether or not there would be agreement amongst those within the institution of Zande witchcraft as to whether a certain person is a witch, Winch claims that agreement would be 'overwhelming' and 'usually reached', implying – however slightly – that agreement is not guaranteed and unanimous.

Now, according to Winch, our responses to the interpretive dilemma of making sense of other beliefs and practices may have the effect of leading us to reflect back on our own concepts, distinctions and practices – especially our 'ready-made distinction between science and non-science' – which, for the most part, lie buried in our dominant discourses and forms of life, and which are thus taken for granted. So while Winch disavows any explicit evaluation of the Azande, and is certainly opposed to an unreflective projection onto Zande practices and institutions of supposed emancipatory possibilities of Western science and modernity, he suggests that we need to focus more on our relationship to our 'own' form of life, that is, modern Western democracies. This is Winch's major concern here: *our* relation to the Azande, and what our understanding of the latter says about *ourselves*.

It is clear, then, that Winch does not easily fall into the trap of moral relativism, of which he is so often accused.[16] As he tirelessly repeats, his project is to show the difficulties of making moral judgements when confronted with beliefs and actions that arise from cultures and forms of life very different from 'our own'. In his view, we need to take these difficulties seriously, and then formulate an approach that can render these beliefs and practices intelligible in their own terms. Only when they have been properly understood can beliefs be considered legitimate candidates for evaluative judgements. Thus, our difficulty with Winch is not his bracketing of universal rationality in order to interpret and evaluate the beliefs of an alien society in a non-prejudicial fashion, but his tendency to dispense with any presumption whatsoever – an attitude which is in keeping with his 'charity in interpretation'. In other words, we *cannot* proceed in a completely presup-positionless fashion. Maximising a 'principle of charity' may help us to render an alien world more intelligible in a less prejudicial way, but it also runs the risk of suggesting that we can describe, interpret and evaluate in a presuppo-sitionless fashion. In our view, the necessary presuppositions of investigation have as far as possible to be rendered visible, and decisions have to be taken about their precise content. In other words, the social ontology underlying the inquiry has to be acknowledged and clarified.

From this point of view, we think it is telling that in his discussion of the Azande, Winch admits to taking 'the institution of witchcraft for granted' and then asking questions 'about the position of particular judgements made within the context of that institution' (Winch 1977: 213). But, of course, this is to foreclose the possibility that the institution itself might not be completely sedimented and taken for granted from the point of view of both actors and analysts, as Winch has himself hinted. Indeed, the primary role that politics plays in our social life is to question and contest – in short, to reactivate – the sedimented sets of social relations and practices in our societies. As we will see in Chapter 4, our poststructuralist ontology helps highlight the political dimension underlying institutional practices by making it explicit and axiomatic that no social order is completely closed or saturated. Instead, it considers such an order to be marked by a plurality of competing tendencies and interpretations, and riven by internal inconsistencies and by exclusions, which ideologies cover over.

It is striking that our conception converges to some degree with Winch's later reflections on these questions. In one of his final essays, 'Can We Understand Ourselves?', Winch argues that:

> A culture is not a seamless web and this is true in more than one sense. On the one hand individuals are variously exposed, in the course of their upbringing and after, to different facets of a single culture. But at least as important as this is the fact that different individuals *respond* to what they encounter in enormously varied ways. The importance of this factor is obscured by the passive sounding term 'internalization', so beloved of sociologists and social psychologists. We do not merely imbibe or absorb those aspects of our culture with which we come into contact, we *react*. The characters of individual reactions to what we may be prepared to call the 'same' cultural manifestation, are enormously diverse. The diversity may extend to quite radical conflict; in some areas of life, indeed, this is very characteristic (Think of morality, politics, religion.).
>
> (Winch 1997: 198)

He even goes on to stress 'the possibility that an individual may fail to respond significantly to, and hence to see any sense in, most of the culture into which he is born' (Winch 1997: 198–9). And with respect to the Zande poison oracle he suggests that 'there is something about the Zande practice that we do not, perhaps even that we never shall, understand' (Winch 1997: 199). Indeed, it is precisely this affirmation of limits which we seek to highlight by having recourse to a poststructuralist ontology (though our lack of understanding applies not just to others but to ourselves), thus furnishing us with resources with which to amplify and complexify the grounds of a *critical* explanation.

Even though Winch may acknowledge the need to engage in a process of interpreting subjects' self-interpretations and thus partake in a kind of 'war of interpretations' within the community of social scientists there are no systematic attempts to tackle this head on. However, Charles Taylor does do precisely this, for he offers us criteria to decide upon the relative epistemic gains of one interpretation over another: a superior interpretation will make more sense of a phenomenon by resolving contradictions in other accounts or by explicating implicit or occluded meanings in the object that are not explicit in 'proto' or rival interpretations. Indeed, it might well be claimed that the most important criterion guiding Taylor's choice of the validity of an interpretation is measured in terms of its practical effects, namely, its relation to the deeper goal of bringing about 'emancipatory outcomes' in the subjects and social practices investigated. In this sense, the truth value of a theory is determined not so much in terms of its accuracy in representing an independently existing objectivity, but 'in the way our practices fare when they are informed by the theory' (Smith 2002: 127). In an important sense, then, guided by the notion of emancipation as the most relevant validity criterion, Taylor's approach is at times more comfortably located in the tradition of critical social theory, rather than an interpretive (*Verstehen*) school of inquiry.

In a style that recalls Alasdair MacIntyre's moral theory, Taylor addresses these questions by elaborating a story of moral progress, wherein people must strive to 'improve' themselves by discerning and articulating the overall *telos* in Being or history, which can then be realised or actualized collectively (MacIntyre 1984). But how do we know that our highest values really are our highest values? What are the criteria for adjudicating between conflicting goods, and of providing an overall evaluation of their historical development? Taylor addresses these questions of moral progress – at the level of the human self and at the level of culture more broadly – in part with the notion of an 'epistemic gain' in the movement from one form of life to another. As he puts it:

> We are convinced that a certain view is superior because we have lived a transition which we understand as error-reducing and hence as *epistemic gain*. I see that I was confused about the relation of resentment and love, or I see that there is a depth to love conferred by time, which I was quite insensitive to before. But this doesn't mean that we don't and can't argue. Our conviction that we have grown morally may be challenged by another. It may after all be illusion. And then we can argue; and arguing here is contesting between interpretations of what I have been living.
>
> (Taylor 1989: 72; emphasis added)

Running alongside Taylor's idea of an epistemic gain in the movement from one form of life to another is a particular understanding of practical reasoning and rationality. To begin with, he refuses to equate the concept of rationality with instrumental reason. Moreover, though logical inconsistency places important constraints on rationality for him, it is not reducible to this either. He seeks instead to develop a broader, more comprehensive conception of rationality, in which we have 'a rational grasp of something when we can articulate it', when we can 'distinguish and lay out the different features of the matter in perspicuous order' (Taylor 1985b: 137). It is this fairly strong conception of rationality which allows Taylor to talk about people being mistaken about their choices or preferences, thereby underpinning his notion of 'strong evaluation' (Taylor 1977, 1989: 14; see also Smith 1997: 21–3).

More specifically, Taylor's gaze is simultaneously directed upwards and downwards (see Taylor 1989). It is directed upwards towards 'transcendent goods' or a 'higher direction in Being', which can 'command' us in various ways, or towards which we ought to 'attune' or 'aspire' in the quest for our 'higher selves'. But it is also focused downwards to the 'deeper sources' of our goods and ideals, to the underlying ontological grounds of our values and moral beliefs. Thus while his more epistemological concerns produced concepts such as inter-subjective and common meanings, his moral concerns have produced concepts such as 'hypergoods', and 'constitutive goods'.

The rhetoric of Taylor's major treatise on moral theory – the *Sources of the Self* – is suffused with images and injunctions to orient ourselves to goods and commands that transcend our worldly moral frameworks, thus investing our actions with worth and giving them direction. 'High standards need strong sources' is Taylor's neat way of capturing these two spatial dimensions in his account (Taylor 1989: 516). They get fleshed out in terms of 'hypergoods', which enable us to discriminate between and evaluate 'first order goods' (Taylor 1989: 63), and 'constitutive goods', which are linked to the moral source of goods, the feature by virtue of which a good is deemed worthy or 'a something the love of which empowers us to do and be good' (Taylor 1989: 92, 93). Possible constitutive goods might include God, Nature, and autonomous human beings, while concern for others, universal justice, benevolence, 'universal and equal respect' and 'modern self-determining freedom' are possible hypergoods (Smith 2002: 114; Taylor 1989: 101). Taken together, hypergoods and constitutive goods help generate frameworks of qualitative and perspicuous contrast that provide subjects with orientation, and thus the basis for their – and our – critique of social and political practices (Smith 2002: 90–3).

There is much to admire in Taylor's project, especially his critique of positivism and his endeavour to weave together the normative and the descriptive dimensions of analysis within an overarching ontological framework. This endeavour is evident especially in his concept of the 'social imaginary', by which he means 'something much broader and deeper than the intellectual schemes people may entertain when they think about social reality in a disengaged mode'. It concerns, rather, 'the ways people imagine their social existence, how they fit together with others, how things go on between them and their fellows, the expectations that are normally met, and the deeper normative notions and images that underlie their expectations' (Taylor 2004: 23).

Far from being simply a set of ideas, a social imaginary 'is what enables, through making sense of, the practices of a society' (Taylor 2004: 1); it is 'that common understanding that makes possible common practices and a widely shared sense of legitimacy' (Taylor 2004: 23). Taylor suggests that we can shed light on issues about modernity 'if we can come to a clearer definition of the self-understandings that have been constitutive of it', and that on this view Western modernity 'is inseparable from a certain kind of social imaginary', comprising the social forms of 'the market economy, the public sphere, and the self-governing people, among others' (Taylor 2004: 1–2).

Though insightful and rich, our view is that Taylor's work provides a somewhat unwieldy analytical framework for purposes of concrete social and political analysis. Moreover, there is no sustained theoretical, as opposed to an historical-descriptive, account of how common meanings, hypergoods, and moral sources, are constituted and reproduced. Nor indeed is there a convincing account of the ontological conditions under which they are challenged, contested, and transformed. While Taylor is concerned with the emergence of new forms of subjectivity and identity from an epochal perspective, and while he seeks to develop a theory of subjectivity that embeds human beings in systems of meaning, and which has the capacity via a notion of reflexivity to evaluate its choices and to develop a more rational articulation of its purposes and projects, we are not provided with a convincing account of the processes by which social practices – hypergoods and common meanings inclusive – are constituted, reproduced, and transformed through political identification and collective mobilization. More specifically, we feel that his moral ontology has to be displaced towards a more politically-inflected ontology.

In other words, while he seeks to articulate the moral and the explanatory dimensions, it is evident (especially in his later writings) that it is the normative dimension which comes to dominate Taylor's efforts to elaborate a coherent and convincing interpretive theory. What we see instead is a fairly strong conception of rationality, which risks a kind of 'normativism' that effectively severs his account both from its ontological grounds, predicated on the idea of self-interpreting animals, as well as from its explanatory aspirations.[17] In this view, his ontology becomes moralized because of the positive richness he pours into it (see Smith 2002: 113–19, 132–8). By contrast, while the approach we develop from Chapter 4 onwards is capacious enough to encompass normative and sociological aspects, and thus some articulation of a positive conception of the good, crucially, it is predicated on a negative ontology from which a set of logics can be constructed and deployed in generating critical explanations. By fleshing out our negative ontology we hope to suggest why the aim of ascertaining and realizing ideals or hypergoods, summarized in Taylor's phrase 'high standards need strong sources', need not exhaust the critical field. The notion of radical contingency, which is central to our negative ontology, opens up for us an ethical dimension that we think enables us to understand critique in terms which are not just normative in character.

Finally, we claim that the adoption of this ontology helps us to avoid a 'super immanentism', which tends to secure only a minimal critical purchase (the Winchean tendency). But it also enables us to circumvent a kind of 'super transcendentalism' – a 'super-order between . . . super-concepts' to use Wittgenstein's apt phrase (Wittgenstein 1967: §97) – which leans more to the side of securing a critical bite that ends up being largely 'external' to the practice being judged (the Taylorian tendency). In sum, despite his normativist tendencies, Taylor's approach has much to commend it, especially the attention he pays to the *sources* of motivation, not just the ideals and goods themselves. Even so, the epistemological and ontological framework he develops, precisely because of its richness, ends up being too unwieldy, being more suited to philosophical or epochal-historical analyses than more modest social and political analyses.

Bevir and Rhodes' work, on the other hand, has the merit of developing a framework which is more parsimonious and thus more readily deployable for purposes of social and political analysis. Of equal importance, however, is the fact that they align themselves more with Taylor than with Winch in according the task of critique an integral role in their interpretive approach. They do so by drawing an initial distinction between evaluation as a 'policy audit' and evaluation as 'critique'. The former involves a logic of 'fault-finding', which examines the strengths and weaknesses of particular policies, practices or programmes, while the latter involves the use of narratives to 'unmask' the particularity and contingency of a political interpretation. The task of 'unmasking' is achieved 'by showing how [a party such as New Labour or a movement such as the Third Way] arises against the background of an inherited tradition that is held by a particular group in society' (Bevir and Rhodes 2006: 97). The process of 'unmasking' a political party or social movement, for example, would show how such collective actors may be mistaken about their own natures, or how they 'elide' their own natures with the interests of a particular group or class (Bevir and Rhodes 2006: 97). However, as is the case more with Winch than with Taylor, there is a tendency to consider their analytical exercise of description and 'unmasking' (as opposed to the *results* of their exercise) as neutral and apolitical, and we think this is because they are wedded to the idea that it is possible to at least approximate the ideal of unadulterated contextualised self-interpretations.

But the central problem with Bevir and Rhodes' hermeneutical approach concerns the theory of language and subjectivity that underpins it. At the heart of their account, as we have noted, is an effort to interpret the beliefs of social agents, understood as 'individual viewpoints'. This is achieved by locating beliefs within a wider system of meanings, and by analysing the intentions of the authors that speak or write them.[18] The difficulty with this account is that it effectively bypasses the complexities of representation and subjectivity in the name of a problematic model of communication, wherein a sovereign agent *first* forms ideas and beliefs, and *then* expresses them in a linguistic utterance or written statement (see Derrida 1976, 1982). In short, in this model, messages are transmitted and received by sovereign subjects, and language is relegated to the role of a transparent medium of such communicative practices.

Admittedly, they situate agents and authors within particular intellectual traditions and belief systems, thus weakening their complete sovereignty, but they do not really question the capacity of language to convey meanings and beliefs in a transparent and unproblematic fashion, nor do they problematize the 'presence' of both the 'speaking' and 'receiving' subject in formulating and transmitting ideas. The closest they come to compromising this aspect of language and subjectivity is in their discussion of the role of rhetoric, where people's expressed and actual beliefs differ (Bevir and Rhodes 2005: 179). But even here rhetoric is viewed as an instrument of communication, which can be rationally and consciously deployed by calculating agents. 'When people *use* a rhetorical pattern', say Bevir and Rhodes, 'they do so because they believe it will get a suitable response to their ideas' (Bevir and Rhodes 2005: 179; emphasis added). Thus the social scientist 'can explain people's choice of rhetoric by identifying their relevant beliefs and preferences', situating the latter within their appropriate language games, and then relating these language games to wider belief systems and intellectual traditions. What we see here is a prioritization of an instrumental over what might be termed a constitutive conception of rhetoric. In this latter view, 'rhetorical patterns' are not just chosen, but actually shape our language use and meaning in non-conscious ways (see Howarth and Griggs 2007). Of course certain tropes may be consciously employed for strategic reasons, but even when they are they often come to structure our way of thinking in a constitutive way. Copernicus's concentric and geocentric model, or the 'war on terror' metaphor, would be clear examples in which the constitutive rather than instrumental dimension of rhetoric is evident. From this point of view, not only do such tropes introduce unintended and unanticipated connotative consequences, but this 'overflowing' of possibilities is best seen as an intrinsic part of language and rhetoric.

In fact, Bevir and Rhodes' presupposed theory of language and subjectivity also explains their rather problematic account of distorted beliefs, which include beliefs that are characterized as 'deceptive', 'self-deceptive' or 'irrational'. One difficulty in this regard is the apparent separation this implies between belief and action, given that Bevir and Rhodes's interpretivism is grounded on a constitutive link between beliefs and actions. Bevir's analysis of distortions (Bevir 1999: 265–308) suggests that distortions, as opposed to transparent belief formation and communication, arise because of the illegitimate intrusion of actions, such as those of the unconscious or the desire to deceive, into the beliefs or views of a given individual, thus establishing a difference between expressed and actual beliefs. Here, certain actions of the unconscious, for example, cause distorted beliefs to occur. Rather than a constitutive connection between action and belief, certain actions *cause* certain types of beliefs to occur. Quite apart from this apparent inconsistency, the worry here is that Bevir simply redescribes distorted beliefs in terms of rogue 'pro-attitudes' that produce illegitimate effects, rather than furnishing a more clearly ontologically-grounded and thus convincing explanation of the phenomena described.

In order to vindicate these allegations, take first a case where an agent affirms a particular ideal, say a work ethic centred on the completion of certain tasks on time, but that her practices lead her constantly to engage in forms of displacement activity that compromise its realisation. On the one hand, the agent may deceive herself into thinking that her procrastination rituals are not really forms of displacement activity, but necessary to the achievement of the task. In Bevir's model, such distorted belief could be 'explained' by a rogue pro-attitude – the desire to waste time by playing computer games for example – exercising an illegitimate influence on her expressed beliefs. But all that has been accomplished here is that distorted beliefs are traced to an underlying motivation causing the agent to deceive herself, but which itself remains unexplained. We have the grammar, perhaps, to describe and characterize, but not necessarily to explain. On the other hand, the agent may recognise and indeed acknowledge her time-wasting rituals as forms of displacement activity. In other words, she may believe in the ideal, believe also that the displacement activity compromises its realisation, desire not to practice such rituals (and thus complete her tasks), and yet still engage in the displacement activity. Here there is no self-deception, and Bevir would (we suppose) assume a gap between belief and action. The failure would be the result of laziness or a weakness of the will for example. Again, we have a potential re-description that pinpoints the problem as one of (lack of) will, but the description still begs the question as to why there is weakness of the will at all (or, indeed, what 'weakness of the will' actually amounts to).

In short, this discussion of distorted beliefs helps to illuminate Bevir and Rhodes's work precisely because it highlights how their critical explanations rely upon the identification of beliefs that fall short of a rationalist ideal, which is not explicitly affirmed or grounded in a normative or ontological framework. One possible explanation of these 'distortions', for example, might take its bearings not only from the beliefs and desires of agents, but from an explicit theory of subjectivity in which subjects organise their 'enjoyment' (*jouissance*) in different ways. Thus a 'logic of self-transgressive enjoyment' may help explain and evaluate transgressions of ideals by recourse to the enjoyment a subject procures through such transgressions (Glynos 2003a, 2008). We shall return to the psychoanalytic category of enjoyment later, when we spell out our own ontological framework.

These aspects of Bevir and Rhodes's argument, which highlight their presupposed theory of language, are made more explicit in their rather dismissive critiques of poststructuralists such as Jacques Derrida, Michel Foucault, Ernesto Laclau, and others. To begin, Bevir questions the way poststructuralists conceive of the relationship between language and reality, in which the key issue is 'whether our signs refer to reality'. Here, Bevir alleges that 'post-modern sceptics . . . argue that we cannot have knowledge of anything outside of language' because 'our language does not refer to reality' (Bevir 1999: 119–20). Equally, while they endorse poststructuralist critiques of strong human autonomy, which do away with any form of structural constraint or empowerment, Bevir and Rhodes are opposed to what they present as the complete abandonment of agency by poststructuralist theorists for whom individuals are 'mere effects of discourse' (Bevir and Rhodes 2006: 91, 105). Poststructuralists are thus mistaken 'to conceive of traditions as reified quasi-structures that somehow determine the beliefs that people come to hold' (Bevir and Rhodes 2005: 180). A final and related critique concerns the relationship between language and subjectivity, in which Bevir argues that poststructuralists 'imply that meanings exist as quasi-structures that possess a kind of immanent logic or that respond to random fluctuations of power' (Bevir 2005: 22). This means that 'interpretivists should be wary of words like "language", "discourse", and even "ideology", which evoke quasi-structures as constitutive of intersubjectivity rather than emergent properties of it' (Bevir 2005: 23). 'If an interpretive approach', argues Bevir and Rhodes, 'relies on discourse to do explanatory work, this concept can suggest a worrying neglect of agency'. In short, 'if post-structuralists use discourse as an explanatory concept, they adopt a form of determinism that cannot account for change' (Bevir and Rhodes 2005: 172).

We think Bevir and Rhodes' view of language has implications for what we take to be the most promising explanatory dimension in their work, namely their provision of concepts to account for social and political change in a way that supplements exercises in re-description and ascription. More precisely, their concepts of tradition and dilemma seek to supply a conceptual grammar to account for the relationship between wider social formations and individual agency. But the key question one must ask in this regard is how to connect traditions and dilemmas with individual beliefs and desires to explain change. It is here that Bevir and Rhodes insist on the importance of what they call 'situated agency', which they develop by establishing a contrast between their position and their particular gloss of poststructuralist critiques of autonomy. Their alternative categories of traditions, dilemmas and situated agency entail neither the valuing of order as such, nor the idea that structures constitute insurmountable obstacles to change. Instead they are compatible with a form of methodological individualism in which agents can alter their beliefs and traditions. As Bevir puts it, '[i]ndividuals are agents capable both of modifying traditions and of migrating across traditions' (Bevir 1999: 197).

The first problem with this account is that it tends to encourage a far too mechanistic way of linking self-interpretations to background contexts, and overemphasizes the individual's creativity in coping with dilemmas by recourse to various strands of tradition (cf. O'Doherty and Willmott 2001: 471). As Bevir and Rhodes put it, 'individuals are not autonomous since they always experience and reason against the background of tradition, but they are agents who have the capacity to modify and reject *any* aspect of a tradition' (Bevir and Rhodes 2004: 16; emphasis added). Yet this raises a key question: Why might some aspects of traditions exert greater appeal than others, or why might some aspects resist modification? This suggests a potentially promising line of thought which appears to escape the critical scope attributed by Bevir and Rhodes to their narrative interpretations. For the critical aspect of their explanations appears to be centred primarily upon unmasking 'the partiality of a political interpretation' and 'the contingency of traditions and their interpretations' (Bevir and Rhodes 2004: 16). This reveals that the relationship between agency and structure is not sufficiently theorized, especially in terms of categories like power and ideology (see also Finlayson 2004). Indeed, we feel that this is partly because Bevir and Rhodes are over-enthusiastic in their rejection of the ontological – as opposed to a simple contextual – import of structure, leading to an underdeveloped social ontology.[19] In Chapter 4 we shall argue that an ontology which foregrounds the radical negativity and contingency of structure itself opens up a way of affirming the continued importance of structure without reifying it. This, in turn, opens up a way of thinking about the relationship between subject and structure along a range of dimensions, among which feature the political and ideological dimensions, thus making possible both a normative and ethical critique of social and political forms.

By implication, the second and related problem with Bevir and Rhodes' account is that it misrepresents the poststructuralist account of structure and agency, at least as it has been developed by Laclau, for he has sought precisely to provide a much more complicated picture of subjectivity by deconstructing the structure/agency opposition. In their critique of poststructuralism, Bevir and Rhodes present us with a series of classical 'either/ors': either language is constituted in a 'bottom-up' fashion on the basis of individual utterances and meanings, or it is a fully-fledged and all-determining structure that fixes meaning from above, thus trying to 'avoid all appeals to human agency' (Bevir and Rhodes 2003: 22). Either the words and concepts of our language represent the world, or there is no representation and reference at all. Yet it is not clear why one should accept such loaded choices. After all, the whole point of *post*structuralist theories of language and human subjectivity is to problematize the idea of a fully-present subject *and* a fully-constituted linguistic structure, so that we are not forced to choose between, on the one hand, an atomistic and referential conception of language, which is composed of individual utterances that refer to states of affairs or reality, and on the other hand a concept of language as an all-pervasive substance which is completely closed and thus altogether external to subjectivity (cf. Derrida 1976, 1978). Following Heidegger and Wittgenstein, and as developed by Cavell and Derrida, we argue that linguistic signs and grammar have a different, more complex and intimate relationship with 'reality'. Indeed, rather than simply referring to a separate realm of pre-existing objects, the articulations of language make reality possible for us, that is, intelligible and meaningful, by furnishing the criteria for identifying and individuating objects (Mulhall 2001: 93–7, 240–3).

So instead of prioritizing totalised and determining social structures on the one hand, or fully constituted subjects on the other, we begin by accepting that social agents always find themselves 'thrown into' a system of meaningful practices, an immersion that both shapes their identity and structures their practices. However, we also add the critical rider that these structures are ontologically incomplete. Indeed, it is in the 'space' or 'gap' of social structures, as they are rendered visible in moments of crisis and dislocation, that a political subject can emerge through particular 'acts of identification'. Moreover, as these identifications are understood to take place across a range of possible ideologies or discourses – some of which are excluded or repressed – and as these are always incomplete, then *any* form of identification is doomed to fall short of its promise.

In sum, social structures and forms of life are not only composed of relations of hierarchy and domination; even more pertinently, they are marked by gaps and fissures, and forged by political exclusions. And the making visible of these gaps in the structures through dislocatory experiences makes it possible for subjects to identify anew, and thus to act differently. Expressed in a slightly different idiom, this moment of identification is neatly captured by Hannah Arendt's rethinking of freedom, which runs counter to the current liberal hegemony. In her essay 'What is Freedom', free decisions and actions are likened to miracles, which are characterized as an ability 'to begin something new', that is, to set in motion events and practices that cannot be controlled and whose consequences cannot be foretold. Indeed, echoing her once-mentor Heidegger, freedom involves the '*abyss* of nothingness that opens up before any deed that cannot be accounted for by a reliable chain of cause and effect and is inexplicable in Aristotelian categories of potentiality and actuality' (Arendt cited in Žižek 2001: 113). In short, following Heidegger, subjects are 'thrown' into a world not of their choosing, but have the capacity under certain conditions to act differently. But more than this we need also to be able to explain the constitution and reproduction of the social relations into which they have been thrown, and we need also to account for the way in which subjects are gripped by certain discourses and ideologies. Our poststructuralist approach strives to unfold a social ontology adequate to these tasks.

Conclusion

It is important to stress at the outset that the three hermeneutical accounts examined are at their strongest in their powerful critiques of positivism. Moreover, despite their differing presuppositions regarding the nature of language and discourse, there is substantial convergence in their writings when it comes to the role and status of self-interpretations in social science explanations and critique. What then are we to make of their contributions in developing a viable project of critical explanation? We begin with the epistemological and methodological aspects, and then consider the critical aspect of their approach.

As we described, Winch's project is focussed primarily on the endeavour to understand social actions and practices, in which the identification and characterization of rule-governed activities goes a long way to explaining the social phenomena under investigation. However, his endeavour to render a practice intelligible is not reducible to our initial understanding of it, for as we noted there are often occasions when our 'immanent' or 'empathic' understandings of a subject's self-interpretation or action fall short of their target. Instead, they need to be supplemented by a reference to concepts that may be 'external' to the practice investigated. But even here Winch insists that the persuasiveness of any such explanatory account is measured against our initial understandings (and the latter constitute an important condition for getting any explanatory practice off the ground), in which its purpose is to improve upon our initial understandings of social practices and institutions. Nevertheless, while Winch is aware of these issues, he fails to furnish an appropriate set of concepts and logics for the concrete analysis of problematized phenomena, and does not offer a convincing account of the relationship between theoretical concepts and the phenomena examined.

Taylor is equally concerned to render social practices, institutions and systems of meaning more intelligible. He is also aware of the need to go beyond the subject's own self-interpretations, and to use the process of critical investigation to reflect both upon the objects of investigation and our own theoretical understandings. For example, his intervention into the debates sparked by Winch's account of 'primitive' cultural forms and practice develops 'a language of perspicuous contrast', which seeks to provide a better account of the relationship between practices, while also enabling the evaluation and critique of contemporary forms of life. Now, it is clear in this regard that Taylor, unlike Winch, seeks to build more conceptual and theoretical content into his schema. But as we argued, while richly informed at the ontological level, this content does not furnish the means with which to explain social and political phenomena in a clear and parsimonious manner.

As with all variants of hermeneutics, orientated as they are around an ethnographic sensibility that seeks to make sense of practices 'from within', we have seen how Bevir and Rhodes strive to describe the particular and contingent beliefs of agents, without imposing an unnecessary layer of interpretation onto their objects of inquiry. To do so, they elaborate a three-fold set of concepts – dilemma, tradition and situated agency – which provides them with a more parsimonious conceptual framework to explain and interpret social practices and institutions. None the less, while the elaboration of these concepts correctly acknowledges the necessity of developing a richer framework to analyse and explain, we raised two difficulties in their approach. First, the triumvirate of concepts rely on some problematic ontological presuppositions.

Second, and more concretely, their concepts are not sufficiently developed to deal with the complex task of explaining the political constitution of beliefs and social practices, as well as their continued sedimentation and reproduction. Instead, we still face the challenge of elaborating a set of concepts which can furnish the requisite theoretical bridgehead to develop adequate explanations.

An attractive feature of many strands of the hermeneutical tradition is the intertwining of explanation and critique. Resisting the bald separation of fact and value, hermeneutical approaches seek simultaneously to render intelligible and to evaluate the practices they investigate in the social world, while also disclosing novel possibilities in the present and for the future. But how well do the approaches canvassed in this chapter fare in this goal? Winch follows a classic 'hermeneutics of retrieval' in seeking to suspend epistemological and normative judgement before furnishing an account of a practice.[20] However, the problem with his approach is that the substantive perspective from which his evaluation is made, as well as the concrete alternatives which he seeks to disclose, are – perhaps deliberately in his case – left vague and empty. Taylor is also intent on a 'hermeneutics of retrieval', as he seeks to tap into and make explicit the ontological and moral commitments which ground our highest values and ideals. Nevertheless, he also seeks to articulate these values in a way which can transcend existing beliefs and practices in the name of a better way of living. Critical of some of the distortions in modern identity and subjectivity, his work also flirts with a 'hermeneutics of suspicion' that seeks to unmask the repressed motivations at work in the 'malaise of modernity' in the name of something more fulfilling (Taylor 1991a: 1–12). However, his incipient normativism/rationalism runs the acute risk of severing his evaluative programme from his explanatory hermeneutics.

Finally, Bevir and Rhodes also stress the importance of critical evaluation in their interpretation of social phenomena. The main thrust of their project involves an initial comparison of rival narratives followed by a critique of substantive social practices and policies, which consists of unmasking the partiality of particular projects (such as New Labour's 'Third Way') in the name of an immanent critique of a project's self-understanding. But this unmasking of partiality is also done in the name of other possibilities that are suppressed, where appeal is explicitly made to normative considerations regarding social democratic values, 'open community', and the interests of exploited or downtrodden groups or classes (Bevir 2005: 137–53). However, though there are many promising aspects here, this is one of the more underdeveloped facets of their programme.

In making normative concerns relevant to the explanatory practice, hermeneutical approaches to social and political analysis provide us with a welcome alternative to the dominant positivist understanding of social science explanation. Explanation is understood not in terms of *universal subsumption à la* the causal law paradigm (subsuming particularities under universal causal laws), but rather in terms of the production of *particular normatively informed descriptions*. While their accounts do in varying degrees offer the means to describe, characterize and critically evaluate phenomena at the ontical level – that is, with respect to a series of positive objects and processes that occur in specific regions of society – the explanatory framework does not furnish the analyst with helpful guidance, partly because its presupposed ontology suggests that such explanatory concepts remain very close to the ground. One consequence of this is that the political dimension of the explanatory exercise is elided; first, the very process of using concepts to redescribe phenomena has sociological and normative implications for the analyst and, second, the canvassed approaches underplay the political aspects of the *constitution* of beliefs, traditions, and meanings. Another consequence of adopting the hermeneutical ontology is that the critical dimension of the explanatory exercise ends up being too weak (Winch), underdeveloped (Bevir and Rhodes), or potentially overbearing (Taylor). The problem is that these hermeneutical approaches end up opposing the universalism of the causal law paradigm with a normative and descriptive particularism. It is a problem because a too firm embrace of particularism or immanentism leads either to a diminishing of our critical capacity, or to its opposite: an overbearing *external* critique, usually rooted in some notion of strong rationality.

As we will see later, however, we entertain a way out of this opposition between immanence and transcendence. We do this by developing an ontology which affirms the insights of a minimal hermeneutic ontology, but which is distinct from it. More specifically, our critical-explanatory concepts (what we call social, political, and fantasmatic logics) are explicitly linked to the radical contingency at the heart of Being, or more particularly the 'lack' or 'void' in any given symbolic order. This enables us to carve out a critical space external to, yet *within*, the practice or regime under study, and to highlight the ethical dimension of our approach. In this view, questions about ethics speak to the different ways a subject relates to the radical contingency of social relations. In short, reflection on what we shall term the ethical is important not only because it allows us to explore the conditions of possibility and impossibility of any concrete morality, but also because ethical questions intersect with – and have to be related to – the concepts that enable us to characterize and explain the constitution and maintenance of social reality. The specification of our own critical-explanatory concepts, including their inter-relation and articulation, will be explored in detail in Chapters 4–6. Before we tackle these tasks, however, we shall consider a second response to the failures of the causal law paradigm: the turn to causal mechanisms.

3 Causal mechanisms

[C]ausal mechanisms must be distinguished from predictions. Sometimes we can explain without being able to predict, and sometimes predict without being able to explain. True, in many cases one and the same theory will enable us to do both, but I believe that in the social sciences this is the exception rather than the rule.

(Elster 1989: 8)

Plumbing resources in the hermeneutical tradition, the previous chapter explored the plausibility of contextualized self-interpretations as a productive alternative to the causal law paradigm in the social sciences. Our conclusion was that while self-interpretations were an indispensable element of any social science *explanans*, the hermeneutical account was still found wanting on a number of counts. The general problem we address in this chapter can be expressed as a question. Is it possible to come up with a general account of the nature and scope of social science explanation, which is distinct from both positivist accounts that are modelled on the causal law paradigm in natural science, and hermeneutical accounts for which the self-interpretations and intentions of the subjects under study are conceded a foundational status?

A more specific question emerges if we accept two related assumptions. These are, first, that the contextualized self-interpretations and intentions of subjects comprise an indispensable element of any properly constituted explanation in the social sciences, but secondly that a complete explanation is not reducible to the contextualized self-interpretations or intentions of subjects. The more specific question can thus be formulated as follows: Can we come up with an approach to social science explanation that incorporates the non-intentional dimension, but avoids an overly descriptive or particularistic solution (*à la* hermeneutics)?

This chapter explores the role of causal explanations as a possible answer to our questions. More precisely, we examine the work of Jon Elster, who we take to be one of the most important advocates of the 'social mechanisms' approach to social science explanation (Hedstrom and Swedberg 1998).[1] Elster's work, of course, is famously broad-ranging and multi-disciplinary, including pioneering interventions in the philosophy of social science, rational choice theory, Marxism, political psychology, and normative political theory, to name but a few.[2] But there are some common threads in his approach, notably his commitment to a form of methodological individualism, in which the intentions and actions of individuals constitute the bedrock of any social order, as well as a strong attachment to the role of causal mechanisms in explaining individual behaviour and its consequences. It is also striking that while Elster operates in the very mainstream of social and political science, an important effect of his writings has been to erode from within some of the more impermeable shibboleths of these traditions of thought. In particular, he has punctured the belief that a science of society can be predicated on the discovery of causal laws with predictive powers; indeed some of his most recent writings have queried the very possibility of a complete and definitive explanation of macro-social change and continuity (see, for example, Elster *et al.* 2000: 685, 692, 694; cf. Tilly and Goodin 2006: 15).

In addition, though Elster's work is located primarily within the analytical tradition, an evaluation of his arguments is equally relevant for our assessment of those social and political theorists drawing on other traditions, who also deploy the category of mechanism to explain social practices and institutions. Of particular note in this regard are those critical realists who take their lead from the work of Roy Bhaskar, which we examined in our chapter on retroduction. For example, Ian Shapiro has counter-posed causal mechanisms to the law-like and formal models of positivism and rational choice theory, thus embedding his advocacy of 'problem-driven' theory within a realist framework (Shapiro 2005: 8–11).

Against this background, the first part of this chapter describes the role and general character of the category of mechanism in Elster's work, before analyzing the notion of *causal* mechanism in greater detail. In his attempt to capture the non-intentional dimension of explanation in social science, Elster refuses to privilege the value of prediction, which would skew the search in favour of law-like explanations (as in Duverger's or Michel's laws *à la* Riker (1982)), and he avoids over-emphasizing the contingency of human action, which would skew the search in favour of particular, case-specific thick-descriptions (à la Geertz (1973)). However, while Elster is successful in offering us a general account of social science explanation that is free from the unrealistic demands of prediction, we argue that it is ultimately unsatisfactory. Principally, this is because a residual positivism occludes a more productive alternative. Overcoming the deficiencies associated with the notion of causal mechanisms, especially the way it is related to intentional mechanisms, is crucial in reworking the idea of mechanisms in a more fruitful direction.

Put more fully, this residual positivism comes in two forms. In the first place, the notion of a causal law continues to play a determining role in Elster's worldview, in which case mechanisms do not succeed in offering us a distinctive enough alternative to the causal law model. Secondly, the causal chain language deployed by Elster belies how the grammar of causal mechanisms is only one of several possible, and indeed contestable, grammars of intelligibility. The question then becomes one of articulating an appropriate grammar of intelligibility in the social sciences.

In Chapter 5 we develop one such grammar of intelligibility in terms of social, political, and fantasmatic logics, which we believe avoids the twin fallacies of psychologism and idealism that bedevil Elster's account. However, before setting out our alternative approach, we need to outline the nature of these fallacies, which we do in the second part of this chapter. We argue that the fallacy of psychologism is a result of a particular articulation of causal mechanisms with methodological individualism. And we argue that if mechanisms come to be seen as the basic unit of explanation, their employment runs the risk of misunderstanding their nature and status, resulting in the fallacy of idealism.

Causal mechanisms

For Elster, the most basic element of explanation in the social sciences 'is the individual action guided by some intention' (Elster 1983a: 20).[3] This means that the notion of an intentional explanation, which involves a triadic relation between action, desire, and belief, serves as the key feature demarcating social science from natural science (Elster 1983a: 63). More specifically, an intentional explanation of an action involves furnishing the end state which the action was intended to bring about given a particular set of beliefs (Elster 1983a: 70).[4] Of course, this is not to say that intentional explanation exhausts the scope of social science explanation. On the contrary, while Elster is clear that the intentions or self-interpretations of subjects are central, explanations are never wholly reducible to them. Causal analysis has an indispensable role to play here, whether at an individual or collective level (Elster 1983a: 69).

Mechanisms in social science

The way Elster chooses to flesh out the notion of causality is interesting, for he explicitly rejects the option of conducting such causal analysis in terms of *laws*, opting instead for what he calls causal *mechanisms*. In this conception, social science explanation is not only distinctive because of the prominent place that intentional explanations occupy, for even when intentional analysis is supplemented by a causal dimension, the latter has to be couched in a distinctively social science fashion.[5] From this perspective, the social sciences comprise a toolkit of mechanisms (Elster 1989: 168), in which mechanisms are 'understood broadly, to cover intentional chains from a goal to an action as well as causal chains from an event to its effect' (Elster 1983a: 24). To explain, in other words, is to furnish a combination of intentional and causal mechanisms that can account for a particular social phenomenon.

However, even at this early juncture, it is possible to identify the *complementary* nature of the relationship between intentional and causal mechanisms in Elster's picture. The complementary status of the relationship arises because intentional and causal chains are conceived as entirely autonomous of one another. As Elster puts it, 'to say that the agent's doing p was caused by the desire to do p, is not to give a causal explanation. It is only to rephrase the intentional explanation in such a way as to indicate the existence of some (unknown) causal explanation' (Elster 1983a: 22). Intentional explanation is in this sense entirely *sui generis*.[6] Intentional and causal mechanisms are thus connected with one another to form larger and more complex chains and networks of chains, but they do not in any way modify one another in this process.

As we have seen, causal explanations enter the explanatory scene in the social sciences because their explanations are not reducible to the intentions or self-interpretations of subjects. At its limits, an intentional explanation calls for the employment of non-intentional mechanisms, *which are not subject to will or intention*. Elster shows, moreover, how such causal mechanisms can be conceived *intra*personally as well as *inter*personally; or, as he sometimes puts it, they can be understood at the sub-intentional or supra-intentional levels. They are important in helping to explain the emergence of a particular set of reasons for action, which is in turn a product of beliefs and desires. Or they are useful in accounting for the resultant action of an individual given competing tendencies in a particular context and/or to explain the interaction between individual actions in generating the social phenomenon investigated.

Causal mechanisms are thus understood to *complement* intentional mechanisms, where by complementarity we mean to capture the features of additivity, exteriority, and exhaustiveness. Causal mechanisms are *added* to intentional mechanisms, and together they *exhaust* the field of social science explanation. Importantly, though, causal mechanisms do not in any way modify intentional mechanisms; they must thus remain *external* to them. Having offered a general account of Elster's intentional and causal mechanisms, as well as identifying the complementary nature of their relationship, we need now to examine the character and scope of causal mechanisms themselves.

The character and scope of causal mechanisms

In his *Alchemies of the Mind*, inspired by the writings of Montaigne and especially Tocqueville, Elster issues a plea for mechanisms (Elster 1999). As we have already pointed out, causal mechanisms are offered explicitly as a distinct and robust alternative to causal laws (or 'covering laws') when thinking about the irreducibility of social science explanations to the self-interpretations of subjects. However, it is also worth noting that they are offered as an alternative not only to the covering law paradigm, but also to the descriptive or narrative paradigm of social science explanation.[7]

According to Elster, causal mechanisms are 'frequently occurring and easily recognizable causal patterns that are triggered under generally unknown conditions or with indeterminate consequences' (Elster 1999: 1). This formulation already hints at the reason why Elster endows the notion of mechanism with explanatory capacity without prediction, and why from our own perspective it is a candidate for filling out the content of a retroductive explanation. Though mechanisms cannot predict, they 'can at least explain individual events after the fact' (Elster 1999: 44). Take 'wishful thinking' for example, which refers to a situation in which desiring something to be true sometimes leads a person to believe it is true. 'Ex ante', as Elster puts it, 'we cannot predict when [people] will engage in wishful thinking – but when they do, we can recognize it after the fact' (Elster 1999: 5). And it is partly for this reason that proverbs provide a potentially rich source of mechanisms for Elster. Entrenched in a culture, proverbs tend to 'be simple and robust' and tend not to 'survive unless they illuminate behaviour that is widely observed'. They also tend to come in paired opposites: 'like attracts like'/ 'opposites attract', 'out of sight-out of mind'/'absence makes the heart grow fonder', 'the more the merrier'/'one can have too much of a good thing', 'don't put all your eggs in one basket'/'jack of all trades and master of none', 'haste makes waste'/'he who hesitates is lost' (Elster 1999: 10–13).[8]

Given the problems we have already pinpointed with respect to predictions in social science, the use of causal mechanisms as an explanatory device appears to be a promising way forward. Indeed, though Elster does not use the term retroduction, the way he invokes the notion of mechanism supports our claim that social science explanation is retroductive in character. As he puts it, if 'a covering-law explanation amounts to explaining an instance of [an event] E by demonstrating the presence of [conditions] $C_1, C_2, \ldots C_n \ldots$ [then] a statement about mechanisms might be "If $C_1, C_2, \ldots C_n$ obtain, then *sometimes* E" ' (Elster 1999: 5; emphasis added).

Elster acknowledges that 'If p, then sometimes q' appears to be a near-useless insight (Elster 1999: 10). But explanation by mechanisms only works when and because we can identify a particular causal pattern that we recognize across situations and that provides an intelligible answer to the question: 'Why did he do *that?*' (Elster 1999: 10) Elster's answer is that a 'mechanism provides an explanation because it is more *general* than the phenomenon that it *subsumes*' (Elster 1999: 6). Clearly the subsumptive operation is saddled with a critical share of the explanatory burden, where the only difference between mechanisms and laws is the scope of the category under which particular instances are subsumed: while causal laws are universal in their scope, mechanisms are general in scope, hovering closer to the context in which they operate.

Indeterminacy partly accounts for this difference in scope, though it also serves as a means to distinguish between at least two kinds of causal mechanism. Elster labels these type A and type B mechanisms. Whereas type A mechanisms do not allow us 'to predict which of two opposing mechanisms will be triggered', type B mechanisms do not allow us 'to assess the net effect of two opposing mechanisms when both are triggered' (Elster 1999: 8).

In one case, we don't know 'under what conditions a given mechanism will be triggered or, in the case of several mechanisms that operate simultaneously or successively, [we don't know] what their net effect will be' (Elster 1999: 9).

In type A mechanisms, then, there is an indeterminate triggering of *one* of several possible, but mutually exclusive, causal chains. Elster offers many illustrations of this type A mechanism. For example, an animal in shock may fight or flee, but its particular reaction cannot be determined by the prevailing environmental conditions (Elster 1999: 3). Equally, a child of alcoholic parents may become an alcoholic or teetotaller, either because the child does what the parents do, or because it does the opposite, but it is not possible to tell which of these mechanisms will be triggered (Elster 1999: 1). And similarly indeterminate triggering conditions may mean that democracy yields either 'spillover effects' in the form of reduced religiosity, or 'compensatory effects' in the form of increased religiosity (Elster 1999: 18–19). Or, to use the idiom of rational choice theory, dissonance reduction can obtain via wishful thinking (which we have already mentioned) or via the notion of 'sour grapes', that is, through the modification of one's preferences (Elster 1999: 21). Equally, an event may trigger adaptive preference formation, as in the figure of 'sour grapes', which yields dissonance reduction, or it may trigger counteradaptive preference formation, exemplified in the notion of 'forbidden fruit', which yields dissonance creation (Elster 1999: 21–3). In short, in all type A mechanisms, the effect of one or another causal chain is clear, but which one of them is triggered is indeterminate.

In the case of type B mechanisms, there is a *determinate* triggering of *multiple* causal chains but with *indeterminate effects*. Again, Elster provides many illustrations of this mechanism. For example, democracy may trigger two determinate causal chains, one which tends to religiosity as a way of *compensating* for the permissiveness of democracy, and one which tends towards the realization of opportunities for greater licentiousness and dangerous activities, precisely *because* of the permissiveness of democracy (Elster 1999: 19). Here the outcome of their *interaction* is indeterminate, not their triggering. Similarly a person with a 'good past' may trigger two determinate causal chains with indeterminate effects, one which tends to improve the present (which Elster calls the 'endowment effect'), and one which tends to make the present worse (which Elster calls the 'contrastive effect') (Elster 1999: 26–7).

Staying with the last theme, the co-presence of two memories may trigger two determinate causal chains with indeterminate effects: a good memory tends to devalue the present (contrastive effect) and a bad memory tends to improve the present (endowment effect), but the overall effect is indeterminate. As a further example, take a case in which there is an increased availability of opportunities for advancement (Elster 1999: 30–2). One causal chain moves from increased opportunities to higher aspirations to greater discontent, while another causal chain moves from increased opportunities to increased satisfaction and less discontent. As a final example, take the paradox of the ex-lover (Elster 1999: 32–3). If the ex-lover is redescribed as less attractive this leads to less pain (through adaptive preference formation). But re-describing the ex-lover as less attractive also leads to less pleasant memories of past experiences and thus more pain (via the contrastive effect). The net effect of this re-description is indeterminate. In short, in all type B mechanisms Elster claims that '[t]he exact course of events depends on the relative strength of the different mechanisms at work' (Elster 1999: 33). In type B mechanisms, then, 'the separate effects are robust propensities, but the net effect is more contingent' (Elster 1999: 8).

If the previous section identified the general character and complementary nature of the relation between intentional and causal mechanisms, this section has sought to show in greater detail the nature and scope of causal mechanisms more specifically. The appeal of the category of causal mechanism comes from its moving beyond the standard fare of causal laws and thick descriptions. What distinguishes causal mechanisms from causal laws is the *indeterminacy* of the former, and the death knell this sounds for any attempt to make prediction a constitutive feature of social science explanation. More precisely, the lack of determinacy is understood as a serious epistemological obstacle to the elevation of mechanisms to the status of laws, whether this indeterminacy is linked to not knowing the identity of relevant triggering conditions, or to not knowing with sufficient precision the relative force of individual mechanisms acting simultaneously. Elster's intervention thus decisively discredits one of the central pillars of the positivist paradigm by decoupling prediction, and thus a strict deductive-nomological form of reasoning, from social science explanation. While it may still be possible to offer predictions in social science, these predictions are understood to be constitutively precarious and, in any case, non-essential for purposes of explanation. It is for this reason that we feel justified in regarding his approach as conforming to a retroductive form of explanation in the social sciences.

But if Elster offers us a plausible alternative to positivist conceptions of social science explanation, he also appears to offer us a plausible alternative to dominant strands of hermeneutical conceptions of explanation. Clearly, his approach eschews any attempt to reduce social science explanations either to universal causal laws which seek to subsume particulars in an entirely context-free manner or to contextualized self-interpretations. What distinguishes causal mechanisms from thick contextualized self-interpretations is also linked to indeterminacy, but could be more explicitly understood in terms of *generality*. While thick descriptions are always particular and case-specific, and while causal laws are universal in scope, mechanisms are general enough to be used across a wide range of historical contexts for purposes of social science explanation, though they never achieve a law-like status.

Ideals and languages of causality

Elster's emphasis on mechanisms in the field of the social sciences is both insightful and significant. But we now subject his approach to critical scrutiny, arguing that while the category of causal mechanism is fruitful insofar as it contests the false choice between causal laws and thick descriptions, its terminological connotations and conceptual substance betrays a residual positivism which occludes a more radical and productive approach. While it is clear that the demotion of prediction would suggest a move via retroduction away from a positivist conception of explanation, this demotion is not in our view decisive enough to move him beyond positivism.[9] We adduce two reasons for this claim. In the first place, we argue that despite his talk of mechanisms, causal *laws* are still the yardstick against which mechanisms are understood and measured. Secondly, after pointing to the centrality of the 'chain' language of causality in Elster's work, we argue that the attractiveness of such language only makes sense from the perspective of the dominant conception of causality in the natural sciences. This attractiveness belies both the misleading character of such language within the natural science domain itself and, more to the point, its inappropriateness for the social sciences. We elaborate each of these claims in turn.

Despite Elster's emphasis on the idea of explanation by mechanisms, the ideal of an explanation by laws is never far away. He explicitly states, for instance, that he is 'not advancing explanation by mechanisms as an ideal or a norm. Explanation by laws is always better – but also more difficult, often too difficult' (Elster 1999: 10).[10] In this vein, he proposes some fairly straight-forward steps for moving from mechanisms to laws (Elster 1999: 36–44). For example, we can try to eliminate spurious mechanisms by noting how *prima facie* distinct mechanisms are actually the same mechanism, which are just described in different terms. Or, by clarifying the identity and workings of the precise triggers at stake, we might be able to show how particular mechanisms are in fact localised causal patterns of a common causal structure underlying them. As Elster puts it, the 'generalizing strategy [here] is to identify a particular aspect of the *situation* that allows us to *predict* which mechanism will be triggered' (Elster 1999: 40).

The precise role and status of causal laws as an ideal, for Elster, can also be seen in relation to the category of subsumption. As we noted earlier, explanation by mechanisms possesses the feature of generality: 'The mechanism provides an explanation because it is more *general* than the phenomenon that it *subsumes*' (Elster 1999: 6). Explanation in the domain of natural science also works on the basis of subsumption, only this time it 'works by *subsuming* events under causal *laws*' (Elster 1983a: 26). But we also saw that explanation by mechanisms is characterized by indeterminacy. Both generality and indeterminacy acquire their sense and significance in opposition to two other features linked to the notion of law: universality and necessity. And just as the category of subsumption gathers laws and mechanisms together, in the same breath it also excludes other potential candidates that purport to explain in the social sciences, such as thick descriptions of contextualized self-interpretations. In contrast to both causal laws and mechanisms, the latter are presented as entities which cannot speak to any form of generality, universal or otherwise, as they are unable to transcend the particularity of the case from which they emerge.

In this way, the highly significant structuring effects of the causal law ideal are revealed. The category of subsumption enables us to visualize a spectrum of possibilities, with the causal law ideal of universality and necessity at the one end, and thick descriptions of contextualized self-interpretations at the other. Between these poles we can locate the positions of generality and indeterminacy, which together help define the idea of a causal mechanism. In relation to mechanisms, the force of the causal law *ideal* is evident in Elster's account, and can be cast in the form of an imperative: Aim to *universalize* the scope of mechanisms by rendering determinate their *prima facie* indeterminate interactions and triggering conditions. In sum *mechanisms are conceived as stunted or 'proto' causal laws rather than as alternatives to causal laws.* From this point of view, then, Elster fails the challenge he sets himself, which is to offer us a distinct enough alternative to positivist conceptions of explanation, which in this case is explanation by causal laws.

Indeed, it is precisely because Elster does not manage to escape the shadow of the causal law ideal that he remains oblivious to the fact that his actual instantiations of explanation by mechanisms disclose deficiencies in the positivist understanding of the concept. We can thus only glimpse an alternative conception of explanation in Elster's work, as he himself occludes the valid intuition upon which it is based. This intuition, which also structures our own argument, is that the content of a social sciences explanation cannot and should not be reduced to the contextualized self-understandings of actors themselves. In Elster's language, though intentional explanation is the most important element in the social sciences, it is not exhaustive. Elster's first move in fleshing out this intuition is to appeal to *causality*. If intentional mechanisms cannot exhaust the content of social science explanation, these must be supplemented by *causal* mechanisms. More precisely, they must be supplemented by sub-intentional causal mechanisms, which explain how beliefs and desires arise within an individual, and by supra-intentional causal mechanisms, which explain how individuals interact to generate social phenomena (Elster 1983a: 20). In this way, the modifier 'causal' constitutes a *residual* category by qualifying as causal *all* social processes which are not governed by will or intention. For example, one cannot come to believe what one desires to be the case simply through sheer will power. But if one does succeed in deliberately becoming a victim of wishful thinking or sour grapes, this is more likley to be a product of coincidence rather than design. Deliberately willing oneself to become a victim of wishful thinking, or the deliberate intention to modify one's desires through sour grapes, can never bring about these states in the 'right way'. Like falling in love, their triggering is better conceived as a 'by-product' of something else (Elster 1983b). It is thus better to conceive of wishful thinking and sour grapes as species of *causal* mechanism.

However, while we agree that self-interpretations should not exhaust the content of a social science explanation, the move to causality in Elster is too quick. Despite an initial plausibility, there is a problem here because of Elster's particular conception of causality. In fact, his language of causality indicates a misunderstanding about its role in *any* kind of explanation, including natural science. We can call this dominant conception of natural science causality by a variety of names, which include the causal chain, causal sequence, linear, or 'billiard ball' paradigm of causality, all of which are metonymically represented by the term 'mechanism'. Importantly, we argue that this 'mechanistic' conception of causality is actually contested, or, more generally still, that it is only one possible instantiation of a grammar of possible usages.

Central to Elster's conception of causality are the principles of determinism, locality, and temporal asymmetry (Elster 1983a: 26). With this in mind, therefore, the 'mechanistic' dimension of causality is clearly brought into relief when juxtaposed with what Elster regards as the fundamental role of mechanisms: that of reducing the time lag between an *explanans* and *explanandum* (Elster 1983a: 24). The causal sequence or billiard-ball paradigm conjures up a picture of narrow, though ever expanding, causal sequences, which bridge the gap between *explanandum* and *explanans*. From this point of view, what is required — perhaps the most that can be hoped for — is the extension of the causal chain by the addition of extra steps. Let us assume that B believes W. This may already form part of an intentional chain explaining B's action given a certain desire. However, we can extend this chain if we can show how W came to be B's belief. Wishful thinking may provide one such account: If B strongly desired W, he may as a result have come to believe it.

However, according to the philosopher of science Norwood Hanson, this mechanistic image condenses a highly contestable, though no doubt still hegemonic, conception of causality. As he puts it,

> [t]he first scientific theories were those of astronomy and mechanics. These apply to animate and inanimate objects alike. Causal explanations were from the start expressed in terms of impact, attraction, momentum — in short, pushes and pulls. This led to the notion that all causes were impacts, attractions, pushes and pulls, and all effects the result of pushes and pulls. The conviction that sooner or later all science is mechanics dies hard: for three centuries science has been dominated by notions of inertia, impact and resultant velocities. This has affected our understanding of causation.
>
> (Hanson 1961: 65)[11]

But if our understanding of causation has been sedimented along mechanistic lines, what are the other ways of understanding causation? As we shall see, Hanson displaces the causal chain conception of causation, relativizing the concept of causality itself to a particular field of intelligibility, and in this way subordinates the language of causation to explanation. Since causation does not have an essential mechanistic feature, which is shared across all propositions understood to have a causal dimension, causality is relativized to the conceptual framework within which causal statements acquire sense. The corollary of this is that mechanistic causality is no longer a necessary feature of explanation. Rather, causal statements themselves, including their sense and significance, are parasitic upon the explanation itself and the field of intelligibility in which the latter is couched. Causality is thus simultaneously pluralized and demoted.

Consider the following statements:

The primary reason for referring to the cause of x is to explain x. There are as many causes of x as there are explanations of x.

(Hanson 1961: 56)

We can infer an effect from some cause only when the 'cause-word' guarantees the inference; but which words are cause-words and which effect-words is for the context to determine ... Cause-words are charged: they carry a conceptual pattern with them.

(Hanson 1961: 60)

Questions about the nature of causation are to a surprising degree questions about how certain descriptive expressions, in definite contexts, coupled together, complement and interlock with a pattern of other expressions.

(Hanson 1961: 62)[12]

From this point of view, then, mechanistic causality is just one of a range of possible ways of making events in the physical world *intelligible*. And the mechanistic conception can only be made synonymous with causality *per se* if the conceptual network that makes it possible lies buried in the background. Indeed, Hanson's intervention exposes the way in which the mechanistic model not only tends to define causality, but intelligibility as such, at least within the natural science domain and within some (positivist) quarters of social science. From Hanson's perspective, mechanistic causality is just one of a series of possible grammars within which to make physical events intelligible.

Of course both Elster and Hanson take issue with Hempel's covering law model of causality. But while Elster wishes to *correct* its over-inclusivity by admitting within its ambit only those correlations capable of being parsed into – or redescribed as – causal sequences of the causal chain type (Elster 1983a: 26), Hanson wishes to *supplement* the Hempel model by imposing an intelligibility criterion:

[G]enuine laws of nature, although they have a logical form identical to that of generalizations ... nonetheless exert a 'conceptual grip' on the elements of experience – a grip often absent in an actuarial regularity. The mere fact that x and y have always occurred together provides no reason for thinking of x as 'y-ish'; x and y as related inside a theoretical framework, however, 'hooked together' within what we know, may have just this effect on us. In terrestrial space, unsupported bodies *are* 'freely falling' kinds of things. Classical mechanics provides a conceptual structure in terms of which that relationship is articulated. The theory 'makes' the relationship intelligible, or at least captures whatever it is in the relationship which can be made intelligible. *In fact* all unsupported bodies do (as a matter of actuarial generalization) move toward the centre of the earth! This fact makes *sense* only when appreciated as an instantiation of that theory of classical mechanics.

(Hanson 1972: 54; see also 42–5)

Treating causality in terms of intelligibility allows us to see causal mechanisms as a specific and very precise articulation of several elements. In the case of Elster we have at least three ingredients: subsumption, reductionism, and the chain paradigm. Whereas subsumption is also common to laws, the distinction *within* causality is maintained by specifying the permissible values of subsumption. If 1 represents universality (laws) and 0 represents particularity (thick descriptions), causal mechanisms are represented by the range $1>X>0$, where X denotes generality. Elster's conception of causality is then given further content by articulating to it the two central roles with which he invests mechanisms: 'First, they enable us to go from the larger to the smaller: from molecules to atoms, from societies to individuals. Second, and more fundamentally, they reduce the time lag between *explanans* and *explanandum*' (Elster 1983a: 24).

While it may be true that reductionism and the chain paradigm are not essential to causality as such, they both find a place within Elster's conception of mechanistic causality. Indeed, the fact that Elster uses the collocation '*intentional* mechanisms' reveals at least two things. First, it shows that reductionism and the chain paradigm are elements that are not for him exclusive to causality as such. Though reductionism appears to be essentially linked to causality, since smaller units tend to make possible the subsumption of a greater number of phenomena – think of cells in relation to different animal species, or hadrons in relation to different chemical elements – this need not be considered necessary. Thus, intentional mechanisms involve the articulation of reductionism and the chain paradigm to *reasons* (*qua* desires and beliefs) rather than causes. Secondly, insofar as these elements *are* standardly articulated with a conception of causality drawn from the natural sciences, it furnishes further evidence of the force that the causal law ideal still exerts on Elster.

We have thus far identified the key elements of Elster's notion of causal mechanism, showing that his conception is tied to a positivist problematic, which itself is contestable. However, it is still not clear what is wrong with this particular articulation or indeed with its elements. In the next part, we argue that the causal mechanism picture leads to two fallacies – the fallacies of psychologism and idealism – which can be avoided if mechanisms are abandoned, or rather re-understood, as the basic elements of a social science explanation. The question thus becomes: What grammar of intelligibility is appropriate in a social science context? It will be the task of Chapters 4 and 5 to present an alternative grammar of intelligibility as a function of *logics*, which assimilates the intuition underpinning Elster's appeal to the notion of causal and intentional *mechanisms*, but which overcomes some of the problems associated with it.

Problematizing causal mechanisms

We have already suggested that Elster's account is not as distinct from the causal law paradigm as he claims it is, both because the notion of a causal law still functions as a universalizing ideal, and because he remains committed to a subsumptive picture of explanation. The spectre of positivism still haunts his account. In this section, we problematize the causal mechanism picture in a more decisive fashion. We do not argue that causal mechanisms have no role to play in the social sciences, but problematize the status and role that Elster attributes to them. More specifically, we take issue with the way he abstracts causal mechanisms from the contexts in which they function, and we argue that their decontextualized status renders their explanatory adequacy suspect.

Explanation through contextualization

In order to better explore the sense in which causal mechanisms are decontextualized *explanantia*, let us begin with an example. Consider wishful thinking. We can imagine a case in which this mechanism is invoked to explain why the British prime minister Tony Blair believed there were weapons of mass destruction (WMD) in Iraq before the invasion of that country by British and American troops in March 2003: he so strongly desired that Saddam Hussein possessed WMDs that he came to believe it was true. Though we could not predict that Blair would become a victim of wishful thinking in this way – other mechanisms may have been triggered, or other mechanisms may have interacted with it – we can use this mechanism in a retroductive fashion, that is, we can explain Blair's belief after the fact.

Since the mechanism is, as Elster puts it, 'an easily recognizable causal pattern', it is something that will appear intact in – and thus can be 'applied' to – a variety of contexts. Every time someone comes to believe what he or she wishes to be the case *because* he or she wishes this to be the case, we have an instance of wishful thinking. To say, therefore, that Blair's beliefs or actions can be explained by reference to the causal mechanism of wishful thinking has an initial plausibility. But this plausibility is quickly revealed to be partial in character because it elides the question of sense. The essential question is not whether a particular instance embodies wishful thinking, but in what *sense* it is the case that this particular person is a 'wishful thinker' in a particular set of circumstances. And for this one requires some background theory, such as an account of subjectivity, together with the contextual conditions which make this action intelligible. To stay at the level of mechanism is thus to stay at the level of an *abstract essence*.

While it can be said that the identification of such mechanisms shows us potentially interesting causal patterns, the latter have *to be explained through greater contextualization*, and should not be seen as the foundational units with which to *develop* an explanation. The enumeration and designation of causal chains as mechanisms is akin to the equally problematic process of constructing abstract sociological categories such as class, ethnicity, gender, and so forth, and then employing these abstract notions as key elements of a social science *explanans*, without adapting these concepts to suit the particular situations under investigation. Such use of mechanisms is problematic in a social science context because it ignores how their meaning and significance is parasitic upon the practices in which they are embedded. The demotion of context implied in the notion of causal mechanism offers a preliminary rationale for using the qualifier 'social' in *social logic*, about which we shall say more in Chapter 5.

The subject-independence of causal mechanisms

What accounts for this apparent readiness to disavow the context-dependence of mechanisms? Our view is that this is a direct result of the conception of causal mechanism in play, which in turn is fundamentally connected to the problematic way in which it is linked to intentional mechanisms. Recall that for Elster the concept of a causal mechanism is a residual category, which speaks to the intuition that social science explanations are not reducible to the contextualized self-interpretations or intentions of subjects. The category of causal mechanism thus emerges as an instance of X, where X is any process operating along the non-intentional, non-descriptive dimension of social science explanation. From this point of view, causal mechanisms appear as potential contenders for X. However, from the fact that X *qua* process is not *reducible* to the contextualized self-interpretations or intentions of subjects, it does not necessarily – or only – follow that X is *independent* of those contextualized self-interpretations or intentions. But this is precisely what is implied by Elster's conception of causal mechanism. As we noted from the outset, causal mechanisms bear a relation of *exteriority* to intentional mechanisms, such that causal mechanisms can be discussed entirely on their own, with no necessary *internal connection* to intentional mechanisms.

Of course, the subject-independent feature of causal mechanisms is very attractive from the perspective of a positivist programme seeking to import the causal law ideal and its correlative promise of (a certain conception of) objectivity into the social sciences. After all, one of the central ingredients of a natural science conception of causality is its subject-independence. The causal process is unaffected by what any of us think about it or do in relation to it.

Take the law of gravitation for instance. At the very most, we as subjects can act *in light* of such causal laws, but we cannot modify, or be considered supports of, the laws themselves, whether intentionally or otherwise. The *functioning* of comparable processes (X) in the social sciences, however, *is parasitic upon human practices, in the sense that they are constitutively sustained and mediated by the discursive activity of subjects.* If we insist on calling such a process a mechanism, then we must accept that, unlike laws, it has the property of fungibility, that is, it can suffer dissolution. At any point, the mechanism may find that it has lost its necessary support – intentional or otherwise – in the relevant subjects. Thus, mechanisms are not 'proto' laws that may one day be transformed into 'proper' causal laws. This is because the *functioning* of causal laws does not require the passage through the subject: the content of causal laws is not parasitic upon the subjects' self-interpretations. This is why we prefer the term 'logic' to 'mechanism'. The term logic better avoids the connotations of subject-independence that talk of causal laws and mechanisms suggest. At the same time, it allows us to maintain the central insight which prompted the turn to mechanisms in the first place, namely, that not all is reducible to the contextualized self-interpretations of subjects: logics are thus meant to capture the subject-dependent aspect of social processes, as well as aspects which are not reducible to the empirical context.

Avoiding the fallacy of psychologism

When mechanisms are conceived in terms of patterns or abstract essences, and then combined with Elster's methodological individualism, this very easily leads to the fallacy of psychologism. By fallacy of psychologism we denote the tendency to transform outer conditions and relations into characteristics or properties of the individual's inner self. Let us return briefly to the Blair example. There we offered an explanation of his belief in the existence of WMD by reference to the mechanism of wishful thinking. If we accept the mechanism of wishful thinking as having the status of an atom in our social science *explanans*, it is a small step from there to say that we can explain Blair's belief because of his *disposition* to wishful thinking. We get a kind of truncated explanation wherein beliefs, desires, and actions are explained by reference to a fixed set of unexplained dispositions or robust propensities. Thus we enter the terrain of psychologism.

That Elster is not immune to this danger is clear when he makes his plea for disaggregation:

> [I]t has often been observed that human beings are subject to two very strong desires: The desire to be like others and the desire to differ from others, conformism and anticonformism. If some individuals are strongly dominated by the former desire and others by the latter, the aggregate effect might be very weak, supporting the idea that people are mostly autonomous rather than heteronomous. Theories of voting behaviour,

for instance, have identified both an underdog mechanism and a bandwagon mechanism. Those subject to the former tend to vote for the candidate who is behind in preelection polls, whereas those subject to the latter vote for the front-runner. If the two types are evenly mixed, there might be no noticeable effect, so that the polls would be good predictors of the actual vote. The lack of influence of polls on voting in the aggregate does not show, however, that individuals are unaffected by the polls. The neutral aggregate could mask a homogeneous population of unaffected individuals – or a heterogeneous population of individuals who are strongly affected but in opposite directions.

(Elster 1999: 46)

The explanatory weight falling upon mechanisms *qua* dispositions is striking. However, once we take seriously the need to pass through the subjects' self-interpretations on the way to an adequate explanation of social phenomena, the issue of language and discourse is put centre stage. Indeed, once the central importance of discourse is acknowledged, the psychologistic tendencies of mechanistic explanations are brought into relief and thereby thrown into doubt.

There is a considerable literature that puts into question precisely this understanding of psychology, which is conceived as a function of 'internal' states (beliefs, attitudes, predispositions, and so forth). Some of the more trenchant critiques of this 'psychologistic' tendency of orthodox psychology arise from discursive psychology and psychoanalysis. Taking its cue from intellectual sources such as Wittgenstein's later philosophy, ethnomethodology, and conversational analysis, the discipline of discursive psychology eschews talk about 'inner' processes (Billig 1997b; Edwards 1994; Harré 1995; Parker 1992; Potter & Wetherell 1995). Instead, phenomena that are usually treated as inner mental processes by mainstream theories of psychology are seen to be 'constituted through social, discursive activity' (Billig 1997a: 139). In other words, psychological language entails outward, not inner, criteria, implying that emotions are socially constructed. 'If one wishes to study "feelings"', argues Billig, 'psychologists should be paying attention to what people are doing when they claim to have feelings' (Billig 1997a: 141).

One very important consequence of taking seriously the need to focus upon the outward criteria for inner states is that individuals are dethroned from the privileged position usually ascribed to them vis-à-vis their self-interpretations. Indeed, from our point of view, the discipline of psychoanalysis is at one with this approach when it talks about a patient's 'repression' or 'unconscious desires'. What justifies the use of this talk is not any access to 'inner' unconscious states, but rather the 'outward' appearance of what Freud calls the parapraxes of everyday life, namely, slips of the tongue, bungled actions, and so on. In other words, 'because language is socially shared, there must be public criteria for the use of psychological words' (Billig 1997a: 142). In short, the flaws or failures that interrupt conversation and social interaction, index desires outside the subject's conscious control. Far from implying the existence of a separate causal domain which is independent of the subject, these failures demonstrate the *social* dimension of their constitution.

In reference to studies of politeness, for example, Billig notes how

> [t]he temptations of impoliteness do not stand outside the dialogic process, but are constituted within it. The desires to be rude, to contradict, 'to speak one's mind', to have done with the constraints of politeness are formed within dialogue. Such desires cannot antedate, nor stand outside, the constrictions of politeness. In this respect, it makes sense to talk of the unconscious being dialogically constituted.
>
> (Billig 1997a: 151)

The argument here is that detaching psychological propensities from social context is rendered problematic from a psychoanalytic perspective and by recent developments in discursive psychology. This is because 'inner' states or mechanistic propensities have 'outward' criteria, thereby also pointing to their highly *contestable* nature, both from the perspective of the participants and from the perspective of the social scientist studying a practice.

The move from mechanisms to what we call logics thus opens up the possibility of not simply providing a more robust and reliable social science explanation, but also the possibility of a *critical* explanation. This possibility follows once one acknowledges the error of moving too quickly from the claim that a process is not reducible to subjects' self-interpretations, to the further claim that the functioning of such processes is causal, asocial, and subject-independent in character. However, in order to make more visible the critical component of a social science explanation, more needs to be said about a key dimension of the ontology of the social world.

Avoiding the fallacy of idealism – from epistemological indeterminacy to an 'ontology of lack'

Our account thus far may suggest that the problem with a mechanistic approach to social science explanation can be remedied simply by contextualizing psychological propensities or other mechanisms within a wider set of social and relational structures. However, this is not the case because it turns out that both methodological atomism *and* methodological structuralism tend to appeal to the principle of reductionism, which in turn leads to the fallacy of idealism. Elster operationalizes what we call the principle of methodological atomism, where the aim is to explain social phenomena in terms of smaller, more fundamental units. In a first move, then, the basic unit of an explanation in the social sciences for Elster is the individual action. This forms the basis of his methodological individualism. But in a more fundamental sense the basic unit is the mechanism, since actions and interactions can themselves be explained in terms of mechanisms. That is to say, intentional mechanisms comprise intentional chains connecting goals to actions via beliefs, while causal mechanisms comprise causal chains connecting events to effects. In short, according to Elster, mechanisms are the ultimate units in terms of which all social science explanations are to be constructed.

Now, we have already suggested why mechanisms cannot serve this foundational function, and we have hinted instead at the role of logics as more promising candidates for a social science *explanans*. However, as we have just seen, Elster's account of mechanisms also appeals to the principle of reductionism. By treating mechanisms as the basic 'atoms' of explanation, we argue that he misunderstands their nature and status, which in our terms leads to the fallacy of idealism. Revealing and rectifying the character of this fallacy does, nevertheless, help us to supplement our conception of social science explanation by furnishing it with an underlying materialist ontology.

According to Laclau and Mouffe, idealism involves the claim that the 'innermost nature of...objects is identical to that of mind – that is to say, that it is ultimately *thought*' (Laclau 1990: 106). Idealism in this sense presupposes a realist outlook, as the idealist project is characterized as an attempt to reduce the real to the rational or conceptual. From this point of view, many theorists who consider themselves to be materialist are actually idealists in disguise. Indeed, it is clear that Elster's attempt to close the gap between the *explanans* and the *explanandum* by furnishing ever-more basic mechanisms conforms to this idealist project. As Laclau points out, Hegel was aware of this to such an extent that in his *Greater Logic* he presented ancient materialism – atomism – as one of the first and crudest forms of idealism. Laclau marshals a relevant passage from the Hegel scholar, W.T. Stace, to drive this point home:

> Atomism alleges that this thing, the atom, is the ultimate reality. Let it be so. But what is this thing? It is nothing but a congeries of universals, such perhaps as 'indestructible', 'indivisible', 'small', 'round', etc. All these are universals, or thoughts. 'Atom' itself is a concept. Hence even out of this materialism proceeds idealism.
>
> (Stace cited in Laclau 1990: 107–8)

The real division, then, between idealism and materialism according to Laclau and Mouffe, hinges on 'the affirmation or negation of the ultimate irreducibility of the real to the concept', where materialists insist on the constitutively deficient or lacking character of the conceptual field itself (Laclau 1990: 107). This is a general argument in favour of a materialist ontology, and from this point of view, it carries important implications for the way we develop our conception of critical explanation. More specifically, what we might term an 'ontology of lack' carries implications both from the perspective of the theorist or analyst, and from the perspective of the subjects and practices being analysed.

In the first place, it can apply to the analyst's own activity insofar as he or she draws on a theoretical/conceptual framework. From this point of view, a materialist ontology involves an affirmation that the conceptual network of the analyst is constitutively lacking. As Fink puts it, the proclivity to fill in the 'gap' between cause and effect in scientific discourse 'progressively eliminates the content of the concept "cause", events being viewed as leading smoothly, in accordance with well-known "laws", to other events. Science, attempting to suture the subject [here, the subject of the scientist] – that is, trying to evict subjectivity from its field – tends also towards a suturing of the cause' (Fink 1995: 31). The never-ending search for a cause leads paradoxically to the formulation of laws which empty causality of its substance.

Perhaps, then, cause ought to be retrieved and re-understood in terms that are opposed to the idea of a causal chain, and in favour of a *breach of a conceptual pattern or routine*. As Hanson puts it, we may ask

> 'What is its cause?' selectively: we ask it only when we are confronted with some breach of routine, an event that stands out and leads us to ask after its nature and genesis. Thus Sagredo might learn that Galileo was indisposed and ask 'What is the matter?' On being told that he had cut his arm Sagredo might then ask for the cause of the cut. It is unlikely, however, that on any ordinary Tuesday morning Sagredo would ask after the cause of Galileo's moderate good health. Why should he? Only if he expects Galileo to be otherwise (at a time, for instance, when Padua had been hit by a contagious illness) would the question be in place.
>
> 'What caused the clock to stop running?' is a request for news about the one thing responsible for the stoppage, the 'link' immediately preceding cessation of movement. One less frequently asks 'What makes the clock keep running?' If one does, it is with an awareness that it is different from the former query. No tick-tock account is appropriate here, as it might have been in the former case; a complete account of what makes the clock run will involve a lot of horological theory and physics.
>
> (Hanson 1961: 68–9)

In short, 'cause' emerges as relevant at those moments when our conceptual field is revealed as deficient, indicating the irreducibility of the real to the concept. When Elster, for example, talks about the indeterminacy attaching to type A and type B mechanisms, the status of this indeterminacy is epistemological and the obstacle preventing us from making it determinate is empirical. Here, on the contrary, the obstacle is ontological and the incompleteness of social structures is constitutive. We are thus bringing about a shift from epistemological indeterminacy to an ontology of lack.

However, the critique of idealism does not just apply to the analyst's own attempt to render the real fully intelligible by reference to conceptual or theoretical categories without remainder. Most importantly, it applies to the system of meaning relied upon by the subjects under study. The reason social science explanation cannot be entirely reduced to the contextualized self-interpretations of the subjects under study is not simply because these are structured by broader social processes that are too complicated and complex in their interactions to grasp, but more fundamentally because social structures are themselves constitutively lacking. But, again, the social structures making possible the subjects' self-interpretations, and the limits of social structures themselves, are locatable and understandable only by identifying correlative limit experiences by passing through, and relating them explicitly to, the self-interpretations of subjects. Lapses, bungled actions, and slips of tongue comprise examples of just such limits within the psychoanalytic domain.

Conclusion

This chapter has examined a second alternative to the perceived inadequacies of the law-like model of explanation. While Elster's notion of causal mechanisms seeks to break with both the hermeneutical tendency to reduce explanations to contextualized self-interpretations, and the positivist tendency to subsume particulars under universal causal laws, we have shown how his position fails to bridge the gap between historical contextualization and theoretical idealization. In the end, as Elster himself admits, he is not prepared to give up the ideal of strong causal explanation and the logic of subsumption this entails. In part, this is because he is not prepared to develop what we have called a *materialist* ontology, which is predicated upon a relational conception of reality and the radical contingency of social relations and identities. Indeed, in keeping with his positivist background, he is reluctant to countenance a role for ontological questions at all. In our view, by contrast, any legitimate candidate for a social science *explanans* must be compatible with such a materialist ontological framework. It is to our ontological framework, and then our concept of logics, that we now turn.

4   Ontology

> It will be expected that ontology now takes the subject as [an] exemplary
> entity and interprets the concept of being by looking to the mode of being of
> the subject – that henceforth the subject's *way of being* becomes an ontologi-
> cal problem ... The motive is ... to know precisely *that* and *how* being and
> being's structure can be clarified.
>
> (Heidegger 1982: 123)

In our critique of existing logics of explanation in the social sciences, and
in the development of our alternative approach, we stress the ontological
rather than just the epistemological and methodological aspects of
interpretation, analysis, and critique. While Elster's theory of causal mechanisms
responds to certain limitations of the causal law paradigm, he nevertheless
accepts the search for laws as an ideal. And one of the reasons for this is the
atomistic ontological grounding of his account, in which the world consists
of discrete events, facts, and mechanisms. But while Elster eschews the task of
ontological reflection, Bhaskar's account of causal mechanisms explicitly
locates his concept of causal mechanisms within a clearly elaborated ontological
framework. Nevertheless, his approach falters because his aim to furnish a
positive ontology of objects and processes pushes him to make very abstract
theoretical claims whose relevance for conducting empirical enquiry is
unclear. Finally, while hermeneuticists are also often explicitly concerned
with ontological questions – more so in the case of Taylor, less so in the case
of Bevir and Rhodes – the analytical frameworks emerging from their
ontological reflections do not produce robust or convincing enough critical
explanations, and we think this is partly because of their presupposed ontology.

In this chapter, we advance the ontology that underpins our own
poststructuralist approach to critical explanation. It is against this ontological
background that we will in Chapter 5 counter-pose logics to both contextualized self-interpretations and mechanisms. We begin now by introducing a
simple paradigm for our objects of investigation in general, namely, the
transformation and/or stabilization of regimes and practices. We then present
the latter's conditions of possibility and impossibility, which involves setting

out four ontological dimensions of social reality – the social, political, ideological and ethical dimensions – as well as clarifying the concepts implicated in them. We conclude our ontological investigation by returning to – and enriching – our account of regimes and practices.

Practices, regimes, logics

Consider the impact of a major economic depression that dislocates communities across the globe, bringing the closure of factories and businesses, mass unemployment, the loss of savings, spiralling inflation, a rise in crime and social disorder, and so forth. Social actors in general can interpret and respond to these new situations in a variety of ways, ranging from passive resignation, despair and alienation, to a mounting anger and outrage that leads to new grievances which can be articulated as claims and demands. The latter may even lead to the construction of new identities and subjectivities, and these constructions in turn may disclose ways of linking various demands together into new political projects or social movements. Indeed, there may emerge a radical political subjectivity and ideology that seeks to transform social relations along fundamentally different lines. Equally, of course, these developments may provoke renewed efforts by power holders and political elites to meet or deflect claims and demands, thus channelling and reshaping the grievances into the existing institutions and structures of power. A dislocatory experience such as an economic depression may thus reveal the contingency of taken-for-granted social practices, highlighting the fact that the existing system represents only one way of organizing social relations amongst others.

In a more theoretical vein, we can formalize these processes by inscribing them in a broader framework of concepts. Let us start by defining social practices as the ongoing, routinized forms of human and societal reproduction. They are thus largely repetitive activities that do not typically entail a strong notion of self-conscious reflexivity – what we might term a series of sedimented practices – which have been inscribed on our bodies and ingrained in our human dispositions (see Bourdieu 1977). A whole host of acts and activities, from making breakfast in the morning to the successful delivery of children to school, followed by the plotting of one's journey to work, contribute to the successful reproduction of various systems of social relations – the family, the school, the transport system, or the workplace – and they are (usually) carried out without it even occurring to someone to put into question the rules animating these practices. Whether they are intended to or not, such practices contribute to the reproduction of wider systems of social relations.

Importantly, however, for our account, every social practice is also *articulatory*, as human beings constantly engage in the process of linking together different elements of their social lives in these continuous and projective sequences of human action. Catching a bus to work in the morning is an activity we engage in on a regular basis, and consequently has a repetitive character. Nonetheless, as we saw in our discussion of Wittgenstein in Chapter 2, it is slightly different each time we do so, thus requiring minor modifications and adjustments in its accomplishment. This means that all social practices comprise temporal and iterative activities, which by necessity connect the present with the past and the future.

However, while social practices and the identities they sustain tend to conceal the inherent contingency that inhabits social systems, this does not mean that its spectre can be banished once and for all. The irreducible presence of negativity means that any social edifice suffers from an inherent flaw or crack which may become visible in moments of dislocation (Heidegger 1962; Lacan 2006: 693). In such situations, new possibilities become available, enabling a subject to identify differently. Indeed, there are a number of ways in which human beings can fill in the gap between experiencing dislocation and responding to it. For the moment, however, we will consider how the dislocation of social relations can provoke *political practices*. These comprise struggles that seek to challenge and transform the existing norms, institutions and practices – perhaps even the regime itself – in the name of an ideal or principle. This entails the construction of political frontiers, which divide the social space into opposed camps. But political practices also involve efforts on the part of the power bloc to disrupt the construction of antagonistic frontiers by breaking down the connections that are being forged between different demands.

Clearly, then, insofar as political movements are successful in challenging norms and institutions in the name of something new, political practices bring about a transformative effect on existing social practices. Indeed, to the degree that such movements become hegemonic by managing to link various demands together across a variety of social spaces and sites of struggle, they can exercise a transformative effect on an entire regime of practices, resulting in the institution and sedimentation of a new regime and the social practices that comprise it.[1] We summarize this interrelationship between practices and regimes in Figure 2.

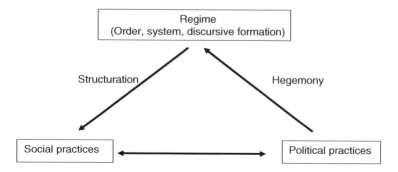

Figure 2 A simplified model of practices and regimes.

This figure displays a triangular relationship between regimes and two sorts of practices. To begin, *regimes* have a structuring function in the sense that they order a system of *social* practices, thus helping us to characterize the latter. This is because the institution of a particular regime (say the Thatcherite regime) is always defined in opposition to a contested regime (say the Keynesian Welfare State regime), and this oppositional contrast colours the regime's practices. On the other hand, *political* practices can shape, modify, or reorder the regime itself. Insofar as these practices are successful in constructing a new hegemonic order, they come to redefine key parameters of a range of practices. In this sense they are responsible for the institution of a new regime. Finally, it is worth noting how the model already allows us to introduce in a very preliminary way our three-fold typology of logics – social, political and fantasmatic – which when articulated together constitute the basic explanatory schema of our poststructuralist approach to critical explanation. This complex of logics provides us with the theoretical resources to characterize practices and regimes, to account for their dialectical relationship, and to explain how and why they change or resist change.

Social logics comprise the substantive grammar or rules of a practice or regime, which enable us to distil their purpose, form and content. Moreover, in characterizing a regime, we also describe the context of the practices under study, since a regime is always a regime *of* practices. The Thatcher regime, for example, comprises a heterogeneous set of practices linked to welfare, business, the passage of legislation, measures targeting local government, and so on. *Political logics*, by contrast, enable us to understand the way a social practice or regime *was* instituted or *is being* contested or instituted, thus contributing to our description and analysis of it. Since the very identity and significance of a social practice depends upon its institution, as well as the subsequent forgetting of its ignoble origins, political logics assist in the characterization of a practice or regime by showing how they emerge and are sedimented.

Political logics derive from a post-Saussurian ontology of signification. Saussure, of course, identifies two fundamental relations in language – the associative (or substitutive) and the syntagmatic (or combinatory) – but these are transformed by Laclau and Mouffe into two dynamic and politically inflected logics, which they call logics of equivalence and difference (Laclau and Mouffe 1985: 130; Saussure 1983: 121–32). Insofar as political practices entail the construction of new frontiers to challenge old social structures in the name of an ideal or principle (thus implying a new set of inclusions and exclusions), one can say that the political logic of equivalence predominates. But insofar as there is a breaking down of those frontiers so as to maintain existing social structures (thus retaining the old distribution of inclusions and exclusions) we say that the political logic of difference predominates.[2] We shall explain and illustrate the nature and operation of these political logics in more detail during the course of Chapter 5. For now we would like to complete our three-fold picture of logics by introducing our final type of logic: the logic of fantasy.

Fantasmatic logics furnish us with the means to account for the *grip* of an existing or anticipated social practice or regime. They derive from a Lacanian ontology of *enjoyment*, insofar as fantasy is understood as the frame which structures the subject's enjoyment. However, enjoyment is not to be understood as a synonym for pleasure, if only because such enjoyment is often – though by no means always – consciously experienced as suffering.[3] Lacan, in fact, defined enjoyment in *opposition* to pleasure (Lacan 1992: 185). Closely associated with the Freudian notions of libido and primordial loss, enjoyment is a category used in conjunction with a set of other terms like fantasy, desire, repression, and so on, to account for a symptom's *inertia*. Thus the notion of enjoyment captures a subject's mode of being, whether individual or collective. The guilt which may accompany the transgression of an officially affirmed ideal is a possible, indeed fairly common, mode of experiencing enjoyment. So if one insists on using the term pleasure, this must be understood as *unconscious* pleasure.

In the field of social and political analysis, the notion of enjoyment has been used to characterize and account for the resilience of a host of practices and rituals (Glynos 2001a; Žižek 1989). Žižek, for example, suggests that 'a nation *exists* only as long as its specific enjoyment continues to be materialized in a set of social practices and transmitted through national myths that structure these practices'. Of central importance here is 'the remainder of some real, non-discursive kernel of enjoyment which must be present for the Nation *qua* discursive entity-effect to achieve its ontological consistency' (Žižek 1993: 202). Žižek summarizes the significance of the category of enjoyment for the analysis of nationalist discourses as follows:

> What is at stake in ethnic tensions is always the possession of the national Thing: the 'other' wants to steal our enjoyment (by ruining our 'way of life') and/or it has access to some secret, perverse enjoyment. In short, what gets on our nerves, what really bothers us about the 'other', is the peculiar way he organizes his enjoyment (the smell of his food, his 'noisy' songs and dances, his strange manners, his attitude to work – in the racist perspective, the 'other' is either a workaholic stealing our jobs or an idler living on our labour). The basic paradox is that our Thing is conceived as something inaccessible to the other and at the same time threatened by him.
>
> (Žižek 1991b: 165)

In sum, by invoking fantasmatic logics we suggest that one condition for subscribing to an existing or promised social practice concerns the extent to which it can tap into the subject's existing mode of enjoyment and thus fantasmatic frame. When working in tandem with political logics, fantasmatic logics may be invoked to help explain why certain demands – or responses to demands – succeed in gripping or interpellating a particular constituency. Equally, they can be mobilized to account for the way explicit challenges to existing social structures or institutions are blocked.

Roughly speaking, we could say that our three types of logic correspond to three sorts of question we address in accounting for a problematized phenomenon, each of which is valuable in generating critical explanations: what, how, and why questions. If social logics assist in the process of characterizing *what* a practice is, and political logics show *how* it is challenged and defended, then fantasmatic logics can be said to generate reasons for *why* practices are maintained or transformed. All are necessary in any account of a problematized phenomenon and thus mutually implicate one another. It is, however, heuristically helpful sometimes to think of them as picking out different aspects of a critical explanation.

Ontological presuppositions

Our initial sketch of practices and regimes, as well as our typology of logics conceals considerable complexity. For one thing, our model is predicated upon a social ontology that comprises four dimensions of social reality, which we call the social, political, ideological and ethical dimensions. This means that in order to elaborate our model in more detail we need to clarify our ontological presuppositions, and the concepts and distinctions upon which they rely. We will then be in a position to revisit and complexify our picture of regimes and practices, before going on in Chapter 5 to examine each of the three logics in a more systematic fashion.

The need to clarify our notion of ontology is important because the turn to ontology is by no means obvious. As Maurice Duverger notes perceptively in *The Study of Politics*, modern science is no longer concerned with 'a search for "the being" of things', but rather with generating 'a collection of coordinated prescriptions enabling one to act upon things and individuals' (Duverger 1972: 5). To be sure, in our view, the role of political study should *not* be to make 'reality judgements' – to discover the true nature of things in the world. However, we do not think ontology can or should be bracketed in the name of simply developing pragmatic concepts with which to investigate and intervene in politics and society. Instead, an ontological inquiry, for us, focuses attention on the underlying presuppositions for any analysis of politics; it focuses on the 'basic concepts' mobilized by a discipline in any empirical and normative investigation (Heidegger 1962: 30–1).

In order to develop this idea, let us begin by reactivating the origins of the ontical/ontological distinction in Heidegger's early work. In *Being and Time*, Heidegger argues that an ontical inquiry focuses on particular types of objects and entities that are located within a particular domain or 'region' of phenomena, whereas an ontological inquiry concerns the categorical pre-conditions for such objects and their investigation. For instance, a political scientist might investigate the construction of national identity in a variety of contexts, or she might examine the changing role of teachers and university lecturers in societies that are increasingly marked by new audit regimes and markets. If the researcher takes for granted the notions of 'national identity', 'audit regime' or the 'market', which are given in the practices themselves, as well as in second-order accounts of them, then her research operates at the ontical level. If, on the other hand, the research inquires into the underlying presuppositions that determine what is to *count* as an identity or role, *how* these phenomena are to be studied, and *that* they exist at all, then the research incorporates an ontological dimension. In other words, the more an inquiry is directed at the categorical and existential preconditions of a practice or regime, the more the ontological dimension is foregrounded.

Marxist theory, for example, can be said to engage in an ontological inquiry insofar as it connects the construction of social and political identities to the underlying economic relationships and class structures of a society, which are accorded explanatory primacy. In fact, this account of identity and social role is itself rooted in the idea that humans are primarily 'productive beings' or 'tool-making animals', as 'man' for Marx is *Homo Faber*. But Olson's 'logic of collective action' (Olson 1965, 1982) is also animated by a set of ontological presuppositions concerning the nature of human beings, rationality, and interaction, though these are generally taken for granted. From a Heideggerian point of view, then, all theories and approaches in the social and political sciences, including positivist social science approaches, presuppose a distinctive ontology, which structures their more specific theories and explanations.

We shall return briefly to the way in which the ontical/ontological distinction informs our concept of logics in the next chapter.[4] For now, we need to return to our model of practices and regimes, and begin the task of setting out its precise ontological presuppositions. Our first premise is that all practices and regimes are discursive entities, in the sense in which Ernesto Laclau and Chantal Mouffe understand the 'discursive' nature of all actions, practices and social formations. For them, the notion of discourse signals the centrality of meaning to practices. Although, as they put it, a 'stone exists independently of any system of social relations . . . it is, for instance, either a projectile or an object of aesthetic contemplation only within a specific discursive configuration' (Laclau and Mouffe in Laclau 1990: 101). In other words, an object's identity is conferred by the particular discourses or systems of meaning within which it is constituted. In short, social practices can coalesce into constellations or systems of practices which we call regimes, and both practices and regimes are located within a field of discursive social relations.

Crucially, however, a further axiomatic premise of our ontological framework is the idea that any field of discursive social relations is marked by radical contingency, where radical contingency refers to the inherent (as opposed to accidental) instability of an object's identity. As we have argued in previous chapters, the significance of *radical* or *ontological* contingency is highlighted when contrasted with *empirical* or *ontical* contingency, as evident in Bhaskar's critical realism or in Popper's commitment to epistemic fallibilism. By empirical contingency we aim to capture a sense of possibility: the possibility that contingency *may* be absorbed by a higher order process.

For example, what appears to us now as a contingent event – a solar eclipse say – may be represented or spatialized by its being subsumed under a higher-order process – the planetary laws of motion. However, the appeal to radical contingency in a social science context contests this familiar subsumptive move which is characteristic of the natural sciences. Radical contingency opposes empirical contingency's sense of possibility with a sense of *im*possibility: the *constitutive* failure of any objectivity to attain a full identity. Other formulations of radical contingency as an ontological premise include 'lack in the Other' (Lacan), 'structural undecidability' (Derrida), and so on, all of which question the idea of a fully constituted essence of a practice, regime or object, in the name of an irreducible negativity that cannot be reabsorbed (see Coole 2000).

The way this ontological premise is affirmed is critical for us, because radical contingency not only shapes our understanding of different elements of our discourse theoretical approach, such as practices, regimes, and logics, but it also ties them together. To see this, we flesh out our ontological postulate along two axes, yielding four dimensions of socio-political reality: the political, social, ideological, and ethical dimensions.

Dimensions of socio-political reality

In elaborating these four dimensions, two further notions need to be specified. These are the category of *dislocation* and the notion of *public contestation*. The former enables us to sketch out the ideological-ethical axis, while the latter provides conceptual resources to develop the political-social axis. The intersection of these two axes generates a parsimonious conceptual grammar which can enhance our practice of critical explanation.

One way of understanding dislocation in terms of the radical contingency of social relations is to restate the latter postulate in the following way: the structure of social relations is constitutively incomplete or lacking, or, more pointedly, '*every* identity is dislocated' (Laclau 1990: 39; emphasis added). However, in his discussion of dislocation Laclau also refers to the dislocatory effects of commodification, bureaucratization, technologization, and globalization in creating the conditions for the rise of the 'new' social movements (Laclau 1990: 52–3, 56, 67; see also Laclau and Mouffe 1985: 159–71). Here dislocation can be understood as a moment when the subject's mode of being is experienced as disrupted. In this sense, then, we could say that dislocations are those occasions when a subject is called upon to confront the contingency of social relations more directly than at other times.

However, it does not follow that the subject will engage with contingency in a more authentic way because of this confrontation. In using the term authenticity we simply aim to capture a subject's *generalized sensitivity* or *attentiveness* to the always-already dislocated character of existing social relations, wherein creativity and surprise are accorded prominent roles. But this implies that an inauthentic response to a dislocation is also possible.

We call the authentic response ethical, and the inauthentic response ideological. In other words, the radical contingency of social reality and identity can be acknowledged and tarried with, or it can be denied and concealed. This, then, suggests one way we can use the category of dislocation to redescribe social relations in terms of our fundamental ontological premise, making possible the following sort of question: To what extent do subjects engage authentically with the radical contingency of social relations (where the ethical dimension is foregrounded), or to what extent are they complicit in concealing it (where the ideological dimension is foregrounded)? As we shall argue later, these different ways of mediating and coming to terms with radical contingency have important implications for discharging our task of critical explanation.

While a reference to dislocation enables us to develop two dimensions in terms of which to characterize aspects of a practice or regime, the concept of *public contestation* enables us to develop two further dimensions. By public contestation we mean simply the contestation of the norms which are constitutive of an existing social practice (or regime) in the name of an ideal or principle. Just as dislocation served as a device for articulating our fundamental ontological postulate (the radical contingency of social relations) in an analytically fruitful direction, so too, we claim, does the notion of public contestation.

Public contestation can, of course, be seen as just another response to dislocation, which we can add to the repertoire of ethical and ideological responses. This is true, but for us public contestation (*qua* response) operates at a different analytical level. It is possible in our approach, for example, to characterize public contestation as *itself* ethical or ideological. More importantly, however, the notion of *public contestation* is relevant to the present discussion because of its privileged status in relation to the radical contingency of social relations, and because of its association with the concept of the political. As Laclau and Zac put it, 'it is only in ... [the publicly articulated] antagonistic relation to other projects that the contingency of particular acts of institution is shown, and it is this contingency that gives them their political character' (Laclau and Zac 1994: 4). Or to put it in Lacanian terms, '[t]he political becomes one of the forms in which one encounters the real', so that 'political reality is the field in which the symbolization of this real is attempted' (Stavrakakis 1999: 73).

The political-social axis can thus be constructed with reference to this notion. To the extent that aspects of a practice make visible the instituting moment of a social practice, either through public contestation, or the active absorption of public contestation, or the resolution of public contestation by means of collective mobilization and decision, then the political dimension is foregrounded: 'It is this instituting dimension – constitutive of social practices – that [post-marxists] call "the *political*" ' (Laclau and Zac 1994: 4). Conversely, to the extent that public contestation does not arise, or is actively prevented from arising, we could say that the social dimension is foregrounded.

Consider the experience of many academics who suddenly find that certain administrative tasks actually have a negative impact on their teaching and research, despite being explicitly designed to enhance them. Now this moment of dislocation can be experienced and responded to in a variety of ways, with the ideological and ethical dimensions adding an extra layer to this process of characterization. From the point of view of the political-social axis, however, the way in which the dislocation is articulated is largely a result of its discursive construction and enactment. For example, one may complain to colleagues at every available opportunity about the nature of this bureaucratic madness, just as one would complain about depressing weather. In this case, public contestation is kept at bay, and so the social dimension is foregrounded. Alternatively, the dislocation may be politically constructed. One may begin to wonder how it is that she came to be in this situation in the first place, and may begin to publicly challenge it in the name of something different. In other words, the way the dislocation is constructed and enacted does not follow from the simple fact of dislocation. It may be gentrified (or absorbed) by an existing social practice or regime, or it may provoke a political practice.

Dislocation and public contestation allows us therefore to translate our fundamental axiom concerning the radical contingency of social relations into a schema comprising four dimensions, which is represented in Figure 3. The *social dimension* in this figure refers to that aspect of social relations in which subjects are absorbed in their practices, that is, for whom the radical contingency of social relations has not been registered in the mode of public contestation. This formulation of the social dimension resonates strongly with Heidegger's remark that 'Dasein ... is nothing but ... concerned absorption in the world' (Heidegger 1985: 197; see also Heidegger 1962: 80–1). In contrast, the *political dimension* captures that aspect of social relations in which subjects articulate their experience of dislocation by (re)activating the contingent foundations of – and challenging – existing social relations in the

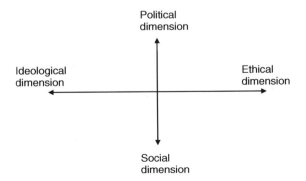

Figure 3 Four dimensions of social relations.

name of a principle or ideal. The *ideological dimension*, on the other hand, designates that aspect of social relations in which subjects are complicit in concealing the radical contingency of social relations. By contrast, the *ethical dimension* aims to grasp the aspect of social relations in which subjects engage in their practices in a way that is attentive to the radical contingency of social relations.

In sum, then, our claim is that any concrete practice or regime can be understood in terms of these four dimensions of social reality. But before we examine these concrete articulations in more depth, we need to clarify the concepts that underpin these ontological dimensions. We begin by elucidating our concept of the political and its relationship to the social, before moving to the concepts of ideology and ethics.

The political and the social

The concept of the political in our approach is not restricted to the ongoing practices of politics within a pre-defined set of institutional forms. Instead, it concerns the contestation and 'radical institution' of social relations through acts or decisions (Laclau 1990: 172; Laclau and Zac 1994: 4; see also Marchart 2007). The concept of the political is thus not confined to a particular domain or social space. As Lefort states:

> The political is . . . revealed, not in what we call political activity, but in the double movement whereby the mode of institution of society appears and is obscured. It appears in the sense that the process whereby society is ordered and unified across its divisions becomes visible. It is obscured in the sense that the locus of politics (the locus in which parties compete and in which a general agency of power takes shape and is reproduced) becomes defined as particular, while the principle which generates the overall configuration is concealed.
>
> (Lefort 1988: 11)

Similarly, Schmitt's definition of the political does not confine itself to any particular domain of practices, such as practices linked to the state for example. Since a central aspect of Schmitt's concept of the political concerns antagonism and conflict, which he captures with his distinction between friend and enemy, it is clear that the construction of friends and enemies can occur in any social space or site (see Howarth 2006). As he puts it,

> the distinction of friend and enemy denotes the utmost degree of intensity of a union or separation, of an association or dissociation. It can exist theoretically and practically, without having simultaneously to draw upon all those moral, aesthetic, economic, or other distinctions. The political enemy need not necessarily be morally evil or aesthetically ugly; he need not appear as an economic competitor, and it may even be

advantageous to engage with him in business transactions. But he is, nevertheless, the other, the stranger; and it is sufficient for his nature that he is, in a specially intense way, existentially something different and alien, so that in the extreme case conflicts with him are possible. These can neither be decided by a previously determined general norm nor by the judgement of a disinterested and neutral third party.

(Schmitt 1996: 26–7)

The central point we wish to take away from the above – a point expressed, of course, by many besides Lefort and Schmitt[5] – is the idea that the political is not tied in any a priori fashion to a particular site such as the state. As Gramsci (1971) shows in his reworking of the distinction between state and civil society, where he introduces the concept of an 'integral state' to encompass both aspects, the task of demarcating the social and the political dimensions is difficult if one holds onto a rigidly topographical division of social reality. Private issues within the domestic sphere, for example, are often politicized, and public institutions are often privatized. Indeed, modern governance structures and practices often straddle the public and private domains (Rose 1999; Sorensen and Torfing 2006). Politics is about the taking of decisions in a contingent and 'undecidable' terrain, which involves radical acts of power and institution. This is why for us the political is first and foremost an ontological category that is distinct from the social, rather than an ontical or regional category.

Understood in ontological terms the political is thus irreducible to the social in this sense, and vice versa. The social is not reducible to the political, for this would lead to a kind of politicism, in which all social relations were understood to be political in character. Here the political would be everything and nothing. But neither does the category of the political refer to a particular empirical domain of relations and objects, whether this is conceived as the political 'instance' or 'superstructure' of a social formation, such as the state in Marxist theory, or as the sub-system of the social system, as argued by system theorists (see, for example, Easton 1965). This would lead to the opposite problem of reducing the political to the social, which theorists such as Hannah Arendt argue is the dominant tendency of modernity itself. For her, the political ought not to be reduced to what she calls the 'social question' (Arendt 1958: 47; cf. Zerilli 2005). As already hinted, in Marxist theory political institutions such as the state, or political practices such as class struggles, are ultimately rooted in definite sets of social relations, in which the latter determine both their form and content. Indeed, there is a strong imperative in Marxism to call for the abolition of politics altogether, so that (following Saint-Simon) in a future communist utopia 'the government of persons . . . [would be] replaced by the administration of things' (Engels 1978: 713).

There is much to be said about Arendt's critique of the overweening effects of the social in the contemporary world, and the consequent downgrading of political life by the omnivorous logics of society and the culture industry, as well as her valorization of the importance of active citizen involvement, public deliberation and collective decision-making about common matters affecting a community of equals. Of course, we do not want to suggest that there are no unproblematic features or tensions in her account (see, for example, Habermas 1986; Zerilli 2005: 3), only that we find particularly helpful the view, inspired by her work, that what counts as political are not 'interests as such but the world-building practice of publicly articulating matters of common concern' (Zerilli 2005: 22; 14–16). The 'public' in 'public contestation' thus captures for us the minimal notion of contesting social norms in a particular site or space where persons addressed are publicly recognized as taking on official roles. This concept of the public is helpful – perhaps essential – in enabling us to distinguish between social and political practices, in which the latter are defined as having a distinctively public import. More precisely, political issues and demands are those which in principle are of concern to all who participate in the process of deciding about the affairs of the communities they inhabit. However, we need to specify how the notion of public contestation gets hooked up with our concept of the political, after which we must return to and clarify our distinction between the political and the social.

In addressing the first objective, we can build upon Laclau's theoretical discussion of populism (Laclau 2005), and Laclau and Mouffe's discussion of radical democracy (Laclau and Mouffe 1985). In *On Populist Reason*, Laclau begins, as we do, with the experience of contingency for a subject – a dislocatory event – and the various responses to it. One such response is to construct the moment of contingency as a grievance: as something that constitutes an issue for people, which can be expressed publicly as a request that is directed at the appropriate authority. A satisfactory response by the authority can end the matter there, but the failure to respond adequately, at least from the perspective of the aggrieved subject, can lead to the hardening of a request into a demand. And if this demand publicly challenges the norm(s) of an institution or society then, in our terms, it becomes political. As Laclau and Mouffe put it, 'when we speak . . . of the "political" character of . . . struggles, we do not do so in the restricted sense of demands which are situated at the level of parties and of the State. What we are referring to is a type of action whose objective is the transformation of a social relation which constructs a subject in a relationship of subordination' (Laclau and Mouffe 1985: 153). That is to say, *a demand is political to the extent that it publicly contests the norms of a particular practice or system of practices in the name of a principle or ideal.*

This formulation allows us to distinguish between radical political demands and hegemonic political demands. A *radical* political demand would be one that publicly contests a *fundamental* norm of a practice or regime.[6] In this view, only demands and struggles that contest the fundamental rules of a practice and seek to institute new rules and institutions count as radical political demands. For example, the simple demand for more wages by teachers or university lecturers may do little or nothing to question the dominant rules of the institution, whereas a demand that challenges the exclusion of minorities or the poor as teachers, lecturers, or students, or which rejects marketization in the name of a different organizational principle, may make the demand radical. A *hegemonic* political demand, on the other hand, is a demand – whether radical or not – which comes to represent a challenge to aspects of a *regime* of practices by successfully *generalizing* its relevance to other institutions and practices. A demand for more wages and better conditions by workers in one sector of the economy (e.g. university lecturers), may be taken up by workers in adjacent social spaces and sites (e.g. nurses, teachers, and council workers), thereby becoming hegemonic. A demand that is both radical and hegemonic may thus have the effect of reconfiguring an entire regime of practices in the name of a new order. Finally, it is important to note that the way we propose to conceptualize the categories of the political and the social helps make visible the sociological and normative aspects presupposed by such an approach. Briefly, the sociological aspect emerges in the very identification of a norm as more – or less – fundamental to a practice or regime, while the normative aspect emerges because the implication is that a particular norm is *worthy* of public contestation.

Our second objective is to develop a more relational and dialectical conception of the relationship between the social and the political. Here we follow Laclau in saying that 'any political construction takes place against the background of a range of sedimented practices', in which 'the boundary of what is social and what is political in society is constantly displaced' (Laclau 1990: 36). Laclau draws upon Husserl's distinction between sedimentation and reactivation to flesh out the relationship between these two dimensions of reality. The late Husserl invokes these concepts to account for the way the original subjective intuition that makes possible the constitution of an intellectual object or truth, such as a geometrical theorem, is often eclipsed at the moment it is formalized. He thus calls for the need to 'reactivate' the moment of its animating origin so that the truth of the original intuition is not forgotten. In Husserl's terms, the routinization and forgetting of origins is 'sedimentation', while the recovery of the 'constitutive' activity of thought is labelled 'reactivation' (Husserl 1970: 353–78).

Laclau posits a parallel between Husserl's dialectic and the way we can conceive of the relationship between the social and the political. Whereas the former consists in the forgetting of the acts or decisions of 'originary institution' (which involved the rejection of those options which were actually attempted), the latter requires a reactivation of the contingent moment of foundation, thus disclosing the potential for different constructions. Of course, as Laclau notes, in a new situation, the options on offer will be different from the ones rejected in the original moment of institution: 'Reactivation does not therefore consist of returning to the original situation, but merely of rediscovering, through the emergence of new antagonisms, the contingent nature of so-called "objectivity" ... The moment of antagonism where the undecidable nature of the alternatives and their resolution through power relations becomes fully visible constitutes the field of the "political" ' (Laclau 1990: 34–5). For us, this emphasizes why the concept of the political – and the social for that matter – is an ontological rather than an ontical category, whose effects can be registered in any social site. Indeed, its character is one of contesting sedimented social relations in the name of new ones in situations where undecidability and power have been brought to the fore.

Both the political and social dimensions of social reality presuppose an intimate connection to the radical contingency of social relations, for both are understood in relation to a particular ontical manifestation of this radical contingency, namely, the public contestation of a social norm. Insofar as public contestation does not arise or is eschewed, we say that the social dimension is foregrounded. Insofar as this public contestation is initiated or affirmed through action, we say that the political dimension comes to the fore. In our view, the two dimensions are always present in social reality, as there is never a complete disappearance of political practices, nor a complete politicization of all social relations.[7] Though we are about to complicate our picture by introducing two further ontological dimensions of social reality – the ideological and ethical dimensions – we can at this stage say that because of the inherent unevenness of the social field, and because different practices are politicized at different times, the boundary between the social and political is not fixed, but in a state of constant flux.

Ideology and ethics

We turn now to the concepts of ideology and ethics. Earlier we discussed the way in which a dislocatory experience in the field of social relations can provoke a political response. However, it can also provoke an *ideological* response, which aims to repair and cover over the dislocatory event before it becomes the source of a new political construction. For us, the ideological dimension signals the way in which the subject becomes complicit in covering over the radical contingency of social relations by identifying with a particular discourse. In this sense, ideology involves the way a subject *misrecognizes* its real conditions of existence. Indeed, the hold of this misrecognition inures or insulates the subject from the vagaries of the structural dislocation that always threaten to disrupt it. What we term the 'grip of ideology' thus comprises a myriad of practices through which individuals are turned into subjects with an identity, and through which such identities are sustained and reproduced. The ideological can thereby induce the 'forgetting of political origins' and it can enable subjects to live as if their practices were natural.

These claims recall, of course, Louis Althusser's famous materialist theory of ideology, in which ideology is understood to represent 'the imaginary relationship of individuals to their real conditions of existence' (Althusser 1971: 162). More precisely, as he puts it, *'ideology has the function (which defines it) of "constituting" concrete individuals as subjects'* (Althusser 1971: 171). And this function in turn involves the twin operations of recognition and misrecognition: ideology 'imposes' an 'obviousness as obviousness', which 'we *cannot fail to recognize* and before which we have the inevitable and natural reaction of crying out (aloud or in the "still, small voice of conscience"): "That's obvious! That's right! That's true!"' (Althusser 1971: 172). But at the same time it leads to the necessary *misrecognition* of social reality, as the production of obviousness and normality covers over the ultimate contingency of social existence.

Our ontological commitments resonate, therefore, with Althusser's thought that the ideological dimension constitutes 'an organic part of every social totality', which 'human societies could not survive without' (Althusser 1969: 232). This means that the 'systems of representation' and practices that constitute the ideological instance of a social formation can never be erased in the name of a society which is completely transparent to itself – a social form that is not marked by something which always escapes it. In other words, the concept of ideology is for us an ontological category. As Althusser puts it, '[h]uman societies secrete ideology as the very element and atmosphere indispensable to their historical respiration and life', so that only 'an ideological world could have imagined societies *without ideology* and accepted the utopian idea of a world in which ideology (not just one of its historical forms) would disappear without trace, to be replaced by *science*' (Althusser 1969: 232). Concealment and misrecognition are thus necessary features of any identification and identity, and thus any concrete social formation.

Although Althusser's path-breaking work in this regard is essential to our understanding of the ideological dimension of social reality, it is not without difficulty. As we have suggested, the ideological realm is not a separate, even if 'relatively autonomous', region of practices that is connected to a social formation by, for example, the determining role of the economy. Nor is it simply functional to the reproduction of capitalist relations of production. Instead, it resonates with the way in which Michael Freeden conceives the key feature of any ideological act to be 'the decontestation of the essentially contestable' (Freeden 2005: 119), or with the way Ernesto Laclau reconceptualizes the category of the ideological (see Norval 2000). For Laclau, the ideological does

> not consist of the misrecognition of a positive essence, but exactly the opposite: it would consist of the non-recognition of the precarious character of any positivity, of the impossibility of any ultimate suture. The ideological would consist of those discursive forms through which a society tries to institute itself as such on the basis of closure ... The ideological would be the will to 'totality' of any totalizing discourse.
>
> (Laclau 1990: 92)

But an equally problematic aspect of the picture proffered by Althusser is that it does not provide us with an adequate account of how individuals are turned into subjects in the first place. As critics such as Paul Hirst have argued, Althusser's model of 'interpellation', in which individuals are constituted or 'hailed' as subjects by recognizing certain signifiers and discourses as addressed to them, seems to presuppose an already constituted subject, which is able to 'recognize', 'desire', 'know', and so forth (Hirst 1979: 64–8). And when coupled with Althusser's insistence that the ideological domain is directly functional to the reproduction of the existing relations of production, this restricts the role of agency to the mere 'bearer of a structure', which ultimately underestimates the complexity of social relations. After all, for Althusser, '*individuals are always-already subjects*', whose 'places' in the existing social structures have been determined and fixed beforehand (Althusser 1971: 176).

By contrast, we accentuate Althusser's suggestion that the category of the subject, which is 'the constitutive category of all ideology', is marked by a fundamental misrecognition that can never be transcended. The subject is thus no more than a void in the symbolic order whose identity and character is determined only by its identifications and mode of enjoyment (Žižek 1989). Indeed, it is precisely here that we have to supplement our account by introducing the correlative concept of the ethical.

In our view, the space of the ethical – like the political, social, and ideological – is understood in relation to the radical contingency of social relations and the way in which the subject 'responds' to this 'ontological lack'. But we reserve the concepts of the ethical and the ideological to speak about the different *ways* in which a subject engages in practices, be they social or political. This means that the concept of ethics in our approach is not reducible or equivalent to questions about normativity – at least not in any straightforward way. We are not concerned with questions of right conduct or questions about our proper obligations to others; nor are ethical questions about the construction of binding norms that may or may not be agreed upon by all affected social agents. And nor finally is our concept of the ethical to be understood in terms of the inculcation of an appropriate set of virtues or dispositions that enables human agents to live the good life,[8] though the concern with issues about 'ethos' move in the direction we want to go.

Instead, in our view, questions of ethics (and ideology) centre on the subject's particular *mode* of enjoyment. They address issues that arise from the different modalities of subjectivity in relation to the ultimate contingency of social existence. How does a subject relate to the contingency of social life that is disclosed in dislocatory events? How does it identify anew? How does it translate its 'radical investments' into social and political practices? How does a subject relate to its identifications and consequently to its own contingency? It is perhaps worth emphasizing here that these modes of subjectivity should not be understood in cognitivist or intellectualist terms. In other words, what we are trying to capture here with the categories of ideology and ethics has nothing whatsoever to do with the idea that someone can apprehend and even consciously affirm a particular ontological schema rooted in the radical contingency of social relations. This is because modes of subjectivity are also modes of *enjoyment*, and modes of enjoyment are always *embodied* in material practices, and thus not completely reducible to conscious apprehension. It is with this in mind that one should approach the question of subjectivity and identification. For example, does the mode of identification privilege the moment of closure and concealment (ideological dimension), or does it keep open the contingency of social relations (ethical dimension)? In the following chapter we shall speak to these latter two ontological dimensions by elaborating our logic of fantasy.

To conclude this section, it is worth saying that in keeping with our commitment to the ultimate contingency of social relations, we stress 'the primacy of the political' insofar as it has a key role in shaping the form and ultimately the content of social relations. Of course, the political is not freestanding, because it presupposes the social, ideological and ethical dimensions. But the political dimension is given priority in our account, both because of its role in structuring social practices and regimes, and also because in our conception it is – often in conjunction with certain ethical preconditions – the source of novelty in the social world.[9]

Practices and regimes revisited

Having clarified our conceptual and ontological presuppositions, we can now revisit our model of practices and regimes by relating them to the ontological dimensions of social reality in a more systematic fashion. We must engage, therefore, in what might be termed a more middle-range style of theorizing, which involves the use of our ontological categories to redescribe ontical entities like practices and regimes. For instance, practices can be understood in terms of the way different dimensions of social relations – comprising the social, political, ideological, and ethical dimensions – are foregrounded or backgrounded, how they are articulated, and so on. We claim that this provides us with significant analytical purchase to describe and explain the socio-political world in a non-topographical fashion.

In more concrete terms, we can begin by considering cases in which the social dimension of a practice is foregrounded. We might want to characterize such a practice as a social practice. There are at least two related ways of complexifying the picture of a social practice here: let us call them, amplifying insights offered by Laclau and Mouffe, 'the subordination way' and 'the domination way' (Laclau and Mouffe 1985: 153–4).[10] The 'subordination way' points to those *aspects of a practice which appear not to invite or need public contestation of social norms*. Existing social relations would thus be actively and iteratively reproduced without public contestation because there are no dislocations. Everyday activities such as picking up kids from school, gardening, going to school or work, holidaying, and so on, may comprise just these aspects of a practice. All these activities may in fact involve and rely upon relations of subordination, but they need not be experienced as oppressive, nor regarded as unjust by the analyst.

The 'domination way' points to those *aspects of a practice which appear to actively prevent the public contestation of social norms from arising in the first place.* Here existing social relations are actively and iteratively reproduced without public contestation because, though there are dislocations, these are processed privately or informally. For example, they may take the form of 'off the record' complaints made by employees amongst themselves, or even toward their managers, who then elicit, deflect, or satisfy requests, or it may involve individuals who cope alone with dislocation by enrolling on stress management courses, and so on. Of course, it is our hunch that this will be accomplished most completely and effectively if subjects become ideologically complicit in this process, but this is of course not necessary. More generally, then, in the context of a set of dislocatory experiences, these pre-emptive aspects of a practice seek to maintain existing social structures by muffling or guiding the process by which grievances are articulated, so that the existing social structure remains unthreatened.[11] An important part of contemporary labour process theory, organization theory, and critical management studies literature deals with precisely these aspects of social practices.[12] Moreover, since such activities are geared towards keeping public contestation at bay, they tend to be unofficial in character, in the sense that they operate in the interstices of official institutional practices, whether state or otherwise. Insofar as social practices are understood to keep public contestation at bay, they share an affinity with what Gramsci calls the institutions of civil society, or what Althusser calls 'ideological state apparatuses', which encompass various educational, religious, economic, aesthetic, and other practices.

But characterizing aspects of a practice as fostering or reinforcing relations of domination immediately highlights the sociological and normative character of the kind of analytical practice we are advocating. After all, the very identification of a social norm as *worthy* of public contestation (which is a prerequisite for identifying those aspects of a practice one claims to be keeping public contestation at bay in the first place) presupposes some view of society and domination. It implies that we already have some grasp of the practice, both sociologically and normatively. As we will see in the following chapters, social logics are helpful in making explicit the sociological and normative aspects of this process of characterization. Already, therefore, our approach indicates ways in which we can address the 'normative deficit' problem imputed to discourse theory and analysis, which we alluded to in our Introduction. All we want to suggest here is that this normative deficit is in no way constitutive of poststructuralism or Laclau's theory of hegemony. On the contrary, our approach allows us to locate its status and role more precisely and productively.

We have thus far considered practices in which the social dimension is foregrounded. Consider next those cases in which the political dimension of a practice is foregrounded. Call them political practices. To highlight the political dimension of a practice, we simply point to those *aspects of a practice which seek to generate, maintain, contain, or resolve the public contestation of social norms*, or, in the wake of the institution of a new social norm, *aspects of a practice which seek to bed down the new social structure* by providing incentives and disincentives which tempt subjects to more actively accept and identify with it. In other words, political practices involve attempts to challenge and replace existing social structures, as well as attempts to neutralize such challenges in a transformist way (Gramsci 1971: 58–9). Such practices might include various newspaper campaigns and other media interventions, interventions through novels, movies, documentaries, theatrical productions, even deconstructive and genealogical studies, lectures, and so on.

But of course such practices can also involve projects which explicitly set out to change or maintain a set of existing social relations through collective mobilization. For example, the modern environmental movement challenges the dominant logic of industrialization in contemporary societies by seeking to transform our attitudes to the natural world, and by pressing for new public policies and principles which would lead to changes to a whole host of sedimented social norms and practices (Griggs and Howarth 2007). Groups and movements have thus merged to challenge the norms governing modern transport systems, for example, which are manifest in our over-reliance on private car use and its consequences for road-building projects. And they have used a variety of strategies and tactics, ranging from petitions and formal representations to direct action protest, in order to articulate and prosecute their demands. More recently, these campaigns have extended to the norms and practices governing air transport, where there have been growing demands for 'sustainable aviation' and 'demand management', as well as a series of challenges to the expansion of airports (Griggs and Howarth 2004). One could also argue that celebrity chef Jamie Oliver's school meals campaign in the UK, which started in 2005, set out to challenge and transform a fairly basic social norm governing the culinary practices of schools and the eating habits of youngsters in Britain. Here subjects are mobilized with reference to signifiers which promise a fullness that is lacking in the subject and its practices. Certain signifiers or linguistic expressions – 'sustainable environment', 'health', 'justice for all', and so forth – function as names that stand in for the absent fullness of a dislocated community or life. Though they are metaphors with no corresponding facts – they are moments of naming in a radical sense – they strive to represent the failure of a signifying system or language. At least in part, this is why Laclau calls these signifiers 'empty signifiers' (Laclau 1996: 36–46).

Our emphasis on the notion of public contestation implies that the specifically political aspect of a practice is largely linked to the fact that grievances are articulated *publicly* as demands, rather than simply in private conversation. But we can further qualify political practices as having official and unofficial features; as being more or less hegemonic; or more or less ethical. We shall comment on these features in turn. There is an official side to political practices, in the sense that *political demands are typically addressed to and expressed by individuals acting in their official capacity*. But there is also an unofficial side to political practices, in the sense that official rationales for demands and how they are to be met are often bolstered by some justifications which *resist public official disclosure*. Insofar as it can be shown that there is such a link between unofficial discourse and a particular publicly and officially articulated discourse, both can be considered to be sides of a political practice or regime.

Of course, this link between the official and unofficial sides of a practice can be understood in terms of hypocrisy or straightforward deceit. But there are other ways of conceptualizing it. For example, it has been suggested that key Thatcherite policies concerning the economy and state centralization were sustained by forms of enjoyment inherent in discourses of race and sexuality, which tended to resist public-official disclosure, but which were nevertheless focused around very public events such as the Falklands war between Argentina and Britain, and the debates over Section 28 of the *Local Government Act* (1988), which concerned the teaching and/or promotion of homosexuality in schools (Smith 1994). Second, political practices can be characterized as *more or less hegemonic depending on the degree to which the political demands articulating a grievance are formulated in terms that succeed in having more or less universal appeal*. And, finally, political practices can be characterized as more or less ethical depending on the degree to which subjects are *attentive to the radical contingency of their political practice*. In the cases where such attentiveness is prominent it can be said that a political practice is informed by a radically democratic *ethos* (Glynos 2003b; Howarth 1998, 2006).

It should be clear from what we have said thus far that the social and political dimensions of a practice can find expression alongside either the ideological or ethical dimensions. Aspects of aesthetic or religious practices, for example, can be characterized as ethical from our point of view, even though they are not accompanied by the public contestation of social norms. Conversely, aspects of a practice in which the political dimension is foregrounded can also be characterized as ideological, insofar as subjects are complicit in concealing the radical contingency of social relations in the *way* they advocate and fight for a new order.

With this fuller, more nuanced, account of practices as a function of dimensions, we can complexify our initial model of practices and regimes as shown in Figure 4. The grammar of dimensions we have developed here means that there is no typology of practices as such, only practices for which one or more ontological dimensions are foregrounded, backgrounded, or articulated. For this reason, the boundary between social and political practices is blurred, as is the boundary between regimes and practices. This is why we have modified our diagram in a way that represents these three entities as three intersecting and overlapping figures. Though we acknowledge the risk of misrepresentation inherent in any attempt to capture all relevant conceptual links diagrammatically, we claim that our grammar does enable us to distinguish between different concrete practices.

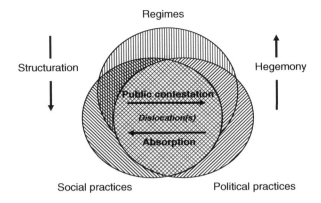

Figure 4 A complex model of practices and regimes.

Consider, for example, a religious conversion – a 'road to Damascus' experience so to speak – in which a subject confronting a tragic event in her life finds in God the source of peace and salvation. This may make possible a greater attentiveness to the radical contingency of social relations, which could form the basis for a new beginning and a new form of subjectivity in which the ethical dimension of her social practice is foregrounded. However, we can also imagine the 'road to Damascus' experience partaking of a social practice in which the ideological dimension is foregrounded. After all, much of the religious (and psychodynamic) counselling that targets prison inmates – not to mention the public at large – appears to bring about a new closure in the wake of dislocation, instead of allowing the latter to function as an opening to another (ethical) mode of being. Whatever the case, the turn to God represents an experience of transcendence, which provides the subject with resources to positivize and explain the traumatic event she confronts, while also pointing the way to a future life inflected with different principles and values.

Of course, these experiences of transcendence are varied because they depend on the historical circumstances in which they take place. Indeed, foregrounding the ethical or ideological dimension of social relations does not exhaust the characterization of a practice. After all, the way this conversion takes place can set the subject on a political path. In other words, if it results in the life we have so far suggested, namely, a life devoted to the church and one's family, which is led in accord with one's religious beliefs, we may be tempted to characterize it as a social practice. On the other hand, if it produces in the subject a missionary zeal that leads her to proselytize on behalf of the church and its doctrine, and/or to a life committed to bringing about social justice for all, we may be tempted to characterize aspects of this life as political and her associated practices as political practices.

Whereas the first translation of one's investment into practice might be social, the latter response is aimed at the radical institution of new practices and discourses, and is better characterized as political. Finally, as was the case with social practices, a political engagement may be characterized in terms of whether it foregrounds the ideological or ethical dimension. Does such political practice embody an ethos where it is clear that subjects are attentive to the radical contingency of social relations? Or do subjects prosecute their political aims in a totalizing way, betraying their complicity in covering over this contingency?

We have thus far concentrated on practices, and how we might characterize such practices in terms of our four ontological dimensions. But we also need to revisit our conception of regimes in light of the more complex picture we have sketched out. It is clear that regimes remain both entities which structure practices, and entities which are produced by practices. Equally, we have noted the discursive and constructed character of regimes. But it is also important to reiterate our claim that every regime is marked by an outside that partially constitutes its identity, and which carries the threat of subverting it. And this ontological assumption is linked to our claim that every order and practice arises as a political construction that involves the exclusion of certain possibilities.

What more can we say about regimes that does not simply repeat what we have said about practices? In a first move, we can say that it is empirically the case that many of the examples and cases studied by those who are sympathetic to the approach developed here focus on the nation state.[13] But this focus and level of analysis does not exhaust our concept of regime. On the contrary, we have been content to keep the concept at a high level of abstraction, thus making it possible for regimes to be apprehended analytically at different levels depending on the context.

The analysis of any concrete regime must therefore begin by articulating it in relation to precise circumstances and contexts. But the identification of the latter depends upon the specific problem under investigation. For example, we can talk about the practices of a department or faculty in relation to the regime of a particular university, or we can talk about a particular university's practices in relation to the regime defined by the higher education sector as a whole. Equally, we can talk about educational practices in relation to a regime of practices at the level of the state (comprising, for example, the dominant historical bloc of a nation state, to use Gramsci's terms), or we can talk about a particular state's practices in relation to an international regime. In this sense, a regime is just another term denoting the particular context of a practice or set of practices. It denotes the broader context that structures social practices, as well as the new social structure that emerges out of hegemonic political practices. However, the term regime has for us the advantage of denoting something that is more individuated than context, and this is because it already flags the fact that some work has already taken place in characterizing that context in a particular way. In other words, this characterization process implies that the analyst adopts an active role in constructing the context *as a particular regime*.

For example, while various schools of international relations have stressed the importance of international regimes, they tend to put forward rival conceptions of such regimes, which they conceptualize in terms of inter-state codes of conduct, and they generally accept that regimes themselves comprise various types (Hasenclever, Mayer and Rittberger 1997). So while the realist Stephen Krasner defines regimes as 'implicit or explicit principles, norms, rules and decision-making procedures around which actors' expectations converge in a given area of international relations' (Krasner 1983: 2), Oran Young takes regimes to be 'more specialized arrangements that pertain to well-defined activities, resources, or geographical areas and often involve only some subset of the members of international society' (Young 1989: 13). Expressed in an idiom that is much closer to our approach, Robert Cox draws upon Gramsci to focus on the construction of hegemony and historical blocs at the global level. For him, regimes comprise three basic elements – ideas, material capabilities, and institutions – which are concretely articulated into different historical configurations at both the national and international levels. More precisely, at the international level Cox's object of study centres on the dialectical interaction between social forces (situated principally below the national state level), national state actors, and an overall 'world order' or regime – say *Pax Britannica* in the nineteenth century or *Pax Americana* in the twentieth – that has achieved hegemony. According to Cox, then, a hegemonic world regime only obtains if there is a coherent fit between material economic power, a dominant collective image of the world order, and a particular set of global institutions that can regulate and administer a specific order (Cox 1981a, 1987).

The above suggests that regimes and practices acquire more precise specification, with respect to both the level and scope of analysis, through the process of concrete analysis itself. It is important therefore not to reify such spatial specificities by forgetting their close connection to the problem being investigated. In short, the regime/practice complex is primarily a heuristic device that enables us to conduct concrete analyses. Of course, out of such concrete analyses, it is possible that some sort of typology might emerge on the basis of different *structural configurations* and various *qualities* of regimes. For instance, we could distinguish between regimes that are explicitly divided by political frontiers into two camps (insiders versus outsiders) and those in which the explicit exclusion of others has been pushed to the margins of a social formation. In more idiomatic terms, and focussing on the level of the nation state, the first sort of regime involves a 'two nation' project, whereas the latter is often identified with a 'one nation' project. Or we might find it fruitful to characterize regimes in terms of their qualities, focussing for instance on the relative weight of its authoritarian versus democratic characteristics. For example, a two-nation project may be authoritarian or democratic depending on its openness to otherness and difference, the level of popular accountability, and the kinds of interests that are represented in its policies and political interventions. Equally, a one-nation project may be authoritarian or democratic, depending on similar considerations. Perhaps an authoritarian one nation project is more likely to be marked by the predominance of the ideological dimension insofar as it successfully covers over and displaces any potential demands and antagonistic constructions.

It is important to stress that in this to and fro movement between the ontological and ontical levels, which after all is constitutive of the logic of middle range theorizing, such typologies are empirical and contingent. Even so, what our discussion so far highlights is how our account of regimes and our account of practices as a function of four ontological dimensions relies on a set of sociological and normative assumptions. These assumptions are linked to our capacity to identify social norms underpinning practices, our ability to attribute to them relative weight in terms of their foundational status, our suggestion that particular norms are more or less worthy candidates for public contestation and/or transformation, and so on. We made a similar point earlier in the chapter, where we pointed out how the very claim that a particular dimension is foregrounded, or that a particular dimension is being actively backgrounded, presupposes a sociological and normative view about the practice or regime. This suggests that we need to develop a language with which to characterize and critically explain the existence, maintenance, and transformation of concrete practices and regimes that is sensitive to our four ontological dimensions, and which makes explicit the normative aspects of our critical explanations. It is precisely to this task that we shall turn in the following chapters, where we develop this language as a function of three types of logic: social, political, and fantasmatic logics. Before doing so, however, we intend to make explicit another aspect of our approach, which concerns the category of subjectivity.

Subjectivity

Though central to our perspective, the notion of subjectivity has thus far remained more or less implicit in our discussion. Of course, our account of subjectivity is predicated on our core ontological assumption that each system of meaning or each symbolic order is essentially incomplete or lacking. While meaning is holistic, in the sense that the identity of an element depends on its relationships to other elements within a wider social structure, each structure is never closed. Each structure is marked by an impossibility – what Lacan captures with the register of 'the real' – which prevents the full constitution of meaning. This means that in keeping with our ontological presuppositions every subject is a discursive construct or entity, whose identity depends on its relationship to other subjects and objects. However, because each discursive construct is never fully constituted, but essentially incomplete or lacking, the subject is also lacking and incomplete.

We are already in a position to see how our conception of subjectivity challenges many (contradictory) attributions made to poststructuralist understandings of subjectivity. On the one hand, there is a tendency to accuse poststructuralists of privileging the dimension of structure at the expense of the dimension of agency. Here the subject is reduced to an *identity* determined by, and coterminous with, 'reified quasi-structures' such as discourses or ideologies, which function to subject individuals to the prevailing power structures (e.g. Bevir 2005: 137; Bevir and Rhodes 2005: 172–3). On the other hand, there is the opposite tendency of accusing poststructuralists of privileging agency over structure, in which the subject is identified with a kind of textual *dispersion* and is considered to be as infinitely malleable as the identities she or he constructs (e.g. Bhaskar 1989; Taylor 1995: 16). The latter is often considered to be complicit with voluntarist or sovereign conceptions of subjectivity.

We do not, of course, accept these criticisms of poststructuralism – and this simply because their target has been wrongly described as poststructuralist. The first criticism misses completely the significance of 'post' in 'poststructuralism' (or even the 'quasi' in 'quasi-structure'), taking the target to be structuralism *simpliciter*. Althusser's reworking of Marx might better fit the profile of such critiques, for he emphasizes the idea of the subject as 'a bearer of structures' (Althusser and Balibar 1997). The second criticism misses the significance of the 'de' in poststructuralism's '*de*centred subjectivity', taking the target to be some form of ego psychology or sovereign rational chooser. Both Foucault and Derrida, for example, make statements that radically decentre the subject. In the *Archaeology of Knowledge*, for example, Foucault treats the subject as an enunciative position within a discursive formation from which one can speak and pronounce with authority, whereas Derrida's critique of transcendental conceptions of subjectivity often leads to the view that the subject is an effect of the play of signifiers (Derrida 1981a, 1981b, 1982; Foucault 1972; Howarth 2002a).

So we must decisively reject the widespread, yet unproductive, choice in which subjectivity is thought either as a passive effect of structures or as an active self-determination. Situating subjectivity in relation to radical contingency, in our view, is a key step in breaking out of this apparent impasse. As Laclau puts it,

> if the subject were a mere subject position within the structure, the latter would be fully closed and there would be no contingency at all ... [Radical contingency is possible only] if the structure is not fully reconciled with itself, if it is inhabited by an original lack, by a radical undecidability that needs to be constantly superseded by acts of decision. These acts are, precisely, what constitute the *subject*, who can only exist as a will transcending the structure. Because this will has no place of constitution external to the structure but is the result of the failure of the structure to constitute itself, it can be formed only through acts

of identification. If I need to identify with something it is because I do not have a full identity in the first place. These acts of identification are thinkable only as a result of the lack within the structure and have the permanent trace of the latter. Contingency is shown in this way: as the inherent distance of the structure from itself.

(Laclau 1996: 92)

One implication of this conception of subjectivity is that it offers a novel perspective on the so-called 'structure/agency' debate in social and political theory (e.g. Hay 1995, 2002; Hollis 1994; Stones 2005; Wendt 1999). On the one hand, it problematizes essentialist conceptions that privilege the determining role of either structure or agency, while on other hand it contests dualistic conceptions which are predicated on an external relationship between structures and agents. It begins instead with a 'thrown' subject – a subject that is nothing but the identities conferred by its culture or 'world'. However, as this structure is marked by a fundamental lack – an impossibility which becomes evident in moments of dislocation – it is able under certain conditions to engage and act. This moment of identification is the moment of the radical subject, which discloses the subject as an agent in its world. Nevertheless, as lack is constitutive both of the structure and of the subject, the construction of any identity – or the linking together of identities into a common project – is always contingent and precarious. In this sense, identities are always 'failed identities', which never fulfil the telos of subjective identification, thus rendering them vulnerable to further dislocation. In sum, 'far from being a moment of the structure, the subject is the result of the impossibility of constituting the structure as such' (Laclau 1990: 41). Situated within this poststructuralist horizon, our aim is thus to plot a path away from thinking about the subject as simply a discursive position, to thinking about it as constitutively incomplete and split. This conception of subjectivity is predicated on four notions: *lack, identity, identification*, and *enjoyment*.

To begin, we take the subject to be marked by a constitutive *lack* or, to put it differently, by an *identity* which is impossible to fully suture. It is an ontological feature of subjectivity which is empirically disclosed in moments of dislocation when it is no longer clear how the subject is to 'go on', that is, when it is undecided as to how it is to follow the rules, for instance, or engage in its routinized practices. In short, lack is revealed when identities fail, that is, in situations where the contingency or the undecidability of social structures is made visible. It is in these situations of structural failure that we see the emergence of subjectivity in its radical form: subjects are literally compelled to engage in acts of *identification*, whose aim is to fill the void made visible by a dislocatory event with new signifiers and discourses. Here the subject is 'merely the distance between the undecidable structure and the decision' (Laclau 1990: 39). A person becomes a subject in this sense, for example, when she mislays her paper five minutes before the lecture is about to begin, and has to scramble around in a panic trying to fathom how best to cope. Or, less prosaically, consider the black schoolchildren and youth in Soweto in June 1976, who became radical political subjects when they took on the might of the South African police and army with the demand to end Bantu Education in the name of 'Black Power' and *'Amandla!'* But practices of identity reproduction and new acts of identification also presuppose a subject of *enjoyment* that is structured around certain fantasies. Though we shall be discussing the notion of fantasy in greater detail in Chapter 5, we note here how fantasy is understood as a narrative that covers-over or conceals the subject's lack by providing an image of fullness, wholeness, or harmony, on the one hand, while conjuring up threats and obstacles to its realization on the other.[14] When successfully installed, a fantasmatic narrative hooks the subject – via the enjoyment it procures – to a given practice or order, or a promised future practice or order, thus conferring identity. This suggests that the categories of enjoyment and fantasy are relevant for thinking about issues of ideology and ethics.[15]

To conclude this section, we make more explicit the connection between our conception of subjectivity and our earlier discussion of the four dimensions of social reality. Consider first the social and political dimensions of reality. An initial implication of the above conception of subjectivity for social and political analysis is that we must distinguish between identity and identification. As Laclau puts it, 'the incorporation of the individual into the symbolic order occurs through *identifications*. The individual is not simply an identity within the structure but is transformed by it into a subject, and this requires acts of identification' (Laclau 1990: 211). Here we could say that the subject of identity is linked to the social dimension, while the subject of identification is linked to the political dimension.

In clarifying the distinction between identity and identification, we could say that *identification* is linked to the *enigmatic* dimension of the signifier, the dimension of the signifier that functions as a raw question mark that troubles the subject, and defies his or her attempts to discern its meaning. For example, a dislocation may give rise to the public contestation of social norms and identities in the name of an ideal or principle, and yet the vision of this ideal may not be clear. To put it more concretely, in the case of an ecological *identification* in the wake of a dislocation the signifier 'ecology' may be conceived by a subject not so much as a site of fluid and/or overlapping meanings (though, no doubt, it is this too), but as an *enigma that promises meaning*, as the site of a hegemonic struggle *over* meaning (Glynos 2000a). Here 'ecology' holds the place of the *gap* separating 'ecology' from its many possible meanings and associated identities, thus making political struggle possible. When this dimension of the signifier emerges (what Lacan can be said to capture with *master signifier* and Laclau with his *empty signifier*[16]), it signals the introjection of this signifier as 'enigma-plus-promise' that accounts for a *common identification without (yet) a common identity*. It literally marks the incompleteness of the symbolic order, that is, the structural lack that inhabits the order of discourse, and yet it also engages subjects in a concerted effort to decipher it, thereby uniting them.

It is because the master signifier simultaneously promises a meaning, and yet withholds it, that subjects can be politically engaged. They are engaged in a search for identity and a struggle over meaning. A signifier that functions in this way is called a master signifier because it is as if it were issuing the command 'Let the search begin! I guarantee there is something to be found!' It is only at the conclusion of a hegemonic struggle that a particular meaning may be 'naturalized' *as* ecology. In this case, 'ecology' ceases to appear so enigmatic – its meaning, if not fixed, is determinate enough to eclipse its enigmatic dimension to a considerable degree.

Identity is therefore conceived as the meaning attributed to ecology, while *identification* is conceived in terms of the enigmatic pure signifier of 'ecology'. It is the *enigma* of 'ecology' – What does 'ecology' *mean?* – that provides a focus for political struggle, not some shared positive content. In this way, identification avoids the problem of having to suppose a common set of properties. In addition, it suggests how it is possible for a signifier to condense two or more meanings that are mutually exclusive at the level of content. Ecology, for instance, may be conceived in pro-market terms or in anti-market terms. What links the master signifier to particular identities is the *subject*, not an underlying biological essence, nor some sort of extra-discursive social force. At a fundamental level, the master signifier holds the place of the lack in the structure and simultaneously constitutes it and the subject (Žižek 1991b: 132).

We are now in a position to consider what is involved in the *ideological* or *ethical* aspect of subjectivity. When a political struggle is brought to a close (through a vote for example), there is the possibility of attributing to ecology an essence which appears natural and obvious. To be a *feminist* ecologist, say, already implies subjective involvement. But this can be experienced in a variety of ways, each summarizing a different mode of enjoyment and thus engagement. For instance, we may confront 'ecology' with an 'aha' exclamation: what once made no determinate sense (on account of its empty character) has now become meaningful (ecology means *feminist* ecology). Or the installation of 'ecology' as *feminist* ecology may be taken as an experience of error ('all these years I had been deceiving myself by thinking of ecology as socialist in essence, I had been labouring under false-consciousness'). Alternatively, the contingent aspect of the experience may be strongly affirmed. In other words, one suddenly realizes that 'it could very easily have been otherwise'. It is this experience of contingency that may usher in a new *modality* of the identity-identification dialectic as a function of enjoyment, where ethics and ideology take on a central role. Insofar as the mode of enjoyment can be characterized as one involving the subject's complicitous concealment of the radical contingency of things, we are dealing with a case in which the ideological dimension is foregrounded. Insofar as the mode of enjoyment can be characterized as one involving the subject's attentiveness to the radical contingency of socio-political relations, we are dealing with a case in which the ethical dimension is foregrounded. As we will see in the following chapter, what we call the logic of fantasy provides us with the means to talk about the subject's mode of enjoyment, and thus about the way the ideological and ethical dimensions of socio-political reality are foregrounded or backgrounded.

Conclusion

This chapter set out our basic ontological framework. It has presented our understanding of the underlying dimensions of social reality and subjectivity in the context of more ontical categories like regimes and practices. Pride of place in this schema is accorded to an ontological negativity or radical contingency that penetrates social structures and identities. In the next chapter, we elaborate our basic units of explanation, which we call logics of critical explanation. Our aim in this regard is to continue to construct a group of middle range concepts – a particular grammar or vocabulary – with which we can both explain and criticize the practices and regimes that constitute our concrete objects of analysis.

5 Logics

Formal analysis and abstraction are essential for the study of concrete historical processes – not only because the theoretical construction of the object is the requirement of any intellectual practice worthy of the name, but also because social reality itself generates abstractions which organize its own principles of functioning. Thus Marx, for instance, showed how the *formal* and *abstract* laws of commodity production are the core of the actual concrete workings of capitalist societies. In the same way, when we try to *explain* the structuration of political fields through categories such as 'logic of equivalence', 'logic of difference' and 'production of empty signifiers', we are attempting to construct a theoretical horizon whose abstractions are not merely analytical but *real* abstractions on which the constitution of identities and political articulations depends.

(Laclau 2000a: 87–8, note 8)

The previous chapter outlined our underlying ontological presuppositions and our associated ontology of social relations. Among other things, it provided us with the theoretical and conceptual resources to develop our basic units of explanation, which we conceive in terms of logics. In this chapter, we show how our conception of a logic in the social sciences, and the particular logics we elaborate, enable us to characterize and elucidate the transformation, stabilization, and maintenance of regimes and social practices. In a nutshell, we suggest that a social science explanation involves the mobilization of three types of logic, which we name social, political and fantasmatic respectively, that are articulated together to account for a problematized phenomenon.

Put briefly, *social logics* enable us to characterize practices in a particular social domain, say the practices of consumption and exchange within an economy, or an entire regime of practices, whether Thatcherism, apartheid, or the audit regime of a particular university for example. *Political logic*s provide the means to explore how social practices are instituted, contested, and defended. Here we invoke Laclau and Mouffe's logics of equivalence and difference to investigate the way in which the traces of radical contingency associated with the original institution of practices and regimes can in certain circumstances be reactivated by subjects, thus enabling them to construct new meanings, practices and identities. Finally, if political logics are most closely associated with the political dimension of social relations, *fantasmatic logics* are closely linked to the ideological dimension. More precisely, with the logic of fantasy we aim to capture a particularly powerful way in which subjects are rendered complicit in concealing or covering over the radical contingency of social relations.

Since all dimensions are to some degree present in a practice or regime, each logic has a role to play in furnishing us with a complete explanatory account. Our aim in this chapter is thus to establish the distinctive features and status of each of these logics by relating them to our overall social ontology, thereby enabling us to distinguish our approach from those which appeal to contextualized self-interpretations and causal mechanisms. While in our view logics are subject-dependent, in the sense that our explanations require a passage through a subject's contextualized self-interpretation (which is the hermeneutical insight), they also require something more, which comprises the key naturalistic intuition of positivists and critical realists. We seek to articulate the intuitions of both approaches through our notion of logics, thus carving out a space beyond hermeneutical and naturalist accounts of social phenomena. We begin by elaborating the concept of a logic, before turning our attention to each of the types we have identified.

The concept of a logic

A trawl through the internet using one of the many available search engines shows clearly the pull of the collocation 'logic of . . .'. We find the 'logic of scientific discovery', the 'logic of decision and action', the 'logic of suicide terrorism' or the 'logic of terror', the 'logic of withdrawal', the 'logic of cultural capitalism', the 'logic of authentication', the 'logic of appropriateness', and so on. Like Wittgenstein's 'game', the term *logic* connotes a range of grammars in which 'logic' is uttered, articulated, implied, and so on. However, from a Wittgensteinian point of view, the identification of all these grammars as grammars *of* logic does not mean that we have to isolate a feature or set of features they all have in common. Of course, they may happen to share some feature(s), but this is not what is responsible for such a gathering under 'logic'. Rather, again following Wittgenstein, they share a set of *family resemblances* (Wittgenstein 1967: §67). The notion of 'family resemblance' formalizes our intuition about 'actual' family resemblances: language games criss-cross and overlap in an open-ended network, against particular background contexts of history, purposes, motivations, and so on. In our view, the difficulty of grasping the linkages between the different usages, as well as the boundaries demarcating correct and incorrect usages, can be offset by attempting to articulate a paradigm case or set of paradigm cases.

We can start by saying that when we talk about the *logic* of a practice or a regime of practices we seek to capture those aspects which make it tick. A logic distils what Wittgenstein calls 'the essence' of a practice, though we need to add his important rider that this is not an essentialist operation that penetrates below the surface to its singular ground, but seeks instead to investigate the ' "possibilities" of phenomena' – 'the kind of statements that we make about phenomena' – in various spatial and temporal contexts (Wittgenstein 1967: §§ 90, 92). This means, first, that the concept of a logic does not refer to the formal analysis of propositions in order to determine their validity or truth-value, or to establish the logical essence of a practice, for this runs the risk of 'subliming' logic by conceding it a super-hard, transcendental status in relation to the world of empirical propositions (Wittgenstein 1967: §§ 97–8).

Equally, a logic is not a causal law, as in Duverger's law or Marx's laws of capitalist society (Duverger 1963: 217; Marx 1976). Take Marx's general law of capital accumulation for example. Even though he concedes that laws are 'modified in [their] working by many circumstances', his notion of 'natural laws of capitalist production . . . working themselves out with iron necessity' is too strong and deterministic to be compatible with the ontological presuppositions of our approach (Marx 1976: 798, 91). Nor are logics synonymous with tendencies that are conceived as weak or 'soft' laws, such as Marx's 'tendency of the rate of profit to fall', which are more akin to empirical generalisations of a causal mechanistic sort that may or may not be triggered, or which interact indeterminately. (Indeed, the latter often presuppose more deterministic causal laws at higher levels of abstraction.) Finally, logics are not reducible to contextualized self-interpretations, however crucial these are in getting the explanatory process off the ground. In other words, our idea of a logic is not only set against the universalizing and necessitarian tendencies of the causal law paradigm, but it is also opposed to the particularistic tendencies of the interpretivist paradigm.

Instead, let us start with Laclau's initial attempts to clarify the concept. In his exchange with Butler and Žižek, Laclau characterizes a *social logic* as 'a rarefied system of objects, as a "grammar" or cluster of rules which make some combinations and substitutions possible and exclude others', making it virtually synonymous with his category of 'discourse' (Laclau 2000a: 76). Elsewhere, however, he claims that the concept enables him to grasp

> the type of relations between entities that makes possible the actual operation of that system of rules. While the grammar enounces what the rules of a particular language are, the logic answers to a different kind of question: how entities have to be to make those rules possible. Psychoanalytic categories such as 'projection' or 'introjection', for instance, presuppose processes whose logic is different from those that operate in the physical or biological world.
>
> (Laclau 2000b: 283–4)

In contrast to his specification of social logics, logic appears now to be conceded an ontological status. Indeed, in another statement, Laclau appears to clarify this latent ambiguity by distinguishing more sharply between 'social' and 'political' logics, in which the former involve 'rule-following' while the latter concern 'the institution of the social' (Laclau 2005: 117).

More positively, then, we could say that *the logic of a practice comprises the rules or grammar of the practice*, as well as *the conditions which make the practice both possible and vulnerable*. Consider first the logic of chess playing. Here we can obviously discern the characteristic grammar of the practice of playing chess. In other words, we can reconstruct the dominant pattern of sequences or actual moves comprising the strategies and counter-strategies, tactics and counter-tactics involved in chess playing. On the other hand, there are also the presupposed *basic entities and types of relationships*: the fundamental rules of the game (Laclau 2000b: 282–3). After all, these are precisely the types of relationship that make possible the myriad moves at the level of tactics and strategy. In other words, chess playing embodies and presupposes the basic rules of the game, the way pieces can move on the board, their different capacities ('capturing', 'checking', or 'being promoted'), as well as more informal rules such as 'pinning' or 'forking'.[1] Together they furnish us with the general grammar or 'rules' of chess playing. In addition, however, while the practice of playing chess involves the elaboration and revision of various strategies and tactics on the basis of a presupposed set of basic rules, the fundamental rules themselves can evolve in the face of changing circumstances and demands.

Now consider the 'logic of the market'. Clearly, the way we conceptualize the market depends on whether it is a supermarket, a market in energy supply, a market in educational goods, and so on. In other words, the meaning of expressions such as the 'efficient allocation of resources', 'fair price' or 'supply and demand' depends on the way we understand the key actors and terms associated with the specific market paradigm we have adopted. There is a clear relational network at stake here which the concept of a logic must try to capture and name. Crucial in this respect is the way actors themselves interpret their roles and activities. In abstract terms, we can say that a particular market comprises a particular set of rules or grammar that govern the arrangements and meanings that bring together the buyers and sellers of goods and services. Hence the logic of the market comprises a particular set of subject positions (buyers and sellers), objects (commodities and means of exchange) and a system of relations and meanings connecting subjects and objects, as well as certain sorts of institutional parameters (such as a well functioning legal system). However, our concept of a logic also aims to capture the conditions that make possible the continued operation of a particular market practice, as well as its potential vulnerabilities. And this involves answering a set of connected questions: What were the conditions under which the institution of this market was made possible? What political struggles preceded its institution? What processes ensure its maintenance or question its hegemonic status? Logics must also provide the means with which to answer these sorts of questions.

Having adumbrated our general concept of a logic, we can now offer a more detailed elaboration of social, political and fantasmatic logics. To start with, we note that social logics are always contextual entities, arising in particular historical and political circumstances. This means we can add little more to social logics by way of conceptual substance at this level of abstraction, and yet we still need to clarify their function and status in relation to our overall logic of critical explanation. By contrast, political logics and the logic of fantasy have more content at the ontological level – they are 'quasi-transcendental' categories – even though their operation and functioning is contextual and iterative. Each of these logics thus calls for greater specification. We begin with social logics.

Social logics

We have argued that social logics are in the first instance understood in terms of rules (cf. March and Olsen 1989). But we need to clarify the relationship between rules and practices. As we noted in our critique of Winch's concept of 'applying a rule' in Chapter 2, practices are not subsumed or exhausted by rules. Social practices always exceed any particular system of rules, because they contain possibilities and a contextual richness that cannot be captured by any one expression of them. Nevertheless, the search to discern the rules surrounding or informing a practice is still important in helping us to determine the meaning and character of a social practice. In fact, as investigators or interpreters of the world, the passage through rules is almost forced upon us. As Bourdieu notes, the anthropologist or social scientist is 'condemned to adopt unwillingly for his own use the representation of action which is forced on agents or groups when they lack practical mastery of highly valued competence and have to provide themselves with an explicit and at least semi-formalized substitute for it in the form of a *repertoire of rules*' (Bourdieu 1977: 2). In short, rules serve the important purpose of enabling the researcher to recover the meaning and function of a particular practice.

When we talk of *social* logics, therefore, we are primarily interested in *characterizing* a particular social practice or regime. Take, for instance, the Thatcher regime in the UK, which can be characterized in terms of a network of social logics, including the logics of marketization and centralization, both of which were rooted in the philosophy of the New Right (Gamble 1994; Hall 1988). Once sedimented, the Thatcherite discourse signified the practices and aspiration of liberating the capitalist economy, with its attendant entrepreneurial practices, from the stranglehold of an overloaded and bureaucratic state, as well as from over-powerful trade unions which were smothering enterprise and innovation (King 1975). On the other hand, Thatcherism came to represent a demand for a more restrictive, though more powerful, state that would regulate less, but more intensively.

Or consider the 'logic of apartheid' in South Africa, which involved separating different 'races', 'national groups' or 'peoples' (*Volkere*) into distinct entities, as well as the provision of 'separate but equal' institutions and resources for these differentiated units, whether in the form of 'Bantustans', 'homelands' or spatially segregated 'group areas'. Although this imposed form of ethnic identification was grounded on dubious anthropological theories and historical sources, it was lived out by those held in its sway (Dubow 1989). The new dispensation and its underlying rationale were sketched out in 1968 by the Chairman of the Bantu Affairs Commission in the following terms:

> The Government does not view all Bantu as one single people, but the Bantu are in fact divided into several peoples or nations, namely, the Xhosas of the Transkei, the Zulus of Zululand and Natal, the Swazi's of Swaziland and Bantu areas contiguous or near to Swaziland, the Bapedi of Sekhukhuniland and neighbourhood, the Venda of the Zoutpansburg, the Shangaans of the Transvaal Lowveld, the Tswanas of Botswana and Bantu areas of the Republic contiguous or near thereto occupied by Republican Tswana tribes, the South Sotho of Lesotho and Witzieshoek. Fortunately for each of these people or nations, history left to them within the borders of the present Republic large tracts of land which serve as their homelands. The Government's policy is, therefore, not a racial policy based on the colour of the skin of the inhabitants of the Republic, but a policy based on the reality and the fact that within the borders of the Republic there are found the White nation and several Bantu nations. The Government's policy is, therefore, not a policy of discrimination on the ground of race or colour, but a policy of differentiation on the ground of nationhood of different nations, granting to each self-determination within the borders of their homelands – hence this policy of separate development.
>
> (Cited in Platzky and Walker 1985: 114)

In the justifications and self-interpretations of its proponents and supporters, the logic of apartheid was thus cast in terms of signifiers such as 'separate but equal' and 'separate development'. In reality, of course, the fantasy of a pure and homogenized system of group difference underpinned policies and practices that divided 'non-white' groups into discrete units, so as to ensure their continued economic exploitation and political domination by 'whites' (Norval 1996; Wolpe 1988).[2] We could say that these logics of 'enforced separation' contrasted with the pre-existing logics of 'segregationism', and was opposed to logics of 'non-racialism' and 'democracy'.

In a first approach, then, the logic of the apartheid regime captures the rules or norms governing the practices of apartheid domination, inclusive of its subject positions and objects. Apartheid thus constituted certain sorts of subject positions – 'whites', 'non-whites', 'Afrikaners', 'Zulus', and so forth – as well as certain spaces, places and institutions (objects), such as 'bantustans', 'homelands', 'group areas', 'tribal authorities', and so on. It is true, of course, that in order to identify this logic we need to pass through the self-interpretations of the social actors involved in the regime and practices under investigation. In this case, those who were interpellated by apartheid discourse either saw themselves as separate from and superior to other racial groups, or accepted their inferior positioning within the social order and were complicit in its reproduction. But, as we shall emphasize in Chapter 6, social logics are also *constructed* and *named* by the analyst. Thus, even though they take their cue from existing self-interpretations such logics are not reducible to them. As we have suggested, the apartheid regime comprised social logics of 'enforced separation' for domination and exploitation, and this characterization provides a starting-point for us both to explain *and* criticize the practices and regimes under investigation. As we shall go on to show in the next sections, these tasks will also require the introduction of political and fantasmatic logics. However, before we do this, we need to formalize the intuitions embedded in our foregoing illustrations of social logics.

Laclau develops the notion of a social logic to characterize the overall pattern or coherence of a discursive practice. For him, 'social logics consist in rule-following' and so involve 'a rarefied system of statements, that is, a system of *rules* drawing a horizon within which some objects are representable while others are excluded. We can thus speak of the logics of kinship, of the market, even of chess-playing (to use Wittgenstein's example)' (Laclau 2005: 117). A social logic of the market, then, aims to capture the unity of a market practice or discourse. However, this coherence or unity is not guaranteed by a subject standing outside the discourse, nor is it captured by simply enumerating the rules that subsume all instances of a practice by providing a rigid definition of its pattern. 'A discursive formation', as Laclau and Mouffe put it in another context, 'is not unified either in the logical coherence of its elements, or in the a priori of a transcendental subject, or in a meaning-giving subject *a la* Husserl, or the unity of an experience' (Laclau and Mouffe 1985: 105). Here, they accept Foucault's rejection in *Archaeology of Knowledge* of 'four hypotheses concerning the unifying principle of a discursive formation – reference to the same object, a common style in the production of statements, constancy of the concepts, and reference to a common theme' (Laclau and Mouffe 1985: 105). Instead, again following Foucault, the type of unity attributed to a discursive formation by Laclau and Mouffe is conceived as a '*regularity in dispersion*', which neatly summarizes what is at stake in conceptualizing social logics, as it allows us simultane-ously to hold on to the idea of a pattern *and* an open-endedness.

In summary, then, the focus on rules furnishes a crucial insight regarding our concept of a social logic. But this insight has to be qualified in important ways. On the one hand, rules are not reified entities that subsume practices and discourses; instead, they enable us to *describe* and *characterize* the latter. This conception closely approximates the later

Wittgenstein's understanding of logic, especially the way he opposes orthodox understandings (including his earlier work) which accord logic a 'sublime' or 'super-hard' status, whose identity can survive independently of the contexts within which it is instantiated or operative (Wittgenstein 1967: §38). Logic, for Wittgenstein, is not separate from – nor suspended in – the empirical contexts in which it functions, but is ultimately indistinguishable from the language games and circumstances within which it subsists (Mulhall 2001: 95). Or, as Laclau and Mouffe put it in more sociological terms, 'social logics...acquire their meaning in precise conjunctural and relational contexts, where they will always be limited by other – frequently contradictory – logics' (Laclau and Mouffe 1985: 142). This observation simply reinforces for us why social logics should not be seen as synonymous with causal mechanisms.

Equally, however, it is important to stress that social logics *qua* rules are not reducible to empirical contexts. We can still talk about social logics as a function of paradigms which allow some cross-contextual travel. The difference with the 'hard' conception of logic is not that social logics cannot move from context to context, only that one cannot do so unproblematically and without explicitly forging new links with the new context. In sum, we could say that with social logics, we aim to capture the 'patterning' of social practices, where such practices are understood in this regard as a function of the contextualized self-interpretations of key subjects. Social logics of competition, for example, might describe the way that actors interact with, and understand, each other as competitors. Or social logics of 'individualization' might capture those patterns of discursive articulations which, in the self-understanding of actors, individuate persons, isolating them from each other.

In Chapter 6 we shall have the opportunity to revisit themes concerning the relationship between social logics and rules on the one hand, and between social logics and their empirical contexts on the other, especially insofar as they raise questions about how we should best understand the 'application' of logics in general to particular cases (the so-called 'application problem'). For now, however, we reiterate what we stated at the outset of this chapter, namely, that social logics are not by any means exhaustive of our understanding and characterization of practices. In order to *explain* the formation and character of social practices it is also necessary to focus on the processes through which they are constituted. And in order to *criticize* them it is necessary not only – as we saw in Chapter 4 – to develop a normative and sociological perspective, but also to examine the practices through which subjects are gripped in different ways by the discourses with which they identify. For us, this requires the development and employment of political and fantasmatic logics. In short, our initial focus on social logics has to be supplemented with political and fantasmatic logics, and it is to the latter that we now turn.

Political logics

If social logics assist in the task of directly characterizing practices and regimes along a synchronic axis, political logics can be said to focus more on the diachronic aspects of a practice or regime, whether in terms of how they have emerged, or in terms of how they are being contested and/or transformed. Political logics aim to capture those processes of collective mobilization precipitated by the emergence of the political dimension of social relations, such as the construction, defence, and naturalization of new frontiers. But they also include processes which seek to interrupt or break up this process of drawing frontiers.

Consider again the apartheid regime in South Africa. In this context, political logics manifest themselves in the very formation and constitution of apartheid practices, as well as their sedimentation and naturalization. More precisely, their construction was engineered, first, by dividing the 'white' ruling bloc between the proponents of Afrikaner nationalism, with their policy of apartheid, and those supporting the existing 'segregation' policies, who in the discourse of Afrikaner nationalism were presented as the lackeys of British imperialism. But it also involved a sharpening of the frontier between the emergent forces of Afrikaner nationalism and African nationalism, in which the proponents of apartheid presented the latter as seeking to bring about a communist takeover of the country. The spectre of communism was thus used to demonize those who were opposed to apartheid as enemies of the Afrikaner *volk*, and indeed of any authentic nationalist sentiment. Against the morally acceptable and pure Christian nationalism of Afrikanerdom, there were the unacceptable and impure discourses of non-racialism, socialism and democracy, which were articulated by the ANC, the South African Communist Party, and their allies (Norval 1993: 233–9).

As Diederichs, a leading Afrikaner nationalist put it in the period leading up to the victory of the National Party (NP) in 1948:

> All attempts to maintain and strengthen the unity of a people, and all efforts to bring the different parts, groups, classes or stands of the *volk* to unanimous co-operation, is condemned in principle by [the communist]. The notion '*volk*' itself is rejected to be replaced with the notion of 'class'...For [the communist], no peoples exist; only classes...Class hatred and class struggle is therefore a fundamental tenet of the communist doctrine. The unity of society must be destroyed, and in its place, a new form of sociality has to be established.
>
> (Diederichs 1946: 5)

The opposition to communism was also directed at the possible and actual articulation of communism and nationalism. This was expressed in a fundamental difference between the communist and the NP's conceptualization of nationalism. In 1950, for example, Diederichs argued the point in the second reading of the *Suppression of Communism Bill*:

> By 'nationalism' we understand respect for what is one's own; pride in one's own...and a respect for others. But the nationalism preached by communists is something quite different. It is not love of their own, but hate for the other; not solidarity with one's own people; it is people who do not want to return to serve their own communities...That is not true nationalism.
>
> (Cited in Norval 1996: 137)

Here, an authentic nationalism is demarcated from a fraudulent articulation of nationalism with socialism, democracy, or communism, on the grounds that Communist nationalism equates the nation with the false universals of equality and non-racialism, rather than with homogeneously defined ethnic particularities.

In short, then, the apartheid project involved an intensification of the divisions between whites and blacks, in which blacks were presented as a dangerous other, who would 'swamp' and thus endanger the interests of whites, especially Afrikaners. And following the victory of the National Party in 1948, the new ruling party, and the reconfigured South African state, struggled to sediment these new divisions by domesticating otherness in the name of legitimate, though subordinated, ethnic and national particularities. Indeed, these 'authentic' forms of nationalism were sedimented into the project of constructing 'separate but equal' institutions, social spaces, territories, and means of representation, thereby preventing the creation of overlapping linkages or combinations between demands and identities.

Having illustrated the ontical manifestations of political logics, we now need to elaborate the conceptual underpinnings of these political practices of constitution, contestation and sedimentation in a more theoretical fashion. Let us start with Ernesto Laclau's claim that whereas 'social logics consist in rule-following, political logics are related to the *institution* of the social', where the process of institution 'proceeds out of social demands' rather than an 'arbitrary fiat' and is 'inherent to any process of social change' (Laclau 2005: 117). A few exegetical remarks are called for in order to unpack this dense passage.

To begin, if political logics are concerned with the *institution* of the social, they are also related to its possible *de-institution* or *contestation*. This is because the very institution of a new regime or social practice presupposes the possibility that a previous social order is successfully displaced from its hegemonic position and thus de-instituted. In short, then, political logics are integral to the processes of contestation and institution of social practices and regimes. In addition, Laclau's remarks imply that the contestation of a hegemonic discursive formation and the possible institution – or failed institution – of a new one via political logics can never be totally external, and thus arbitrary, in relation to the social formation itself. Instead, the radical institution of the social emerges from concrete empirical demands within a particular order.

If the political dimension of social relations indicates, via a dislocatory moment, the *limits* of a social formation, political *logics* have to be related to this moment. To put it in Lacanian terms, a dislocation signifies the presence of 'the real' in the symbolic order, which can be characterized as a moment when a sense emerges, however localized or diffuse this may be, that 'things are not quite right', whether this is registered by the researcher or the subject affected by the dislocatory event (see Evans 1996: 159–61; Fink 1995: 24–31). Political logics thus formalize our understanding of the ways in which dislocation is discursively articulated or symbolized. Taken together, political logics, dislocation, and the political dimension help us to redescribe the ontical level in terms that emerge out of our poststructuralist ontology of social relations.

The reference here to our ontological framework enables us to elaborate the content of political logics in a more precise way. Since in this schema *all* practices are *signifying* practices, political logics must in the first instance be a species of logics of signification as such. More precisely, adapting Saussure's conceptualization of linguistic relation as either associative or syntagmatic, we can posit the operation of two signifying logics: the logics of equivalence and difference. While the former involves the expansion of the associative or paradigmatic pole, the latter involves the expansion of the syntagmatic pole of language (Laclau and Mouffe 1985: 130). Insofar as these signifying logics are instantiated in situations wherein the political dimension of social relations is at the forefront, and in which there is some sort of collective mobilization in play, we could say that they manifest themselves as *political* logics.

Consider, for example, the political situation in South Africa during the 1980s, when the discourse of the United Democratic Front (UDF) was constructed in opposition to the crisis-ridden apartheid order (Howarth 2000b, 2005b). Its very name promised a future South Africa that would be completely free of apartheid domination – 'non-racial', 'democratic' and 'united'. But the logic of this discourse can be captured in its guiding slogan – 'UDF Unites, Apartheid Divides' – as the movement sought to link together a range of groups and identities into an equivalential chain that was opposed to national oppression and racial domination. More precisely, the UDF articulated a series of demands in different sites of the social – demands for better housing, lower rents, education, wages and conditions of employment, medical care and so forth – by presenting the apartheid state as a common enemy that denied national self-determination and basic political rights to the majority. It thus simplified and politicized the entire national social space by transforming it into two hostile camps.

We are now in a position to see why social logics have to be supplemented by political logics. While social logics speak to ongoing social practices in different regimes – 'regularities in dispersion' – there is an important question about how they become individuated, which is also a question about their *limits*. Where and how do we draw the boundaries between concrete practices? And how are we to account for their institution and transformation? As Laclau and Mouffe insist in their critique of Foucault's archaeology of discourse, for these concrete social practices and regimes to exist and function as systems, there must be logics 'which produce effects of totality capable of constructing the limits, and thus of constituting the formation' (Laclau and Mouffe 1985: 145–6). Political logics thus provide a conceptual vocabulary to show how these limits are constituted, transformed, and absorbed, and they do so by focusing on the way the logic of equivalence comes to predominate over the logic of difference, and *vice versa*. In short, then, if the logic of equivalence involves the simplification of signifying space, the logic of difference involves its expansion and complexification (Laclau and Mouffe 1985: 130).

In developing this idea, we reiterate our assumption that the elements of discourse – signifiers – always exist in relational networks that exhibit varying degrees of structuration. This means that we can characterize the relations between discursive elements in terms of two dimensions. Linked to the two fundamental relations identified earlier in the context of structural linguistics (associative and syntagmatic relations), they generate a two-dimensional matrix comprising the dimensions of equivalence and difference. The dimension of equivalence captures the *substitutive* aspect of the relation by making reference to an 'us-them' axis: two or more elements can be substituted for each other with reference to a common negation or threat. That is to say, they are equivalent not insofar as they share a positive property (though empirically they *may* share something in common), but, crucially, insofar as they have a common enemy. The dimension of difference, by contrast, captures the *combinatory* or contiguous aspect of the relation, which accounts not simply for differences in identity among elements, but also for keeping elements distinct, separate, and autonomous. Both dimensions are always present in the sense that each presupposes the other. But since discursive structures are contingent and not fixed, we have a means of specifying the *dynamic* aspect of this politically-inflected signifying ontology. *Logics* of equivalence and difference thus emphasize the dynamic process by which political frontiers are constructed, stabilized, strengthened, or weakened. They elucidate the way one or another dimension acquires greater or lesser significance, even while each presupposes the other (cf. Laclau 2005: 79).

Put in other terms, the logic of equivalence entails the construction and privileging of antagonistic relations, which means that the dimension of difference on each side of the frontier is weakened, whether differences are understood as a function of demands or identities. For instance, a national liberation struggle against an occupying colonial power will typically attempt to cancel out the particular differences of class, ethnicity, region, or religion in the name of a more universal nationalism that can serve as a common reference point for all the oppressed; indeed, its identity may be virtually exhausted in its opposition to the oppressive regime. By contrast, the logic of difference draws on other discourses in an attempt to break down these chains of equivalence. The age-old practice of 'divide and rule', for instance, in which an occupying power seeks to separate ethnic or national groups into particular communities or indirect systems of rule, is invariably designed to prevent the articulation of demands and identities into a generalized challenge to the dominant regime.

In sum, the *political* logics of equivalence and difference comprise a descriptive framing device which is derived from a particular understanding of discourse and the importance accorded to processes of signification. They enhance our approach to social science explanation by furnishing us with a conceptual grammar with which to account for the *dynamics* of social change. They help show how social practices and regimes are contested, transformed, and instituted, thereby extending our grammar beyond social logics.

Fantasmatic logics

We turn now to fantasmatic logics in order to add a further explanatory and critical layer to the process of accounting for change or continuity. If political logics provide a politically-inflected signifying frame within which to show *how* social practices come into being or are transformed, then fantasmatic logics provide the means to understand *why* specific practices and regimes 'grip' subjects. To use Laclauian terms from a different though related context, if political logics concern *signifying operations*, fantasmatic logics concern the *force* behind those operations (Laclau 2005: 101). Or, to put it in Lacanian terms, if political reality involves a symbolic construction produced through metaphoric and metonymic processes and articulated around master signifiers, 'it nevertheless depends on fantasy in order to constitute itself' (Stavrakakis 1999: 81). For us, then, fantasmatic logics contribute to our understanding of the resistance to change of social practices (the 'inertia' of social practices), but also the speed and direction of change when it does happen (the 'vector' of political practices).

Consider first the relationship between fantasmatic logics and social practices. Though social practices are punctuated by the mishaps, tragedies and contingencies of everyday life, social relations are experienced and understood in this mode of activity as an accepted way of life. The role of fantasy in this context is not to set up an illusion that provides a subject with a false picture of the world, but to ensure that the radical contingency of social reality – and the political dimension of a practice more specifically – remains in the background. In other words, the logic of fantasy takes its bearings from the various ontical manifestations of radical contingency. Consider fantasy in relation to the political dimension of social relations for instance. As we pointed out in Chapter 4, the very process of problematization and critical explanation involves the identification of an aspect of a practice which is deemed *worthy* of public contestation, thereby imputing to it some normative import.

In this context, we can say that the role of fantasy is to actively contain or suppress the political dimension of a practice. Thus, aspects of a social practice may seek to maintain existing social structures by pre-emptively absorbing dislocations, preventing them from becoming the source of a political practice. In fact, the function of many management and governance techniques could be seen in this light.

Several studies on employee cynicism, for example, suggest how transgressive acts can sometimes serve to stabilize an exploitative social practice which they ostensibly seek to subvert (Willmott 1993; du Gay and Salaman 1992). Taking their cue from Michael Burawoy's study of factory workers in *Manufacturing Consent* (1979), they draw the conclusion that informal games that transgress the control systems and company rules imposed by management often have the effect of sustaining the oppressive system with which they have ceased to identify. In a related vein, and referring to Gideon Kunda's study of cynical workers in *Engineering Culture* (1992), Fleming and Spicer emphasise how 'employees performed their roles flawlessly and were highly productive' despite their recourse to 'humour, the mocking of pompous official rituals and sneering cynicism'. Thus as they conclude:

> The ideology of cynicism ensures that [the company] operates akin to a well-oiled machine because the corporate culture does not necessarily need to colonize employees' minds..., only their discursive practices. Employees are cynically enlightened about the realities of corporate exploitation, but *they act as if they are not*. In fact, cynicism in a context like this may often lead us to feel that we are not fully reducible to the company line, [thereby allowing us to indulge in the fantasy that we] are 'unique individuals'.
>
> (Fleming and Spicer 2003: 164)

That such cynical-transgressive acts sustain the social practice being transgressed appears to be corroborated by studies which show how personnel officers of many companies actually advise workers not to identify with corporate culture ideals too strongly, and to retain a healthy distance from the company script (Ashforth and Humphrey 1993, Leidner 1993, Sturdy *et al.* 2001). These transgressive 'indulgency patterns' (Gouldner 1955; Mars 1982) 'have long been recognized by researchers as an important part of maintaining workplace relations of power. In turning a blind eye to minor infringements such as petty pilfering and "fiddling", for example, more consequential disruptions are avoided' (Fleming and Spicer 2003: 167).

The operation of fantasmatic logics can thus reinforce the social dimension of practices by covering over the fundamental lack in reality and keeping at bay what we have labelled 'the real'. In this respect, logics of fantasy have a key role to play in 'filling up' or 'completing' the void in the subject and the structure of social relations by bringing about closure. In Žižek's words, they 'structure reality itself' or, as he puts it in his rephrasing of Lacan's formulation, fantasies are 'the support that gives consistency to what we call "reality"' (Žižek 1989: 44).

But how do fantasmatic logics relate to *political practices*? For is it not the case that political practices represent a *rupture* with the logic of fantasy, which we have described in terms of concealment? After all, political logics are linked to moments of contestation and institution, all of which presuppose contingency and all of which involve the attempt to defend or challenge existing social relations through the construction of social antagonisms. Nevertheless, though social antagonisms indicate the limits of social reality by disclosing the points at which 'the impossibility of society' is manifest, social antagonisms are still forms of social construction, as they furnish the subject with a way of positivizing the lack in the structure. As we noted in Chapter 4, while the construction of frontiers presupposes contingency and public contestation, this process does not necessarily entail attentiveness to radical contingency. In other words, radical contingency can be concealed in political practices just as much as it is in social practices. If the function of fantasy in social practices is implicitly to reinforce the natural character of their elements or to actively prevent the emergence of the political dimension, then we could say that the function of fantasy in political practices is to give them *direction* and *energy*, what we earlier referred to as their vector. As Stavrakakis puts it, 'it is the imaginary promise of recapturing our lost/impossible enjoyment which provides the fantasy support for many of our political projects and choices' (Stavrakakis 2005: 73). In addition, during the institution of a new social practice or regime, there are invariably political practices that actively seek to naturalize a newly emerging social structure or regime by backgrounding its political dimension through decision, institutionalization, and other means. This entails marginalizing whatever contestatory aspects remain from the struggle to institute the new social structure.

In sum, whether in the context of social practices or political practices, fantasy operates so as to conceal or close off the radical contingency of social relations. It does this through a fantasmatic narrative or logic that promises a fullness-to-come once a named or implied obstacle is overcome – the beatific dimension of fantasy – or which foretells of disaster if the obstacle proves insurmountable, which might be termed the horrific dimension of fantasy. For example, images of omnipotence or of total control would represent the beatific dimension, while images of impotence or victimhood would represent the horrific dimension of such fantasmatic attempts to achieve or maintain closure (Glynos 2001b: 93–6; Stavrakakis 1999: 108–9). Of course, the logic of fantasy (in the singular) appears ontically in many guises – hence our use of the term fantasmatic *logics* (in the plural). Moreover, such logics typically rely upon narratives which possess features distributed between public-official and unofficial forums. This is because fantasies seek directly to conjure up – or at least presuppose – an impossible union between incompatible elements. They partake of a 'have your cake and eat it' logic and so one way for subjects to cope with this impossibility is to distribute the appearance of incompatible elements among different registers. This observation helps us to identify the fantasmatic elements of social reality, for it generates an important methodological rule of thumb: empirical evidence indicating the presence of a fantasmatic object can often be identified by asking *whether or not it resists public official disclosure*. In addition, we could say that aspects of social reality having to do with fantasmatically structured *enjoyment* often possess contradictory features, exhibiting a kind of extreme oscillation between incompatible positions.

In order to illustrate these claims, consider the political practices and struggles that eventually resulted in the UK's *Criminal Justice and Public Order Act* of 1994. In explaining what made possible the legitimization of its draconian anti-nomadic character, Dave Lewis has shown how the passage of the Bill through Parliament in 1992 was accompanied by an outpouring of virulent and often irrational attacks on 'New Age Travellers' in the tabloid press (Lewis 2005: Ch. 3). New Age Travellers were constructed as an obstacle to the morally upstanding communities of the British nation, and a threat to Tory promises of a healthy economy and a harmonious society. Moreover, though these attacks resisted public-official disclosure in the sense that they were rarely voiced in the serious broadsheets, or by politicians in parliament speaking in their public-official capacity, they did appear at the margins of public-official discourse, that is to say, in private 'off-the record' accounts, in the tabloid press, and so on. And they often appeared in the context of narratives imputing to new age travellers contradictory features. For example, they were often described as being both lazy and anarchic on the one hand, and as very organized and disciplined on the other hand. In one breath New Age Traveller camps were regularly represented as comprising thousands who 'heave, sweat and jump in that weird raving style, fingers and arms twisting through the mist', their every van serving simultaneously as 'a café, an orgy and a drug den' (*The Daily Mail*, 28 July 1992). But at the same time there were 'rumours of a leadership' (*The Times*, 3 August 1992) and allegations to the effect that '[n]obody knows and plays the system better than the travellers' (*The Sunday Times*, 2 August 1992).

As a further illustration, consider how policy debates in the US, which typically assume the welfare system is inefficient, are often underpinned by a fantasmatic narrative in which single African-American mothers are alleged to sponge off hard-working, tax-paying citizens (Hancock 2004). Again, this aspect of the narrative typically resists public official disclosure, thereby hinting at its possible *enjoyed* and thus fantasmatic status (Žižek 1997a; Glynos 2001a). Or take the way certain British Euro-sceptics have resisted attempts to construct a common European identity and project. In this context, Stavrakakis suggests that the strength of these opposition discourses resides not simply in the official counter-narrative of Europe as an inefficient bureaucracy that suffers from regulatory over-reach, but also by unofficial counter-narratives that emphasize how European officials and politicians are out to 'steal' their nation's enjoyment. And here one only has to think of tabloid headlines that invoke images of Brussels bureaucrats hatching plans to replace the British 3-pin plug and loo with European versions, or to legislate that rhubarb, bananas, and cucumbers be ideally straight, or at least not excessively curved (Stavrakakis 2005: 88).

Consider finally the way in which Afrikaner nationalists constructed the discourse of apartheid in the 1930s and 1940s by naming a series of 'others' that blocked the interests of Afrikaner workers, farmers, the petty bourgeoisie, and a growing Afrikaner capitalist class (Davies *et al.* 1984: 18–19). The figure of 'Hoggenheimer' – the 'Jewish international financier and capitalist' deemed responsible for the exploitation of Afrikaners – is exemplary in this regard. For example, in a public speech on 12 April 1937, D.F. Malan – leader of the purified Nationalists who was later to become the first Afrikaner nationalist Prime Minister in 1948 – described the 'fusion' of the United Party and Herzog's National Party in 1934, and its subsequent electoral success in the following terms:

> Coalition and Fusion were to a great extent the result of Jewish organization. The Jews did everything in their power to keep the Afrikaners from uniting, as they feared that South Africans would rise from their lowly and insignificant position to save South Africa for the South Africans ... Throughout the world the Jews avail themselves of democratic institutions for their own profit and that was why they joined the Labourites. There is yet another aspect of Jewish communism in South Africa. The Jews oppose discrimination because they fear discrimination against them. In South Africa this means miscegenation.
>
> (Cited in Furlong 1991: 65; see also Shain 1994: 145–51)

In this typical set of remarks, and in the figure of 'Hoggenheimer', we see the classical workings of *enjoyment*: the Jew is both a rapacious capitalist who is exploiting Afrikaner workers, but at the same time a radical Bolshevik leading Afrikaner workers away from 'the *Volk*' into the hands of communists and militant trade unionists. Ultimately, in its various manifestations and ideological connotations – international capitalist, British imperialist, Bolshevik revolutionary, and so forth – the Jew is stealing enjoyment from Afrikaners thus blocking their identity.

In this emergent ideology, then, the fantasy of a pure, uncontaminated and homogenous white Afrikaner '*volk*' was threatened and undermined by figures such as the 'Hoggenheimer' and the 'British imperialist', who represented foreign controlled monopoly capitalism, as well as the '*swaart gevaar*' ('black peril'), which augured a process of '*oorstrooming*' – the overrunning of the 'white' cities by the native masses (Norval 1996: 57–100). It was later to evolve into the fantasy of a 'White's Only' South Africa, of a world with 'no black South Africans', that is, of a white South Africa populated only by black migrant workers from other nations. As Piet Koornhof, then Deputy Minister of Bantu Affairs, put it in Parliament in 1971,

> [t]he fact of the matter is that we on this side of the House have a vision
> and a policy ... the policy of multi-nationalism ... Whether a Bantu was
> born in Soweto or any other prescribed area, he is and remains first of all
> a member of his people ... Nor does it matter how long he has been
> living there. He remains a member of his people'.
>
> (Cited in Greenberg 1987: 140)

Despite the major practical impediments in realizing these goals – the
need for black labour and the consequent growth of African urbanization in
white areas – problems which were recognized by apartheid ideologues
themselves, they were still pursued with ruthlessness and systematic efficiency.
Thus, while Heribert Adam's landmark description of Afrikaner nationalists
as 'a pragmatic race oligarchy' captures something of their character and
practices, it misses the important unconscious investments in the ideals of
apartheid ideology by its leaders and supporters alike (Adam 1971). How else
to explain the fanatical zeal accompanying the removal of 'black spots',
the policing of 'group areas', the enforcement of 'pass law' violations, and the
creation of independent homelands? Indeed, given our theoretical perspective,
we can hypothesize that perhaps it is the resulting transgressions of the
impossible apartheid ideal, and then the increasingly baroque solutions
required to deal with them, which sustained its grip and the identities it
fostered. This suggests that it is only by examining the failure and
disintegration of these fantasmatic objects that we can begin to explain the
failure of the Afrikaner discourse to sustain its grip beyond the apartheid
period (see Howarth 2002b).

In thinking about the links between political and fantasmatic logics we
could say that the articulation of fantasy and the political dimension varies,
depending on whether or not the equivalential or differential aspects of a
discursive construction predominate. For example, the predominance of the
logic of equivalence, in which the articulation of political discourse is
dominated by a logic of substitution that links different demands together,
harbours the possibility of a more *populist* or *revolutionary* politics. In this
context, fantasmatic logics may take the form of a narrative in which an
internal obstacle (or 'enemy within') is deemed responsible for the blockage of
identity, while promising a fullness or harmony to come. This logic is clearly
evident in Leninist forms of Marxist discourse, in which a particular class
enemy has to be forcibly overthrown (usually through revolutionary means)
in the name of a universal class (the proletariat), so as to bring about complete
human emancipation. But it can equally apply to projects such as Thatcherism
in which a failing social democratic consensus (condensed in the figure of the
trade unionist *qua* 'enemy within') was opposed in the name of a 'strong state
and a free economy' (even though in many respects the latter ideal harked back
to a golden age of capitalism in the nineteenth century).

By contrast, the prominence of the logic of difference in political practices, in which the articulation of political discourse is dominated by a logic of combination that decouples demands, and addresses them in a punctual fashion by channelling them into the existing system of rule, harbours the possibility of a more *institutionalist* or *reformist* politics. Here fantasmatic logics may be articulated by means of a narrative in which an external obstacle or enemy is deemed to be a threat to an already existing fullness and harmony. For example, a 'Marxist' or 'Communist threat', allegedly orchestrated by the Soviet Union and Cuba, was presented by military strategists as a direct threat to South Africa's 'free enterprise', 'Christian values' and 'Western freedoms'. This 'Total Strategy' doctrine emerged in the aftermath of the Soweto uprising, which in turn was important in precipitating an organic crisis of the state during the late 1970s and early 1980s, and was articulated alongside measures to reform the apartheid system by making economic and political concessions designed to win support amongst certain strata of the black middle classes and amongst the permanently settled urban masses. These included the creation of 'acceptable' forms of trade unionism, minor political reforms, and attempts to concede certain rights to urban workers in 'white' areas of South Africa. In short, we witness efforts to disarticulate the growing political opposition to the apartheid state in the naming of an external enemy which threatens the internal stability and prosperity of the country (initially, at least, internal protest is typically construed as provoked by 'external agitators'), coupled with the defence of a fully constituted and harmonious order in the here and now (Saul and Gelb 1986). And a similar logic can be said to be at play in the current 'war on terror' discourse, in which the values and stability of liberal democracies are confronted by a foreign 'axis of evil', 'international terrorism', and an 'arc of extremism' (see Blair 2006; Bush 2002).

We have emphasized above the ways in which political logics can be linked to fantasmatic logics. But we can also mention how ethics is related to the logic of fantasy. As we have intimated, while political logics can be resolved into two main components – the logics of equivalence and difference – the logic of fantasy is defined solely by the function of closure. Moreover, in concealing – suturing or closing off – the contingency of social relations, fantasy structures the subject's mode of enjoyment in a particular way: let us call it an 'enjoyment of closure'. Thus, ethics is directly linked to the logic of fantasy because, whatever its ontical instantiation, the latter has closure as its principle of intelligibility, whereas ethics is related to the 'traversal' of fantasy in the name of an openness to contingency corresponding to an 'enjoyment of openness'.[3] For us, then, fantasy and ethics pick out the subject as a subject of enjoyment. Though social practices are capacious enough from our point of view to enable us to capture those aspects in which subjects are attentive to the radical contingency of social relations, it should be clear that fantasmatic logics are operative in social practices where the ideological dimension is foregrounded. However, we have also seen that fantasmatic logics are equally operative in political practices. But whereas political logics are used to explain the discursive *shifts* in the wake of a dislocatory moment, fantasmatic logics describe and account for the *vector* and *modality* of those discursive shifts, capturing the way in which the subject *deals* with the radical contingency of social relations as a subject of enjoyment.

So far we have developed the idea that logics furnish us with the means to characterize social practices and regimes, and to account for their transformation or resistance to change. But this raises a number of questions about their role, their precise ontological status, as well as the way in which their operationalization can be infused with a suitably self-reflexive ethos. We shall now tackle these issues.

Logics and the tasks of critical explanation

As our ontological framework implies, our different sorts of logic always work together in the practices under investigation. This means that any 'logic of critical explanation' involves the linking together of different logics, along with the empirical circumstances in which they occur, in order to construct an account that is descriptive, explanatory, and critical. More specifically, social, political, and fantasmatic logics come together to elucidate processes of social change and stabilization within a general theory of hegemony, which presupposes the existence of a social field criss-crossed by social antagonisms and the availability of contingent ideological elements – or 'floating signifiers' – that can be articulated by opposed political projects striving to confer meaning on them (Laclau 2005: 133; Laclau and Mouffe 1985: 134–5; Žižek 1989: 87–129). Of course, our three logics and their inter-relationships are underpinned by the premises of our poststructuralist ontology – the discursive and contingent nature of all objects and identities, the subject's modes of enjoyment, and so on – which together constitute their conditions of possibility. In short, social, political, and fantasmatic logics are articulated together in an overarching explanatory logic that combines descriptive, explanatory, and critical aspects.

Thus, for instance, to return to the example of South Africa, the social logics of apartheid distil certain core characteristics of South African society between 1948 and 1976, thus providing a descriptive account of its underlying processes of control and structuring. But the language of logics also enables us to describe and explain the emergence and constitution of the apartheid order through the interplay of the political logics of equivalence and difference, as well as the grip exercised by the apartheid regime on those subjects interpellated by its discourse. For instance, the logic of fantasy is important in accounting for the way racist ideologies such as apartheid discourse holds subjects in its sway, but it also helps us explain the operation and sustenance of racist ideology via the psychoanalytic theoretical framework in which it is inscribed. Our ontical inquiry is here supplemented ontologically through a reference to the subject's structure of desire and the fantasmatic objects that function as the 'object cause' of such desires. As we noted earlier, this was evident in the desire of Afrikaners – and later 'whites' in general – to achieve a pure 'whites only' homeland wherein its identity could be secured and protected from the '*swaart gevaar*' (the 'black peril'), the 'British', or the figure of 'Hoggenheimer' (the figure of Jewish-Imperial enslavement) (see Howarth 2002b).

Finally, the function of logics in social scientific analysis is not only to make social processes more intelligible, but in the process of *describing* and *explaining* it should also furnish the possibility of a *critical* engagement with the practices and processes under investigation. Indeed, *all* logics carve out a space for a *critical* conception of explanation because they all presuppose the non-necessary character of social relations. As we shall show more concretely in the next chapter, this means that the very identification, characterization, and naming of a discursive pattern as a social logic is already to engage in a process with a normative and political valence. And this is simply to emphasize that the identity of a practice cannot be taken for granted. In fact, the process of invoking and deploying political logics to show the contingent institution of social practices is already to signal their non-necessary character, and to begin the normative task of contemplating alternative practices and regimes. But the same is true of fantasmatic logics. While the latter contribute to our account of the *grip* or ideology of racism in a descriptive and explanatory sense, they also furnish the ontological resources with which to open up ethical possibilities and thus to engage critically with the practices under investigation.

On the status of logics

The three interrelated component logics of our overarching 'logic of critical explanation' can also be grasped by relating them to the ontical/ontological distinction and to the cognate notion of a *quasi-transcendental* inquiry. Recall first that whereas social logics are substantive, in the sense that their identity is virtually coterminous with the social practices and contexts they inform and make possible, political logics have a formal aspect, enabling us to specify them with some precision independently of the fields of meaning within which they operate. And the same is true of fantasmatic logics because we can separate out the ontological from the ontical aspects in a more robust way than is possible in the case of social logics. More fully, when we talk about the *logic* of fantasy (in the singular) we draw attention to the *onto*-logical dimension of the concept: the process by means of which the subject *enjoys* in such a way as to conceal the radical contingency of social reality. But when we talk about fantasmatic *logics* (in the plural) we refer to the myriad ways in which the logic of fantasy, conceived ontologically, is rendered manifest at the ontical level. Thus, consonant with the epigraph to this chapter, when we talk about the logic of equivalence, the logic of difference, and the logic of fantasy, we foreground the ontological dimension of our inquiry because each of them are understood to be constitutive of our practices and regimes, including the different ways in which subjects experience and mediate social reality.

As to the quasi-transcendental aspect of our approach, it is important to stress that our concept of logics not only provides our objects of critical investigation with their conditions of *possibility*, but also furnishes their conditions of *im*possibility (see Derrida 1989: 76–7). On the one hand, as we have stressed, our different types of logic enable us to describe and explain social practices by setting out their social, political and fantasmatic conditions of possibility. In the first instance, social logics enable us to specify the rules governing a particular social practice, as well as associated features and phenomena. But in addition, political and fantasmatic logics provide the resources to account for the emergence, formation and maintenance of particular social practices, focusing especially on their political constitution and the ways in which subjects are gripped by certain discourses and not others. On the other hand, however, because our concept of logics is predicated on the ultimate contingency of social relations, we can also account for the conditions of impossibility of a practice. In this regard, our three logics furnish us with the means to recover the options that were excluded or foreclosed in its constitution. But they also provide the conceptual resources with which to explore the way in which those excluded possibilities and/or the various forces that are constitutively excluded in the construction of any identity or regime render that identity vulnerable to being subverted and eventually transformed. In short, logics speak both to the possibility and impossibility of regimes and social practices.

Finally, we note that, for us, the appellation 'quasi-transcendental' also captures the fact that our logics are *themselves* contingent and finite constructs that are contestable and revisable in the light of changing conditions and theoretical developments. This is most clear of course with respect to social logics, which we use to characterize particular social practices. But it is also true of political and fantasmatic logics, which we use to draw out the implications associated with the contingency of regimes and social practices. Though political and fantasmatic logics *qua* ontological categories are highly formal, they are nonetheless the concrete products of history. (In Laclau's terms, following Marx's analysis of capital, they are 'real abstractions'.) In other words, no matter how robust political and fantasmatic logics are in relation to social logics and practices, their subject-dependence and their quasi-transcendental status serves to remind us of their historical character. This means that our *ontological framework is itself historical and ultimately contingent and contestable*. While ontological logics are axiomatic and universal, and exhibit for us something with real effects, they constitute nothing more – though nothing less – than the horizon of our theoretical world view. They comprise, in short, a *theoretical* horizon, which emerges from our *quotidian* experience and is thus in principle subject to historical displacement and contestation. As we will see shortly, the methodological possibility of incorporating this self-reflexive and self-critical ethos forms part of what William Connolly calls an onto-political interpretation.

The primacy of the political and the ethos of an articulatory practice

What then does the task of incorporating a self-reflexive and self-critical ethos into the concrete problematization and explanation of social phenomena entail? On the one hand, the ontological postulates of our approach concerning radical contingency have to inform the construction, investigation and explanation of social phenomena. On the other hand, we must develop a style of research that builds contingency into its very *modus operandi*, and which is open and attentive to possibilities disclosed by the research itself.

For us, the focus on contingency is also tied to the practice of critique. One mode of critique combines Derrida and Foucault, thus generating a 'deconstructive genealogy' of a social practice or regime. The task here is to reactivate and make evident options that were foreclosed during the emergence of a practice – the clashes and forces which are repressed or defeated – in order to show how the present configuration of practices relies on exclusions that reveal the non-necessary character of the present social formation, and to explore the consequences and potential effects of such 'repressions'. On the other hand, in the mode of what we could call an *onto-ethical* critique the task is to critically interrogate the conditions under which a particular social practice or regime grips its subjects *despite* its non-necessary character. This mode of critique furnishes us with a means of critically interrogating the will to (fantasmatic) closure. However, both modes of critique are informed by an ethos of exercising a fidelity to contingency itself, by displaying other possibilities for political decision and identification, as well as other modalities of identification. Together they contribute to a practice of *ethico-political interpretation*.

The practice of *ethico-political* interpretation shares certain affinities with cognate approaches. Of particular relevance in this regard is the work of Connolly, who highlights the centrality of the *ontopolitical* dimension involved in any socio-political analysis. The 'onto' in ontopolitical is impor- tant for him because it 'invokes a set of fundaments about necessities and possibilities of human beings', including what they are composed of, how they relate to nature, to each other, and so on (Connolly 1995: 1). By emphasizing the ontological dimension of experience Connolly questions a range of social science practices which deny their contestable ontological presuppositions by presuming one or another version of the 'primacy of epistemology' (Connolly 1995: 6–9). And to concede primacy to epistemology he explains 'is to think either that you have access to criteria of knowledge that leave the realm of ontology behind or that your epistemology provides neutral test procedures through which to pose and resolve every ontological question' (Connolly 1995: 5). Thus '*every* interpretation of political events, no matter how deeply it is sunk in a specific historical context or how high the pile of data upon which it sits, contains an ontopolitical dimension' (Connolly 1995: 1; emphasis added).

The master ontological postulate for Connolly is explicitly related to what Foucault has identified as the 'transcendental-empirical' doublet, which arises from the famous 'doubling of man' in the modern episteme, where the figure of 'man' appears in the 'ambiguous position' of being both 'an object of knowledge and . . . a subject that knows' (Foucault 1970: 312).[4] The need to emphasize the ontopolitical aspects of socio-political analysis is intimately linked to the role played by contingency in human affairs, and how we endeavour to cope with it: do we deny, register, or confront it? Taking this postulate as his *ontological* starting point, Connolly argues that positivists deny or repress it, or in registering it, as is the case with Charles Taylor and Michael Walzer, hermeneuticists try as far as possible to close it off. Though hermeneuticists may be more forthright and explicit about their turn to ontology, and though they may not deny contingency, they tend to domesticate the experience of contingency by rhetorically deploying their ontology in the service of closure. In short, Connolly advances an argument in favour of 'an ethicopolitical orientation that both asserts that the fundaments of being are mobile and that, in the ordinary course of events, social pressures accumulate to present particular formations of life as if they were intrinsic, solid, or complete' (Connolly 1995: 34). Critical reflexivity of this sort he argues may promote agonistic respect and critical responsiveness (Connolly 1995: 39–40), or what he and others elsewhere term 'presumptive generosity'. Here he advocates the loosening up of 'sedimented forms' in order 'to cultivate further a care for life (hopefully) *already there in protean form* – to incite energies on behalf of extending diversity where it is possible to do so' (Connolly 1995: 34; emphasis added).[5]

However, while Foucauldian genealogy and Derridean deconstruction provide important theoretical and ethical resources for Connolly, they are also *insufficient* for him (and for us) to pose an effective challenge to dominant modes of analysis, because they 'refuse to pursue the trail of affirmative possibility very far, out of a desire to minimize its implication in ontological assumptions'. He thus supplements these 'strategies of detachment' with a 'strategy of attachment' which emphasizes the positive dimension of an ontopolitical interpretation (Connolly 1995: 36):

> To practice this mode of interpretation, you project ontopolitical presumptions explicitly into detailed interpretations of actuality, acknowledging that your implicit projections surely exceed your explicit formulation of them and that your formulations exceed your capacity to demonstrate their truth. You challenge closure in the matrix by affirming the contestable character of your own projections, by offering readings of contemporary life that compete with alternative accounts, and by moving back and forth between these two levels.
>
> (Connolly 1995: 36)

Ethico-political interpretations of this sort require the mobilization and articulation of all three sorts of logic, each of which has to be understood in relation to the political dimension, as well as to the experience and registering of contingency. More precisely, within the context of our ethico-political interpretations, social logics are most relevant when the social dimension of practice is prominent. Here dislocatory experiences might be denied, concealed, or responded to in an ethical fashion, but the political dimension of practices and regimes are not foregrounded. On the other hand, political logics presuppose subjects for whom the dimension of the political is 'active', in the sense that the moment of dislocation has been taken up politically. Finally, fantasmatic logics have an important role to play in both social and political practices, for in both cases they account for the way in which contingency is concealed, thereby speaking to the ideological dimension of discursive relations. As we noted earlier, the ideological dimension combines readily with either the political or social dimensions. Indeed, it is worth recalling how the very identification of a political dimension as backgrounded presupposes some sense that there is a social norm which ought to be contested. And given that the ethical dimension can also be foregrounded in a political practice, it is clear that both normative and ethical aspects are constitutive features of our practice of critical explanation.

Logics versus self-interpretations and causal mechanisms

Our objective thus far has been to sketch out the character and status of logics. In this section, we return to the themes of Chapters 2 and 3 because we are now in a better position to contrast our conception of logics with contextualized self-interpretations and causal mechanisms. While the passage through self-interpretations is in our view a necessary starting point for any social science investigation, our understandings and explanations cannot rest on them alone. We share this insight with hermeneuticists, neo-positivists, and critical realists alike. However, we claim that logics offer us a way to move between the world of self-interpretations and practices on the one hand, and our social science explanations and critiques on the other, in a way that avoids some of the problems associated with the hermeneutical and naturalist approaches. This section fleshes out these various propositions.

It will be recalled that for hermeneuticists such as Winch, Taylor, and Bevir and Rhodes, self-interpretations constitute an essential starting point in social science research. Positivists and behaviouralists, by contrast, tend to concentrate exclusively on observable facts and 'public opinions', consigning the conditions of such facts and opinions to the background. This follows from the fact that positivists and behaviouralists inhabit a world of normal and routinized science, where issues of ontology have been naturalized and thus excluded from view. Whereas positivists reduce meanings and self-interpretations to facts and observable behaviour, hermeneuticists focus on the meanings and self-interpretations of actors. Indeed, the hermeneutical gesture adds something more to self-interpretations, either by rendering the implicit practices more explicit by adducing the rules that govern them, or by offering interpretations of the self-interpretations, which themselves are guided by certain ethical and normative impulses. This process generates what we have termed contextualized self-interpretations.

Importantly, however, there are moments when the background conditions that form our normal practices come to the fore. These are moments of failure or breakdown when the normal ways of going on are interrupted and their contingency is potentially disclosed. In Heidegger's terms, the figures of the 'broken hammer' or the 'misplaced screwdriver' are indicators of the taken-for-granted background conditions of existence. In the case of a broken or misplaced tool, for instance, we encounter an object's 'unreadiness-to-hand', in which our normal relationship with the tool, and its relationship with other tools and equipment, no longer holds. This leads us to focus on an important, if backgrounded, quality of objects as such: that we encounter them primarily as 'ready-to-hand' (i.e. available to do things with) rather than as 'present-at-hand' (i.e. available to be inspected in purely theoretical or cognitive terms).

We are thus led to focus on the being of such objects – their status as equipment which we use for certain assignments and tasks – as well as the ways in which we encounter things (their 'readiness to hand'). More fully, it shows that we encounter things in 'worlds' of related objects, whether it be the workshop, the classroom, or parliament, and that we ourselves are always 'in' these worlds, both in the sense that we are involved with things in this world, and in the sense that we inhabit these worlds. These experiences can, in short, help us to clarify the 'worldhood' of the world, the nature of our involvement in it, as well as the nature of ourselves. In Heidegger's terms they lead us to see ourselves fundamentally as 'being-in-the-world', not as agents or subjects that are outside and acting upon such worlds.

Moments of disruption and contingency are equally important in social and political terms, because they make possible new identifications and novel political practices. This, of course, recalls our discussion of the dimensions of practices and regimes – the social, political, ideological and ethical dimensions. But it also brings us to our three logics of critical explanation, whose role is to connect the world of practices and self-interpretations to our critical explanations of them. How exactly does this occur, and how does our account differ from the hermeneutical and naturalist alternatives?

As we noted above, a hermeneutical inquiry not only pushes the study of society beyond the given facts and behaviour to the meaning and interpretation of facts, but it also moves beyond self-interpretations to the study of rules and the interpretation of self-interpretations. Hermeneuticists thus seek to render the implicit explicit and to interpret self-interpretations, yielding contextualized self-interpretations. And while this investigative practice is particularly evident when we encounter institutions and activities that are not readily understood, such as those of a 'primitive society', it is also required to make sense of practices that are 'closer to home' so to speak. This is because those involved in a practice may not be conscious of the rules they follow, nor able to explicate the rules they follow with any certainty, nor defend them if challenged. Think, for instance, of our normal use of a language, where people speak and write without necessarily being able to furnish the explicit rules it presupposes.

Notwithstanding the advantages of the hermeneutical perspective, our use of logics goes further than this, for the latter not only focus our attention on the rules or grammar that enable us to characterize and even criticize a phenomenon, but they also allow us to disclose the structures and conditions that make those rules possible. Importantly, both tasks are discharged in an ontologically-informed and analytically parsimonious way. The first task is accomplished by what we have called social logics, while the second involves the mobilization of our other two sorts of logic – political and fantasmatic logics – in order to critically explain practices. These logics enable us to account for the institution, contestation and sedimentation of social practices and regimes. They 'go beyond' contextualized self-interpretations because they speak to the latter's contingent constitution and sedimentation, focusing attention on the way their 'ignoble origins' are generally forgotten or covered over as the practices and their self-understanding are then lived out (Nietzsche 1973: 177).

Now it is clear that those who stress the role of causal mechanisms also go beyond the field of self-interpretations. For example, though Elster stresses the indeterminacy of their triggering and interaction, he uses mechanisms to provide a causal connection between phenomena and events. But he brackets the ontological conditions of possibility of these mechanisms, and underplays their organic and dynamic relation to self-interpretations and their contexts. More precisely, according to this model, mechanisms are atomic units which can be combined to form molecular units in which the identities of the atomic units are not moderated by the context in which they are used.[6] This view ignores the parasitic relationship between social processes and human practices. In other words, Elster short-circuits the passage through the subject by conceiving mechanisms as a set of 'abstract essences' or free standing 'tools' that are not tied to any ontology, and which can be applied to different contexts without modification.

For us, by contrast, logics are always linked to a particular field of self-interpretations. Social logics, in particular, provide access to the practices under investigation, enabling us to grasp the point of a practice or institution, as well as the rules and structures that organize them. And while concrete social logics may occasionally yield a paradigm with which to explore and explain similar cases – they may in other words be generalizable – they are nonetheless understood as entities which are modified through articulation in each particular case. Social logics require therefore a 'passage through the self-interpretations of subjects', and they provide a bridge between description/characterization and explanation/critique. Political and fantasmatic logics are, of course, also tied to specific practices and self-interpretations when deployed, even if their conceptual character can be formalized to a greater degree than is possible for social logics. In any fully-fledged critical explanation of a phenomenon, political and fantasmatic logics have to be *articulated* with a range of social logics together with the empirical contexts they inform and within which they function. The entire logic of explanation thus requires the passage through self-interpretations.

In contrast to Elster's picture, Roy Bhaskar's stress on causal mechanisms does move us to the ontological level. He begins by correctly rejecting the 'epistemic fallacy', which reduces and thus restricts the investigation of being to our knowledge claims about it. Thus, as we saw in Chapter 1, Bhaskar and his school are concerned with the way the world has to be in order for knowledge claims to be possible at all. And his answer is that the world is composed of an underlying set of *real objects* or *structures* with specific properties and generative mechanisms. The latter are presupposed in our actions and experiences at the phenomenological level, and they make possible our knowledge of the world at the epistemological level.

The problem with this approach, however, is that it restricts the understanding of ontology to an elaboration of the sorts of objects and mechanisms that make up the (social) world. By contrast, our ontology is not reducible to an inventory of the kinds of things in the world – the 'furniture of the world', so to speak. Indeed, in our view this does not really break with the 'epistemic fallacy' at all, but displaces the latter to a deeper level of 'real objects', which though not necessarily visible in our experience of them, still bring about certain outcomes or effects. Ontology in our view is not only about the different *kinds* of things in the world, but is more importantly about the *being* of these beings. We follow Heidegger here by focusing on the historicity and contingency of beings – and not just on the contingent interaction of fully constituted causal mechanisms – wherein the meaning and identity of beings depends on the historical and relational contexts in which they appear.

As against Bhaskar, therefore, we cannot sever beings from the relational contexts in which they appear, and from the particular interpretations that constitute their meaning. And while it is possible to speak of political and fantasmatic logics under the ontological aspect in isolation from the relational contexts in which they function, these constructs are not to be understood as entities with a fixed set of properties at all – 'real things' as it were – but purely formal constructs or logics, which we call 'real abstractions', that come into operation in particular situations. They are better understood as quasi-transcendental 'infrastructures' (cf. Gasché 1986: 109–251), which render phenomena possible and impossible, rather than real and fixed things with definite properties as Bhaskar maintains. Once again, in Bhaskar's account there is a short-circuiting of the necessary and complex relationship between the ontical and ontological levels of analysis. Social structures (or 'society') – 'the ever-present condition (material cause) and the continually reproduced outcome of human agency' (Bhaskar 1998: 34–5) – are ultimately privileged in this picture, as they constitute the essential and necessary 'properties' that make societies 'possible objects of knowledge' (Bhaskar 1998).[7] They are what Bhaskar calls 'intransitive objects': 'things [that] exist and act independently of our descriptions' (Bhaskar 1975: 250). In his account of structure and agency, then, he thus privileges the role of structures, which are separated from subjects and agency, but which define for them the potential range of outcomes and strategies (Hay 1995, 2002). What this does not fully take on board, as Laclau has pointed out, is the transitive nature of the transitive-intransitive distinction (Laclau in Laclau and Bhaskar 1998: 10, 13).

Several consequences follow from our account of logics. Methodologically, we argue that the development of an explanation must start with intentions and self-interpretations. It is absolutely crucial to pass through subjects' self-interpretations, not only as part of the process of problematization, but also to arrive at an understanding of the character of social logics, as well as political and fantasmatic logics. In conceptual terms, logics are aligned with self-interpretations against causal mechanisms, because it is through self-interpretations and thick descriptions that the ontic is connected to the ontological, and social logics connected with political and fantasmatic logics. However, as we will see in more detail in Chapter 6, reference to self-interpretations and thick descriptions does not preclude the possibility of generalizability. Contextualized self-interpretations are necessary but not sufficient components of a social science explanation. Showing why and how this is possible allows us to carve out a space beyond the domains of causal laws and mechanisms on the one hand, and self-interpretations and thick descriptions on the other.

Two further implications flow from our account. In the first place, it is clear that social logics are context-dependent constructions that are retroductively posited as a function of the rules and structures that inform practices and regimes. They thus allow us to characterize the relational practices and identities under investigation. By contrast, political and fantasmatic logics are formal constructs that enable us to account for orders and practices in a variety of historical contexts. However, except in forming the basis of our theoretical horizon, they do not predetermine our explanations and critical engagements. In other words, while they provide the means for critical explanation, political and fantasmatic logics do not determine the outcomes. Instead, they make the latter possible by directing our attention to those dimensions and aspects of phenomena that make explanations and critiques possible. They offer us an ontologically-informed grammar with which to conduct our empirical investigations, enabling us to generate explanations which are always concrete and singular.

This means, in the second instance, that the process of social science explanation ought to be understood in terms of *articulation* rather than subsumption. It is evident from our account that any fully-fledged *explanans* contains a *plurality* of different kinds of logics and concepts, which have to be linked together to critically explain. This raises a question about the conditions under which it is possible to bring together these heterogeneous elements into an explanation without subsuming them under higher-order laws or abstractions and without falling into a pure descriptivism. In the following chapter, we argue that we should understand critical explanation as part of an articulatory practice, by which we mean 'any practice establishing a relation among elements such that their identity is modified as a result of the articulatory practice' (Laclau and Mouffe 1985: 105).

Conclusion

We now have the elements in place to show how our conception of social science explanation provides a more persuasive alternative to its hermeneutical and naturalist counterparts. Siding with hermeneutics against naturalism we argue that contextualized self-interpretations are an essential and ineluctable aspect of any critical explanation. But now siding with naturalism, we argue that critical explanations cannot be reduced to contextualized self-interpretations, because we bring to each particular object of study a set of concepts and logics that necessarily transcends the particularity of context.

The ontological framework that makes possible our approach has two key dimensions, which centre on the notion of subjectivity. These are what might be called the hermeneutic-structural and the poststructural dimensions. The former highlights the presumptive centrality of the self-interpretations of subjects in social science explanations. But it is also important to recognize in this regard that discursive practices exhibit varying degrees of sedimentation, ranging from regimes and institutions to social habits. While the social logics structuring them are literally buoyed up by subjects – they do not exist except through the activity of subjects – they are not necessarily cognitively accessible to subjects, at least not immediately and without some form of intervention. This means that logics can have significant explanatory and critical leverage independently of the consciously held self-interpretations of agents. Certainly, social logics are products of past understandings, interpretations and decisions, but they tend to secure a degree of autonomy and not insignificant force when sedimented into practices and regimes. This is one reason why the assent of agents is not conclusive or exhaustive of an explanation's validity.

On the other hand, the poststructural dimension highlights the way in which social structures are never complete in themselves by foregrounding the dislocatory nature of the symbolic order (the 'real' in Lacanian terms) and thus the possible emergence of political subjectivity as such. This means that the hermeneutic-structural dimension fails to exhaust our particular ontological framework. It is at this point that political and fantasmatic logics come into play, thus enabling us to generate critical accounts of the constitution and dissolution of social structures themselves. This is because they assist in the process of revealing and explaining the non-necessary character of social logics and the practices they sustain and animate. This enables us to generate critical explanations that are both sensitive to context and explicit about their ontological, ethical, normative, and sociological presuppositions.

We can approach the character and relation between the three logics, as well as the implications they carry for issues of critique, by means of a question. If social logics are firmly embedded in what Laclau calls 'descriptive-normative' complexes (Laclau 2004), what is the status of political and fantasmatic logics? For while it is clear that the content of social logics will be as varied as the cases being analysed, it is tempting to suggest that political and fantasmatic logics are far more robust, travelling more or less in tact from one case to another; after all there appear to be only *two* political logics which are closely connected and *one* logic of fantasy. There is a sense in which this is right, but also a sense in which it is misleading. It is right because political and fantasmatic logics lend themselves to quasi-transcendental formalization. This is because their formal identity arises out of an inquiry into the conditions that make possible (and impossible) the operation of discursive practices or social logics as such. Or, to put it in more pointed terms, they come as answers to questions about the conditions of possibility of descriptive-normative complexes themselves. And this, in turn, relies on presuppositions that are valid for *all* signifying and libidinal practices, namely, the constitutive openness of the social, the two fundamental axes of discourse, and the two fundamental axes of enjoyment. In other words, these presuppositions function as axioms. However, this way of speaking can be misleading for two separate reasons. First, the empirical instantiation of political and fantasmatic logics can be as varied as the practices being analysed. The rhetorical moves involved in constructing chains of equivalence or in breaking them down are as varied as the social contexts in which they function. And the same is true for fantasmatic logics: there may only be one fantasmatic mode of enjoyment (conceived as a function of closure), but the way this is fleshed out will be as varied as the contexts in which it is operative.[8] The second reason why it is misleading to suggest that political and fantasmatic logics escape the parameters of the descriptive-normative complex is related to the character of social science as such, namely, its inability to resolve what Foucault calls the empirico-transcendental doublet. This does not only mean that we, as analysts, must be open to the possibility that political and fantasmatic logics may in confronting a set of cases require modification or even abandonment. It also means we should be as explicit as possible about the sociological, ethical, and normative parameters of our critical analysis.

Consider the ethical aspect for example. Here, the very positing of fantasmatic closure as a response by the subject to an ontological openness raises the question of what other possible responses there might be; and, indeed, whether one or another response might be more attractive. In fact, a subject's possible responses to such (ontologically presupposed) openness is precisely what carves out for Lacan the domain of ethics, because it suggests the possibility of 'crossing the fantasy' (cf. Boucher *et al.* 2005).[9] Taken together, then, the ethical and political dimensions of social reality underline the radical historicity of social practices as such and thus the possibility of engaging with them critically.

We can focus on the character of our critical explanations to develop one final contrast between our poststructuralist approach, on the one hand, and the hermeneutical and naturalist approaches on the other. As we argued earlier, if naturalists offer the prospect of a causal explanation by *subsuming* the phenomena under *universal laws* or *general mechanisms*, and if hermeneuticists explain via the use of *particular contextualized interpretations*, our approach conceives of explanation in terms of a *critical and articulated assemblage of logics*. Our parsimonious theoretical grammar consisting of logics and dimensions thus contributes to a kind of 'middle-range theorizing', which moves between empirical phenomena, consisting of self-interpretations and practices, and our underlying ontological premises. Our task is thus 'to *re-describe* the ontical level in terms of the distinctions brought about by [our] ontology' (Laclau 2004: 323; emphasis added). With this in mind, we move to a more systematic investigation of the methodological, epistemological, and critical implications of our approach.

6 Articulation

> There is no general law, there is no general rule ... There are only contexts, and this is why deconstructive negotiation cannot produce general rules, 'methods'. It must be adjusted to each case, to each moment without, however, the conclusion being a relativism or empiricism.
>
> (Derrida 2002: 17)

In the last chapter we delineated our understanding of logics in the social sciences and set out three types of logic that constitute the main components of our explanatory framework. Nevertheless, a number of methodological and epistemological questions were either left unaddressed or not addressed systematically enough. How do we conceptualize the relationship between theoretical categories and empirical analysis? On what grounds, for example, do we identify empirical features as features of a social or political logic, or how do we distinguish between a dislocation and an antagonism in social reality? And how should one best understand the way in which different theoretical and empirical elements come together to form an explanatory narrative? What is the epistemological and methodological status of a single case study within our approach, and what is the role of comparative research in deepening, modifying and 'testing' our critical explanations? Finally, what are the implications of our approach for questions about hypothesis-generation, validation, generalization, and theory-building?

This chapter responds to these questions by developing the concept and practice of *articulation*. For us, articulation serves as a means to conceptualize the way we conduct research in the social sciences, while also contributing to our overall understanding of the logic of critical explanation. Following the logic of our approach we begin with the practice of problematization, taking the opportunity to illustrate our understanding of this concept by problematizing recent changes in the UK's higher education system. Then, in endeavouring to address some of the theoretical and methodological issues that arise from our empirical illustration, and taking our cue from Derrida's remarks in the epigraph of this chapter, we construct the question of social science explanation as a *problem of subsumption*.[1] We take the latter to consist of four inter-related elements. First, a conception of employing laws, general rules, or causal generalizations to explain specific cases, in which a variety of empirical elements, or a set of empirical cases, are subsumed under overarching universal laws, causal mechanisms, or law-like causal generalization. Second, a particular understanding of the relationship between a concept and an object, in which the former is seen to exhaust completely or contain the latter. Third, the idea that the process of applying abstract concepts to concrete phenomena leaves the former untouched by the practice of application itself. Fourth, in what amounts to a pure inversion of the foregoing, a kind of 'empiricism' or 'pure descriptivism', in which particular empirical cases or self-interpretations are assumed to constitute 'explanations in themselves'.

Throughout our book we have contrasted our own understanding of social science explanation with the positivist and hermeneutical conceptions. From the point of view of naturalism, a particular empirical instance is ideally explained when it is *subsumed* by a universal causal law, law-like statement or causal mechanism. In this conception of explanation, individual variations between cases are secondary to the law or mechanism, the latter remaining intact as they are 'applied' to explain successive cases. From a hermeneutical point of view, a particular empirical instance is ideally explained in so far as this case is contextualized through the process of thick description and by interpreting the self-interpretations of relevant actors. Whereas naturalism tends to affirm subsumption as an ideal, hermeneutics tends to reject subsumption as an ideal. At one extreme we have a kind of pure universalism, and at the other extreme we have a form of pure particularism. Thus, at one end of the spectrum 'we find claims for universal principles that cut across particular social contexts', while at the other we encounter 'claims that attempts to describe and explain political phenomena' which 'have no means of escaping particular social contexts' (Tilly and Goodin 2006: 9).

Of course, these are no more than ideal types, which means that in practice various representatives of these traditions will fall somewhere on a spectrum ranging from laws to mechanisms to contextualized self-interpretations. Nevertheless, it is significant that this spectrum has been defined with reference to the causal law paradigm which we construe in terms of the subsumptive ideal, which is not so surprising given the powerful hegemonic sway of naturalism in the social sciences. In the place of subsumption, therefore, we open up an alternative theoretical space that is defined by the principle of articulation. After presenting our understanding of this concept, as well as the way it modifies our conception of social science explanation, we explore the epistemological and methodological implications that follow from its adoption. We show how the concept of articulation allows us to develop a particular understanding of judgement and naming, while also shedding light on the notion of logics as against contextualized self-interpretations and mechanisms. We then spell out the implications of our 'method' of articulatory practice for issues of critique. Finally, focussing on the role cases and comparison can play in our approach, we reflect on how a practice of articulation transforms our understanding of research methodology into one better conceived in terms of research strategies.

Problematization

Our approach to social and political analysis is a species of *problem-driven*, rather than *method-* or purely *theory-driven* research. In Chapter 1, we noted that method-driven approaches are motivated more by the techniques of data-gathering and analysis than by a concern with the empirical phenomena under investigation, while theory-driven research aims 'to vindicate a particular theory' rather than illuminate a problem that is specified independently of the theory' (Shapiro 2002: 601). At the same time, our problem-driven approach ought not to be confused with problem-solving research, as the latter tends to assume the existence of certain social structures or rules, as well as the assumptions of the dominant theories of such reality, and then operates within them (Cox 1981b: 129–30; cf. Popper 1999).

For us, by contrast, an object of study is *constructed*. This means that a range of disparate empirical phenomena have to be constituted *as* a problem, and the problem has to be located at the appropriate level of abstraction and complexity. Thus our approach shares a family resemblance with Foucault's practice of problematization, which in his view synthesized the archaeological and genealogical methods of analysis.[2] In a classic formulation, Foucault argues that the technique is not a matter of analysing 'behaviour or ideas, nor societies and their "ideologies", but the *problematizations* through which being offers itself to be, necessarily, thought – and the *practices* on the basis of which these problematizations are formed' (Foucault 1985: 11–12). More specifically, to *problematize* in the domain of 'politics' for Foucault is to interrogate the latter about what 'it has to say about the problems with which it [is] confronted' (Foucault 1997: 115). It concerns 'a movement of critical analysis in which one tries to see how the different solutions to a problem have been constructed; but also how these different solutions result from a specific form of problematization' (Foucault 1997: 118–19). The very terms 'constitution', 'construction' and 'formed' already hint at the centrality we will attribute to the category of articulation.

The strategy of problematization has been adopted by a number of poststructuralists and critical theorists. In *National Deconstruction*, for example, David Campbell problematizes the dominant practical and academic problematizations of the conflict in Bosnia, concentrating on the main political forces which were party to the conflict inside the country, as well as those involved in the former Yugoslavia 'at arm's length' (such as the EU, USA and so forth). He shows how 'the Bosnian problem' was thought and constituted primarily in terms of a struggle between primordial ethnic and national groups, arguing that this ideological convergence among the dominant representations precluded any political solution other than those of modulating or ameliorating an insurmountable ethno-nationalist conflict (Campbell 1998).

In a similar vein, Nikolas Rose follows Foucault in pointing out how the 'problem of government' has tended to be framed by a certain understanding of freedom as the absence of coercion or domination, generating very specific questions about 'who holds power', 'how it can be secured and maintained', and 'whether it is legitimate', questions which shaped a wide range of fields, involving the state, the law, the market, the family, and so on. Rose seeks to problematize this series of problematizations by conducting a genealogy of freedom. By showing how the conception of freedom that dominates much of our thought and action is not a necessary one, he seeks to open up a space from which to gain a certain critical leverage, as well as exploring other ways of becoming. He takes the present as 'an array of problems and questions' that demand problematization so as to make current practices amenable 'to action by the action of thought' (Rose 1999: 11). For example, he argues that we 'must abandon the political calculus of domination and liberation' because concrete analysis reveals that 'power also acts through practices that "make up subjects" as free persons' (Rose 1999: 95).

Problematizing higher education reforms in the UK

Initial research into the changing face of higher education in the UK should also, in our view, start by problematizing the different ways it has been problematized by key social actors. For the last twenty years, especially since the publication of the 1985 green paper 'Higher Education into the 1980s', successive governments and politicians of various hues have constructed the problem of the universities as one of making the latter serve the national economy 'more effectively'; as one of expanding the numbers of students who attend universities; as one of developing globally competitive tertiary educational institutions; as one of driving down the unit costs of this expansion for the state and taxpayer alike; and so on. The 'solutions' to the problems identified have included a greater role for markets and private capital to encourage competition between and within universities, the expansion of tertiary institutions, the introduction of student loans and the charging of student fees, as well as the development of a range of audit practices to increase the accountability of researchers and teachers working in universities, such as the Research Assessment Exercises (RAE) and the Teaching Quality Audits (TQA).[3]

This problematization has resulted in policies and programmes that have led to rapid changes in the nature and functioning of UK universities. Stated baldly, there has been a shift from a mainly elitist, self-regulating, publicly funded system of higher education, where research was principally 'pure' and supposedly disinterested, to a more mass-based system that is only partially funded by the public purse (Trow 1994, 1998). In this new regime of practices, university teaching and research is strongly encouraged to support the interests of the wider society and economy, and universities have become more tightly regulated through a variety of economic and audit measures.[4]

Senior university managers and administrators, for their part, have constructed the problem of the universities largely in terms of adjusting and reforming their respective institutions to respond rationally and reasonably to the challenges within the constraints of the new regime. Acting individually and collectively, for example, vice chancellors and senior managers have sought at times to modify the new audit practices in ways that soften the impact of the changes on their staff and students, or have striven to interpret and implement the changes in a creative fashion. In the main, however, they have been unable or unwilling to challenge the construction and implementation of the new policies and practices.

The convergence between governments and senior managers arises in part because both sets of problematizations are underpinned by a similar understanding of the character and role of universities in relation to the wider institutional and structural contexts within which they function. From this perspective, the restructuring of the university system is perceived to be a necessary response to the wider political and socio-economic shifts associated with the inexorable developments of market economies and economic globalization (see Fairclough 2000). Viewed against this background, if universities are to provide the appropriate goods and services for their respective clients and consumers in an efficient fashion, they can do little more than accommodate themselves to these new contexts by behaving even more like corporations and businesses. Such interpretations suggest that the phenomena under consideration are governed by causal laws, implying that the changes are akin to natural processes beyond social and political control. Not only does this partake of a subsumptive logic of explanation, in which a variety of effects in a number of different contexts are accounted for by means of robust causal statements, but there is little questioning of the supposed inevitability and over-powering force of socio-economic development itself, and little or no prospect for developing alternative conceptions of the university in liberal democratic societies.

While government officials and manager-academics have tended to advocate, implement, and accommodate themselves to higher education reforms, students and employee-academics have tended to be more sceptical about the benefits of these reforms. While the growing commercialization and consumerization of higher education (Willmott 2003) has not been the central target of student protests, a related concern has: tuition fees and the prospect of long-term loan debts. The generally accepted view is that ordinary academics, for their part, have also tended to experience negatively the immediate consequences of the new regimes and practices on their identities, work practices and wages. Though this category of 'ordinary academics' is by no means homogenous, one could say that they and their unions have focussed their critical gaze on the changing ways in which governments and senior managers have sought to control and dominate academic staff, in their endeavours to make them more productive, competitive and efficient.

In this general context, an apparent puzzle has emerged concerning the lack of meaningful resistance by academics to the new regime of audit practices: in spite of the 'increasingly vocal dissatisfaction' with the new regimes, there appears to be no effective and 'publicly articulated' critique of audit rationality (Shore and Wright 2000: 80). For purposes of illustrating our logics approach, then, we shall pick up and develop this problem into a problematization. The problem itself has often been posed in the following terms: Why have academics proved so compliant, even complicit, in accepting the changes they are experiencing, especially when they recognize them to be contingent and problematic? Some radical critics have noted the passive and complicitous response of academics by correlating changes in the academic labour process – the 'intensification of tasks', deskilling, the loss of autonomy in the work process, and so on, all of which reduce job satisfaction – with their mute and ineffective complaints.[5] Indeed, it is sometimes argued that academics often collude in these practices of 'coercive accountability' by reluctantly or willingly 'policing . . . their colleagues and themselves' (Brenneis, Shore, and Wright 2005: 8)[6] or by maintaining a 'disgraceful silence on these matters' (Howie 2005: 5–6).[7]

However, there is a problem with invoking the 'force' of change, in conjunction with 'passivity' or 'lack of will power', as the key to accounting for the 'audit revolution' in higher education. This is largely because it encourages one to overemphasize the absence of effective resistance to the virtual exclusion of other types of response. In short, this interpretation presents an overly homogeneous picture that tends to reinforce the 'causal law' paradigm, while smoothing over the 'combined and uneven' effects and responses in the academic field.

Another group of scholars has questioned this simple picture by focussing more closely on the full scope of academics' self-interpretations.[8] They suggest that passivity and ineffective resistance is not a particularly accurate way of characterizing the situation 'on the ground'. For a start, it does not reflect the ways in which academics have interpreted and used the reforms to their own advantage. In addition, it does not acknowledge the existence of resistance, nor the varied forms this may take. For example, Worthington and Hodgson sketch out a typology of resistance strategies or subject positions adopted by academics, classifying them as 'devolvers', 'shirkers', 'ditherers', and 'deceivers' (Worthington and Hodgson 2005). Trowler, too, proposes a nuanced approach which acknowledges that policy implementation will meet with a range of academic responses: 'with compliance (both enthusiastic and reluctant), with resistance, with coping strategies, and with attempts to reconstruct the policy during the implementation phase' (Trowler 1998: 153), though it is worth pointing out that in her research Morley found that 'for every one informant who celebrates audit, there are at least ten who decry it' (Morley 2005: 86).

These interpretations not only highlight the uneven and varied terrain of higher education, in which only about 50 per cent of academics are on permanent contracts, while the rest make do with fixed-term, part-time, or hourly-paid contracts, but they also caution against the monolithic compliance hypothesis implied by 'causal law' models relied upon by both enthusiasts and detractors of market and audit reforms. Importantly, they open up a research agenda that focuses on the diverse range of responses that do not comply with the new practices (see Prichard and Willmott 1997: 292; Trowler 1998; Worthington and Hodgson 2005).

Contextualized self-interpretations are thus crucial in helping us to better refine and understand our problem. We are thus able to formulate the question in broader and less pre-emptive terms. Why are higher education audit reforms frequently not abandoned or actively resisted by academics? Or, to put it in even stronger terms, why are these reforms often allowed to intensify further, becoming even more deeply institutionalized and sedimented in UK universities? Indeed, our problematization of existing problematizations can be reiterated and expressed in more Foucauldian terms. Why is it that academics have insisted with such vehemence that they are increasingly exploited and dominated by the new regime, and yet powerless and impotent to resist such changes?

Viewed from our logics perspective, we seek to connect this problematization to a range of related questions: How are we to characterize the new phenomena and practices? Where did this new regime of practices come from, and how and why has it been installed so rapidly? Where there is discontent amongst academics why does this rarely translate into effective political protest and resistance? How can we account for the way in which these new discursive practices have managed to grip subjects, especially when they are opposed to them?

The turn to logics: towards a retroductive explanation

We recall from Chapter 1 that problematization constitutes the first of three moments in the overall logic of critical explanation. The second moment entails the furnishing of a retroductive explanation that addresses key features which emerge out of our initial problematization. In our approach this involves identifying the relevant social, political, and fantasmatic logics. In furnishing this retroductive explanation, we must thus start by *characterizing* the practices under investigation. To phrase it in Foucauldian terms, we begin with a process of archaeological bracketing that seeks to identify a domain of objects and practices in need of analysis and critique, before then providing a genealogical accounting that explains their political and ideological emergence. This involves the task of retroductively identifying the assemblage of *social logics* that are currently being installed in UK universities. For purposes of illustration, we start by positing the operation of four such logics – competition, atomisation, hierarchy, and instrumentalization – which when articulated together enable us to characterize the emergent regime of audit practices.

To begin, we could say that the rules of many practices linked to the audit regime are governed by a *logic of competition*, which in our view captures the ways that actors interact with each other as rivals. They capture the way in which universities *qua* producers of knowledge and skill commodities compete to secure income from students and from research councils and private companies; the way *students* compete to secure positions and scholarships in highly ranked universities; and the way *schools, departments, and individual academic staff* compete to maximize their share of university resources.[9] This logic of competition, which is of course central to market practices generally, has to be artificially triggered in contexts such as universities by means of audit techniques which make diverse products and services comparable.[10]

It is clear that the social logics of competition interact with other social logics in the context of new public management, marketization, and commodification discourses. For example, *logics of atomisation* could be said to describe patterns of discursive articulation that individuate institutions and persons as independent entities, thus isolating them from each other, while abstracting from them their virtues, skills, and other attributes. They operate in such a way as to downplay the social or structural aspect of success and failure in the self-understanding of persons and institutions, leaving them to view themselves as individually responsible for their successes and failures. *Logics of hierarchy* embrace a range of top-down modes of governance, including some forms of collegial governance structures. Here, they describe the way universities are increasingly understood by academics to be governed in the way that firms are governed, namely, by chief executives who have Hobbesian-like authority to make snap decisions and thus respond quickly and firmly to external audit demands and (global) market trends, seeking out entrepreneurial advantage wherever possible (Robins and Webster 2002: 13; Wright 2004: 84). Finally, we could add *logics of instrumentalization*, which operate in such a way as to downplay the potentially intrinsic and processual qualities of teaching and research in favour of their instrumental or exchange value, whether from the point of view of academics or students (Howie 2005: 4; Willmott 1995: 1021).

We can thus pinpoint four possible social logics informing the practices of the new regime. The underlying drive of the logics of competition is to render all things commensurable and comparable, which in turn tends to feed and reinforce logics of atomisation and hierarchical governance, as well as processes of instrumentalization, in which academic activities are converted into commodities whose quality – via the various audit regimes – can be ascertained and enhanced numerically. The important point to keep in mind here is how, for us, the identification and operation of social logics requires some reference to – or passage through – the self-interpretations of subjects. Nevertheless, having gone some way to establishing *what* the logics structuring the various audit practices in higher education are, we can also ask *why* and *how* they came about and continue to be sustained. This turns our attention to the operation of political and fantasmatic logics.

Political and fantasmatic logics

In order to account for the installation and grip of the audit practices in UK universities – the logic of its emergence and radical institution, and the way in which it recruits, grips and governs subjects – we have to consider the problem at both the 'macro' and 'micro' levels, even though we accept that this distinction is not ontological, but pragmatic or 'technological' (Rose 1999: 5–6). The macro-micro contrast is connected to our distinction between regimes and practices, though the precise elements of these contrasts depends on the problem being investigated. For heuristic purposes, then, let us fix the notion of regime here at the level of the state government and audit practices at the level of the university. This suggests that we focus our analysis both on the role of the New Right project in challenging and re-structuring the crisis-ridden post-war consensus in the 1970s and 1980s, in which the universities were but one element in an overall hegemonic project designed to install a new political settlement, *and* on the micro-dynamics by which these new ideas and practices were installed in the universities themselves.

Obviously, in this limited illustration, we cannot provide a comprehensive account of these complex processes. Nonetheless, we can suggest ways in which an analysis of regimes at different levels reveals how political logics of equivalence were mobilized to shift the terrain away from the post-war consensus. In the context of a deepening crisis and dislocation, New Right politicians, ideologues and activists during the 1970s sought to link together a range of diverse demands into a project that publicly contested the failing Keynesian welfare state project, which had been installed in the UK after the Second World War. They did so in the name of a project that welded together the demands for a 'free economy', a 'strong state' and traditional morality in a radical new mix (Gamble 1994). As many analysts have shown, this involved a form of populist politics that successfully divided the existing 'one nation' welfare state consensus into two camps, pitting those in favour of the newly proposed project against those associated with the post-war consensus (Gamble 1994; Hall 1983, 1988; Jessop *et al.* 1988; King 1987; Smith 1994).

Amongst the many institutions and groups that were made equivalent, and then targeted, by this new project – public sector workers, trade unions, teachers, doctors, lawyers, immigrants and gays, and so forth – it is not surprising that universities, academics and state-subsidized students also came under fire. Indeed Thatcher's higher education reforms began in dramatic fashion in 1981, less than two years after her election, when funding to universities was cut by an average of 17 per cent, pitching annual increases thereafter at below inflation rates. But it was the 1985 Jarratt Report that explicitly re-envisioned universities in the mould of corporations competing in a higher education market and requiring much tighter management structures (Jarratt 1985; Shore and Wright 2000: 67; Wright 2004: 84). From then on, 'Vice Chancellors were re-baptized as "chief executives", departments became "cost centres", and university administrators became "managers"' of educational providers (Shore and Wright 2000: 104). Subsequent Reports have reinforced this view, praising what advances were made, and calling for still further reform (e.g. the Dearing Report (1997) and the Lambert Report (2003)) (Wright 2004).

In this incipient discourse, academics and universities were easily targeted as an outmoded and inefficient obstacle to realizing the ideals of market competition, lower public spending, and greater consumer accountability. For example, in the period preceding the new legislation, Mrs Thatcher slyly summed up her antipathy to the universities in an interview with *The Daily Telegraph* by asking: 'Why is it that a lot of the people who want to build up a business never get to university, don't want to go to university, but will employ a lot of university people?' (*Daily Telegraph*, 18 September 1984 cited in Young 1989: 414). It is not difficult to discern the logic of fantasy at work in her discourse in these and similar representations of universities and academics. The latter are unfavourably compared with hard-working, self-made 'men' who do not require a university education to succeed in the competitive world of business and industry. By contrast, lecturers and students are often portrayed as 'privileged', 'lazy', 'inefficient', 'sexually corrupting', 'morally deviant', and so forth.[11] What is important to highlight here is that for something to function fantasmatically – the image of the lazy or free-riding academic or, somewhat contradictorily, the academic who industriously sets out to 'milk the system' – it needs to come to embody the general public's view, or at least the relevant audience's view, of the *typical* academic, especially if this is officially denied when individuals are confronted with the 'facts', or indeed even if – as no doubt is the case – there are some academics who 'in fact' conform to this image. The function of these fantasies is to organize a subject's own mode of enjoyment by imagining how academics enjoy themselves, usually at its expense.

From our perspective, political and fantasmatic logics help us to furnish an account of how and why the institutionalization of audit practices became a goal at state level. They do this because they make visible and enable us to construct a narrative that typically comprises a threat, an obstacle, and the formulation of the problem which sets the terms of debate, and the range of possible policy solutions (see Levidow 2002: 234). In the case of the universities in this context, academics and students were often named as an obstacle to the goals of economic competitiveness, efficient public spending, and consumer accountability. They were thus ripe for neo-liberal 'solutions' requiring the implementation of market competition, greater transparency, and consumer accountability.

In sum, then, the recent university reforms make sense against the background of a Thatcher legacy of civil service and public sector reforms, which sought to reduce public expenditure by introducing simulated market environments that were structured around centrally managed targets (via the creation of the National Audit Office in 1983). And in this new regime public servants and individuals generally would compete with one another to cut through bureaucratic inefficiencies. As far as higher education was concerned, it was clear that the Thatcher government considered universities to have failed the economy (DES 1987; Kogan and Kogan 1983: Chapters 1 and 8; Shore and Wright 2000: 67). Moreover, higher education reforms were not halted in the Major and Blair years. In fact one could argue that they have been accelerated by the post-Thatcher Conservative Party and New Labour, who have both striven to implement and even extend many aspects of the New Right programme. The main architects of New Labour appear to be still very much in the thrall of a fantasy in which the market functions as a kind of panacea, promising to solve all problems through increased competition, greater choice and consumer responsiveness (see Wright 2004).

If we turn now to discern the logics through which audit practices were instituted at the level of universities, we can point to the various ways in which many senior university administrators and a new cadre of 'manager academics' embraced them. Though they would often seek to ease the impact upon their staff, such reforms were clearly compatible with the prospects of restructuring their institutions and advancing their careers. In a similar way, the new audit practices offered avenues for some 'ordinary academics' to advance their careers. But, overall, the responses have been multiple and uneven. For example, there have been instances of resistance, where some of the more extreme elements of the new programmes were contested. One such instance of overt resistance took place in 1988 when the AUT successfully challenged vice-chancellors' attempt to link targets with appraisal for differential pay and promotions (Pollitt 1993: 80). Similarly, while the security of tenure was lost in the 1988 *Education Reform Act*, the profession successfully lobbied for 'the insertion of a formal statement of academic freedom' (Shore and Wright 2000: 68). Of direct relevance to the attempt to install audit practices was the successful revolt against the QAA in March 2001 led by the LSE, and followed closely by UCL, Oxford, Cambridge, Edinburgh and Birmingham, who threatened to set up their own separate quality assurance schemes (see also Apple *et al.* 2003; Bruneau and Savage 2002: 109–14). And yet these acts of resistance are perhaps better understood as battles won in a losing war. Moreover, they have been largely conducted from above, whether by the higher-ranked managers in select universities or by the leaders of the then AUT and/or NATFE, without the active support of ordinary academics. At issue here, then, is the extent to which these public contestations and political demands are either radical or potentially hegemonic, and we suspect that in the eyes of many they are neither.

In the main, one could argue that universities have complied with the structures of the new audit and market practices in a variety of ways. On the one hand, the new elites identified with the idea that UK universities needed to compete in an increasingly competitive global market, and that closer links with business and industry, the charging of student fees, and the demands for greater productivity were necessary evils in the survival and expansion of UK universities. They have also employed a variety of means to implement higher education reforms generally and install audit practices specifically. Of course, greater ethnographic specificity is required to explore the precise logics through which these practices were installed in different institutions, as well as their considerable impact on the structure and function of these institutions. Nevertheless, it is apparent that audit practices have already been deployed to justify the closing down of 'failing departments', to pressurize academic staff to 'publish or perish', and/or to raise greater research funds and recruit more students. 'Modernizers' have constructed a series of antagonistic equivalences in order to establish political frontiers that make possible the installation of the new practices. Thus we have seen the ideological construction of 'surplus' versus 'deficit' departments, 'research active' versus 'research inactive' members of staff, 'good recruiters' versus 'bad recruiters', 'traditional' versus 'innovative' modes of service provision, and so forth. On the other hand, and at the same time, university managers and administrators have – by means of various logics of difference – sought to manage change by addressing demands and by changing the structures of governance, so as to prevent or displace public contestation. This active production of manageable difference leads us directly to our final set of questions.

What, then, about the reproduction and maintenance of this new complex of practices in the face of apparent discontent? Why so little effective political resistance? There are a number of factors that can help us to address these questions without reducing their answers to a function of the 'law-like force' of the changes or the lack of will power ('passivity') on the part of 'ordinary academics'. This, of course, is not to deny that reforms have in many cases been imposed on academics and students through pressure, coercion and enforced compliance. Putting pressure on 'failing' academics, or even entire departments, schools or universities, to meet required targets or face the prospect of 'early retirement', closure or 'restructuring', has certainly ensured a measure of compliance. Equally, academics face the perennial problem that arises from the logic of collective action, in which the individual's costs of collective action are often perceived to outweigh her potential benefits. This means that sporadic student protests and occasional strike actions by lecturers for better wages and conditions are frequently seen as the only possible means of protest, and even these actions are often unevenly supported and carried out.

But as we have suggested these elements of an explanation acquire sense and significance against the backdrop of the social logics of competition, atomization, hierarchy, and instrumentalization. And these, in turn, are integrally connected to the installation of the new audit practices in which they are operative, especially the way these new social practices and logics render significant numbers of academics complicit with their dominating aspects. For instance, we can hypothesize that the grip of these social logics is linked to the fact that they resonate strongly with relations of rivalry and the fantasmatic logic that underpins the latter. From this point of view, the social logic of competition, along with its commensurating preconditions, draws upon and is sustained by an underlying logic of fantasy, which it would be the task of detailed and subtle ethnographic research to shed light on. What sorts of market fantasies and modes of enjoyment – whether beatific ones of success or horrific ones of victimization – are operative in the university audit context?

It is also the case that the fantasies of rivalry, of 'winning' the various competitions and successfully 'passing' various institutional tests, strongly resonate with the broader social context in which they operate. In other words, given a wider discursive context in which a culture of instrumentalist consumption and exchange dominates, it is not fanciful to suppose that key signifiers which exhibit a clearly positive valence for subjects, whether they are 'quality', 'professionalism', 'knowledge', 'excellence' or 'freedom', should be suitably rearticulated to better resonate with the market ethos (see Mautner 2005: 100; Readings 1996). 'Quality' and 'knowledge' are thus no longer presented as different, antithetical, or simply autonomous in this new discourse from consumer ideals or the market ethos. Given a dislocation, and the drawing of a political frontier via logics of equivalence, key terms acquire the status of 'floating signifiers' – signifiers that for relevant subjects are no longer fixed to a particular meaning. Once detached, they begin to 'float', and their identity is only (partially) stabilized when they are successfully hegemonized by groups that endeavour to naturalize meaning in one way rather than another.

It is not surprising, then, that academics often bear an ambivalent and complicitous relation to such reforms, especially when they are closely associated with the ideals of greater transparency and accountability, giving rise to feelings of guilt and shame if they are opposed or transgressed. And this in turn acts as a 'restraint' on their impulse to protest. But the context surrounding the introduction of the higher education reforms in the UK is also relevant in understanding this ambivalence, for there is evidence that the Thatcher government succeeded in drawing a political frontier that enabled it to drive through the reforms. By criticizing universities for failing the economy throughout the 1980s, accusing academics of being snobbishly out of touch with the real world, and by painting a general picture of higher education as overly bureaucratic and inefficient in the face of an imminent and threateningly aggressive global market, 'modernizers' facilitate the process by which certain key signifiers are detached from their signifieds and rearticulated to reinforce market-friendly equivalences.

Articulation

The foregoing illustration constitutes no more than an 'explanation-sketch' to use Hempel's felicitous phrase (Hempel 1942). But it will serve our purposes well here, first, because it gives rise to a number of pertinent theoretical and methodological questions worth addressing; second, because it furnishes us with some relatively familiar empirical material which can serve as backdrop to the more abstract discussion that follows; and third, because it allows us to pursue some of these questions at least in a more empirically-sustained, albeit hypothetical, fashion. We have already noted that one of the main difficulties addressed in this book is the problem of subsumption, and the problem is rendered more explicit in our empirical illustration.

Two particular issues can be singled out. On the one hand, it is evident that any full-fledged explanation of a social phenomenon will invariably involve a plurality of heterogeneous theoretical and empirical elements that need to be assembled together into a complex, though singular, explanation. This requires some account of the relationship between the universal and the particular that is neither subsumptive nor its ideographic inverse. On the other hand, our illustration also makes clear the need for a theoretical and methodological answer to the question of how to *identify* features of a phenomenon or practice as features *of* a particular logic – a logic of competition for instance – or how we *name* that logic. More generally, how do we understand the process by which we identify a particular empirical instance as an instance of theoretical significance? When is something a floating rather than an empty signifier for example? Once again, we must guard against the temptation of subsuming empirical phenomena under abstract theoretical categories, as this can result either in a naïve empiricism in which phenomena are simply given, and thus not mediated or constructed by our concepts, or a theoreticism in which abstract categories are simply imposed onto a complex social reality without mediation or construction. Of course, both these temptations stem from a kind of idealism which – as we saw in the context of Chapter 3 – posits a complete overlapping between thought (concepts) and reality (objects).

In this section, we introduce and develop the concept and practice of articulation to counter the problem of subsumption, showing how any concrete application of our approach involves the synthesis of a plurality of elements. But this practice of articulation is in turn linked to practices of judgement and naming, both of which are required if we are to flesh out the concept of articulation in more detail. Finally, our complete logic of critical explanation involves a process of critique, evaluation and intervention, which must also be integrated into our overall approach. We thus examine each of these aspects in turn, starting with our concept of articulation.

The notion of articulation appears as an organizing concept in a number of theoretical contexts. In the field of structural linguistics, for example, Saussure stresses the idea of 'language articulation' to justify his identification of 'linguistic structure' as the proper object of study in developing a conventional (rather than natural) science of language use (Saussure 1983: 10). After first recalling that in Latin the word *articulus* 'means "member", "part", "subdivision in a sequence of things" ', he argues that in language articulation refers 'to the division of the chain of speech into syllables, or to the division of the chain of meanings into meaningful units' (Saussure 1983: 10).

Thus, in his view, a 'linguistic structure' can be described as 'the domain of articulations', in which each 'linguistic sign is a part or member, an *articulus*, where an idea is fixed in a sound, and a sound becomes the sign of an idea' (Saussure 1983: 111). A second source of theoretical reflection on the concept of articulation can be found in the work of Charles Taylor, which we discussed in Chapter 2. The notion of articulation plays a critical role in all of his work, but it is particularly evident in his account of moral theory. Allied to an expressivist conception of language, the process of articulation for Taylor involves the rational explication of the implicit grounds of our moral intuitions and responses (Taylor 1989: 77, 80; 1991a: 61).

Ernesto Laclau can be seen to respond to the structuralist and rationalist overtones associated with Saussure and Taylor respectively by developing a fully-fledged poststructuralist account of articulatory practice. Though developed originally in the context of his *Politics and Ideology in Marxist Theory* (Laclau 1977), it is only in his later writings that Laclau (sometimes with Chantal Mouffe) extends his concept of articulation into a general theory of articulatory practice. In *Hegemony and Socialist Strategy*, Laclau and Mouffe (1985) break with an original commitment to fundamental social classes charged with the tasks of articulating the meaning of ideological elements such as 'the people' or 'the nation'. Instead, ideological *elements* are now conceived as floating signifiers or differences that – in the context of a hegemonic practice – can be transformed into the *moments* of a discourse by *any* group, whether class-based or not. Here, privileged moments of signification are articulated into what they call nodal points or empty signifiers that function to stabilize the flow of meanings, thus constituting identities.

Expressed in more theoretical terms, Laclau and Mouffe characterize the practice of articulation as '*the construction of nodal points which partially fix meaning*' (Laclau and Mouffe 1985: 113). And meaning is always partial because of what they call '*the openness of the social*', in which the latter follows from the '*constant overflowing of every discourse by the infinitude of the field of discursivity*' (Laclau and Mouffe 1985: 113). They thus widen the logic of political articulation because contingency now inhabits not only the different elements that are linked together to form a discourse, but also the hegemonic projects or subjects that strive to fix meanings, as well as social structures themselves. Indeed, as we have insisted, social structures are best conceptualized as systems of meaningful practices marked by an inherent lack and undecidability (Laclau 1990). Laclau and Mouffe thus valorise the role of articulatory practices in the structuring of social relations. It is now the case that *every* social process of putting together elements is to some degree articulatory, and this is because they (and the agents of articulation) are not governed by any underlying metaphysical principle or ground.

We can summarize our trajectory thus far by saying that the crucial ingredient of an *articulatory* practice involves conceptualizing the relation between articulated elements as non-necessary or contingent. Articulation, therefore, 'is the primary ontological level of the constitution of the real', and will thus always involve 'the creation of something new out of a dispersion of elements' (Laclau 1988: 16). Or, to put it differently, the gathering of heterogeneous elements under a name is necessarily a singularity: '[t]he less a society is kept together by immanent differential mechanisms, the more it depends, for its coherence, on this transcendent, singular moment' (Laclau 2005: 100). However, as we have also noted, Laclau and Mouffe add the further claim that the identity of each element that is articulated is always 'modified as a result of the articulatory practice' (Laclau and Mouffe 1985: 105). More formally, then, we can isolate the contingency, singularity, and modification of elements, as three key aspects of an articulatory practice.

We suggest that all three aspects are relevant when thinking of social science practice in terms of articulation, even if their relative importance varies with respect to the case investigated. As we have seen, articulation is invoked by Laclau and Mouffe primarily to understand concrete social practices in which social actors 'articulate' discursive elements along the axes of equivalence or difference. The important thing to note here is that in line with the 'double hermeneutic', which is characteristic of social science practice, articulation is a concept that can be invoked to understand the practices being studied, as well as the practices of social scientists themselves. In this chapter, we invoke the concept primarily to reflect upon and better understand our own social scientific practice.

Laclau and Mouffe thus provide us with a general theory of articulation, which is predicated on the ultimate contingency of social relations and objectivity. In this view, empirical and theoretical elements can be combined together to generate three sets of articulatory relations: among empirical elements, among theoretical elements, and between empirical and theoretical elements. But how exactly does this theory enable us to tackle the various issues that fall under the problem of subsumption? As we have intimated, social science explanation involves the articulation of different theoretical concepts together in a concrete empirical context, in an effort to provide a singular critical explanation of a problematized phenomenon.

Consider our question about the failure or reluctance of academics to resist the installation of new audit regimes and work practices in UK universities. Our explanation sketch involved the identification of a number of different logics – social, political and fantasmatic – as well as a set of (theoretically mediated) empirical observations, which were combined to forge a hypothetical explanation. But under what set of ontological conditions is this operation possible? Here the task is to avoid the temptation to subsume a particular empirical instance under an over-arching law-like generalization, and to resist an eclecticism that would simply combine (potentially) incommensurable elements in an unstable explanatory amalgam. It is precisely in this regard that the concept of articulation provides the conditions of possibility for conceptualizing the 'double operation' of simultaneously linking different theoretical elements together, and then connecting the latter with specific empirical phenomena. This is because the practice of articulation is predicated on the idea that all elements and relations are ultimately contingent and partial, and that their meaning and function is relative to the singular explanatory chain within which they are linked.

In short, it is only by linking theoretical and empirical elements in a non-subsumptive and non-eclectic fashion that one can produce a singular explanation of a problematized phenomenon. And, if achieved, to use Marx's apposite terms, it would comprise 'a rich totality of many determinations and relations' (Marx 1973: 100). However, this formulation raises, in turn, an important question about those theoretical concepts or empirical generalizations (whether causal or correlational) that have emerged in traditions of thought whose ontological presuppositions are at odds with our own, but which we wish to use in our own explanations.

Our claim here is that these sorts of concepts and generalizations *can* be brought within the fold of our framework, though this will involve the closely inter-related moments of reactivation, deconstruction, commensuration and articulation. In fact, it is precisely these sorts of tasks that make our investigation not simply an ontical inquiry but also an ontological inquiry. Consider, first, how we might treat a theoretical concept from another tradition of thought. Drawing on Husserl, reactivation involves a return to the 'original' sorts of questions and problems that were addressed in the development of a theoretical concept. For instance, Marx's theory of class struggle can legitimately be understood as a response to the problem of collective agency in capitalist societies. However, the initial formulation of a theoretical (or, indeed, empirical) response to a problem may in certain respects be problematic: it may partake of an essentialist form of reasoning or may be ensnared in a reductionist framework. The aim of deconstruction in this regard is to lay bare these sorts of ambiguities and exclusions, thus weakening any essentializing projections into the concept and/or exploring repressed possibilities foreclosed by reductionist proclivities. It may turn out, for example, that class struggles are only one form of collective agency amongst others; indeed, its particular embodiment may be overdetermined by other forms of struggle and identity, such as race, gender or ethnicity. If this is the case (which we think it is), then a practice of commensuration is required to rework the theoretical concept so as to render it compatible with our ontological presuppositions, while the practice of articulation involves its reinscription in a new explanatory framework.

Consider our use of Olson's logic of collective action to account for the failure of a group such as university teachers to form and mobilize in pursuit of their perceived interests. Olson's theory can be seen as a legitimate response to the paradoxes of collective action, in which the strictures of individual rational self-interest produces collective irrationalities. But while his logic may be a useful component of any singular account of mobilization and protest, its strong assumptions about rationality, individual self-interest, and so on, render it incommensurable with the ontological assumptions underlying our approach. In this case, it is only by weakening some of Olson's initial assumptions, and then grafting his logic into our alternative explanatory chain, that we can avoid the twin difficulties of subsumption and eclecticism, where the latter would involve taking on board a set of inconsistent assumptions.[12]

So far we have considered how we might use a theoretical concept derived from a different tradition for purposes of our own research. The kind of caution implied in such 'importation', however, is equally necessary when it comes to using empirical generalizations from other sources. In Chapter 1, we showed how 'Duverger's Law' could be suitably reinterpreted as an empirical finding and then rendered compatible with a hermeneutical framework of analysis. But it may also be fruitful here to think about the use of empirical generalizations in relation to another example. In this vein, it is worth examining Przeworski, Alvarez, Cheibub, and Limongi's well-known study of 141 countries from 1950 to 1990, in which they looked at the relationship between regime type (democracies, dictatorships) on the one hand, and *inter alia* economic development and demography on the other (Przeworski *et al.* 2000). Consider the empirical claim that democratic regimes are more likely to survive crises the richer they become, or that economic growth rates are independent of the type of political regime. In his discussion of this study, Keith Topper illustrates the potential dangers of a too hasty bracketing of context and self-interpretations in presenting one's findings and their significance (Topper 2005: 202–7).

Moreover, these dangers can be located at both a descriptive and normative level. It is necessary, therefore, to reactivate and deconstruct the assumptions underpinning the generalizations before deciding whether these findings can serve one's own research purpose. It turns out, for example, that the generalizations of Przeworski and his co-authors rely on a highly contestable understanding of democracy. They define democracy in terms of multiparty electoral competitions, leaving aside a whole host of other features we often associate with the concept, such as the protection of basic human rights, or the scope and content of the electoral franchise. Paradoxically, in attempting to be as 'value-neutral', and thus 'scientific', as possible they also end up reinforcing a very specific normative outlook.[13]

From our point of view, it is futile to try and purge terms like freedom and democracy of their normative connotations (see Connolly 1993). In doing so, not only do we risk misrepresenting a state of affairs, but we also risk reinforcing prejudices and views defining the status quo. As Topper points out, Przeworski *et al.*'s conception of democracy, 'which classifies the US as democratic during a period in which African Americans were substantially disenfranchised in several Southern states, obscures rather than spotlights' the 'inconvenient fact' that the US has 'not always, or even very recently, been democratic' (Topper *et al.* 2006: 740). This, we feel, is a direct result of not engaging openly with the constitutively normative and ethical aspects of social science research. In any case, it should be clear that using empirical generalizations derived elsewhere in order to advance our own research requires considerable preliminary groundwork. After the reactivation and deconstruction of such findings, one must then undertake the further tasks of commensuration and articulation, so as to make them consistent with the presuppositions underpinning our own approach, and to bring them together into an explanatory narrative. As long as these preconditions are met, then empirical generalizations – whether law-like, probabilistic, or statistical – can have both descriptive and explanatory roles to play *within* an overall research strategy.

Judgement

As we have suggested, an articulatory practice puts together theoretical and empirical elements that have no logical or necessary links into a new configuration that, if warranted, makes possible a critical explanation of the phenomenon under investigation. However, we are still faced with the problem of *identifying* what in social reality instantiates one or another theoretical concept. It is here that we turn to the vitally important roles that subjectivity and judgement play in our approach. We begin with a discussion of judgement, after which we examine the implication of the latter for the practices of naming, generalizing, and justifying.

We begin with the claim that because any singular explanation involves a plurality of contingent theoretical and empirical elements whose unification cannot be conceived in subsumptive terms, then it is necessary for the researching subject to *articulate* them. This means that the process of articulating different elements together in order to construct a critical explanation always requires *practices of judgement* enacted by a particular researching *subject*. To phrase the issue in Kantian terms, these practices involve a reflective rather than determinative form of judgement. In the second of his introductions to the *Critique of Judgement*, Kant distinguishes between the two forms in the following fashion:

> If the universal (the rule, the principle, the law) is given, then judgement, which subsumes the particular under it is *determinative* (even though [in its role] as transcendental judgement it states a priori the conditions that must be met for subsumption under that universal to be possible.) But if only the particular is given and judgement has to find the universal for it, then this power is *reflective*.
>
> (Kant 1987: 18–19)

In other words, as against determinative judgement, in which the subject subsumes individual instances under concepts, in reflective judgement one is confronted with a particularity for which no determinate concept is readily available or given. Instead, if reflective judgement is to produce a synthesis of diverse elements at all, then some kind of universal form has to be constituted by the power of judgement itself.[14]

This account of the power of judgement allows us to revisit the 'application problem', which concerns the relation between theoretical categories and empirical phenomena. For instance, how do we know what counts in social reality as an empty signifier or dislocation? Or how do we identify the operation of a political or fantasmatic logic? As against the naturalist tendency to subsume, we favour an approach based on intuition, theoretical expertise, and the practice of articulation. This means that having immersed oneself in a given discursive field consisting of texts, documents, interviews, and social practices, the researcher draws on her or his theoretical expertise to make particular *judgements* as to whether something counts as an 'x', and must then decide upon its overall import for the problem investigated. The aforementioned theoretical expertise is acquired by the practice of learning and using the specific language games that constitute the grammar of the researcher's theoretical approach. (Indeed, as we shall suggest, it is precisely in the concrete investigation of particular cases that we acquire such expertise.) An integral part of judging whether a particular empirical phenomenon counts as an instance of 'x' consists in deciding what the precise relevance and importance of 'x' is in constructing a narrative that explains a phenomenon. These concepts – intuitions, theoretical expertise, judgements, and so forth – are internal components of what we call the practice of articulation, namely, the practice which links specific theoretical and empirical elements together so as to account for a problematized phenomenon (see also Howarth and Griggs 2007).

Judgement, then, is a kind of *situated ability*, in which a subject – a researching subject in our particular case – acquires and enacts the capacity to connect a concept to an object, or 'apply' a logic to a series of social processes, within a contingent and contestable theoretical framework. The centrality of judgement is also evident in Wittgenstein's later philosophy, as well as those scholars who have developed this aspect of his writings, such as Stanley Cavell and Stephen Mulhall. Wittgenstein's reflections are important because they allow us to say something about how we judge whether features of a practice are best characterized as a function of a social logic, a political logic, a fantasmatic logic, or something else besides. Relatedly, they tell us something about how we judge whether a particular logic – say a social logic – is best characterized and named in one way rather than another – as a logic of atomization, for example. We can shed light on these concerns by turning to Wittgenstein's reflections not simply on 'rules' but more specifically on 'rule following' or 'applying rules'. Is there anything which would give us some guidance in 'applying' our theoretical concepts to particular empirical contexts?

Wittgenstein's comments indicate that theoretical concepts do indeed give us some guidance in the process of 'application'. However, the way this guidance is understood needs to be unpacked and clarified for Wittgenstein approaches this question in a way that avoids the Scylla of pure intuitionism and the Charybdis of pure conventionalism. One of Wittgenstein's entry points here is to focus on instances where there is a problem in rule following: the errant school-pupil, for example, who fails to apply the rule 'add 2' as we might expect him to. For Wittgenstein, this raises crucial questions about how we are to 'go on' in following a rule. In seeking to demystify the various ways we may address the question, he seeks to avoid a pure intuitionism, in which a new Platonic insight is required at each step to follow the rule (Wittgenstein 1967: §186) and a pure conventionalism in which we *choose* a particular course of action, whether deliberatively or through a kind of existential act (Mulhall 2001: 112–14). Instead, for Wittgenstein, rules are *nothing more* (though nothing less) than the norms and customs we acquire – or sometimes fail to acquire – in becoming expert users of a language and practice. The practice of judgement is thus an ability which we master in and through practice – by learning and imbibing the grammar of concepts and logics that make up one's theoretical approach for instance.

Clearly the act of *situated judgement* is crucial in avoiding a pure intuitionism on the one hand, and a pure conventionalism on the other hand. Nevertheless, Wittgenstein has something to say about this 'situatedness' which addresses in a more direct fashion the question of *how* our theoretical concepts, in conjunction with the situational context, can offer some guidance when engaging in these sorts of judgement. This can be understood in relation to his concept of 'family resemblance', which we have already discussed in Chapter 5. In this view, the concept of 'family resemblance' unites a set of patterns on account of a series of overlapping similarities which, though always regional, cover the entire terrain we identify as a concrete practice. For example, the social logic of competition captures the way actors see themselves as rivals, even though this receives slightly different inflections depending upon whether we look at it from the point of view of representatives of universities, ordinary academics, students, and so on. In other words, there will be regional variations in the way that this social logic is instantiated. Nevertheless, this unity is perfectly intelligible and precise, even though 'there is no single common feature – no unique, underlying essence available for analytical extraction' (Mulhall 2001: 95). Therefore a social logic – comprising the grammar or rules of the practice – must be understood as inseparable from, though not necessarily reducible to, the empirical contexts of its instantiation (Mulhall 2001: 90–1).

In sum, a social logic – in this case the social logic of competition – appeals both to a patterning *and* to a context-sensitive open-endedness which we captured in Chapter 5 with the Foucauldian notion of 'regularity in dispersion'. The indefinitely extendable instantiations of the social logic of competition would

> comprise individual items, specific scenarios, that are perfectly definite in themselves, and that can be added to in perfectly definite ways; and yet there are no obvious recipes or concise formulae lying to hand for their construction and expansion. Anyone who knows how to talk knows how the lists might be extended, and reveals in the exercise of that

knowledge how demanding and exact the criteria which inform those extensions really are; but if someone were to ask, 'In what sorts of circumstances is... [this pattern an instance of the social logic of competition], we could not specify a particular *sort* of circumstance – we could only answer by offering some examples together with a similarity rider, and perhaps by evaluating further examples that our questioner may bring up.

(Mulhall 2001: 96–7)

This is one way to understand why Wittgenstein asserts 'that we *judge* any specific *pattern of sayings and doings* to be an instance of... [for example, the social logic of competition] only in certain circumstances' (Mulhall 2001: 95; emphasis added). What enables us to give content to the social logic of competition is thus both the contexts which constitute it as well as the analyst's *judgement*. Moreover, we should add that these insights regarding the relation between judgement and family resemblance are also relevant to the case of political and fantasmatic logics, though of course these insights would need some modification because their theoretical contents possess a greater degree of inter-contextual robustness.

In a key passage in *Philosophical Investigations*, Wittgenstein asserts that 'if language is to be a means of communication there must be agreement not only in definitions but also (queer as it sounds) in judgments' (Wittgenstein 1967: §242). In other words, we need to share judgements, as well as the criteria upon which they are based, in order 'to be able to project' our concepts and logics 'into further contexts' (Cavell 1976: 52). And our agreement on how to use words and apply them in new circumstances stems from our immersion in a particular language or form of life, in which we learn its practices and rules. In analogous fashion, then, our poststructuralist approach suggests that explanatory concepts cannot remain fully intact in the process of explaining. This is because the researching subject leaves its trace through acts of judgement.

Naming

We turn now to the intimately related issue of characterizing, constructing, and naming logics, which we shall continue to discuss with reference primarily to our concept of *social* logics. In a first move, the significance of identification and naming for our approach can be appreciated by opposing it to 'conceptual determination'. Here we rely on Ernesto Laclau's elaboration of this distinction, based on the work of Saul Kripke and Slavoj Žižek (Laclau 2005: 99–110). The central point here is that 'the identity and unity of the object results from the very operation of naming', or as he otherwise puts it 'the name becomes the ground of the thing' (Laclau 2005: 104, 100). Although Laclau is primarily interested in how to apprehend the singularity of a 'people' in concrete populist discourses without reducing it to a conceptual determination, our view is that this insight can be fruitfully, if partially, applied to the act of characterizing a social logic. An 'assemblage' of 'heterogeneous elements' kept together 'by a name' is, he argues, 'necessarily a *singularity*' (Laclau 2005: 100). This means that the very naming and identification of social logics entails a judgement or act of *gathering* that articulates together a set of heterogeneous discursive elements by making their links visible in the process of constituting them. It constitutes them through an act of judgement by laying a claim that cannot be analysed in or reduced to purely conceptual terms, and which can therefore be challenged.

This process of naming and characterizing social logics shares an affinity with the notion of *paradiastole* as defined by Quintillian, who in turn draws upon Cicero's commentary and reworking of Aristotle's account of rhetoric. In the contemporary context, this trope has been most developed by Quentin Skinner, for whom *paradiastole* is a form of rhetorical redescription, whose essence may 'be said to consist of replacing a given evaluative description with a rival term that serves to picture the action no less plausibly, but serves at the same time to place it in a contrasting moral light. You seek to persuade your audience to accept your new description, and thereby to adopt a new attitude towards the action concerned' (Skinner 2002: 183). Using one of Quintillian's illustrations, Skinner shows how 'prodigality' can in this fashion 'be more leniently redescribed as liberality, avarice as carefulness, negligence as simplicity of mind' (as cited in Skinner 2002: 183).

The key point to stress is that the act of naming or (re)description through 'rhetorical displacement or reaggregation has precisely the function of emancipating a name from its univocal conceptual attachments' (Laclau 2005: 109). In a similar vein, Skinner suggests that it is not the conceptual content of events, practices, or actions which through their descriptions determine the invoked name, but rather that conceptual change is the *outcome* of debates over how to characterize or name something – in our case, a social logic: 'The more we succeed in persuading people that a given evaluative term applies in circumstances in which they may never have thought of applying it, the more broadly and inclusively we shall persuade them to employ the given term in the appraisal of social and political life' (Skinner 2002: 186; see also 182). How, then, do these theoretical and methodological reflections impinge upon our critical analysis and explanation of social practices and regimes? The immediate implication is that we can ask what possibilities are excluded by the social logics that are currently operative. And our intuition is that these logics comprise elements which could be reaggregated and *named* differently, or which could be gathered together as a *counter*-logic. We shall develop, and illustrate, this aspect of our approach in relation to the task of critique, which we explore in the next section.

Generalizing

The principles and practice of articulation and judgement in social science explanation also have implications for thinking about the grounds for generalizing beyond the confines of a particular case. The question of generalization can be related, we believe, to what we call the problem of subsumption and, in this way, we can contrast our logics approach with mechanisms on the one hand, and contextualized self-interpretations approaches on the other. More specifically, we argue that our poststructuralist approach refuses the choice between the universal aspiration of mechanisms and the particularist and eclectic tendency of contextualized self-interpretations. A genuine *tertium datur* emerges by undermining the presupposed ideal underpinning this choice, namely, subsumption – whether in the guise of affirmation (in the case of naturalism) or rejection (in the case of hermeneutics). Our view, in other words, is that the opposition between universal or general subsumption on the one hand, and thick-descriptive particularity on the other, is not necessary.

We recall how the subsumptive character of laws and mechanisms is typically understood to carry the bulk of the explanatory burden. Upon rejecting universal or general subsumption, however, it might be tempting to opt for particularity, with little scope for making general claims. But, as we have just noted, this choice rests on a questionable assumption, namely, that explanation can only be subsumptive in character. So if subsumption is rejected, one also rejects explanation, being left with mere descriptive particularity. It is a dichotomy which maps historically onto the opposition between explanation and understanding.

As should be evident by now, our view is not simply that there is an alternative to subsumption, but that subsumption mischaracterizes the practice of social science explanation, even when practitioners invoke the terminology of causal laws and mechanisms. Subsumption relies on the idea that the very process of explanation is exterior to the explanation itself, an assumption which we have sought to undermine. From a poststructuralist point of view, therefore, we can reconceptualize laws, mechanisms, and empirical generalizations, as a function of *reification*, or what we called in Chapter 3 *abstract essences*. The term reification simply signals the effect of bypassing the contextualized self-interpretations of actors. By contrast, reactivation involves a process of de-reification, in which abstract essences are linked to the contexts and self-interpretations relevant to the problem at hand. Understanding such theoretical concepts and empirical generalizations as a function of degrees of reification or sedimentation, of course, differs substantially from the way mechanisms and laws are usually understood in the literature, namely, as representing differences in *subsumptive scope*.

By contrast, for us, the process of explanation is better characterized in terms of *articulation*. This means, as we noted before, that we can deploy theoretical concepts and empirical generalizations derived from other traditions, so long as their use is accompanied by suitable acts of reactivation, deconstruction, commensuration, and articulation. We have already discussed this aspect of an articulatory practice. But what can we say, more specifically, about the task of *generalizing* from a single case?

Clearly, the question of *generalizing* from a case is intimately related to the question of *comparing* cases, which we shall be discussing in a later section. Nevertheless, taking our inspiration from Wittgenstein we claim that the process of generalization takes place on the basis of shared judgements about theoretical terms, about paradigms, and about what constitute cases that converge or diverge from paradigm cases. Logics are thus constructed through the process of *articulating* self-interpretations to contexts *by means of a theoretical framework* consisting of a set of concepts and ontological assumptions. It is this articulatory aspect and its theoretical presuppositions that a mechanistic approach denies and a hermeneutical approach underplays. Accordingly, we suggest that what makes possible the simultaneous singularity *and* generalisability of each case is the background theoretical framework informing the analysis, coupled with the articulatory process itself.

As we noted earlier, the process of articulation means that our account will be singular and involve the judgement of the analyst. However, the fact that we explicitly couch this account in theoretical terms, which find expression in different contexts because they emerge out of our presupposed – and unavoidable – ontological *horizon*, means that we can formulate more general questions and hypotheses that invite comparative research, while also assisting in the exercise of refining our theoretical perspective. For example, how do specific social logics, such as the social logic of the supermarket, function as a paradigm in articulating and characterizing market practices? How might a social logic of competition, used perhaps to characterize aspects of a market practice, acquire a positive or progressive impetus? Do conservative discourses tend to adopt a particular narrative whose form can be defined in contradistinction to progressive utopian discourses? Do empirical manifestations of the former always take on an ontological form, wherein the political logic of equivalence predominates over the logic of difference? How might different totalitarian discourses (Nazism, Italian fascism, Franco's fascism, Stalinism, and so on) be differentiated as a function of fantasmatic logics of enjoyment?

In the main, the search for empirical generalizations in positivist social science is motivated by the desire to test the relationships between the proposed variables of a model or theory, either falsifying proposed relationships or failing to falsify them. We have already questioned the sharp separation between discovery and justification in Chapter 1, and with it the valorisation of the predictive criterion as a constitutive feature of social science testing and explanation. Our approach begins instead with a particular problem in need of a singular retroductive explanation. This means that empirical generalizations arise not through inductive or deductive means. Rather, cases are generalized insofar as they are judged exemplary with respect to a particular field of investigation (see also Dreyfus 1986). In other words, it is by virtue of their paradigmatic status, in conjunction with the theoretical language used to articulate them, that they can contribute to the explanation of related cases and instances. We have already mentioned the paradigm of the apartheid case in this regard, which in our view can shed light on related cases of racist or ethno-nationalist domination. But the way they shed light is not straightforward. Not unlike the analogical type of reasoning found in legal arguments from precedent (see, for example, Sunstein 1993), this is because it requires that one *articulate* the networks of similarities and differences, justifying the claim to a generalized family resemblance in both theoretical and contextual terms.

Justifying

We turn finally, albeit briefly, to explore the implications of our conception of articulation and judgement for questions of justification and persuasion. In line with much contemporary philosophy of science, whether inspired by Popper, Kuhn or Feyerabend, one implication of adopting the principle of articulation, which problematizes correspondence conceptions of language and theory, is that we reject notions of directly accessing or reaching a final or absolute truth (Feyerabend 1975; Kuhn 1970; Popper 1989). Equally, however, we distance ourselves from truth as a kind of 'subjective imposition', which theorists such as Habermas and Taylor often accuse Nietzsche and Foucault of asserting (see Habermas 1987: 95–7; Taylor 1985c: 174–84). Truth and knowledge are not reducible or equivalent to power.

On the contrary, for interpretations to *count* as 'candidates for truth or falsity' – to be regarded as potentially valid – they must first accord with the social ontologies and 'regimes of truth' within which they operate (Foucault 1981). Foucault neatly captures this idea when he claims that '[w]ithin its own limits, each discipline recognises true and false propositions; but it pushes back a whole teratology of knowledge beyond its margins.... [P]erhaps there are no errors in the strict sense, for error can only arise and be decided inside a definite practice' (Foucault 1981: 60). For example, Foucault argues that though we can retrospectively affirm that Gregor Mendel, the so-called father of modern genetics, 'spoke the truth', he was not ' "within the true" of the biological discourse of his time', and thus his statements could not even be called true or false, as they did not constitute *candidates* for knowledge at all (Foucault 1981: 60; see also Howarth 2000a: 56–8).

As we noted in Chapter 1, this means that claims to truth in the social sciences are subject to the usual burdens of reliable evidence, objectivity and internal consistency consonant with the prevalent regimes of truth, although as this book insists we would want to challenge and in certain respects extend the parameters of these regimes. In other words, our explanatory hypotheses and interpretations are subject to the familiar constraints of evidence and the judgement of the relevant communities, although in keeping with the assumptions of our poststructuralist discourse theory empirical 'tests' cannot be understood in terms of a narrow, positivist understanding of verification or falsification, which would presuppose the possibility of theory-independent empirical observations beyond interpretation (see Laclau 1977; Miliband 1969, 1970; Poulantzas 1969, 1973).

In this picture, then, it is difficult to specify meaningful epistemological criteria of validation in advance. And this means that apart from vague gestures towards 'consistency', 'insight', and 'evidential support' – vague because the very meaning of these terms varies from one empirico-theoretical context to another – one can only say that the ultimate 'proof of the pudding' consists in the production of persuasive narratives that better explain problematized phenomena. This reinforces our characterization and advocacy of a retroductive understanding of social science inquiry, which for us consists of three moments: problematization, retroductive explanation, and persuasion. In the next section, we add a further dimension to our overall articulatory approach: the question of critique.

Critique

The critical dimension of our logic of critical explanation has never been far away from our discussions about articulation, judgement and explanation. But while we have affirmed this dimension and explored it in previous chapters, we have not yet explicated it in any detail. To begin, we can say that our approach steers a course between an unapologetic positivism, which denies any role for critique and values in scientific investigation (other than those intrinsic to science itself), and a partisan approach that is prepared to compromise the virtues of scientific study – objectivity, impartiality, systematicity, consistency, and so on – in the name of an explicit set of polit-ical commitments and values. Along a spectrum bounded by these limit points we can plot a number of standpoints. A Weberian, for instance, would accept the importance – even unavoidability – of holding and taking-up particular value orientations, even if they are to be systematically excluded from the practice of scientific investigation itself. Another position may totally refrain from critique in seeking to characterize a practice as faithfully as possible, yet still have recourse to an ideal in order to critically evaluate that practice. On the other hand, a more radical approach may posit an internal relation between facts and values, such that the latter necessarily impinge on the former, but still hold out against a purely partisan orientation in which values trump scientific endeavour. For example, early members of the Frankfurt School such as Max Horkheimer engage in an 'immanent critique' that identifies gaps between the posited ideals of bourgeois society – freedom, equality and solidarity – and the actual practices and social relations of such societies, thus drawing up normative standards that are internal to a particular society to develop a critical perspective (Horkheimer 1986: 108). This approach permits some critical leverage vis-à-vis a practice or text with-out apparently importing an external ideal, though it still relies upon a strong conception of universal reason and a 'rationalist' conception of consistency to enable them to identify gaps *as* gaps in the first place.

This latter conception of critique is closer to our own, though we do not accept the foundational commitments of the early Frankfurt School.

Instead, our approach shares and exploits important family resemblances with a number of related critical approaches, including Foucault's genealogy, Quentin Skinner's reorientation of the history of ideas, and Derrida's 'method' of deconstruction. Derrida's 'deconstructive critique', for example, exposes points of undecidability and torsions within a text, while *simultaneously* disclosing new possibilities for infrastructural accounting and reconstruction. Edward Said's *Orientalism*, despite his protestations to the contrary, instantiates a form of deconstructive critique. He shows how the construction of identity, 'whether of Orient or Occident, France or Britain...involves establishing opposites and "others" whose actuality is always subject to the continuous interpretation and re-interpretation of their differences from "us"' (Said 1995: 332). And in good deconstructive fashion his analysis goes further than just describing these processes of 'othering' by endeavouring to displace and reorient the binary opposition between Orient and Occident in a more humanist direction: 'Can one divide *human* reality, as indeed *human* reality genuinely seems to be divided, into clearly different cultures, histories, traditions, societies, even races, and survive the consequences *humanly?*' (Said 1995: 45).[15]

In other words, as against assertions that Derrida's 'method' is a negative metaphysics, which amounts to a 'totalized critique of reason' (McCarthy 1994: 35), or Gillian Rose's opposite claim that it is not critical enough – in her verdict an empty and 'unknowable legal formalism' (Rose 1984: 162–8) – deconstructive critique challenges particular occlusions or closures *from within* by describing, unravelling and reworking their concrete specificity. In addition, even though a deconstructive ethos presupposes a general system of occlusions implicit in the idea of 'Western Metaphysics', this does not exclude an engagement with particular logics and structures (see Norval 2004; Smith 1994). On the contrary, it is only by engaging with such particulars, uncovering their specific forms of exclusion and domination, that the general system and/or its undermining can be advanced.

Against this background, how shall we conceptualize the practice of critique in our logics approach? At the outset, we can say that our critical standpoint emerges out of the ontological commitments informing our practices of problematization and characterization, including the articulatory nature of our judgements. More precisely, there are two important aspects that are relevant to the critical dimension of our explanations, each of which is rooted in the idea of radical contingency: the normative and the ethical aspects. First, as we have asserted, the experience of dislocation, in which the inherent contingency of social relations becomes visible, is an important condition for the possibility of political practices. The latter involves the public contestation of norms in the name of something new. Significantly, the centrality we accord to the political dimension of practices already implies a normative point of view, which regards certain norms or social logics as *worthy* of public contestation. Reactivating the political dimension thus presupposes the intrinsic contingency and unevenness of power underlying any decision from the point of view of an alternative vision, however implicit this might be. The ethical aspect of our critical explanation is also linked to radical contingency, though this time in a more direct fashion because it concerns the *way* in which a subject confronts it in its various ontical manifestations, whether political or social. We examine the normative and ethical aspects of critique in turn.

Normative critique

As we pointed out in Chapter 4, the key point for questions of *normative* critique centres on the *grounds* for publicly contesting the norms and practices of an institution or way of life. What are the normative grounds for characterizing a relation not simply as a relation of subordination, but as a relation of *domination* (or unfair, bad, unjust, etc.)? Indeed, can there be *any* such normative grounds for an approach predicated on an affirmation of the radical contingency of practices and relations? As should be evident from earlier chapters, our answer to this question is affirmative. Even though sensitivity to the context of a particular problematization is crucial in formulating a more concrete normative position, we can briefly note here that, in more abstract terms, our normative orientation arises from our commitment to the principles and values of radical and plural democracy (see Laclau and Mouffe 1985; Mouffe 1992, 1993, 2000). Combined with concerns arising directly out of a particular empirical context, and drawing upon Connolly's idea of ontopolitical interpretation, this normative vantage point enables us to project alternative values and ideals into the object of study to assist in the production of a fuller critical explanation.

For example, our illustrative analysis of UK higher education at the (national) regime level stressed the initially decisive role of Thatcher's New Right project in shaping the emergence and imposition of the new regime of audit practices. But it is important to recall that this project was only *one* possible solution to the organic crisis of the post-war consensus, and that other options – a reformed status quo, for example, or a more radical left-wing project – were defeated in the hegemonic struggles of the late 1970s and early 1980s. Indeed, there are some that have sought to reactivate and defend the New Left or Labour Left projects that emerged at that time, drawing on their ideas to contest what they take to be the current neo-liberal consensus (see Panitch and Leys 2001).

The same could be said about the rapid installation of audit practices at university level. In order to illustrate and elaborate the critical aspect of our logic of explanation, let us stay with the case of UK higher education, returning to our critical evaluation of the dominant – and we might add *dominating* – social logics that we identified in the university context. Let us consider, for example, the logic of atomization with which we captured and contextualized the atomizing patterns of audit practices, at least as they manifest themselves through the self-interpretations of academics and students. In other words, let us start by assuming that lecturers and students *do* tend to see themselves predominantly as sellers of labour or purchasers of products, in which the value of their skills and talents is taken to be a product of their individual efforts and virtues. We assume, here, that this social logic constitutes a dominant and dominating norm that is worthy of public contestation. Nevertheless, while it is true that the social dimension of this audit practice is at the forefront, it does not mean that the political dimension is necessarily totally foreclosed from view. In other words, there are also academics and students who understand themselves and their skills differently, and there are certainly academics and students who are capable of envisioning themselves differently.

In this situation, a counter-logic of a *plural and democratic community* can be projected into our objects of study in order to serve as a critical counter-point to the belief that the logic of atomization is necessary and inevitable. With this logic we can gather together those (latent and manifest) discursive patterns that in the self-interpretations of actors tend to situate their institutions, themselves, and their attributes in a wider social context. We can also point to the strongly felt need amongst many academics to be consulted about the ongoing changes, which stands in contrast to those social logics which function to abstract or bracket them from wider decision-making structures. And we can affirm the idea of a heterogeneous set of research and teaching practices that ought not to be homogenized in the name of *one* model of a university. In other words, while counter-logics of a plural and democratic community are construed loosely and abstractly, prescribing in this sense only a minimal normative content, they can still point to a contextualizing and democratic impulse in the self-understanding of actors themselves. The aim is thus to articulate such a counter-logic out of '[d]ifferences, resistances, and protean energies [which] flow through the "perpetual gaps" within and between social formations, opening up possibilities for the politics of pluralization' (Connolly 1995: 39). There are, in other words, discursive resources available to people, even if only in protean form, to articulate their varied experiences of dislocation in an alternative normative direction. Thus, for example, if it is accepted that in the particular context of UK higher education reforms, the social logic of atomisation tends to provide fertile ground for the operation of the social logic of competition, and because the more social totalities are broken down into atoms the more scope there is for the logic of competition to take hold, then the counter-logic of a plural and democratic community can have the effect of weakening or contesting it, or at least making it visible.

This highlights the ineliminable connection between analysis and critique in our approach. The very naming of a social logic already involves critical judgement. First, as we explained above, it serves to gather together – understood in terms of articulation – what is ultimately a heterogeneous field of elements that have no 'objective' or 'necessary' connections. Second, this process of naming enables us to conjure alternative names and accompanying socio-political visions, if only because the significance of atomization in this context derives from those names and reaggregations to which it can be opposed.

Counter-logics of a plural and democratic community can thus oppose and problematize those discursive articulations in which the logics of atomization predominate. Take, for example, Willmott's claim that 'skills possessed by sellers of labour, such as academics, are not sensibly theorized as individual capacities that provide their sellers with leverage in the labour market'. Instead, a counter-logic can be used to understand skills in a non-atomistic way. In this view, skills would be seen as 'supported by the way that work is organized in society. It is this organization of work that is productive of, and promotes the attribution of value to, certain skills' (Willmott 1995: 997–8, drawing on Johnson 1980). In other words, when considering the valuation or devaluation of skills, this pattern of self-understanding places great importance on its social and collective character by making visible a broader politico-economic context. As Trowler puts it, 'seeing knowledge and skill as socially distributed within a community of practice alerts us to one of the problems with the notion of "key skills" and the idea that we should "fill" our students with as many and as much of them as possible. This individualistic [or atomistic] way of thinking about knowledge and skill shows the error of attributing to the individual what is in fact a social characteristic' (Trowler 2001: 195–6).

If put together, a view that stresses the values of plurality, community and democracy can provide grounds for reflecting critically about inequality which is conceived primarily in terms of individual choice or capacity. For instance, while a Weberian approach might conceive inequality 'in terms of the capacity of individuals to acquire skills and act collectively to create monopolies and scarcities', a Marxian approach might understand inequality as a function of class domination in capitalist societies, 'in the sense that those who derive an income from capital are obliged to adapt and respond to systemic pressures to commodify their labour as they compete with other sellers of labour to secure the means of subsistence' (Willmott 1995: 997–8). However, it should be stressed that it is only through hegemonic struggle that the adoption of an alternative conception of inequality – say as a function of socio-structural domination – is possible.

We recall that we also identified social logics of hierarchy as capturing those discursive patterns which in the self-interpretations of actors reinforce a specific managerial form of top-down governance. They are logics which are not simply reflected in university governing structures themselves, but also in university-related decision-making structures, such as RAE and TQA panels. For some commentators, of course, these managerialist logics of hierarchy tend to reinforce and exacerbate existing hierarchies of seniority and gender, but this need not be the case. Here again, however, the critical counter-logic of a plural and democratic community suggests that progressive change cannot come about by individual action alone. The problem in this regard is that more and more features of our social lives appear to be excluded from collective control, and academia is not exempt from these processes. Elite managerial technocrats increasingly make important decisions affecting universities, mostly in response to new government targets and/or consumer trends, without tracking the interests of their stakeholders sufficiently – especially their employees and students – through processes of deliberation or even consultation.

In emphasizing the more plural, collective, and democratic dimensions of social life, we can also make visible the different ways in which the logic of competition is articulated with the social logic of atomization, and we can foreground the contingency of the managerialist logic of hierarchy that increasingly structures university organizations. Counter-logics of democracy and non-domination thus become viable and normatively attractive options in this context. Even so, we should note that counter-logics are not pure projections, since they are also immanent – that is, they exist in incipient form – in the self-interpretations of academics, who often complain about the lack of consultation, or the lack of time to make meaningful contributions in the various consultation exercises. These normative options can then receive support and backing by opening them up – via an articulatory practice – to existing normative theories of pluralism, democracy and justice.

In concluding this section, it is worth re-emphasizing the point discussed earlier in the chapter that in *naming* dominant social logics and counter-logics, we engage in a task of rhetorical redescription that foregrounds the contingent and political character of social practices. It does not follow, of course, that objectivity is substituted by a kind of subjectivism in which the analyst's individual preferences become foundational. It only follows that the political analyst is already engaged in a hegemonic struggle, deploying political logics of rhetorical redescription in the very process of characterizing and explaining discursive practices. This is what is at stake in identifying and emphasizing one social logic rather than another. That is to say, it involves the linking together of certain discursive features in equivalential chains, thereby making them part of one rather than another logic. This is precisely what we have done in specifying the nature of social logics and counter-logics.

When we turn to political logics it is thus important to emphasize their *double* operation, for these are not only *explicitly* invoked to render intelligible the discursive and political shifts in a particular case, but are also *implicitly* invoked by the analyst herself in the very process of characterizing features of a practice as belonging to one social logic rather than another. To miss this double invocation of political logics is to risk misconstruing the characterizing exercise as 'natural' or 'value neutral', thus suppressing the normative dimension of critical explanation. As Morley puts it, the 'terms that are used to describe organizational life in the academy are also [the] active forces shaping it' (Morley 2003: ix), thus highlighting the danger that emerges when specific theoretical approaches do not think critically about the fact that they may share the assumptions that are meant to underpin the practices being studied (e.g. classical economics in the case of market practices). From this point of view, markets, as well as audits and democratic forms of life, are not simply 'neutral' entities which can be put to either good or bad uses. Their very apprehension and analysis requires ongoing characterizing *and* evaluative judgements on the part of the analyst, to adapt Ernest Nagel's terms (Nagel 1961: 492). Repressing this double-invocation is akin to denying the role of the analyst's subjectivity, and to be complicit with the way mainstream political scientists strive to avoid the political nature of their own analyses.

All this suggests that the construction of a counter-logic demands that normative and sociological resources be explicitly brought to bear. It is a view which resonates with our discussion in Chapter 4, where we noted how the very identification and characterization of a norm or social logic worthy of public contestation relies on normative and sociological presuppositions. But this analysis already hints at how we may add a further critical vantage point to the normative one described thus far. For we can consider the degree to which the social logics of competition, atomization, hierarchy, and instrumentalization, feed into or reinforce certain fantasies – fantasies of control for example. And these in turn open up a new, though related critical vista. How might specific counter-logics, such as those of a plural and democratic community interrupt or destabilize these fantasies, ushering forth a space for hegemonic struggles informed by a radical democratic ethos?

Ethical critique

There is, then, a second, ethical aspect of critique which is closely associated with the notion of radical contingency. It focuses on the *way* in which subjects identify with a practice or regime, whether new or old. It is here that we have contrasted the ethical and ideological dimensions of a practice or regime, where the former relates to its constitutive *openness* to the radical contingency of things, and the latter to a complicity in *concealing* the lack or void at the heart of social relations. In other words, if the focus on the political dimension can disclose the contingency of the emergence and formation of hegemonic projects, thus focussing our critique on the historical and normative specificity of a practice or regime, as well as those options that have been foreclosed in the latter's institution, then our concept of ethics sharpens the critical focus on the ways in which subjects identify and are gripped by discourses. For example, to return to our discussion of the New Right, is it not the case that an important problem with this project is the way its proponents and supporters *dogmatically identify* with the free market as the *only* solution to all anomalies and crises of the post-war consensus? Indeed, the demands for a 'free market' and a 'strong state' became an ideological panacea – invoking the logic of fantasy – for structuring all kinds of social relations and practices, including those of universities and schools which are arguably not suited to these forms of social organization.

What might be termed our *ethical* critique of social practices thus focuses on the *closure* of subjective identification, which for us is just another name for the ideological. Ideology it will be recalled is related to those practices and forms of identity which conceal or deny the inherent radical contingency of practices. But, as Steven Lukes and others have shown, the concepts of social domination and ideology raise important methodological and strategic questions about the identification of domination, or the exercise of power, if subjects themselves are content to comply with such relations (Lukes 2005; Rosen 1996). The situation is complicated because ideology's very function is to fantasmatically conceal such relations and structures of domination by keeping radical contingency at bay. From this point of view, ethical critique demands detailed analyses of the kinds of fantasies underpinning social and political practices, as well as the exploration of ways such fantasies can be destabilized or modulated.

Nevertheless, it is important in this regard to distinguish between our concept of ethics and our grounds for normative evaluation. It will be recalled that for us ethics entails acknowledging the radical contingency of social existence and responding to *its* demands. It is thus directly connected to the fundamental ontological commitments of our overall approach. By contrast, questions of normativity are directed at the concrete sets of social relations within which subjects find themselves, requiring the analyst to characterize those relations that are perceived to be oppressive or unfair in the name of alternative values or principles. It is important here to stress that we concede a lexical priority to the ethical as against the normative (cf. Rawls 1971: 42–3). This has important implications because it means that our normative stances are always relative to the ultimate contingency of social relations and practices. In other words, the norms and ideals that we project into our objects of study are intrinsically contingent, contestable and revisable. Contingency necessarily penetrates the realm of the normative, which in turn indicates the need to develop a suitable ethos for conducting research.

In sum, then, we maintain that both the normative and ethical aspects of our particular conception of immanent critique are essential for purposes of characterizing and explaining problematized social phenomena. More specifically, our notion of critique discloses the contingent and precarious character of investigated practices or regimes, focussing on – and reactivating – excluded possibilities that follow from any form of radical institution. It concentrates on the naming and contestation of specific relations of domination in particular historical settings, where the identification of the latter presupposes the mobilization of alternative values and ideals that are themselves contingent, contestable and revisable. Finally, our approach also involves critically interrogating the *modes* of identification, focussing in particular on the *way* in which radical contingency is or is not properly acknowledged and negotiated. But having shown the articulation between explanation and critique in our approach, we need also to explore the different research strategies through which these objectives can be realized. Before doing so, however, it may be helpful to return to our illustration, in order to show briefly how the critical aspects of our approach mesh with its explanatory aspects.

Universities revisited

The general question animating our illustration and to which our assemblage of logics and their underlying theoretical framework was addressed concerned the rapid transformation in the UK's higher education's systems of control. This involved a transition from collegial to managerial forms of governance, entailing the introduction of a series of audit regimes. After problematizing the 'passivity' thesis as a popular response to the more specific question of why there has been a relative absence of overt and effective contestation on the part of many academics who are subjected to such reforms, we attempted to construct a set of explanatory hypotheses in the form of an illustrative 'explanation sketch' by articulating together different kinds of logics.

In accounting for the installation of various audit practices in universities, we first had recourse to an analysis pitched at the level of the state regime, showing how they formed one element in a wider New Right project initiated by the Thatcher government. All we would like to do here is to highlight several aspects of our critical explanation concerning the apparent lack of significant and effective resistance to audit reforms, as a way of illustrating the role that logics can play in generating explanations. We can start with the social logic of atomisation which, as we have seen, can reinforce the idea of individual responsibility and fault for the fallout of audit practices. One significant implication of this pattern of discursive articulations, at least as they are taken up in the self-interpretations of academics, is that the very recourse to complaint is rendered less likely. In other words, self-attribution of fault can function to pre-empt the emergence of complaints in the first place.

Yet even where such complaints do emerge, the forums and structures for constructing and expressing them are weak. Here the various logics of hierarchy are important in understanding and explaining why one might stop short of public contestation, whether these logics are operative in academics' place of work or their unions. Once the logic of atomisation is made visible, by hitching one's wagon to some form of democratic community as a counter-logic for example, it becomes more likely that issues of governance will be foregrounded, thereby politicizing hierarchical tendencies. This is because, if fault is not locatable in the individual, but is seen instead to reside primarily in wider structures, the question of how we do and should shape those wider structures will tend to be addressed more directly: Should the balance fall more on the side of hierarchical and elitist forms of governance, or more plural and democratic forms? If the latter, what precise content should the counter-logics of a plural and democratic community take? For example, should they tend towards a republican ideal, a radical democratic ideal, or some other ideal?[16]

But even where powerful democratic counter-discourses are available, there may yet be a tendency to shy away from overt contestation for a number of reasons. For example, academics may feel that the purposes of universities are changing, especially under the influence of wider consumption discourses in which the logic of instrumentalisation is prominent.[17] Moreover, the social logic of competition, and the relations of rivalry which it encourages and with which it resonates, appear to be making life difficult for those who resist their underlying commensurability drives. From their point of view, commensurability and comparability imperatives generate anti-pluralist tendencies, thus marginalizing and excluding practices, especially practices which privilege the qualitative dimension in research and teaching. From this perspective, the status and nature of the social sciences and humanities have undergone (and are still undergoing) fairly dramatic changes.

In this story, of course, political and fantasmatic logics are invoked to highlight how various social logics have become operative in higher education discourse both at the state level and at the level of the university. For instance, the political logics of equivalence and difference can and have been deployed to draw frontiers between modernizers and traditionalists, and to emphasize the similarities between consumer and higher education discourses. But fantasies of control and victimization are also important in enriching our overall account by offering reasons why it may be difficult to destabilize established social logics. Once this assemblage of logics has managed to sediment itself firmly in the academic arena, it requires complex counter-hegemonic work – notwithstanding a major dislocatory event – to experience something different and thus offer some sort of bulwark against what appears to many as an inevitable and natural anti-pluralizing trend.

As we saw earlier, our analysis attributes a certain centrality to the social logic of competition and the relations of rivalry which underpin it. One implication of this is to sound a cautionary note as regards progressive demands, such as demands for equitable wages for university staff, which are justified on the basis that they will ensure universities remain competitive or even enhance their competitiveness. That is to say, it suggests we pause before accepting competition as a fundamental and unproblematic ideal or principle of governance. But another implication is more exploratory in nature. It suggests we investigate in more detail the different ways a social logic of competition can get fleshed out in practice. Are some forms of competition in certain contexts more benign – even desirable? After all, as some have noted (e.g. Evans 2004: 119, 137), academics have always tended to work competitively and in relative isolation from each other. In addition, what sorts of counter-logics can be counter-posed to competition? One way of doing this, of course, would be to proceed by means of counterfactuals. The idea here would be to identify practices that have been marginalized by, or which even actively resist, those for which the logic of competition is central, and then try to discern not only the conditions making them possible, but also subjects' relations to the fantasies underpinning these practices.

This, in turn, may help us to better conceptualize notions of 'resistance', and even generate context-sensitive criteria of cooptation.

Research strategies

We turn finally to a consideration of some of the research strategies that enable us to put our theoretical approach to work in a more concrete fashion. More precisely, we address a set of questions about the character, role and limits of the use of case studies and comparative research in seeking to critically explain problematized phenomena. Of course, the selection of particular case studies, the comparison of cases, or indeed the very choice *between* case study and comparative methods, always presuppose a purpose, which in turn stems from a pressing problem in the present. It is for this reason that we prefer the term *strategy* to *methodology* when thinking about designing and conducting research. Whereas the term 'methodology' tends to connote ideas like neutrality and theory independence, 'strategy' better highlights the ontological, normative, and sociological presuppositions framing and informing our research agenda and its processes. Nevertheless, as we will see shortly, we can benefit considerably from the existing literature that discusses case study and comparative research methodologies, so long as this learning exercise incorporates moments of reactivation, deconstruction, commensuration, and articulation.

The commonsensical view of many positivists and naturalists is that case studies are at best a limited tool for producing knowledge, or at worst misleading and ultimately dispensable. For certain hermeneuticists, interpretivists and ethnographers, by contrast, there is the equally debilitating 'myth of *the* Case Study' that somehow speaks for itself: the thick description of a particular empirical instance, which can produce knowledge of social reality with little or no theoretical mediation, or which unproblematically becomes the placeholder of general knowledge, or which makes no contribution to more general knowledge at all. And, finally, there is the further danger of empirical illustrations and examples masquerading as case studies, when they are little more than explanation sketches of selected phenomena. Since much of the empirical research associated with our approach (either implicitly or explicitly) is based on case studies, it is worth addressing these charges and misconceptions head on.

Bent Flyvberg's *Making Social Science Matter* is a useful starting-point in this regard because he identifies a number of related assertions, objections, or misunderstandings about the case study method (Flyvberg 2001: 66–87). These are, first, that general and theoretical (i.e. context-independent) knowledge is more valuable for social science than the concrete and practical (i.e. context-dependent) knowledge associated with case studies; second, that case studies are most useful for generating hypotheses, but other methods (usually quantitative) are more suitable for testing hypotheses and theory building; third, that the case study method is biased both because it favours verification, rather than falsification, as part of the process of justification, and because it verifies or confirms the researcher's own preconceived ideas, hypotheses, and theories; and finally, that it is risky to establish general propositions and theories on the basis of specific case studies since the principle of induction requires large samples to make these propositions credible. In short, the case study method contributes little to the generation of systematic knowledge of a law-like sort.[18]

As should be clear from our book in general, these objections rest on a highly contestable understanding of the nature and conduct of social science, involving the projection of a very particular model of natural science practice onto the social sciences. As we have argued in our first three chapters, the search for explanatory theories that are both context-independent and rich enough to produce robust predictions is highly problematic in the social and human sciences (Dreyfus 1986: 11–13; see also Flyvbjerg 2001: 69–71). Indeed, our claim throughout has been that context and detail are indispensable because our focus is on the critical explanation of subject-mediated, problematized phenomena. This perspective suggests that the case method should form a privileged element in our overall research strategy. Nevertheless, we feel that there are legitimate reasons for thinking it necessary to incorporate a comparative element, though we need to be cautious about how this element (and its incorporation) should be conceived. We do not, of course, want to imply that the use we make of cases is straightforward. Both case and comparative methods require considerable reworking to make existing discussions of them relevant and fruitful for our poststructuralist approach. We therefore tackle each in turn.

Cases

In Chapter 1, we showed how a more suitably conceived ontology for understanding social processes problematizes the sharp demarcation between discovery and justification. In our view, the acceptance of a proto-explanation as an explanation does not rely on a fetishized conception of empirical testing. We suggest, therefore, that case studies can be used not only as a means of developing our empirical and theoretical understanding of problematized phenomena, or as a way of generating hypothetical explanations, but also as a basis of generalization, comparison, and lending support to proto-explanations.

In fact, there are a variety of ways of conceptualizing cases and their role in enhancing our understanding of social and political phenomena. Flyvbjerg himself outlines four types of case study, and these can be suitably re-read from our ontological point of view to yield a heuristic, and thus by no means exhaustive, typology of cases. *Extreme* or *deviant* cases, for instance, can serve to highlight particular phenomena in a dramatic fashion. In *The Birth of the Clinic*, for example, Foucault begins with a medical report from the middle of the eighteenth century that describes Pomme's treatment of a hysteric. The 'treatment' involved a series of unintelligible 'cures' and practices – ten or twelve hour baths that lasted for ten months and which resulted in the literal disintegration of the woman's bodily parts – which are virtually unintelligible from the point of view of 'modern' medicine with its careful perception and neutral description of the body, a view which was to take hold shortly afterwards (Foucault 1973: ix). In this typical juxtaposition, Foucault heightens our sense of discontinuity, while underlining the contingency of different modes of medical practice. Such is the value of extreme or deviant cases.

Critical cases, by contrast, may lend or weaken support for proto-explanations, as well as accepted explanations. In this regard, it is useful to distinguish between 'least likely' and 'most likely' cases. For instance, it was often held that South Africa's ethnic and racial divisions made it a 'least likely' case for peaceful transition to democracy (Horowitz 1991; Sisk 1995). The fact that it has for the most part succeeded in becoming a functioning democracy in a reasonably peaceful fashion raises doubts about those hypotheses, which held that its ethnic and racial composition and its unequal distribution of resources militated against democratic transition. By contrast, the absence of working-class revolutions in countries such as Britain (or other advanced capitalist societies), which many Marxists regarded as 'most likely' candidates for such transformations, problematized Marxist theories of revolution and social change. The fact that the Russian revolution occurred in the least developed capitalist country – the 'least likely' case so to speak – further problematizes the linear account of historical development in Marxist theory; it led Gramsci, for example, to develop a different perspective and set of hypotheses rooted in the concept of hegemony (Gramsci 1977: 68–72).

Third, *maximum variation* (or 'anomalous' or 'peripheral') cases may enable researchers 'to obtain information about the significance of various circumstances for case process and outcome' because they are as different from each other as possible (Flyvbjerg 2001: 79). For example, a small number of cases might be selected because they are very different in particular respects: size, form of organisation, geographical location, historical background, normative assumptions, conformity to mainstream, and so forth. It is then possible to assess to what extent these aspects affect particular outcomes. For instance, the analysis of populist logics in a wide range of contexts both 'tests' whether the concepts and assumptions 'travel' and, to the extent that they do, provides resources to refine and develop the theory itself.

Finally, *paradigmatic* cases can come to embody in an exemplary way a wider field of phenomena (Flyvbjerg 2001: 80). These cases often function as exemplars or metaphors for a whole class of cases, or as emblematic of an entire kind of society. For example, the logic of apartheid discourse that was discussed extensively in the last chapter can be taken as an exemplary form of racist discourse, which can then be used as a means to characterize and explain similar or different instances (see Norval 1996). On the other hand, Foucault focuses on Jeremy Bentham's 'Panopticon' in order to condense a complete system of disciplinary and surveillance mechanisms that represents the logic of disciplinary society (Foucault 1977: 200–9).

But Foucault's last example raises important questions about the selection of cases. How, for example, does one identify a paradigmatic case? What are the criteria for assessing whether or not a case has metaphorical value? These are difficult questions not least because, *pace* Wittgenstein and Kuhn, there are no general rules to identify cases: the paradigms themselves partly constitute the rules. But once established, paradigm cases are critical for the practice of generalizing certain kinds of logics and practices from individual cases. For instance, Ernesto Laclau treats the case of Peronism in Argentina as an exemplary case of what he calls 'populist reason', from which he is able to construct an entire logic of populist politics that can help explain other empirical cases (Laclau 2005; see also Panizza 2005).

The range of uses to which cases can be put can help dispel accusations of selection bias. After all, researchers who engage in thorough and in-depth case studies commonly report that their preconceptions and assumptions are challenged by their work. Given the oft-expressed scepticism about the possibility of generalizing insights derived from in-depth cases, it is worth stressing that hermeneuticists and poststructuralists agree that an overhasty and unreflective tendency to generalize *is* a risky and ultimately inappropriate way of depicting, explaining and intervening in social reality. From this perspective, one of the virtues of the case study method – its greater attention to detail and its closer proximity to the object of study – is to reveal this risk, which is often overlooked within positivist and naturalist traditions of analysis. In itself, this attention to detail surely cannot be a failing of the case study method.

By unpicking the misconceptions surrounding the role and purposes of the case study method, and stating a more positive case for its legitimate employment, we have suggested that the analysis of single cases can be important for conducting empirical research in political analysis more generally. For us, however, the selection and investigation of in-depth cases is a vital part of our overall logic of critical explanation. This is because case studies provide an important vehicle for critically explaining problematized phenomena by providing the contextually specific knowledge within which to link our more general logics together in a particular instance. But while our approach fosters a sense of caution when it comes to formulating general propositions based on a single study, it certainly does not exclude processes of generalization and comparison, as those who propagate 'the myth of *the* Case Study' would lead us to believe. As we have discussed the question of generalization in an earlier subsection, we move directly to the related question of comparison.

Comparing

The practice of comparing cases is an important methodological device in our approach, especially when used in conjunction with our analysis of case studies. For example, when harnessed alongside the comparative method, a knowledge of 'extreme cases' can – in Wittgensteinian fashion – expose our taken-for-granted practices and invisible norms, just as 'anomalous' or 'peripheral' cases can disclose something unexpected and invisible in apparently more 'normal' cases. Equally, our knowledge of paradigm cases only assumes its full significance when used to cast light on the similarities and differences of other related cases. The practice of comparing cases makes possible the dialectical interplay between our knowledge of the familiar and our desire to understand the unfamiliar.

Nevertheless, the proper conditions and basis for conducting comparative research and generating general propositions is still an issue that requires more systematic attention. On the one hand, there has been very little direct theoretical reflection about the comparative perspective amongst poststructuralists and discourse theorists. In practice, however, whether implicitly or explicitly, the latter often engage in comparative research when generating interpretations and explanations of problematized phenomena. For a start, comparisons are important in rendering phenomena more intelligible. Consider the way Wittgenstein uses 'intermediate cases' to illuminate 'alien' practices that are prone to misinterpretation, either because they are too easily assimilated into our dominant, parochial understandings, or because they are conceded an 'unintelligible otherness' (Butler 2001). Wittgenstein's therapeutic 'technique' is to use intermediate cases to connect the unfamiliar to what is familiar, thus providing a perspicuous representation of the former. For instance, in his critical remarks on James Frazer's *On Golden Bough*, Wittgenstein makes reference to the practice of American pilots during World War Two kissing the pictures of their loved ones before embarking on a mission, so as to draw attention to the expressive, rather than functional or instrumental, characteristics of certain human actions (Wittgenstein 1979: 64). He then shows how this example can help us to understand the way that so-called 'primitive practices', such as 'rain-dancing' in traditional societies, are internally related to the customs and rituals of these forms of life, and not necessarily implausible proto-scientific beliefs about the efficacy of their actions (see Cioffi 1998).

Wittgenstein also invents examples to show the contingency and strangeness of the practices we take for granted. For instance, he asks us to imagine an errant school-pupil who diverges 'irrationally' from conventional modes of rule-following in order to clarify conventional ways of learning and following rules (Wittgenstein 1967: §§185–7). Or consider Winch's study of the Azande which – as we saw in Chapter 2 – was instructive for him in so far as it helped to render his (and our) own modern Western practices more intelligible. It served to de-sediment and de-familiarize his (and our) normal understandings of phenomena by drawing attention to their contingent peculiarity. His understanding of certain primitive practices thus relativized and 'decentred' congealed beliefs about the universal superiority of scientific reasoning, which we often assume to be natural and normal.

In this respect, it is perhaps worth noting here the role that counterfactuals can play in producing plausible explanations of problematized phenomena.

Consider once again the failure of academics to resist the transformation of higher education in the UK. One way to explore this issue is to choose cases in which similar situations have yielded different outcomes, where the point is to search for an explanation of the difference. For example, comparative research into similar groups of professionals or workers facing similar conditions, but who responded in a more confrontational fashion, can perhaps shed light on those more acquiescent reactions. In short, comparative research is vital in enabling us to locate a range of possible counterfactuals that can help to lend or weaken support for our account of a problematized phenomenon.

The central reason for engaging in comparative research from a positivist perspective centres on the pinpointing of decisive factors in the provision of a causal explanation of empirical phenomena. For example, a comparison of maximum variation cases is thought to establish the presence or absence of a critical condition which would justify or invalidate the invocation of a causal law or statement as part of an explanatory story. Of course, from our perspective, which questions the causal law paradigm, this use of the comparative method is problematic, even though there may be good reasons to employ comparative research as one component of an overall research strategy. The dangers of a positivist approach to comparison have been highlighted from a hermeneutical point of view in Alasdair MacIntyre's classic essay 'Is a Science of Comparative Politics Possible?', where he stresses the embeddedness of concepts and terms in particular social and historical contexts that militates against the universalizing impulse in much comparative research (MacIntyre 1973).[19] However, what is still not clear is the legitimating basis of comparative research from the point of view of our own approach.

At the outset, we can say that at least two conditions must be satisfied for comparative research to be undertaken within our approach. First, it is necessary to specify the problems and questions to be addressed, thus circumventing the temptation to subordinate the comparative approach to method-driven research. Instead, for us the practice of comparison is always relative to the specific problems addressed and tackled. In other words, the practice of comparison needs to be related to the practice of interpreting problematized phenomena, and the normative and sociological assumptions underpinning this practice of interpretation. This means that while we can surely go along with so-called 'lower-level' tasks of 'contextual description' and the 'classification of empirical phenomena into distinct categories with shared characteristics' (see Landman 2003: 4–10), we do not view the latter as mere 'precursors' to prediction and the (strong) testing of hypotheses. As we have stressed, the logics of testing and predicting in a strong sense are rendered problematic in our retroductive account of social science.

The second, related condition is that comparative research cannot short-circuit the focus on the concrete specificity of each case within particular historical contexts. The basis for comparing must comprise thick descriptive interpretations of particular empirical phenomena, self-interpretations included, even though our aim may be to discern important similarities among a group or class of phenomena. In short, the use of the comparative 'method' to explain why similar structures give rise to different outcomes, or why different systems produce similar effects, ought to be both problem-driven and grounded on the interpretation of particular cases. While data from 'large-n' comparative studies can sometimes help in establishing overall patterns to assist in the formation of proto-explanations, or may feature as part of an overall explanatory story, they cannot provide the sole basis for accepting interpretations and explanations (cf. Mahoney and Rueschemeyer 2003).

However, in specifying these conditions for comparative research, have we not eradicated the possibility of systematic comparison and generalization? Are we not left with an extreme particularism of single case studies, for which the more universal comparative dimension is rendered casual and *ad-hoc*? We thus need to draw on different theoretical resources to elaborate a legitimate basis upon which to conduct systematic comparative research. Fortunately, these resources are available among the philosophical traditions and thinkers upon which our approach draws. For example, Foucault's archaeological and genealogical methods of analysis involve the making of explicit and implicit comparisons between discursive formations, orders of discourse and systems of power/knowledge (Foucault 1972, 1984). Quentin Skinner's and James Tully's rethinking of the history of ideas help us analyse the past so as to cast light and open up possibilities in the present, thus injecting an explicitly comparative dimension into their accounts (Skinner 2002; Tully 1995). And, in a similar vein, both Peter Winch's project of developing a 'hermeneutics of recovery', and Hans-Georg Gadamer's call for a 'fusion of horizons' to understand and interpret a text or practice, involve a strong comparative component in order to contextualize and decentre our apparently universal forms of life. Not only do these thinkers and theorists furnish a variety of reasons for engaging in comparative research, they also elaborate a range of methods, devices, techniques and therapies to capture the comparative ethos and further its ends.

Building on these different philosophical and methodological insights, then, the key concept we rely upon in elaborating the theoretical ground for comparison is, of course, the concept of *articulation*, which we have developed in opposition to *subsumption*. As we have suggested before, our approach rejects the false choice between, on the one hand, the search for universal laws and mechanisms, and with it the desire for causal explanation and prediction, and our knowledge of particular self-contained case studies and contextualized self-interpretations on the other. Eschewing the extremes of 'frictionless' comparison (pure universality) and the impossibility of comparison (pure particularity), we develop a grammar of concepts and logics that enable the practice of comparison to be conducted and understood more broadly as a way to cast different perspectives on a problematized phenomenon.

Conclusion

The concept and principle of articulation is a nodal point for our entire ontological and theoretical framework, as the construction of all identity involves the linking together of contingent elements into historically particular and incomplete 'totalities'. But to make use of Frederic Jameson's and Žižek's suggestive concept, the articulatory aspect of any practice, whether social, political or methodological, operates like a kind of 'vanishing mediator' (Jameson 1988; Žižek 1991a). That is to say, it functions as the always presupposed, but never present, hinge that links contingent elements together to constitute partial and limited structures.

This chapter has stressed the importance of articulation for making possible the hooking together of different theoretical concepts in a non-subsumptive and non-eclectic fashion, as well as providing the means to connect them to particular empirical circumstances. In our terms, this makes possible the construction of a singular explanation of a problematized phenomenon. Using the recent higher education reforms in the UK as an illustration, we showed how the principle of articulation is also vital for thinking of the way in which the processes of problematization, retroductive explanation, and persuasion and intervention are implicated not just in our descriptions and characterizations of phenomena, but also in the normative and ethical aspects of our critical engagement.

Finally, in thinking about the appropriate vehicles for conducting empirical analysis, we focussed on the role of case studies and the comparative method as part of an overall research strategy. Here again the notion of articulation played an important role. As we argued, case studies are neither dispensable prolegomena to proper scientific research – the generation of hypotheses for the empirical testing of theoretical statements – nor self-sufficient unities that speak for themselves without theoretical mediation. Instead, the case study is only significant in relation to the connected practices of problematization, retroductive explanation, critique and persuasion, in which the latter three moments provide the overall context and conditions for its construction, conduct and contribution to knowledge. This means that case studies are always immersed in a broader theoretical context, where they are informed by more general concepts. Equally, we stressed the way in which case studies and the comparative method, once understood in our terms, are best used in tandem with one another – by being articulated together so to speak – in order for certain problems to be investigated. Among other reasons, comparing cases is important for rendering the unfamiliar familiar and, conversely, in defamiliarizing the familiar by exposing our invested presuppositions.

Conclusion

There is a growing need for a renewed conversation between theorists and practitioners, between advocates of different approaches to empirical research, and between quantitative and qualitative researchers, about the character and purposes of social and political analysis. There are, of course, indications that such a need is being heeded. For example, there have been efforts to connect the study of policy to developments in democratic theory,[1] and to explore and exploit the interchange between theorists and practitioners.[2] Projects have also been launched to carve out a legitimate space for the study and analysis of political ideas and ideologies, which draw upon a wide range of philosophical and theoretical currents that cannot be subsumed by standard models of political science or normative political philosophy.[3] Equally, the analysis and evaluation of public policy and new forms of governance has precipitated the emergence of a powerful interpretive current. And in the field of international relations, the growth of an important constructivist and poststructuralist strand of thinking, not to mention renewed concerns with normative and ethical questions, confirms the existence of a significant engagement between political theory and philosophy on the one hand, and its more empirical and practical concerns on the other.[4]

Our contribution to this conversation can be understood in terms of the question of method. Although the domain of 'methodology' appears to be the sub-field of social and political analysis 'least likely to engage with political theory', as the editors of a recent companion to political theory observe, this is only true to the extent that method is construed narrowly in terms of technique, whether quantitative or qualitative. However, as the editors correctly go on to note, the domain of methodology also furnishes us with a space in which to reflect on what different sorts of method can do, which means that 'political theorists are in an especially good position to mediate between the philosophy of social science on the one hand, and particular methods on the other' (Dryzek, Honig, and Phillips 2006: 28). But of equal importance from our perspective is the need to resist the temptation to divorce the problem of method from deeper issues of ontology, explanation, ethics, and normative evaluation. Indeed, we approach methodological issues by relating them clearly to this wider net of theoretical and philosophical questions, thereby making explicit their political and strategic import. Our strategy in this regard has been to advance on both a *critical* and a *reconstructive* front.

Much of the *critical* thrust of our book focused on the problem of scientism, that is, the conviction that science is not just *a* form of knowledge, but *the only* form of knowledge (Habermas 1978: 4). Under the spell of scientism, subjects engaged in scientific practice do not just fail to reflect critically on their objects and methods of study, giving into a naïve form of objectivism, but there is also a severing of the connection between knowledge, critique and emancipation, as the quest for knowledge serves only an empirical and instrumental interest. For us, and for Habermas, at least as he puts it in *Knowledge and Human Interests*, the problem is especially evident in the growing hegemony of positivism in the social sciences, if not as a general philosophical stance, then certainly as a practice comprising a particular set of methods and research techniques. We see a powerful desire among many social and political scientists to emulate the natural sciences – to discover and anoint their own Copernicus, Newton or Einstein – as well as a concerted effort to bracket their social and philosophical conditions of existence. As Husserl insisted, the problem of scientism stems from a 'forgetting' of the philosophical presuppositions and conditions that make scientific practice – indeed *any* social practice – possible in the first place (Husserl 1970: 110–11).

The problem with scientism is twofold. Not only does it misconstrue natural science practice, but it also seeks to mould the social and human sciences in this (misrepresented) image. Of course, the human and social sciences do have specific features which give them a special inflection in comparison to the natural sciences. In Foucault's formulation, the social sciences are strongly marked by the modern *episteme*'s empirical-transcendental doublet, which for him stems from the epistemologically ambiguous figure of 'Man', who is both the subject and object of knowledge. Thus an unavoidable and irresolvable dialectic decisively problematizes the desire for scientific knowledge in these 'dubious sciences', which we name the 'human', the 'social' or the 'cultural'. Indeed, as Foucault implies, these necessarily unstable and ungrounded systems of discourse can never attain the security of scientificity they crave; we confront instead interminable disputes about the appropriate philosophy and method for their study (Foucault 1970; cf. Visker 1995).

Our more concrete object of critique was the *subsumptive* character of the dominant mode of social and political theorizing. Subsumption in the field of method is evident when mainstream social scientists either deduce explanations from higher order laws or generalizations – the so-called deductive-nomological form of explanation – or deduce predictions which are subjected to exhaustive tests – the so-called hypothetico-deductive form of validation. Empirical objects are thus subsumed under the theoretical concepts, and do not modify or transform the latter, thus giving rise to what Althusser calls 'a relation of exteriority' between theoretical categories and empirical phenomena (Althusser 1990: 49). By contrast, our approach is developed by reactivating, deconstructing, and reworking aspects of hermeneutics and naturalism into a wider poststructuralist frame. In this picture, the mode of explanation involves neither pure *subsumption*, nor mere *description*, but the *articulation* of different theoretical and empirical elements.

The *reconstructive* aspect of our project emerges by means of reactivating a crisis in the social sciences, and more particularly a crisis of social and political analysis, thus enabling us to reconsider the very point and purpose of *critical explanation*. Our first concern was to elaborate a *retroductive form of explanation* in the social sciences that consisted of the positing of a proto-explanation which insofar as it renders a problematized phenomenon intelligible can then be said to account for it. This was developed in opposition to the deductive form of explanation and the associated notion of testing through prediction, an ideal to which many social scientists remain committed, even if they are happy to admit that it is not always attainable in practice. Thus, the bulk of our book explored three possible ways of fleshing out the *content* of a retroductive form of explanation: contextualized self-interpretations, causal mechanisms, and logics.

These different approaches – all opposed to the causal law paradigm – are exhibited and characterized in Table 3. Following the chapter sequence of our book, we began by considering the use of contextualized self-interpretations to account for practices and institutions, where we focused our attention on the writings of Winch, Taylor, and Bevir & Rhodes. In this perspective, there is a search for critical interpretation, conceived as an attempt to describe and understand a phenomenon or practice from the inside. Here, explanation is considered to be an internal component of the process of rendering its object of analysis more intelligible. This approach arises from a rejection of the empiricist conception of knowledge associated with positivism or certain variants of naturalism, which in Taylor's words relies on 'brute data identifications' deprived of theoretical and contextual mediation, as well as its insistence that any theoretical approach must make clear its ontological grounding, even though many social scientists may deny such commitments. But while the hermeneutical approach is compatible with the retroductive form of explanation, and though the search for contextualized self-interpretations may be an essential step in the development of a legitimate explanation, a free-standing hermeneutical approach is insufficient to constitute a fully-fledged solution to our problem. Instead, as we have argued, the hermeneutical stance does not furnish us with a convincing ontological and conceptual framework with which to characterize, explain and criticize.

We then examined accounts of explanation that are predicated on the centrality of causal mechanisms, where we mainly focussed on Jon Elster's approach to explanation, though our assessment was relevant for related traditions that concede an important explanatory role to causal mechanisms. As we noted, critical realists such as Roy Bhaskar, Bob Jessop, and Ian Shapiro,

Table 3 Key approaches in social science explanation

Approaches	Elements of explanation	Aims and ideals	Forms of validation & explanation	Modes of explanation	Minimal ontological presuppositions
Positivism	Causal laws	Explanation and prediction	Hypothetico-Deductive & Deductive-Nomological	Universal subsumption	Regularities between observable phenomena (e.g. events, facts)
Hermeneutics	Contextualized self-interpretations	Critical interpretation	Retroductive	Thick description, historical narratives and understanding	Intersubjective meanings Individual beliefs and desires
Critical realism	Causal mechanisms	Explanatory critique	Retroductive	General subsumption	Real intransitive objects with causal powers (e.g. structures, agents, institutions)
Neo-positivism	Causal mechanisms	Causal explanation & possible prediction	Retroductive	General subsumption	Analytical atomism (e.g. individuals, dispositions)
Post-structuralist discourse theory	Logics	Critical explanation	Retroductive	Articulation	Radical contingency of objectivity (e.g. structures, subjects, discourses)

also ground their approach on a realist ontology, which assumes the existence of real, intransitive objects that have specific causal powers and properties. On the other hand, Elster's sophisticated neo-positivism retains the belief that ontological questions can for the most part be bracketed, though in our characterization his approach still relies on an atomistic conception of the world in which the latter can be conceptually decomposed into discrete elements or units. Given the peculiar circumstances of the social sciences, these perspectives are sceptical about the possibilities of prediction in the social world, but remain firmly wedded to the search for causal explanations. Nonetheless, while these approaches manage to avoid reducing their explanations to the contextualised self-interpretations of the beliefs, desires and understandings of those actors they seek to explain, they do so at a price: their explanatory schemas remain too external to the self-interpretations under investigation. This means that the posited mechanisms are conceived as discrete units whose properties remain intact when applied to one context, then another.

In short, while these two critiques of the causal law paradigm are both helpful in exposing the problems of the dominant paradigm, they are not themselves without difficulty. Advocates of causal mechanisms err on the side of abstracting mechanisms from the historical contexts in which they function, thus reifying them in a way that constrains their contingency and militates against their full contextualization; the universalism of the causal law ideal still exerts too powerful an attraction. By contrast, proponents of contextualized self-interpretations run the risk of over-valorizing the virtues of historical context and concrete particularity, thus precluding the development of critical explanations that can somehow transcend the particularity of a given situation both explanatorily and critically without, however, risking a kind of imposed normativism.

In the place of contextualized self-interpretations and causal mechanisms, we have proposed the adoption of logics as the basic explanatory unit of our approach. Our aim was to reflect on the conditions for advancing convincing critical explanations, and we developed a nexus of political, social and fantasmatic logics that can critically explain problematized phenomena in a way that respects their singularity, but that does not restrict itself to just reporting or describing that singularity. In general terms, our conception of logic is designed to capture the point, rules and ontological preconditions of a practice or regime of practices. More fully, the discernment of *social logics* enables us to characterize practices or regimes by setting out the rules informing the practice and the kinds of entities populating it; *political logics* allow us to account for their historical emergence and formation by focusing on the conflicts and contestations surrounding their constitution; and *fantasmatic logics* furnish us with the means to explain the way subjects are gripped or held by a practice or regime of practices. Taken together, logics are by no means reducible to the empirical phenomena for which they are designed to account, though neither are they accorded a fully transcendental role and function.

Importantly, as we have insisted throughout the book, our logics are not independent of the specific historical contexts in which they operate, or of the particular ontological framework within which they emerge and are rooted. Indeed, it is critical that our conception of logics is sustained by a particular, though more encompassing social ontology, whose basic concepts and underlying presuppositions we elaborated in Chapter 4. But while we agree with critical realists and hermeneuticists that an ontological turn in the social sciences is necessary, our ontology is built on different premises. Of central importance in this regard is our commitment to the *radical contingency* of social objectivity, whether in the form of structures, agents or institutions, which in our view has important ramifications for our understanding of social change, political subjectivity, and the overall structuring of social relations. In sum, our ontological perspective is not just concerned with a detailed listing of the different sorts of entities in the world – *what* is in the world – which, of course, is always relative to particular situations and practices, but it also raises prior considerations about *how* entities are in our social worlds and *that* they are the way they are, which admits of more general reflection.

In the course of discussing the employment of logics as the basic means of critical explanation, and in the various examples and illustrations we used to justify our approach, it became clear that any explanation would comprise a plurality of logics in a historically specific and complex set of social circumstances. This meant that the various types of logic had to be articulated into a singular *explanans* in order to explain a particular *explanandum*. We thus elaborated the character and conditions for an articulatory practice in Chapter 6, which in our view avoided the problems of subsumption, descriptivism and eclecticism. As the name implies, an articulatory practice links together a series of concepts and research activities and strategies – judging, naming, generalizing, justifying, comparing, explaining, and so on – that enables us to put our grammar of concepts and logics into practice.

Finally, and importantly, the work of critique and evaluation in our approach is not separated from the adjacent practices of description and explanation. Instead, the task of social criticism is internally connected to the practices of problematization, characterization, and political engagement. In this regard, we highlighted both ethical and normative aspects of critique. While ethics is directly linked to the constitutive incompleteness of structures (the inverse of our notion of ideological fantasy), normative evaluation centres on historically specific relations of social domination and oppression.

* * *

This study has sought to develop a grammar of concepts and logics with which to problematize, explain, criticize, and evaluate a range of practices and regimes. We have critically engaged with a number of prominent approaches to social and political analysis, while also endeavouring to elaborate an alternative. Much of the reflection has been theoretical, sometimes dealing with abstract discussions in ontology, epistemology and methodology.

And yet the approach we articulate is not conceived as a fully-fledged and free-standing theory of politics and society, which can resolve by itself the pressing problems we encounter as political analysts and social critics. Instead, it constitutes an open-textured grammar of concepts – a theoretical horizon – designed for the purpose of analyzing and learning from concrete empirical practices and regimes. The thought here is that 'it is only through a multitude of concrete studies that we will be able to move towards an increasingly sophisticated theory' (Laclau 1990: 235).

But, equally, our approach also requires a continual engagement with adjacent theoretical approaches, as indeed we require a continual dialogue with those approaches with which we disagree, even if such disagreements are fundamental and prove difficult to overcome. Such is the demand associated with the ethos of agonistic respect that arises from the conception of ethics we develop in this book. It is only if empirical and theoretical research proceeds in tandem that our approach can hope to constitute a 'living' rather than 'dead' tradition of thought. In a similar vein, an intervention can only aspire to be explanatory *and* critical to the extent that it engages with the norms and values of the specific practices and regimes it encounters in particular contexts. Critique and normative evaluation are thus the products of the exploratory interplay between the counter-logics that emerge in particular contexts, and the contestable values and principles we necessarily bring with us to our concrete investigations.

Notes

Introduction

1 By the term positivism we mean to capture the following features usually associated with it: 'unity of method', especially as concerns the hypothetico-deductive method, 'value neutrality', and 'fact neutrality'. But our use of the term is broad enough to include not just what we might call a 'constant conjunction positivism' but also a 'depth realist positivism'. As Steinmetz points out, a significant development in the evolution of positivism during the latter half of the twentieth century saw the empiricism associated with Hume and the logical positivists (which entailed a passage through human experience) disarticulated from the epistemological commitment to constant conjunctions itself. This made it possible for someone working within the positivist tradition to commit to a much stronger notion of causation involving real unobservables with causal properties (Steinmetz 2005: 32). For a good historical overview of positivism in twentieth century social science, see Steinmetz's 2005 collection of essays that charts positivism's vicissitudes, prompting one to ask 'why positivism is perpetually disavowed and unconsciously embraced' (Steinmetz 2005: 31).

2 In Steinmetz's words: 'The so-called glasnost-perestroika movement in political science called for the democratization and reform of the political scientists' professional association and flagship journal and criticized the discipline's preference for rational choice and game theory approaches, econometrics, and mathematical and statistical methods. This movement arose in the wake of concerted efforts during the 1990s to solidify the domination of the field by a basically positivist approach that could encompass both qualitative and quantitative methods' (Steinmetz 2005: 39). For a useful discussion of this movement, see also Topper (2005: 5–10, 181–8), who draws on hermeneutics, pragmatism, critical realism, and poststructuralism to develop a perspective, embodied in the work of someone like Pierre Bourdieu, capable of defending methodological pluralism in political studies.

3 See, for example, Bevir and Rhodes 2004, 2005, 2006; Dowding 2001, 2004; Finlayson *et al*. 2004; Hay 2002; Marsh and Smith 2001; Topper 2005; Yanow and Schwartz-Shea 2006.

4 There has been a growing interest in the history of political science. See, for example, Bevir 2006 and Farr *et al*. 1995.

5 As Tilly and Goodin assert, it may be true that when social scientists 'fight about explanation...they generally pit law-seeking against propensity accounts, with the first often donning the costume of Science and the second the garb of Interpretation' (Tilly and Goodin 2006: 13; see also 6, 9), but explanation by

'robust causal mechanisms' is another powerful contender in this fight, even though it 'has received much less self-conscious attention from social science methodologists' (Tilly and Goodin 2006: 13–14).

6　From this point of view, poststructuralist discourse theory affirms David Apter's recent call that one should focus much more attention on the role of discourse 'in the preservation and alteration of political systems including what might be called languages of action' (Apter 2006: 767; see also Blyth 2003). He says this in the knowledge that there are large numbers of institutes and research centres whose titles refer to 'discourse' in one way or another, where the aim is to understand what affects political beliefs and attitudes. His worry, however, is that there is a tendency in much of this kind of research 'to treat such matters behaviourally and instrumentally... rather than subjecting them to substantive interpretation' (Apter 2006: 768). 'The problem is that such emphases, important as they are, do not deal with the power of discourse itself, the uses of political language, and the power of interpretation to affect people's judgement in important ways. On such matters, political theory remains descriptive rather than analytical, despite efforts to categorize and periodize the relationship between belief systems and the mobilization of opinion and of political groups' (Apter 2006: 769).

7　The primacy we attribute to the political dimension of social life resonates with Michael Freeden's recent call for a 'political theory of politics', construed as 'a significant branch of political theory dedicated to identifying the "political" and making sense of it' (Freeden 2005: 115).

8　See, for example, Campbell 1992, 1998; Dillon 1996; Edkins 2003; Shapiro 2004; Walker 1992.

9　See, for example, Bastow and Martin 2003; Butler 1990; Finlayson 2003; Griggs and Howarth 2004; Howarth, Norval and Stavrakakis 2000; Howarth and Torfing 2005; Laclau 1994, 2005; Norval 1996; Panizza 2005; Salecl 1994; Smith 1994; Zerilli 2005.

10　Chouliaraki and Fairclough 1999; Fairclough 1995, 2000.

11　It is striking that Giddens does not – and in some cases simply cannot – mention the works of Althusser, Balibar, Badiou, Rancière, Butler, Campbell, Castells, Connolly, Copjec, Laclau, Poulantzas, Zerilli and Žižek in his critical appraisal of this tradition of thought.

12　See, for example, Bevir and Rhodes 2006; Geras 1987, 1988, 1990; Žižek 2000.

13　As it has recently and felicitously been observed – at least within the field of political studies – some of the 'fiercest disagreements involve logics of explanation' (Tilly and Goodin 2006: 12).

14　Weber's philosophy and methodology of social science constitutes a vast field of inquiry, and has provoked perennial dispute (see, for example, Owen 1994; Parkin 1982: 17–39; Ringer 1997, 2004; Runciman 1972). Nonetheless, it is possible to say that despite his best efforts to articulate a consistent philosophy of social science, his work remains tantalizingly torn between a desire to satisfy the demands of (subjective) interpretative understanding and (objective) causal explanation. Indeed, alongside the intrinsic question marks surrounding the role and functioning of the various concepts he develops, the relationships between the different elements of his approach are systematically tension-ridden (see Runciman 1972). On the one hand, Weber prioritizes the operation of *verstehen* (interpretive understanding). Understanding the sense and significance of an action or practice from this perspective is a necessary condition for the meaningfulness of cultural science itself, including its 'statistical uniformities' and 'sociological generalizations' (Weber 1978: 12). Without this 'significance test' a law or statistical probability would be 'worthless for the understanding of action in the real world' (Weber 1978: 11). In this respect, laws, empirical generalizations, and ideal types are no more than preliminary devices or heuristic steps in the search for knowledge of historical particulars.

On the other hand, however, the interpretive understanding of subjectively meaningful behaviour sits uncomfortably with the call for 'non-interpretable uniformities underlying what has appeared to be specifically meaningful action', even though he thinks that 'little has been accomplished in this direction thus far' (Weber 1978: 7–8). This is even more evident when Weber appears to consider it 'indispensable' in the social sciences that we verify 'subjective interpretation by comparison with the concrete course of events', in which the latter involves tests of 'subjective adequacy'. By 'subjective adequacy', Weber means 'adequacy on the level of meaning', *as well as* 'causal adequacy', which is predicated on the probability that 'according to established generalizations from experience', an action or sequence of events 'will always actually occur in the same way' (Weber 1978: 11). And while Weber declares the true object of sociological research to be the singular causal analysis of concrete particularities – individual events and processes – he does not explicitly exclude the search for generalities and universals.

15 There are, of course, a number of ways to articulate what we have deemed a 'negative ontology', and then relating it to political theory. For an excellent discussion of these issues, see the work of Diane Coole (2000).

16 In a similar way, Michael Freeden views practices as animated by 'the inevitable tension between the desire for decontestation [or closure] and its impossibility' (Freeden 2005: 123).

1 Retroduction

1 Expressions of this faith are many. Consider, for example, the following: '[T]he sciences . . . consist of a body of related and verified generalizations which describe occurrences accurately enough to be used for prediction' (Riker 1962: 3); or: 'A true science . . . must be able not merely to rearrange the past but to predict the future' (Berlin 1996: 44); or: 'If a descriptive model is to explain anything it must also produce some predictions' (Dowding 2001: 92).

2 In characterizing positivism as a function of the causal law *paradigm* we do not only aim to capture those social science practices which rely upon, or invoke, the term 'causal law'. After all, today many analysts shy away from describing social processes as a function of laws, opting instead for causal tendencies or robust empirical correlations.

3 See for example Galavotti 2003; Schickore and Steinle 2006.

4 As the stark distinction between contexts of discovery and justification has been extensively discussed, contested, and re-articulated in the philosophy of science, it would be worth charting and probing in a systematic way the points of convergence and divergence between the point of view of the history and philosophy of science and the point of view of the history and philosophy of social science.

5 'We will always find political economists on both sides of the question whether cutting taxes leads to increases or decreases in government revenue, and predictive tests will not settle their disagreements. . . . Likewise, political economists have been arguing at least since Bentham's time over whether trickle-down policies benefit the poor more than do government transfers' (Shapiro 2002: 609). Similarly, 'trying to predict election outcomes from various mixes of macro political

and economic variables has been a growth industry in political science for more than a generation. But perhaps the factors that caused people to vote as they did in the 1950s differ from those forty or fifty years later. After all, this is not an activity with much of a track record of success in political science. We saw this dramatically in the 2000 election in which all of the standard models predicted a decisive Gore victory' (Shapiro 2002: 610). However, it is worth noting that even those who are moderately sceptical about predictions and forecasting in political science still retain a commitment to its centrality.

6 Shapiro defends prediction as a criterion against those who claim that prediction is inherently unattainable in the study of human affairs due to free will and contingency. One can still support probabilistic predictions regarding phenomena predicated on free will and predictions regarding those phenomena which are not predicated on contingency or for which contingency can be plausibly bracketed (Shapiro 2002: 607). He suggests that whether and to what extent prediction should play a criterial role depends on the problem and cannot be decided in advance (Shapiro 2002: 608).

7 As Keith Topper shows, following Peter Galison's *Image and Logic*, even a sub-field like high-energy physics is disunified sociologically, ontologically, and epistemologically (Topper 2005: 44–7).

8 This is a simplified version because it omits reference to auxiliary hypotheses – see Lessnof 1974: 18; see also Lakatos (1974) on 'sophisticated falsificationism'.

9 As Hanson puts it, with respect to 'the functioning of theories within technical science, the hypothetico-deductive account seems illuminating vis-à-vis our ideas of hypothesis-*testing*, and terse *expositions of the results* of that testing' (Hanson 1972: 65).

10 In Lakatosian terms, we could say these comprise the 'core' of its research programme (Lakatos 1974).

11 Even as fierce a critic of method and technique-driven social science research as Shapiro appears to share this premise. One difficulty Shapiro mentions in discussing prediction as a problematic sorting criterion is that 'it is usually impossible to disentangle the complex interacting causal processes that operate in the actual world' (Shapiro 2002: 609). This suggests that it is still possible to remain wedded to a Pascalian/positivist dream of total determinism, predictability, and control at the ontological level, while being wary of its complete realization at the epistemological level.

12 Here is another formulation: 'If we are to give the names of Deduction, Induction, and Abduction to the three grand classes of inference, then Deduction must include every attempt at mathematical demonstration, whether it relate to single occurrences or to "probabilities," that is, to statistical ratios; Induction must mean the operation that induces an assent, with or without quantitative modification, to a proposition already put forward, this assent or modified assent being regarded as the provisional result of a method that must ultimately bring the truth to light; while Abduction must cover all the operations by which theories and conceptions are engendered' (Peirce 1957: 237).

13 For Peirce, a hypothesis is any 'proposition added to observed facts' which tends 'to make them applicable . . . to other circumstances than those under which they were observed' (Peirce 1957: 235). 'The first stating of a hypothesis and the entertaining of it, whether as a simple interrogation or with any degree of confidence, is an inferential step which I propose to call *abduction*. This will include a preference for any one hypothesis over others which would equally explain the facts, so long as this preference is not based upon any previous

knowledge bearing upon the truth of the hypotheses, nor on any testing of any of the hypotheses, after having admitted them on probation. I call all such inference by the peculiar name, *abduction*, because its legitimacy depends upon altogether different principles from those of other kinds of inference' (Peirce 1957: 236–7).

14 'The great difference between induction and hypothesis is that the former infers the existence of phenomena such as we have observed in cases which are similar, while hypothesis supposes something of a different kind from what we have directly observed, and frequently something which it would be impossible for us to observe directly' (Peirce 1960: 385). For a useful critical and clarificatory note on Peirce and retroduction (or abduction), see Frankfurt 1958.

15 Note, however, how Peirce also uses the three different forms of reasoning to make distinctions *within* natural science: 'Of the natural sciences, we have, first, the classificatory sciences, which are purely inductive – systematic botany and zoology, mineralogy, and chemistry. Then, we have the sciences of theory . . . – astronomy, pure physics, etc. Then, we have sciences of hypothesis – geology, biology, etc.' (Peirce 1960: 388).

16 Cf. Bhaskar's response to Benton on this point in the Postscript of the third edition of *The Possibility of Naturalism* (Bhaskar 1998).

17 With the term post-positivism we gather together a somewhat disparate set of approaches which all claim to take seriously the basic hermeneutical insight that the self-interpretations of actors are central to – though not necessarily sufficient for – a satisfactory social science explanation. Post-positivism includes within its ambit 'full blown' hermeneutical approaches of course, but it also encompasses many approaches drawing on poststructuralist, critical theory, and critical realist traditions, as well as certain reformed or sophisticated positivist approaches, such as those that take causal mechanisms as their central unit of analysis and explanation.

18 See, for example Popper 1961: Part IV.

19 The widespread practice of ignoring the history of physics when teaching physics reflects this view. Usually it is sufficient to know Newton's or Einstein's theory of gravitation, not *how* and *why* it was posited in the first place. Of central importance, then, is the capacity of a hypothesis, law, or theory to predict and explain. Positivism presents this image of natural science practice as an ideal that social science should aspire to reproduce. Of course, there are reasons to think that this image of natural science practice is itself suspect. Consider, for instance, Lakatos's theory of progressive research programmes or Kuhn's view on the role of paradigms in natural science. However, we can remain largely agnostic on this front, since our only disagreement at this point is with the positivist projection of this particular picture onto social science practice.

20 This does not mean that we cannot address perfectly legitimate questions about which factors may be more important or influential in our overall explanatory account. What we reject is the view that these questions can be answered legitimately only via predictive models that parse out and then test the relative strength of different explanatory factors, thus disregarding the contestable nature of interpretation and contextualization.

21 We can develop this point from a slightly different angle by elaborating a distinction between two orders of reflexivity that are closely related to the category of subjectivity: first-order reflexivity and second-order reflexivity. In both cases, practices are as reliable as the subjects who enact them, and the structures which make such performance possible. This set-up, however incomplete

it is for the time being, already suggests at least two reasons why prediction in the social sciences is so fraught with difficulties. Since predictions are parasitic upon practices, and since practices are mediated by changeable first-order beliefs and meanings, predictions are as fragile as the agents' self-understandings and interpretations that partly constitute such practices. Of course, not all beliefs and meanings change, and those that do change do not necessarily change randomly. While such fragility may force social scientists to abandon all pretence to the kind of certainty promised by deductive forms of reasoning, probabilistic-statistical or inductive forms of reasoning offer a modicum of hope to social scientists who embrace a form of scientism. Instead of laws, in other words, we may have to be satisfied with law-like regularities. Indeed, social scientists have in the main tended to retreat to the realm of statistical probability.

What this overlooks is the fact that the meaning and significance of actors' beliefs and reasons are a function of the context both of the actors and of the problems and objectives animating research. Among other things, this means that the robustness, sense, and significance of law-like regularities are under threat by the subject's capacity for second-order reflexivity. Consider the contingency introduced into the system once an identified practice, however probabilistic in character or however reasonable its underlying rationale, is made public and thus accessible to the subjects being studied. This is the so-called 'feedback effect' (Jervis 1997) or 'looping effect' (Hacking 1995). As Connolly puts it, for example,

> to render the predictions reliable the expert is encouraged to keep established correlations outside the sphere of public discourse. For given the reflexive capacities of the human objects of inquiry, widespread awareness of the antecedents of their own behaviour might provoke them to revise future patterns of conduct. The awareness could diminish both the ability to test the law-like claim (*since one of its preconditions has changed*) and the ability to use the knowledge effectively in social policy.
>
> (Connolly 1981: 20)

Thus, unlike the natural sciences, so-called laws and explanations in the social sciences are inextricably tied to the subjects they purport to cover, such that hypotheses comprise explanatory elements and the conditions under which these explanations hold. This is clear in cases of so-called 'self-fulfilling' prophecies or what we might call 'self-defeating' prophecies. As an example of the latter imagine a dictum which states that queues in theme parks peak on public holidays. This would exemplify the case of a self-defeating prophecy if the wide dissemination and knowledge of the dictum served to provide agents with a reason to avoid theme parks on public holidays, which was then acted upon. We would thus have a new and contrary view stating that queues in theme parks shrink on public holidays. In other words, in the social sciences the contextual features – including the self-interpretations of the relevant social actors – are strongly bound up with the content, and therefore the meaning and significance of, the hypotheses and explanations themselves.

22 As against the covering-law model, which 'reflectively *mis*understands the logic of political explanations' (Farr 1987: 61), Farr thus shows how some of the most well-respected social science laws conform to a 'situational analysis' model rather than to the covering-law model. Paying attention to the situational features yields statements of the following kind: 'In such-and-such a situation, a rational actor, faced with such-and-such a problem, with such-and-such beliefs, intentions, and meanings, will act in such-and-such a way'. This contrasts with the typical covering-law

model explanation: 'All rational actors in such-and-such a situation (like the one to be explained) will believe or act in such-and-such a way' (Farr 1987: 48).

23 Farr draws on Popper in furnishing his account of situational analysis. This may appear slightly odd, since we are using this account to undermine the stark opposition between contexts of discovery and justification, which Popper has been thought to rely upon in strongly advocating the unity of method between natural and social sciences. There are two points we would like to make in this regard. First, Popper's own position on the relation between the natural and social sciences is actually not so clear, as many scholars have pointed out (e.g. Gray 1989: Ch. 2). More recently, in fact, one scholar suggests that Popper came to favour the distinctiveness of situational analysis as more appropriate to the social sciences, despite his plea for the unity of method (Gorton 2006). Second, whether or not Popper has got himself ensnared in a contradiction, and whether this contradiction ends up being fatal to his unity of method thesis, is of secondary concern to us. Of key importance is how we can adapt Farr's use of situational analysis to undermine the detachability thesis, as well as associated notions like causal laws, the stark separation between contexts of discovery and justification, the deductive conception of explanation, and the strong notion of testing based solely or ideally on prediction.

24 Of course, there may be other reasons why one should be sceptical about drawing a stark boundary between the contexts of discovery and justification. For an example from the point of view of the history and philosophy of science see Schickore and Steinle 2006. Among other things, it has been noted that there are serious definitional ambiguities about what elements precisely belong to the respective contexts, and frequent violations of the boundary between contexts have also been observed in the concrete practice of scientists.

25 Or elsewhere: '[T]he experience with negotiation and change in practice and the discontents that arise in response provide a *pragmatic test* of the critical and historical research and the impetus for another round of critical activity' (Tully 2002: 535; emphasis added).

26 Of course, this by no means precludes cases in which we can justify the qualified use of methods and techniques normally associated with natural science practice, or of comparative methods and statistical techniques developed specifically for use in the social sciences. (For a thoughtful discussion of justified uses of such methods and techniques in political science research, see Topper 2005: 192–4.) But such cases would entail the rebuttal of a presumption deeply embedded in much social science practice (i.e., that there is no need, or a limited need, for such contextualization-qualification), thus reversing the vector of 'default' present in a positivist conception of social science testing and explanation.

27 Though the retroductive circle shares a family resemblance with the hermeneutic circle, we keep them separate because of the latter's association with potentially more maximal hermeneutical programmes. For us, as we will see below, the notion of an expansive retroductive circle is compatible with a range of approaches with differing presupposed ontologies, whether they take their bearings from contextualized self-interpretations, causal mechanisms, or logics.

28 See Laclau 1977; Laclau 1990; Laclau 1996; Laclau 2005; Laclau and Mouffe 1985; Mouffe 1979; Mouffe 1993; Mouffe 2005.

29 First person accounts and the academic literature may take for granted the dominant formulation of the problem linked to the 'repressive hypothesis', namely, 'why are people so repressed sexually?' This parallels the dominant hypothesis in the literature concerning audit regimes in UK's higher education

system which we will be considering in Chapter 6, namely, 'why are academics so passive in their submission to the audit regimes?' But Foucault problematizes this formulation of the problem by asking the question 'Why do people insist with such vehemence that they are repressed?' Again, as we will see in Chapter 6, this is paralleled in our illustrative analysis of higher education audit culture via a similar problematization: 'Why are people so insistent that academics passively submit to the audit regime?' Foucault's problematization goes hand-in-hand with a detailed analysis of the literature and the relevant empirical corpus which, under closer scrutiny, reveals a proliferation rather than a repression of sex discourse. Foucault then accounts for this proliferation by identifying and articulating together the logics of disciplinary power and bio-power. And an analysis of the empirical corpus and the literature in higher education also reveals a much more complex picture of academic life in the current audit era, demanding an explanation through the identification and articulation of a range of relevant logics.

30 It is worth pointing out here that from the point of view of an articulatory conception of retroduction, the categories of induction, deduction, and prediction are not of course abandoned, but accorded a different significance and role. It is widely known, for example, that the principle of induction has been continually and heavily criticized for its vagueness in the philosophy of science literature (for a succinct statement of the principle, see Chalmers 1982: 5, where he also discusses its indeterminacy and vagueness). In other words, the articulatory dimension necessarily comes to the foreground when these problematic features of the principle are taken on board (i.e., the interpretation of contextual features and how they shape the 'application' of the principle of induction).

2 Contextualized self-interpretations

1 Part of this quote is cited in Bevir and Rhodes (2003: 1). We, however, stress the internal-external relationship between the 'observer' and the world of objects 'observed', not just the opposition between truth and meaning. On the internal-external distinction in the context of thinking about the character of rules and laws, see Hart (1961).

2 See Bevir 1999, 2005; Bevir and Rhodes 2003; Buzan and Weaver 2003; Campbell 1992, 1998; Dillon 1996; Fischer 2003; Freeden 1996; Hajer 1995; Norval 1996; Stavrakakis 1999, 2005, 2007; Torfing 1998; Yanow 2003; Yanow and Schwartz-Shea 2006.

3 Peter Winch draws on Max Weber and Ludwig Wittgenstein; Charles Taylor draws on classical hermeneuticists such as Dilthey, Heidegger and Gadamer; Mark Bevir and Rod Rhodes draw on post-analytical philosophers like Ludwig Wittgenstein, Charles Taylor and Donald Davidson, as well as 'modern idealists' such as F.H. Bradley, T.H. Green and R.G. Collingwood, whose ideas were in turn rooted in the philosophies of Hegel and Croce.

4 This conception of the relation between reasons and actions can produce a particular account of the relationship between understanding and explanation in the social sciences, where instead of the usual prioritization of causal explanation, or explanation in general, Winch argues that 'understanding is the goal of explanation', while also constituting 'the end-product of successful explanation'. Indeed, understanding is not exhausted by explanation. As Winch puts it, '[u]nless there is a form of understanding that is not the result of explanation, no such thing as explanation would be possible. An explanation is called for only

where there is, or at least thought to be, a deficiency in understanding. But there has to be some standard against which such deficiency is to be measured: and that standard can only be an understanding that we already have' (Winch 1990: x).

5 Winch stipulates two important criteria for determining whether or not someone is 'really applying a rule in what he does', as opposed to just pretending to follow a rule, or following a different rule altogether (Winch 1990: 29). These criteria are, first, the 'reactions of other people' to a particular instance of rule-following, who must in principle be able to discover the rule that is being followed and, second, the possibility of 'making a mistake', which is logically entailed by the concept of rule-following, and which represents 'a contravention of what is *established* as correct' (Winch 1990: 30, 32). In short, then, not all meanings and actions can be made to accord with a particular rule, because following a particular rule is always constrained by the reactions of others, and is bounded by possibilities that clearly do not accord with it.

6 There are another two reasons Taylor considers. The first follows from the fact that the different domains of human events are never 'closed systems' that can be immunized from the effects of 'external interference'. They are instead essentially 'open systems' which are always vulnerable to unpredictable changes, whether dislocations or the eruption of antagonisms. The second reason is principally epistemological. It is grounded on the claim that the human sciences can never achieve 'the degree of fine exactitude of a science based on brute data' (Taylor 1985b: 55), which can be measured and analysed in a precise fashion. The different interpretations articulated in the human and social sciences cannot be judged with this degree of precision and certainty. On the contrary, 'different nuances of interpretation may lead to different predictions in some circumstances, and these different outcomes may eventually create widely differing futures' (Taylor 1985b: 55).

7 Elaborating Heidegger's views in his post-analytical idiom, Taylor argues that moods, emotions, feelings and so forth, are integral to our self-understandings: they involve 'import-ascriptions' to use his technical language. Of central importance here is the fact that language is *constitutive* of emotion: in articulating our feelings and emotions – in rendering them clearer and more refined – language transforms their significance and thus the affect itself. And Taylor draws an important conclusion from this fact for his analysis of human passions, and hence our self-understandings: it is that the character of one's 'import vocabularies' in a specific culture shapes one's experiences; indeed, as he puts it, 'even within one culture, people with different vocabularies have different experiences' (Taylor 1985a: 71).

8 Taylor's emphasis on discrimination as an integral component of the articulation of human emotions leads to his notion of *strong evaluation*. In making a strong evaluation we do not just consider whether or not certain *objects* are good or bad in light of our desires, but we also evaluate desires themselves. Strong evaluation is thus a second-order evaluation because it reflects back on our first-order desires and their justifications to examine their ultimate worth. For instance, it might lead us to revise our initial motivations and desires – say a desire for revenge – in the name of 'a higher way of seeing our relations with others' leading us 'to see ourselves and others more broadly, more objectively, more truly' (Taylor 1985a: 67). Indeed, through strong evaluation we may become 'a bigger person, with a broader, more serene vision', someone who can act out of 'this higher standpoint' (Taylor 1985a: 67). Language is essential for Taylor's logic of strong evaluation because it serves as the means to articulate such insights (Taylor 1985a: 71).

9 For a short summary of Taylor's use of bargaining and negotiation in drawing a contrast between North American and traditional Japanese social life, see Topper 2005: 68–9.

10 Pre-empting mainstream charges of relativism and subjectivism that this view provokes, Bevir and Rhodes begin by rejecting what they term the logics of vindication and refutation advocated by proponents of verification and falsification respectively. Both positions in their view 'ground objectivity or truth in confrontations with basic facts', thus presupposing the idea that we have 'pure experiences' of the external world (Bevir and Rhodes 2005: 182). This leads them to reject the idea of truth as certainty, but not to dispute a commitment to objectivity (Bevir and Rhodes 2005: 183). Instead, they argue that the latter involves a logic of evaluation 'by comparing rival stories using reasonable criteria' (Bevir and Rhodes 2005: 183).

11 See, for example, Jarvie (1977), MacIntyre (1974), Louch (1966), Lukes (1974, 1982, 2003).

12 We discuss our own discourse-theoretical understanding of idealism, in its relation to materialism, in Chapter 3.

13 As concerns idealism, for example, early in *The Idea of a Social Science*, Winch argues that '[a] man's social relations with his fellows are permeated with his ideas about reality'. Indeed, as he puts it, ' "permeated" is hardly a strong enough word: social relations are expressions of ideas about reality' (Winch 1990: 23). Later in the book, he goes on to claim that 'social relations really exist only in and through the ideas which are current in society; or alternatively . . . social relations fall into the same logical category as do relations between ideas' (Winch 1990: 133). At other points in the text, however, he explicitly rejects the privileging of ideas, and reverses his understanding of the relationship between language, meaning and social practice. For example, in his critique of textbook accounts of language in the field of social psychology, Winch states that

> [t]he impression given is that first there is language (with words having a meaning, statements capable of being true or false) and then, this being given, it comes to enter into human relationships and to be modified by the particular human relationships into which it does so enter. What is missed is that those very categories of meaning, etc., are logically dependent for their sense on social interaction between men . . . There is no discussion of how the very existence of concepts depends on group life.
>
> (Winch 1990: 44)

Developing this theme, he argues that '[i]t will seem less strange that social relations should be like logical relations between propositions once it is seen that logical relations between propositions themselves depend *on social relations between men*' (Winch 1990: 126; emphasis added). In the latter formulations, ideas, concepts and statements are related to a more fundamental set of social relations and social practices, and it is the latter which provide a critical locus for meaning and linguistic practices.

14 In fact, we could say that there are two senses in which rules are open for Winch. The first sense pertains to 'following rules' in a settled practice; and the second sense relates to 'applying rules' in a new context. In the first case, the following of a rule, unlike the existence of a causal regularity, always entails the possibility of 'going wrong' or 'making a mistake' as Winch puts it (Lyas 1999: 32; Winch 1990: 32). In other words, unlike phenomena in the physical sciences which are determined by well-formed laws of nature, human actions can always deviate in

both acceptable and unacceptable ways from the norm, and this introduces a necessary contingency into meaningful behaviour understood as rule-governed. And though Winch claims that a practice can be characterized by or subsumed under rules, this does not mean that the practice comprises only activities that can be considered as *conforming* to the rule. As we have said, the practice of 'following a rule' includes making mistakes whether deliberately or not. For Winch, then, rules provide the central reference point when characterizing the practice as *this* practice rather than *that* practice, and the 'open' nature of this conception of rules allows him to distinguish his position from structural or causal deterministic approaches, which seek to characterize practices as a function of laws or mechanisms for example.

The second sense in which a rule could be said to be open for Winch relates to a situation in which it must be applied in circumstances markedly different 'from any in which it has previously been applied'. And while the rule 'does limit the range of possible alternatives', it 'does not specify any determinate outcome to the situation'. Instead, it is only made determinate by the choice between different alternatives – at least until a new choice is required 'in the light of yet new conditions' (Winch 1990: 92). In the new circumstances in which rules must be applied there is always a decision as how best to 'go on', and thus a new instance of the rule in question is disclosed or 'comes into being'. This is especially evident in Winch's analysis of social institutions, where he argues 'that in changing social situations, reasoned decisions have to be made about what is to count as "going on in the same way"' (Winch 1974: 96).

15 As Wittgenstein points out, this leads potentially to the paradox that 'no course of action could be determined by a rule, because every course of action can be made out to accord with the rule' or indeed because every course of action could be interpreted so as 'to conflict with it' (Wittgenstein 1967: §201). Wittgenstein dissolves this paradox by noting that 'there is a way of grasping a rule which is not an interpretation, but which is exhibited in what we call "obeying a rule" and "going against it" in *actual cases*' (Wittgenstein 1967: §201; emphasis added). And this means that 'we ought to restrict the term "interpretation" to the substitution of one expression of the rule for another' (Wittgenstein 1967: §201).

16 See in this regard Jarvie (1977), MacIntyre (1974), Lukes (1974; 2003: 46–62).

17 On this, see Smith 2002: 101–2, 240, 242. See also Benhabib 2002: viii, 56–8, 67–8; Bohman 1991; Hoy 1991; Hoy and McCarthy 1994; Skinner 1991, 1994; Taylor 1991b, 1994, 1995; Weinstock 1994.

18 Expressed more technically, their approach commits them to a form of 'semantic holism' and the concept of 'weak intentionality', as against a conception of 'strong intentionality' that takes intentions as 'conscious and prior to utterances' (Bevir 2000: 298).

19 Though we do not agree with McAnulla's critical realist solutions, he makes a similar point about Bevir and Rhodes' 'neglect of ontology' and their 'procedural individualism' (McAnulla 2006).

20 Paul Ricoeur famously distinguishes between a 'hermeneutics of retrieval' and a 'hermeneutics of suspicion', where the former is a form of interpretation that takes social practices or texts at their face value, and then seeks to recover and reconstruct their meanings so as to render them more intelligible, while the latter consists in the location of a deeper, though concealed, truth that needs to be unearthed and confronted (Ricoeur 1970: 28–32). Ricoeur's 'school of suspicion' comprises three 'modern masters of suspicion' – Marx, Nietzsche and Freud – each of whom seeks to demystify and unmask the 'distorted motivations' underlying

various systems of thought and practice. Radicalizing Descartes's scepticism about our having certain knowledge of the world and ourselves, these thinkers aim to uncover the 'illusions of consciousness', thus decentring its overall importance in our practices and lives. Not capitulating to a complete scepticism or nihilism, however, they also strive to dismantle or 'deconstruct' philosophical texts and intellectual traditions, so as to clear the path for new 'truths' to emerge via a new logic of interpretation, which is centred on the 'deciphering of expressions', rather than spelling 'out the consciousness of meaning' (Ricoeur 1970: 32–6). And, finally, not content to expose 'the real' as against 'the apparent', the masters of suspicion seek to effect change by confronting and ultimately overturning the 'false consciousness' that produces the illusions and repressions in the name of an insight that liberates.

3 Causal mechanisms

1 The editors of a recent handbook in political analysis note that '[e]xplanation by means of robust causal mechanisms has received much less self-conscious attention from social science methodologists' than other candidates, including causal laws and what we have termed contextualized self-interpretations (Tilly and Goodin 2006: 14–15). Nevertheless, there have been a number of social and political theorists other than Elster who have employed the language of causal mechanisms to develop alternatives to mainstream accounts of social science explanation (see Bunge 1997; Hay 2002, 2006; Jessop 1982, 1990, 2002; Little 1998; Shapiro 2005; Shapiro and Wendt 1992, 1997; Stinchcombe 1991; Tilly 2000, 2001; Wendt 1999). Tilly and Goodin venture a rough classification of mechanisms, distinguishing between environmental mechanisms, cognitive mechanisms and relational mechanisms:

> *Environmental mechanisms* mean externally generated influences on conditions affecting social life; words like 'disappear', 'enrich', 'expand', and 'disintegrate' – applied not to actors but their settings – suggest the sorts of cause-effect relations in question.
>
> *Cognitive mechanisms* operate through alterations of individual and collective perception; words like 'recognize', 'understand', 'reinterpret', and 'classify' characterize such mechanisms.
>
> *Relational mechanisms* alter connections among people, groups, and interpersonal networks; words like 'ally', 'attack', 'subordinate', and 'appease' give a sense of relational mechanisms.
>
> (Tilly and Goodin 2006: 16)

2 See Elster 1978, 1984, 1985, 1992, 1993, 1999.
3 Or elsewhere: 'The elementary unit of social life is the individual human action. To explain social institutions and social change is to show how they arise as the result of the action and interaction of individuals. This view, often referred to as methodological individualism, is in my view trivially true' (Elster 1989: 13).
4 Since intentional explanation, for Elster, involves a triadic relation between action, desire, and belief, and if we use 'reason' as a common term for beliefs and desires, then '[i]ntentional explanation involves showing that the actor did what he did *for* a reason' rather than simply *with* a reason. 'The requirement that the actor does what he does for a reason implies that the reason is causally efficacious in bringing about the action, but is not exhausted by that implication. We need to add that the reasons cause the action "in the right way", that is, not by a fluke' (Elster 1983a: 70).

5 For purposes of this paper, we follow Elster in treating the centrality of intentional explanations as homologous to the centrality accorded to self-interpretations in hermeneutics (see Elster 1983a: 16–17).

6 Or, as he puts it elsewhere, 'for practical purposes we may treat intentional and causal explanations as wholly distinct. When using a functional explanation, we usually know at least roughly how it could be backed by a suitable causal story. But in the present state of knowledge, we cannot even see in outline how intentional explanations are related to causal analyses of the same phenomena. Even if at some time in the future Davidson should join the line of distinguished thinkers who have declared it impossible in principle to do something which scientists have then gone on to do in practice, philosophers of science can for the present safely take the two perspectives as being radically different' (Elster 1983a: 23).

7 His work thus constitutes a further development of the notion of mechanism as it was developed in *Explaining Technical Change* (1983) and *Nuts and Bolts for the Social Sciences* (1989). There the antonym for mechanism was not 'covering laws' but a 'black box' (1999: 4).

8 Here it is worth noting that though Elster observes that '[m]echanisms often come in pairs' (1999: 6), his remarks on the whole indicate that they need not.

9 In the introduction to this chapter we noted that our argument with respect to Elster is also relevant for other theorists who adopt causal mechanisms as a central explanatory concept even though they situate themselves in different traditions. For example, our argument applies to Roy Bhaskar who therefore does not escape the shadow of positivism either, even though his naturalist project is intended as a critique of positivism. For a similar point, see Topper 2005: 145.

10 Elsewhere, however, he appears to introduce a little distance between himself and this ideal when he says, for instance, that '[a]lthough it is difficult to establish laws in the social sciences, that goal will always, for better of for worse, continue to guide scholars' (Elster 1999: 36). It is a statement which resonates with the qualified nature of some related remarks. He says, for example, that 'the purpose [of the mechanism approach] is to illustrate and stimulate the imagination rather than to argue for any specific thesis' (Elster 1999: 32). Or, as he puts it later, '[t]he purpose of the discussion is to demonstrate the range and power of mechanism reasoning. I am not trying to prove any particular thesis, only to persuade the reader of the fruitfulness of the approach' (Elster 1999: 20). Indeed, he considers the possibility that 'the resort to explanation by mechanism in the social sciences may not be due to their less developed state or to the complexity of their subject matter, but to more general facts about human understanding or about the world' (Elster 1999: 2).

11 'The tracts, treatises and texts of the last three hundred years of physics rarely contain the word *cause*, much less *causal chain*. In their prefaces and their *obiter dicta* physicists may get expansive; nonetheless the concept is used infrequently in the actual practice of physics, and this fact is important' (Hanson 1961: 52).

12 Or elsewhere: 'Nothing can be explained to us if we do not help. We have had an explanation of x only when we can set it into an interlocking pattern of concepts about other things, y and z' (Hanson 1961: 54). 'This feature of causation and explanation gets lost when concepts are forged in the causal-chain mould' (Hanson 1961: 56). '[C]auses are no more visual data simpliciter than are facts. Nothing in sense-datum space could be labelled "cause", or "effect"' (Hanson 1961: 59). 'Only a hasty view of the vocabulary of mechanics will support a chain conception of causation; classical physics is not like a series of links in its simplicity'

(Hanson 1961: 65–6). 'Causes certainly are connected with effects; but this is because our theories connect them, not because the world is held together by cosmic glue. The world *may* be glued together by imponderables, but that is irrelevant for understanding causal explanation. The notions behind "the cause x" and "the effect y" are intelligible only against a pattern of theory, namely one which puts guarantees on inferences from x to y. Such guarantees distinguish truly causal sequences from mere coincidence' (Hanson 1961: 64). 'This shows what we expect of a causal law. These are not built up in the manner: (A then B)$_1$, (A then B)$_2$, (A then B)$_3$, therefore all As are followed by Bs. This obscures the role of causal laws in our conceptions of a physical world . . . // *The difference between generalizing the repeated occurrence of contiguous, propinquitous, asymmetric, event-pairs and understanding the 'causal' structure of a natural phenomenon is like the difference between having a visual impression of a lunaroid patch and observing the moon.* It is like the difference between contemplating a concavity on the lunar surface, and appreciating the fact that the moon is craterous' (Hanson 1961: 65; emphasis added).

4 Ontology

1 In using the term 'regime' we invoke an ancient concept that can be traced back to the political philosophies of Plato and Aristotle. Aristotle uses the term *politeia* or constitution (regime) to refer to 'a kind of organization of the state's inhabitants', where the latter is conceived as a 'composite thing' (Aristotle 1987: 516). But the term *politeia* or constitution (regime) also captures the broader notion of a community's particular way of life, which 'is in a figure the life of the city' (Aristotle 2001: 1220). In short, the constitution is an immanent organizing principle of a particular state and the community it bounds.

2 In his rise to power, for example, Juan Peron incorporated new popular sectors into his discourse (especially the working class) and excluded old sectors by breaking the sedimented link between citizenship and formal political rights, and reconnecting it instead to a broader social context (Barros and Castagnola 2000). A new dichotomy was thus established between Peron's 'social justice' on the one hand (aligned with the trade unions, youth organizations, right and left-wing groups, and various nationalist groups) and 'social injustice' on the other hand (aligned with the liberal oligarchy, the middle classes, traditional political parties, the Catholic Church, and the armed forces). The case of Peronism also indicates to us that insofar as political struggles are hegemonically successful, political logics provide the means with which to account for not only new social practices, but also regimes of practices. In a more technical language to be explored later, political logics comprise a formal signifying grammar (derived from a post-Saussurean ontology) in terms of which a particular social practice or regime can be shown to have been instituted and maintained, and others rejected.

3 Enjoyment, or what Lacan calls *jouissance*, is closely associated with the Freudian notions of libido and primordial loss (or primary repression). It appeared in his discourse for the first time in the 1950s, and even then occasionally (Evans 1996: 91–2), but it was not until the 1960s, starting with his seminar on the ethics of psychoanalysis, that it comes to be defined in opposition to pleasure (Lacan 1992: 185) and in relation to suffering and the moral law. See also Lacan 2006: 700; 2007, 1998.

4 How, then, does the ontical/ontological distinction relate to our concept of a logic, and help us to clarify the latter's use? While the relationship is complex, it is useful to explore them here in a preliminary way so as to specify further the

notion of a logic, and to define the scope of our investigation. The issue is complicated because our investigation deals with different types of object that are situated at various levels of abstraction. We need therefore to begin by specifying the kind of object being investigated. On the one hand, we might specify a concrete object of investigation: what is the logic of the higher education audit regime in the UK for example? Here we are confronted with a series of empirical phenomena at the ontical level, and our task is to characterize and explain them. By employing our three-fold typology of logics we seek to do this by establishing the rules governing the practices, and the entities that compose the practices under investigation. In a retroductive fashion, we seek to articulate the animating principles of the phenomena investigated, endeavouring to characterize a practice, including what makes it tick, and how it manages to reproduce or transform itself. Our endeavour aims to render the phenomena and practices intelligible both for the subjects involved in the activity studied, and for the subjects who are studying the phenomena. As this investigation requires an analysis of the entities and relationships that constitute the phenomena investigated, our *ontical inquiry necessarily involves an ontological dimension*: an ontical inquiry will therefore always involve the redescription of phenomena in terms of our presupposed ontology. And for us this task requires the employment of social, political and fantasmatic logics.

But this brings us to a second possible investigative focus which is central for our book. While we do attempt to account for specific, problematized empirical phenomena, we are mainly concerned to clarify and develop a kind of 'logic of logics'. And in seeking to explicate the basic concepts and logics of these more abstract objects of investigation we are engaging in a more fully-fledged ontological inquiry. In other words, we are setting out the categorical conditions – the rules, entities and structural relationships – for the investigation of social and political phenomena as such. In sum, we could say that an ontical inquiry, while it presupposes an ontology, yields ontical categories; an ontological inquiry, while it cannot totally escape the ontical field, yields ontological categories.

5 Ranciere's politics/police distinction (Ranciere 1998) and Badiou's event/situation distinction (Badiou 2007) are similarly non-topographical, at least in theory.

6 The idea of a *fundamental* norm bears a certain resemblance to the notion of a 'constitutive' rather than 'regulative' rule (see Searle 1969). A *regulative rule system*, on the one hand, is a system of rules designed to regulate an already existing activity. Here, the relation of such a rule system to its point or purpose is that of a means to an end. Hence the point of a regulative rule system is logically prior to the rule system itself. A *constitutive rule system*, on the other hand, has its point or purpose defined internally. The point does not exist independently of the rule system itself. The traffic rule system is a classic example of a regulative rule system, while the chess rule system is a common example of a constitutive rule system. You would be able to know how to drive your car, even if there were no traffic rules, but you would not be able to play chess without being aware of and following its rules.

7 This is despite the fact that many political theorists, as well as different ideological traditions (whether it be communism, anarchism, radical libertarianism) hold out the prospect of future utopias in which politics is replaced by the fantasy of pure administration or spontaneous organization, or which are predicated on the notion of politics as a continuous and all-encompassing process of permanent revolution.

8 See, for example, Crisp and Slote 1997; Statman 1997.

9 The primacy we attribute to the political dimension of social life resonates with Michael Freeden's recent call for a 'political theory of politics', construed as 'a significant branch of political theory dedicated to identifying the "political" and making sense of it' (Freeden 2005: 115). The task of political theory, then, involves trying to 'distinguish an area [we] wish to term the "political" and then to develop strategies that enable [us] to address directly issues of *political* thought' (Freeden 2005: 115).

10 What Laclau and Mouffe call 'relations of subordination' and 'relations of domination' correspond roughly to what Steven Lukes calls *potestas* and domination (Lukes 2005: 74). On the difficulty of separating analysis from critique in the context of Lukes's work on power, see Heyward (2007).

11 This logic shares an affinity with what we might call 'structural power' or what Lukes terms the 'third face of power' (Lukes 2005). Cf. also the notion of 'premediation' in Grusin 2004.

12 See, for example, Burawoy (1979); Knights and Willmott (1990); Sturdy, Knights and Willmott (1992); Alvesson and Willmott (1992); Willmott (1993); Jermier *et al.* (1994); Sturdy, Grugulis and Willmott (2001); Alvesson and Willmott (2003); and Spicer and Fleming (2007).

13 See for example Howarth 1997; Howarth, Norval and Stavrakakis 2000; Howarth and Torfing 2005; Norval 1996; Smith 1994; Torfing 1998.

14 'Crucial to the notion of the Real is...[the] coincidence of the inaccessible X with the obstacle which makes it inaccessible – as in Heidegger, who emphasizes again and again how Being is not simply "withdrawn": Being "is" *nothing but its own withdrawal*.' (Žižek 1997b: 217).

15 We can organize our thoughts on subjectivity by considering the subject under three aspects. There is the subject of identity (or subject position), the subject of identification (or lack), and the subject of enjoyment (irreducible to meaning or signifying structure). As we will see in the following chapter, these aspects map roughly onto our three logics of critical explanation: social logics, political logics, and fantasmatic logics.

16 On Laclau's work in relation to Lacanian psychoanalysis, see Glynos and Stavrakakis (2004).

5 Logics

1 In Saussurian terms, if the moves correspond to the level of *parole*, the basic rules correspond to the level of *langue*.

2 This emergent logic also finds clear expression in the apartheid discourse on education. Here the Afrikaner's 'right' to difference was extended to the 'Bantu' who were to have their own educational systems designed to cultivate and preserve their own cultures and traditions, as opposed to the universal and liberal educational systems proposed by the 'English', 'Imperial' or 'missionary' traditions (see Molteno 1984: 88–94). For example, in defending the objective of preventing 'non-white' students from entering the so-called 'liberal universities', the Minister of Education argued the need for 'non-whites' to have their own separate institutions in the following way:

> We want to make provision for them in separate institutions which can develop towards independence on their own basis. Second, they must be given the opportunity to develop to the full on the basis of what is peculiarly their own. Third, they must be the bearers of their own culture to stimulate

that culture amongst their own national group. Fourthly, the future leaders should be educated and trained there, not to break down the colour bar but to retain it in the best interest of both whites and non-whites. By this measure the Government wants to give the non-whites the opportunity to develop, to be what they are and to retain their own national roots.

(Cited in Kruger 1969: 319–20)

These ideas were implemented in the infamous *Bantu Education Act* of 1953, as well as the *Extension of University Education Act*, which was passed in 1959. For a fuller analysis of these logics and opposition to them, see Howarth 1997.

3 For a discussion of the notion of 'crossing the fantasy' in the context of Derridian and Lacanian approaches to an 'ethics of the political' see Glynos (2000b).

4 We could add here other intuitively resonant formulations, such as Giddens' 'double-hermeneutic', Gadamer's 'fusion of horizons', Heidegger's *Dasein*, or Lacan's 'lack in the Other'. See Gadamer 1975: 273; Giddens 1976: 162; 1977: 12, 28; 1984: 284; 1987: 18–21; 1996: 75–6; Heidegger 1962; Lacan 2006: 693.

5 'Differences, resistances, and protean energies flow through the "perpetual gaps" within and between social formations, opening up possibilities for the politics of pluralization' (Connolly 1995: 39).

6 As Elster puts it, though his 'focus is on elementary or atomic mechanisms that cannot be broken down further into simpler constituents' (1999: 20), thus comprising the basic units of the social science *explanans*, they can also combine in a range of ways, producing more complex, *molecular* mechanisms (Elster 1999: 32–6).

7 'People', he argues, 'do not create society. For it always pre-exists them and is a necessary condition for their activity. Rather, society must be regarded as an ensemble of structures, practices and conventions which individuals reproduce or transform, but which would not exist unless they did so. Society does not exist independently of human activity (the error of reification). But it is not the product of it (the error of voluntarism)' (Bhaskar 1998: 36).

8 There is nothing, of course, which prevents us from thinking about and further developing the idea of closure in a more theoretically differentiated way. For example, one might think about closure as a function of Lacanian clinical structures (psychosis, perversion, neurosis) or substructures (within neurosis: hysteria, obsession, phobia); or as a function of something else besides.

9 In fact, insofar as the subject's relation to fantasy also defines its very being, then it could be said that what this perspective opens up is the possibility of thinking about ontology as having ethical foundations.

6 Articulation

1 An important lineage of subsumption can, of course, be traced back to Marx's later writings. In his Appendix to the first volume of *Capital*, Marx distinguishes between the formal and real subsumption of labour under capital in order to account for the way in which the wage-labour relation is generalized in the capitalist mode of production. The mechanism of formal subsumption refers to the way the labour process 'becomes the instrument of the valorization process, the process of the self-valorization of capital – the manufacture of surplus-value' – in which 'the labour process is subsumed under capital (it is its own process) and the capitalist intervenes in the process as its director, manager' (Marx 1976: 1019). But whereas in this regard the compulsion to perform surplus labour, and to create the leisure time necessary for development independently of material production, differs only in form from previous modes of production, in the real subsumption

of labour capital directly controls the process of production itself; the latter's 'aim is that the individual product should contain as *much unpaid labour as possible*, and this is achieved only by *producing for the sake of production*' (Marx 1976: 1038). In short, what we see in this movement from formal to real subsumption is not a process whereby external elements are articulated into a more concrete totality, nor a dialectical overcoming of particularity in a higher universal form, but the subordination of all particularity into the abstract universality of capital.

2 While archaeology makes possible the examination of 'forms themselves', genealogy accounts for their contingent emergence and production. By describing the rules that condition the elements of a particular discourse – its objects, subjects, concepts and strategies – in a given period, say the discourse of 'madness' or 'illness' in the nineteenth century, archaeology provides the means to delimit research objects, while genealogy analyses their constitution by recounting the historical practices from which they were constructed. The latter enables the researcher to show the contingency of identities and practices, and foreground possibilities foreclosed by present hegemonic logics. For a fuller discussion, see Howarth 2002a, 2003.

3 On the audit regime more generally, see Power 1997, 2004, 2005.

4 These changes are borne out by a range of statistical indicators. In 2006–7, for example, over two million individuals, about 43 percent of eligible young persons, attended 169 universities and colleges in the UK. The latter received approximately £15 billion in funding, of which about £10 billion came from central government, representing 2 percent of the UK's £0.5 trillion spending, or 1.1 percent of the UK's £1.2 trillion GDP. (Just to put this into context, the government's 2006–7 spending on education as a whole, health, and social protection as a percentage of total spending is 15, 20, and 30 percent respectively.) The remaining £5 billion came from external research contracts, overseas student fees, home/EU 'top up fees', charities, endowments, and other business income linked to universities. Of the £10 billion the government contributed to higher education, £7 billion was distributed via the Higher Education Funding Councils (with a research and teaching funding allocation ratio of about 1:4), and about £1 billion was distributed via the Research Councils (Clark 2006: 13, 16; Hefce 2006; HM Treasury 2006).

   This picture contrasts strongly with the situation in UK universities before Thatcher's New Right reforms in the 1980s. Prior to the creation of 'green field' universities in the early 1960s, as recommended in the Robbins Report (1963), the UK had an elite system of higher education, with only 5 percent of young people going to university. In 2001–2, after the Robbins-inspired expansion and the abolition of the polytechnic-university divide, the proportion of 18–19 year olds attending university had grown to about 34 percent. By 2006 there were about 43 percent of under-30s participating, with the target for 2010 set at 50 percent (Clark 2006: 18–19). Given no corresponding increases in funding, staff-student ratios reflected this trend: 1:9 in mid 1970s, to 1:17 in 1997, projected to be 1:23 in 2010. Association of University Teachers (AUT) surveys conducted amongst the profession in 1998 and 2004 show levels of stress in the academic profession at 70 percent, something confirmed by in-depth interviews reporting numerous instances of 'occupational stress, illness, alienation, fear and resentment' (AUT 2004; Morley 2005: 86).

5 Such commentators include Selway, McMurty, Bocock and Watson, Jary and Parker, among others (as noted by Trowler 1998: 49, 54–5, 97–8, 101–2, 141–2).

6 As one lecturer in English literature put it: 'I think it's extraordinary how quickly academics adjust to a situation which they've all been complaining about. I think we're very spineless in that regard. Or you could say adaptable but, you know, I feel that we accept more or less any kind of imposition that is made on us' (as cited in Morley 2003: 52).

7 From a North American perspective too, 'today's corporatized university – which would have been an unspeakable sacrilege for many less than a generation ago – is now being embraced with hardly any complaint or criticism by the faculty, students, or society at large' (Miyoshi 2002: 52). As early as the 1980s, US researchers were suggesting that heads of departments were effectively colluding with the managerialist thrust towards a human capital approach to achieving higher education aims (Slaughter 1985: 52), reporting 'no identifiable resistance to this from academic staff themselves in any form, the only threat to managerial success being the fact that "managers may be expecting the impossible, asking faculty for higher performance while providing fewer resources and reduced services"' (Trowler 1998: 50).

8 See Johnson 2002; Morley 2005; Prichard 2000; Prichard and Willmott 1997; Trowler 1998, 2002.

9 As one analyst puts it, '[a] major factor contributing to the fragmentation of the notion of a community of scholars is the ideology of competition. The competitive neutrality principle has exacted its toll by making academics compete with one another as though they are on a level playing field. However, this level playing field never exists in reality. Universities are differentiated by history, age, reputation, location, size, types of courses offered, and so on. Departments are equally differentiated by similar factors. And academics by their very location in certain departments, in certain universities, are almost never on an equal playing field. Yet, the notions that the market knows best and that competition brings greater efficiency and that the competition must be based on a neutral stage has meant that formulas that do not differentiate among various types of institutions, departments, or academics are used to set performance indicators and distribute resources. This competitive ethos pits one academic against another, one department against another, and one university against another. This leads to a game of individuals in the survival of the fittest that fragments the university [and subverts its purposes]' (Currie 2004: 52–3).

10 The invocation of a logic of competition is able to capture the following sentiment expressed by Willmott: 'Concepts such as "modernization", "specialization", "professionalization", and, more recently, "rationalization", "specialization" are widely deployed to characterize the dynamics of organizational change in (higher) education. These concepts [*qua* discursive shifts] usefully highlight important aspects of current developments. But they do not directly identify or explore the coupling, which is becoming progressively tightened, between capitalist values and priorities, mediated by political ideologies and programs, and the organization and control of academic labour' (Willmott 1995: 994). A set of criteria are deployed to render the units of production commensurate with one another, which is precisely what the audit systems have helped to bring about in the higher education sector. Since university degrees and academic publications lack many of the usual features we associate with typical goods and services in a market – their frequently repeated sale and purchase which establishes, through an 'invisible hand', a fairly reliable price-quality correlation – teaching and research audits help to *simulate* a market in the higher education sector by furnishing it with the conditions to establish such links.

11 From this point of view, one would also need to focus on the fantasmatic narratives that resist public official disclosure. Indeed, it is critical to note that a range of cultural preconditions were set in place during the 1970s and 1980s, as funding cuts were instituted and new business management discourses were introduced. For example, taking their cue in part from the successful broadcast of Kingsley Amis's *Lucky Jim* in 1957, these preconditions were installed through the televised serialization of Frederick Raphael's *Glittering Prizes* in 1976, Evelyn Waugh's *Brideshead Revisited* and Malcolm Bradbury's *The History Man*, both in 1981, Andrew Davies' *A Very Peculiar Practice* in 1986–8, Tom Sharpe's *Porterhouse Blue* in 1987, and David Lodge's *Nice Work* in 1989. Though based on novels written in and reflecting different periods in the development of the university, they all painted a picture of academic life, with respect to both lecturer and student, that was in its different ways privileged and decadent, out-of-touch, cliquey, vindictive, petty, overly bureaucratic, wasteful, corrupt, revolutionary, and so on.

In fact, one could argue that these views have persisted in the wake of the initial Thatcher attacks on the universities, and they surface at moments when the universities come into public view. For instance, in the 2006 AUT strike, the lazy and inefficient lecturer re-emerged as a figure of fantasmatic representation. Here are some typical expressions:

> Travelling the world to attend conferences? It's a hard life. My friend, who is an academic, goes on several of these a year. She happily admits that they are great fun, that she picks the best places to go to, that they rarely do more than a couple of days' work and spend the rest of the time shopping, lounging on the beach and drinking cocktails. All this (apart from the alcohol) is paid for on top of their salary and normal holiday. She often gives papers that are simply adapted from articles she has already written … There are quite a lot of people who get paid quite a lot less to do similar or longer hours, and with fewer cocktails.
>
> (*Guardian Unlimited* 2006: March 7, 11:02 am)

Or again:

> [L]ecturers have a hard life. Salaries of up to 50k, long hols, contracts with no fixed hours (check out the acres of empty space in the car park on a Friday afternoon) and with as little as 10 hours contact time.
>
> (*Guardian Unlimited* 2006: March 7, 01:39 pm)

The lighter and darker sides of these sentiments are reflected in more recent novelistic representations: Zadie Smith's *On Beauty* and the anonymously written *Campus Conspiracy*.

12 For an attempt to inscribe Olson in poststructuralist discourse theory, see Griggs and Howarth 2002.

13 A similar set of criticisms can be levelled against theories of democratic transition (see Howarth 1998).

14 For an excellent discussion of the power of judgement in the context of Hannah Arendt's interpretation of Kant, see Zerilli 2005: 125–63.

15 By surviving the consequences 'humanly' he means ways 'of avoiding the hostility expressed by the division, say, of *men* into "us" (Westerners) and "they" (Orientals)', which 'limit the *human encounter* between different cultures, traditions and societies' (Said 1995: 45–6; emphasis added). It should be mentioned here that this view diverges importantly from the anti-humanism of poststructuralist thought (on this see Howarth 2000: 70–1).

16 See, for example, Connolly 2005; Mouffe 2000; Norval 2007; Pettit 1997, 2001.
17 A prima facie more bizarre possibility might be that there is an enjoyment involved in the very act of complaining, an enjoyment which would be removed if demands were immediately granted. This idea has been elaborated elsewhere in terms of a logic of self-transgressive enjoyment (Glynos 2003b, 2008).
18 As Hubert Dreyfus (1986: 3–22) and Bent Flyvbjerg (2001: 67–71) suggest, an important intellectual justification of this picture goes back to Socrates and Plato, as represented in the *Meno* and the *Euthyphro*. In these dialogues, Socrates is often frustrated and angered in his efforts to discover the essence of 'virtue' or 'the holy' by those who introduce concrete examples as a substitute (Flyvbjerg 2001: 67–9). Instead, he remains resolutely wedded to a belief in universal truths – even if beyond our available knowledge – such that the status of particular examples and contextual learning is diminished. A further source is, of course, the hegemony of a certain conception of modern science in which physics, with its search for explicit and abstract universal laws, its ideals of complete explanation and prediction, and its commitment to mechanical causality, acquired a paradigmatic epistemological status in the natural and human sciences. Here individual cases were seen largely as a means to the discovery of far more important universal laws.
19 For a discussion on this topic, see also Topper 2005: 196–202.

Conclusion

1 See, for example, Hajer and Wagenaar 2003; Marcussen and Torfing 2006; Yanow and Schwartz-Shea 2006.
2 See, for example, Bevir 1999.
3 See, for example, Freeden 1996; Skinner 2001.
4 See, for example, Buzan and Waever 2003; Campbell 1992, 1998; Frost 1996; Walker 1992; Wendt 1999.

Bibliography

Abbey, R. (2000) *Charles Taylor*, Teddington: Acumen.

Adam, H. (1971) *Modernizing Racial Domination*, Berkeley, CA: University of California Press.

Adorno, T. and Horkheimer, M. (1973) *Dialectic of Enlightenment*, London: Allen Lane.

Althusser, L. (1969) *For Marx*, London: Verso.

Althusser, L. (1971) *Lenin and Philosophy, and Other Essays*, New York: Monthly Review Press.

Althusser, L. and Balibar, E. (1997) *Reading 'Capital'*, London: Verso.

Alvesson, M. and Willmott, H. (1992) 'On the Idea of Emancipation in Management and Organization Studies', *Academy of Management Review*, 17(3): 432–64.

Alvesson, M. and Willmott, H. (eds) (2003) *Studying Management Critically*, London: Sage.

Apple, M. *et al.* (2003) *The State and the Politics of Knowledge*, New York: Routledge.

Apter, D.A. (2006) 'Duchamp's Urinal', in R.E. Goodin and C. Tilly, (eds) *The Oxford Handbook of Contextual Political Analysis*, Oxford: OUP.

Arendt, H. (1958) *The Human Condition*, Chicago, IL: University of Chicago Press.

Aristotle (1987) *Politics*, in J.L. Ackrill (ed.) *A New Aristotle Reader*, Oxford: OUP.

Aristotle (2001) *Politics*, in R. McKeon (ed.) *The Basic Works of Aristotle*, New York: The Modern Library.

Ashforth, B. and Humphrey, R. (1993) 'Emotional Labour in Service Roles', *Academy of Management Review*, 18(1): 88–115.

AUT (2004) *Working to the Limit*, www.aut.org.uk/media/pdf/4/7/workingtothelimit.pdf (accessed July 2006).

Badiou, A. (2007) *Being and Event*, London: Continuum.

Barros, S. and Castagnola, G. (2000) 'The Political Frontiers of the Social', in Howarth, D., Norval, A., and Stavrakakis, Y. (eds) *Discourse Theory and Political Analysis*, Manchester: MUP.

Bastow, S. and Martin, J. (2003) *Third Way Discourse*, Edinburgh: Edinburgh University Press.

Benhabib, S. (2002) *The Claims of Culture*, Princeton, NJ: Princeton University Press.

Benoit, K. (2006) 'Duverger's Law and the Study of Electoral Systems', *French Politics*, 4: 69–83.

Berlin, I. (1978) *Concepts and Categories*, London: Hogarth.

Berlin, I. (1996) 'Political Judgement', in H. Hardy (ed.) *The Sense of Reality*, London: Chatto and Windus.

Bernstein, R.J. (1976) *The Restructuring of Social and Political Theory*, Philadelphia, PA: University of Pennsylvania Press.

Bernstein, R.J. (1991) *The New Constellation*, Cambridge: Polity.

Bevir, M. (1999) *The Logic of the History of Ideas*, Cambridge: Cambridge University Press.

Bevir, M. (2000) 'The Logic of the History of Ideas', *Rethinking History*, 4(3): 295–300.

Bevir, M. (2005) *New Labour*, London: Routledge.

Bevir, M. (2006) 'Political Studies as Narrative and Science', *Political Studies*, 54(3): 583–606.

Bevir, M. and Rhodes, R. (2003) *Interpreting British Governance*, London: Routledge.

Bevir, M. and Rhodes, R. (2004) 'Interpretation as Method, Explanation and Critique', *British Journal of Politics and International Relations*, 6: 156–61.

Bevir, M. and Rhodes, R. (2005) 'Interpretation and its Others', *Australian Journal of Political Science*, 40(2): 169–87.

Bevir, M. and Rhodes, R. (2006) 'Interpretive Approaches to British Governance and Politics', *British Politics*, 1: 84–112.

Bhaskar, R. (1975) *A Realist Theory of Science*, London: Verso.

Bhaskar, R. (1989) *Reclaiming Reality*, London: Verso.

Bhaskar, R. (1998) *The Possibility of Naturalism*, 3rd edn, London: Routledge.

Biko, S. and Arnold, M. (1978) *Black Consciousness in South Africa*, New York: Random House.

Billig, M. (1997a) 'The Dialogic Unconscious', *British Journal of Social Psychology*, 36: 139–59.

Billig, M. (1997b) 'Discursive, Rhetorical and Ideological Messages', in C. McGarty and A. Haslam (eds) *The Message of Social Psychology: Perspectives on Mind in Society*, Oxford: Blackwell.

Blair, T. (2006) *Speech on the Middle East to the Los Angeles World Affairs Council*, 1 August, www.number10.gov.uk/output/Page9948.asp (accessed January 2007).

Blyth, M. (2003) 'Structures Do Not Come with an Instruction Sheet', *Perspectives on Politics*, 1(4): 695–706.

Boggs, C. (1986) *Social Movements and Political Power*, Philadelphia, PA: Temple University Press.

Bohman, J.F. (1991) *New Philosophy of Social Science*, Cambridge, MA: MIT Press.

Boucher, G., Glynos, J., and Sharpe, M. (eds) (2005) *Traversing the Fantasy*, Aldershot: Ashgate.

Bourdieu, P. (1977) *Outline of a Theory of Practice*, Cambridge: CUP.

Brenneis, D., Shore, C., and Wright, S. (2005) 'Getting the Measure of Academia', *Anthropology in Action*, 12(1): 1–10.

Bruneau, W. and Savage, D. (2002) *Counting out the Scholars*, Toronto: James Lorimer & Co.

Bunge, M. (1997) 'Mechanism and Explanation', *Philosophy of the Social Sciences*, 27: 410–65.

Burawoy, M. (1979) *Manufacturing Consent*, Chicago, IL: University of Chicago Press.

Bush, G. (2002) *State of the Union Address*, 29 January, www.whitehouse.gov/news/releases/2002/01/20020129–11.html (accessed January 2007).

Butler, J. (1990) *Gender Trouble*, London: Routledge.

Butler, J. (2001) 'Doing Justice to Someone', *GLQ: A Journal of Lesbian and Gay Studies*, 7(4): 621–36.

Butler, J., Laclau, E., and Žižek, S. (2000) *Contingency, Hegemony, Universality*, London: Verso.

Buzan, B. and Weaver, O. (2003) *Regions and Powers*, Cambridge: CUP.

Campbell, D. (1992) *Writing Security*, Manchester: Manchester University Press.

Campbell, D. (1998) *National Deconstruction*, Minneapolis, MN: University of Minnesota Press.

Cavell, S. (1976) *Must We Mean What We Say?*, Cambridge: CUP.

Chalmers, A.F. (1982) *What is this Thing Called Science?* 2nd edn, Buckingham: Open University Press.

Chouliaraki, L. and Fairclough, N. (1999) *Discourse in Late Modernity*, Edinburgh: Edinburgh University Press.

Cioffi, F. (1998) *Wittgenstein on Freud and Frazer*, Cambridge: CUP.

Clark, T. (2006) OECD Thematic Review of Tertiary Education Country Report: United Kingdom, London: DES.

Clohesy, A.M. (2000) 'Provisionalism and the (Im)possibility of Justice in Northern Ireland', in D. Howarth, A. Norval, and Y. Stavrakakis (eds) *Discourse Theory and Political Analysis*, Manchester: MUP.

Connolly, W. (1981) *Appearance and Reality in Politics*, Cambridge: CUP.

Connolly, W. (1993) *The Terms of Political Discourse*, Oxford: Blackwell.

Connolly, W. (1995) *The Ethos of Pluralization*, Minneapolis, MN: University of Minnesota Press.

Connolly, W. (2005) *Pluralism*, Durham: Duke University Press.

Connolly, W.E. (2006) 'Then and Now', in J. Dryzek, B. Honig, and A. Phillips (eds) *The Oxford Handbook in Political Theory*, Oxford: Oxford University Press.

Coole, D. (2000) *Negativity in Politics*, London: Routledge.

Cox, R. (1981a) 'Gramsci, Hegemony and International Relations', *Millennium: Journal of International Studies*, 10(2): 269–91.

Cox, R. (1981b) 'Social Forces, States, and World Orders', *Millennium*, 10(2): 126–55.

Cox, R. (1987) *Production, Power and World Order*, New York: Columbia University Press.

Crisp, R. and Slote, M. (eds) (1997) *Virtue Ethics*, Oxford: OUP.

Critchley, S. (2004) 'Is there a Normative Deficit in the Theory of Hegemony?' in S. Critchley and O. Marchart (eds) *Laclau: A Critical Reader*, London: Palgrave.

Currie, J. (2004) 'The Neo-liberal Paradigm and Higher Education' in J.K. Odin and P.T. Manicas (eds) *Globalization and Higher Education*, Honolulu: University of Hawai'i Press.

Dallmayr, F. and McCarthy, T. (1977) 'Introduction', in F. Dallmayr and T. McCarthy (eds) *Understanding and Social Inquiry*, Notre Dame: University of Notre Dame Press.

Davidson, D. (1980) *Essays on Actions and Events*, Oxford: OUP.

Davies, R., O'Meara, D., and Dlamini, S. (1984) *The Struggle for South Africa, Organizations and Institutions*, vol. 1, London: Zed Press.

Dearing, R. (1997) Higher Education in the Learning Society: Summary Report of the National Committee of Inquiry into Higher Education, Norwich: HMSO.

Derrida, J. (1976) *Of Grammatology*, Baltimore, MD: The John Hopkins University Press.

Derrida, J. (1978) *Writing and Difference*, London: Routledge.

Derrida, J. (1981a) *Positions*, Chicago, IL: University of Chicago Press.

Derrida, J. (1981b) *Dissemination*, Chicago, IL: University of Chicago Press.

Derrida, J. (1982) *Margins of Philosophy*, Brighton: Harvester Press.

Derrida, J. (1989) *Edmund Husserl's Origins of Geometry*, Lincoln, NE: University of Nebraska Press.

Derrida, J. (2002) *Negotiations: Interventions and Interviews, 1971–2001*, Stanford, CA: Stanford University Press.

DES (Department of Education and Science) (1987) *Higher Education: Meeting the Challenge* (White Paper), London: HMSO.

Diederichs, N. (1946) *Wat die Kommunisme Werklik Is*, Die Sinodale Kommissie vir die Bestryding van Maatskaplike Euwels, Ned. Geref. Kerk in die OVS.

Dillon, M. (1996) *Politics of Security*, London: Routledge.

Dowding, K. (2001) 'There Must be an End to Confusion', *Political Studies*, 49: 89–105.

Dowding, K. (2004) 'Interpretation, Truth and Investigation', *British Journal of Politics and International Relations*, 6: 136–42.

Dreyfus, H. (1986) 'Why Studies of Human Capacities Modelled on Ideal Science Can Never Achieve Their Goal', in J. Margolis, M. Krauz, and R.M. Burian (eds) *Rationality, Relativism and The Human Sciences*, Martinus Nijhoff Publishers.

Dreyfus, H. and Rabinow, P. (1982) *Michel Foucault*, Chicago, IL: University of Chicago Press.

Dryzek, J., Honig, B., and Phillips, A. (2006) 'Introduction', in J. Dryzek, B. Honig, and A. Phillips (eds) *The Oxford Handbook in Political Theory*, Oxford: Oxford University Press.

Du Gay, P. and Salaman, G. (1992) 'The Cult[ure] of the Customer', *Journal of Management Studies*, 29(5): 615–33.

Dubow, S. (1989) *Racial Segregation and the Origins of Apartheid, 1919–1936*, Basingstoke: Macmillan.

Duverger, M. (1959) *Political Parties, their Organization and Activity in the Modern State*, 2nd edn, London: Methuen.

Duverger, M. (1963) *Political Parties*, New York: Wiley Science.

Duverger, M. (1972) *The Study of Politics*, London: Thomas Nelson and Sons.

Easton, D. (1965) *A Systems Analysis of Political Life*, New York: Wiley.

Edkins, J. (2003) *Trauma and the Memory of Politics*, Cambridge: Cambridge University Press.

Edwards, D. (1994) 'Script Formulations: An Analysis of Event Descriptions in Conversation' *Journal of Language and Social Psychology*, 13: 211–47.

Elster, J. (1978) *Logic and Society*, Chichester: John Wiley.

Elster, J. (1983a) *Explaining Technical Change*, Cambridge: CUP.

Elster, J. (1983b) *Sour Grapes*, Cambridge: CUP.

Elster, J. (1984) *Ulysses and the Sirens*, 2nd edn, Cambridge: CUP.

Elster, J. (1985) *Making Sense of Marx*, Cambridge: CUP.

Elster, J. (1989) *Nuts and Bolts for the Social Sciences*, Cambridge: CUP.

Elster, J. (1992) *Local Justice*, New York: Russell Sage Foundation.

Elster, J. (1993) *Political Psychology*, Cambridge: CUP.

Elster, J. (1999) *Alchemies of the Mind*, Cambridge: CUP.

Elster, J. (2000) 'Rational Choice History', *American Political Science Review*, 94: 685–95.

Elster, J., Bates, R.H., Greif, A., Levi, M., Rosenthal, J.-L., and Weingast, B. (2000) '*Analytic Narratives* by Bates, Greif, Levi, Rosenthal, and Weingast: A Review and Response', *American Political Science Review*, 94(3): 685–702.

Engels, F. (1978) 'Socialism', in R. Tucker (ed.) *The Marx-Engels Reader*, New York: W.W. Norton & Co.

Evans, D. (1996) *An Introductory Dictionary of Lacanian Psychoanalysis*, London: Routledge.

Evans, M. (2004) *Killing Thinking*, London: Continuum.

Fairclough, N. (1995) *Media Discourse*, London: Arnold.

Fairclough, N. (2000) *New Labour, New Language?*, London: Routledge.

Farr, J. (1987) 'Resituating Explanation', in T. Ball (ed.) *Idioms of Inquiry*, Albany NY: SUNY.

Farr, J., Dryzek, J., and Leonard, S. (1995) *Political Science in History*, Cambridge: CUP.

Feyerabend, P. (1975) *Against Method*, London: Verso.

Fink, B. (1995) *The Lacanian Subject*, Princeton, NJ: Princeton University Press.

Finlayson, A. (2003) *Making Sense of New Labour*, London: Lawrence and Wishart.

Finlayson, A. (2004) 'Meaning and Politics', *British Journal of Politics and International Relations*, 6(2): 149–56.

Finlayson, A., Bevir, M., Rhodes, R.A.W., Dowding, K., and Hay, C. (2004) 'The Interpretive Approach in Political Science: A Symposium', *British Journal of Politics and International Relations*, 6(2): 129–64.

Fischer, F. (2003) *Reframing Public Policy*, Oxford: OUP.

Fleming, P. and Spicer, A. (2003) 'Working at a Cynical Distance', *Organization*, 10(1): 157–79.

Fleming, P. and Spicer, A. (2007) *Contesting the Corporation*, Cambridge: CUP.

Flyvberg, B. (2001) *Making Social Science Matter*, Cambridge: CUP.

Foucault, M. (1970) *The Order of Things*, London: Tavistock.

Foucault, M. (1972) *The Archaeology of Knowledge*, London: Tavistock.

Foucault, M. (1973) *The Birth of the Clinic*, London: Tavistock.

Foucault, M. (1977) *Discipline and Punish*, Harmondsworth, Penguin Books.

Foucault, M. (1979) *The History of Sexuality*, London: Allen Lane.

Foucault, M. (1981) 'The Order of Discourse', in R. Young (ed.) *Untying the Text*, London: Routledge.

Foucault, M. (1984) 'Nietzsche, Genealogy, History', in P. Rabinow (ed.) *The Foucault Reader*, Harmondsworth: Penguin Books.

Foucault, M. (1985) *The Use of Pleasure*, New York: Pantheon.

Foucault, M. (1997) *Ethics*, New York: New Press.

Foucault, M. (2003) *Society Must be Defended*, New York: Picador.

Frankfurt, H.G. (1958) 'Peirce's Notion of Abduction', *The Journal of Philosophy*, 55(14): 593–97.

Freeden, M. (1996) *Ideologies and Political Theory*, Oxford: Clarendon Press.

Freeden, M. (2005) 'What Should the "Political" in Political Theory Explore?', *The Journal of Political Philosophy*, 13(2): 113–34.

Friedman, M. (1953) *Essays in Positive Economics*, Chicago, UL: University of Chicago Press.

Frost, M. (1996) *Ethics in International Relations*, Cambridge: CUP.

Furlong, P.J. (1991) *Between Crown and Swastika*, Middletown, NJ: Wesleyan University Press.

Gadamer, H.-G. (1975) *Truth and Method*, London: Sheed and Ward.

Galavotti, M.A. (ed.) (2003) *Observation and Experiment in the Natural and Social Sciences*, Dordrecht: Kluwer Academic Publishers.

Gamble, A. (1994) *The Free Economy and the Strong State*, 2nd edn, London: Palgrave Macmillan.

Gasché, R. (1986) *The Tain of the Mirror*, Cambridge, MA: Harvard University Press.

Geertz, C. (1973) *The Interpretation of Cultures*, New York: Basic Books.

Geras, N. (1987) 'Post-Marxism?', *New Left Review*, 163: 40–82.

Geras, N. (1988) 'Ex-Marxism Without Substance', *New Left Review*, 169: 34–61.

Geras, N. (1990) *Discourses of Extremity*, London: Verso.

Giddens, A. (1976) *New Rules of Sociological Method*, London: Hutchinson.

Giddens, A. (1977) *Studies in Social and Political Theory*, London: Hutchinson.

Giddens, A. (1984) *The Constitution of Society*, Cambridge: Polity Press.

Giddens, A. (1987) *Social Theory and Modern Sociology*, Cambridge: Polity Press.

Giddens, A. (1996) *In Defence of Sociology*, Cambridge: Polity Press.

Glynos, J. (2000a) 'Sexual Identity, Identification, and Difference', *Philosophy and Social Criticism*, 26(6): 85–108.

Glynos, J. (2000b) 'Thinking the Ethics of the Political in the Context of a Postfoundational World', *Theory & Event*, 4: 4 http://muse.jhu.edu/journals/theory_and_event/toc/archive.html (accessed December 2000).

Glynos, J. (2001a) 'The Grip of Ideology', *Journal of Political Ideologies*, 6(2): 191–214.

Glynos, J. (2001b) 'There is No Other of the Other', *Paragraph*, 24(2): 78–110.

Glynos, J. (2003a) 'Self-Transgression and Freedom', *Critical Review of International Social and Political Philosophy*, 6(2): 1–20.

Glynos, J. (2003b) 'Radical Democratic Ethos, or, What is an Authentic Political Act?', *Contemporary Political Theory*, 2: 187–208.

Glynos, J. (2008) 'Self-Transgressive Enjoyment as a Freedom Fetter', *Political Studies*, forthcoming.

Glynos, J. and Stavrakakis, Y. (2004) 'Encounters of the Real Kind' in S. Critchley and O. Marchart (eds) *Laclau: A Critical Reader*, London: Routledge.

Goodin, R.E. and Tilly, C. (eds) (2006) *The Oxford Handbook of Contextual Political Analysis*, Oxford: OUP.

Gorton, W.A. (2006) *Karl Popper and the Social Sciences*, Albany, NY: SUNY.

Gouldner, A. (1955) *Wildcat Strike*, London: Routledge & Kegan Paul.

Gramsci, A. (1971) *Selections from the Prison Notebooks*, London: Lawrence and Wishart.

Gramsci, A. (1977) *Selections from Political Writings, 1910–1920*, London: Lawrence and Wishart.

Gray, J. (1989) *Liberalisms*, London: Routledge.

Greenberg, S. (1987) *Legitimating the Illegitimate*, Berkeley, CA: University of California Press.

Griggs, S. and Howarth, D. (2002) 'An Alliance of Interest and Identity? Explaining the Campaign Against Manchester Airport's Second Runway', *Mobilization*, 7(1): 43–58.

Griggs, S. and Howarth, D. (2004) 'A Transformative Political Campaign? The New Rhetoric of Protest Against Airport Expansion in the UK', *Journal of Political Ideologies*, 9(2): 167–87.

Griggs, S. and Howarth, D. (2007) 'Protest Movements, Environmental Activism and Environmentalism in the United Kingdom', in J. Pretty *et al.* (eds) *The Sage Handbook of Environment and Society*, London: Sage.

Grusin, R.A. (2004) 'Premediation', *Criticism*, 46(1): 17–39.

Guardian Unlimited (2006) *Higher Education Mortarboard Blog*, http://blogs.guardian.co.uk/mortarboard/2006/03/post_2.html (accessed 15 March 2006).

Habermas, J. (1978) *Knowledge and Human Interests*, 2nd edn, London: Heinemann Educational.

Habermas, J. (1986) 'Hannah Arendt's Communications Concept of Power', in S. Lukes (ed.) *Power*, Oxford: Blackwell.

Habermas, J. (1987) *The Philosophical Discourse of Modernity*, Cambridge: Polity.

Habermas, J. (1996) *Between Facts and Norms*, Cambridge: Polity Press.

Hacking, I. (1983) *Representing and Intervening*, Cambridge: CUP.

Hacking, I. (1985) 'Styles of Scientific Reasoning', in J. Rajchman and C. West (eds) *Post-Analytical Philosophy*, New York: Columbia University Press.

Hacking, I. (1995) 'The Looping Effects of Human Kinds' in D. Sperber, D. Premack, and A.N. Premack (eds) *Causal Cognition*, Oxford: Clarendon.

Hajer, M. (1995) *The Politics of Environmental Discourse*, Oxford: Clarendon Press.

Hajer, M. and Wagenaar, H. (2003) *Deliberative Policy Analysis*, Cambridge: CUP.

Hall, S. (1983) 'The Great Moving Right Show', in S. Hall and M. Jacques (eds) *The Politics of Thatcherism*, London: Lawrence and Wishart.

Hall, S. (1988) *The Hard Road to Renewal*, London: Verso.

Hancock, A.-M. (2004) *The Politics of Disgust*, New York: NYUP.

Hanson, N.R. (1961) *Patterns of Discovery*, Cambridge: CUP.

Hanson, N.R. (1972) *Observation and Explanation*, London: George Allen & Unwin.

Harré, R. (1995) 'Discursive Psychology' in J.A. Smith, R. Harré, and L. van Langenhove (eds) *Rethinking Psychology*, London: Sage.

Hart, H.L.A. (1961) *The Concept of Law*, Oxford: Clarendon Press.

Hasenclever, A., Mayer, P., and Rittberger, V. (1997) *Theories of International Regimes*, Cambridge: CUP.

Hay, C. (1995) 'Structure and Agency', in D. Marsh and G. Stoker (eds) *Theory and Methods in Political Science*, London: Macmillan.

Hay, C. (2002) *Political Analysis*, Basingstoke: Palgrave.

Hay, C. (2006) 'Political Ontology' in R.E. Goodin and C. Tilly (eds) *The Oxford Handbook of Contextual Political Analysis*, Oxford: Oxford University Press.

Hedstrom, P. and Swedberg, R. (eds) (1998) *Social Mechanisms*, Cambridge: CUP.

Hefce (2006) *Funding Higher Education in England: Summary of Allocations 2006–7*, www.hefce.ac.uk/finance/fundinghe/ (accessed July 2006).

Heidegger, M. (1962) *Being and Time*, Oxford: Basil Blackwell.

Heidegger, M. (1982) *The Basic Problems of Phenomenology*, Bloomington, IN: Indiana University Press.

Heidegger, M. (1985) *History of the Concept of Time*, Bloomington, IN: Indiana University Press.

Hempel, C. (1942) 'The Function of General Laws in History', *The Journal of Philosophy*, 39: 35–48.

Hempel, C. (1965) Aspects of Explanation, and Other Essays in the Philosophy of Science, New York: Free Press.

Hesse, M. (1978) 'Theory and Value in the Social Sciences', in C. Hookway and P. Pettit (eds) *Action and Interpretation*, Cambridge: Cambridge University Press.

Heyward, C. (2007) 'Revisiting the Radical View', *Politics*, 27(1): 48–54.

Hirst, P. (1979) *On Law and Ideology*, London: Macmillan.

HM Treasury (2006) www.hm-treasury.gov.uk/ (accessed July 2006).

Hollis, M. (1994) *The Philosophy of Social Science*, Cambridge: CUP.

Horkheimer, M. (1972) *Critical Theory: Selected Essays*, New York: Herder and Herder.

Horkheimer, M. (1986) 'Materialism and Morality', *Telos*, 69: 85–118.

Horowitz, D. (1991) *A Democratic South Africa?*, Berkeley, CA: University of California Press.

Howarth, D. (1997) 'Complexities of Identity/Difference', *Journal of Political Ideologies*, 2(1): 51–78.

Howarth, D. (1998) 'Paradigms Gained? A Critique of Theories of Democratization in South Africa', in D. Howarth and A. Norval (eds) *South Africa in Transition*, London: Macmillan.

Howarth, D. (2000a) *Discourse*, Buckingham: Open University Press.

Howarth, D. (2000b) 'The Difficult Emergence of a Democratic Imaginary', in D. Howarth, A.J. Norval, and Y. Stavrakakis (eds) *Discourse Theory and Political Analysis*, Manchester: Manchester University Press.

Howarth, D. (2002a) 'An Archaeology of Political Discourse? Michel Foucault and the Critique of Ideology', *Political Studies*, 50(1): 117–35.

Howarth, D. (2002b) 'Ethnic and Racial Identities in a Changing South Africa', *South African Historical Journal*, 46: 250–74.

Howarth, D. (2003) 'Archaeology, Genealogy and Hegemony', *Political Studies*, 51(2): 436–40.

Howarth, D. (2004) 'Towards a Heideggerian Social Science', *Anthropological Theory*, 4(2): 229–47.

Howarth, D. (2005a) 'Applying Discourse Theory', in D. Howarth and J. Torfing (eds) *Discourse Theory in European Politics*, London: Palgrave.

Howarth, D. (2005b) 'Populism or Popular Democracy? The UDF, Workerism and the Struggle for Radical Democracy in South Africa', in F. Panizza (ed.) *Populism and the Mirror of Nature*, London: Verso.

Howarth, D. (2006) 'Space, Subjectivity and Politics', *Alternatives*, 31(2): 105–34.

Howarth, D. and Griggs, S. (2007) 'Metaphor, Equivalence and Catachresis', *Policy and Society*, 25(2): 28–52.

Howarth, D. and Torfing, J. (eds) (2005) *Discourse Theory in European Politics*, London: Palgrave.

Howarth, D., Norval, A.J., and Stavrakakis, Y. (eds) (2000) *Discourse Theory and Political Analysis*, Manchester: Manchester University Press.

Howie, G. (2005) 'Universities in the UK', *Critical Quarterly*, 47(1/2): 1–10.

Hoy, D.C. (1991) 'Is Hermeneutics Ethnocentric?' in J.F. Bohman, D.R. Hiley, and R. Shusteman (eds) *The Interpretive Turn*, Ithaca, NY: Cornell University Press.

Hoy, D.C. and McCarthy (1994) *Critical Theory*, Oxford: Basil Blackwell.

Husserl, E. (1965) *Phenomenology and the Crisis of Philosophy*, New York: Harper and Row.

Husserl, E. (1970) *The Crisis of European Sciences and Transcendental Phenomenology*, Evanston: Northwestern University Press.

Jameson, F. (1988) *The Ideologies of Theory – Essays 1971–1986*, Minneapolis, MN: University of Minnesota Press.

Jarratt, A. (1985) *The Jarratt Report*, London: CVCP.

Jarvie, I.C. (1977) 'Understanding and Explanation in Sociology and Social Anthropology', in F. Dallmayr and T. McCarthy (eds) *Understanding and Social Inquiry*, Notre Dame: University of Notre Dame Press, pp. 189–206.

Jermier, J.M., Knights, D., and Nord, W.R. (eds) (1994) *Resistance and Power in Organizations*, London: Routledge.

Jervis, R. (1997) *System Effects*, Princeton, NJ: Princeton University Press.

Jessop, B. (1982) *The Capitalist State*, Oxford: Martin Robertson.

Jessop, B. (1990) *State Theory*, Cambridge: Polity.

Jessop, B. (2002) *The Future of the Capitalist State*, Cambridge: Polity.

Jessop, B., Bonnett, K., Bromley, S., and Ling, S. (1988) *Thatcherism*, Cambridge: Polity.

Jick, T. (1983) 'Mixing Qualitative and Quantitative Research Methods: Triangulation in Action', in J. van Maanen (ed.) *Qualitative Methodology* Beverley Hills: Sage.

Johnson, R. (2002) 'Resources in the Management of Change in Higher Education', in P.R. Trowler (ed.) *Higher Education Policy and Institutional Change*, Buckingham: Open University Press & SRHE.

Johnson, T. (1980) 'Work and Power', in G. Esland and G. Salaman (eds) *The Politics of Work and Occupations*, Milton Keynes: Open University Press.

Kant, I. (1987) *Critique of Judgement*, Indianapolis, IN: Hackett.

King, A. (1975) 'Overload: Problems of Governing in the 1970s', *Political Studies*, 23(2/3): 284–95.

King, D. (1987) *The New Right*, Basingstoke: Macmillan.

King, G., Koehane, R.O., and Verba, S. (1994) *Designing Social Inquiry*, Princeton, NJ: Princeton University Press.

Knights, D. and Willmott, H. (eds) (1990) *Labour Process Theory*, London: MacMillan.

Kogan, M. and Kogan, D. (1983) *The Attack on Higher Education*, London: Kogan Page Ltd.

Krasner, S.D. (1983) 'Structural Causes and Regime Consequences', in S.D. Krasner (ed.) *International Regimes*, Ithaca, NY: Cornell University Press.

Kruger, D.W. (1969) *The Making of a Nation*, Johannesburg: Macmillan.

Kuhn, T. (1970) *The Structure of Scientific Revolutions*, 2nd edn, Chicago, IL: Chicago University Press.

Kunda, G. (1992) *Engineering Culture*, Philadelphia, PA: Temple University Press.

Lacan, J. (1978) *The Seminar, Book XI: The Four Fundamental Concepts of Psychoanalysis*, New York: W.W. Norton.

Lacan, J. (1991a) *The Seminar, Book I: Freud's Papers on Technique, 1953–1954*, New York: W.W. Norton.

Lacan, J. (1991b) *The Seminar, Book II: The Ego in Freud's Theory and in the Technique of Psychoanalysis, 1954–1955*, New York: W.W. Norton.

Lacan, J. (1992) *The Seminar, Book VII: The Ethics of Psychoanalysis, 1959–1960*, London: Routledge.

Lacan, J. (1998) *The Seminar, Book XX: Encore, 1972–3*, New York: W.W. Norton.

Lacan, J. (2006) *Écrits*, New York: W.W. Norton.

Lacan, J. (2007) *The Seminar, Book XVII: The Other Side of Psychoanalysis, 1969–1970*, New York: W.W. Norton.

Laclau, E. (1977) *Politics and Ideology in Marxist Theory*, London: Verso.

Laclau, E. (1988) 'Building a New Left: An Interview with E. Laclau', *Strategies: Journal of Theory, Culture, and Politics*, 1: 10–28.

Laclau, E. (1990) *New Reflections on the Revolution of Our Time*, London: Verso.

Laclau, E. (ed.) (1994) *The Making of Political Identities*, London: Verso.

Laclau, E. (1996) *Emancipation(s)*, London: Verso.

Laclau, E. (2000a) 'Identity and Hegemony', in J. Butler *et al.* (eds) *Contingency, Hegemony, Universality*, London: Verso.

Laclau, E. (2000b) 'Constructing Universality', in Butler, J. *et al.* (eds) *Contingency, Hegemony, Universality*, London: Verso.

Laclau, E. (2004) 'Reply', in S. Critchley and O. Marchart (eds) *Laclau: A Critical Reader*, London: Routledge.

Laclau, E. (2005) *On Populist Reason*, London: Verso.

Laclau, E. and Bhaskar, R. (1998) 'Discourse Theory vs. Critical Realism', *Alethia*, 1(2): 9–14.

Laclau, E. and Mouffe, C. (1985) *Hegemony and Socialist Strategy*, London: Verso.

Laclau, E. and Zac, L. (1994) 'Minding the Gap', in E. Laclau (ed.) *The Making of Political Identities*, London: Verso.

Lakatos, I. (1974) 'Falsification and the Methodology of Scientific Research Programmes', in I. Lakatos and A. Musgrave (eds) *Criticism and the Growth of Knowledge*, Cambridge: CUP.

Lambert Review of Business-University Collaboration (2003) London: HM Treasury, www.lambertreview.org.uk (accessed July 2006).

Landman, T. (2003) *Issues and Methods in Comparative Politics*, 2nd edn, London: Routledge.

Lefort, C. (1988) *Democracy and Political Theory*, Cambridge: Polity Press.

Leidner, R. (1993) *Fast Food, Fast Talk*, London: UCLA Press.

Lessnoff, M. (1974) *The Structure of Social Science*, London: Allen and Unwin.

Levidow, L. (2002) 'Marketizing Higher Education', in K. Robins and F. Webster (eds) *The Virtual University?*, Oxford: OUP.

Lewis, D. (2005) *Encircling Capital's Blank Figure*, Ph.D., University of Essex.

Little, D. (1998) *On the Philosophy of the Social Sciences*, New Brunswick, NJ: Transaction.

Louch, A.R. (1966) *Explanation and Human Action*, Oxford: Basil Blackwell.

Lukes, S. (1974) 'Some Problems about Rationality', in B. Wilson (ed.) *Rationality*, Oxford: Basil Blackwell.

Lukes, S. (1982) 'Relativism in its Place', in M. Hollis and S. Lukes (eds) *Rationality and Relativism*, Oxford: Basil Blackwell.

Lukes, S. (2003) *Liberals and Cannibals*, London: Verso.

Lukes, S. (2005) *Power*, 2nd edn, Basingstoke: Palgrave Macmillan.

Lyas, C. (1999) *Peter Winch*, Teddington: Acumen.

MacIntyre, A. (1973) 'Is a Science of Comparative Politics Possible?', in A. Ryan (ed.), *The Philosophy of Social Explanations*, Oxford: Oxford University Press.

MacIntyre, A. (1974) 'Is Understanding Religion Compatible with Believing?' in B. Wilson (ed.) *Rationality*, Oxford: Basil Blackwell.

MacIntyre, A. (1984) *After Virtue*, 2nd edn, London: Duckworth.

Mahoney, J. and Rueschemeyer, D. (eds) (2003) *Comparative Historical Analysis in the Social Sciences*, Cambridge: CUP.

Mangena, M. (1989) *On Your Own*, Johannesburg: Skotaville.

March, J.G. and Olsen, J.P. (1989) *Rediscovering Institutions*, New York: Free Press.

Marchart, O. (2007) *Post-foundational Political Thought*, Edinburgh: Edinburgh University Press.

Marcussen, M. and Torfing, J. (eds) (2006) *Democratic Network Governance in Europe*, London: Palgrave.

Mars, G. (1982) *Cheats at Work*, London: Allen & Unwin.

Marsh, D. and Smith, M. (2001) 'There is More than One way to Do Political Science', *Political Studies*, 49(3): 528–41.

Marx, K. (1973) *Grundrisse*, London: Allen Lane.

Marx, K. (1976) *Capital*, vol. 1, Harmondsworth: Penguin.

Mautner, G. (2005) 'The Entrepreneurial University', *Critical Discourse Studies*, 2(2): 95–120.

McAnulla, S. (2006) 'Challenging the New Interpretivist Approach', *British Politics*, 1: 113–38.

McCarthy, T. (1994) 'Philosophy and Critical Theory', in D. Hoy and T. McCarthy (eds) *Critical Theory*, Oxford: Basil Blackwell.

Miliband, R. (1969) *The State in Capitalist Society*, London: Weidenfeld and Nicholson.

Miliband, R. (1970) 'Reply to Nikos Poulantzas', *New Left Review*, 59: 53–60.

Mill, J.S. (1987) 'On Coleridge', in A. Ryan (ed.) *John Stuart Mill and Jeremy Bentham*, London: Penguin Books.

Miller, J.-A. (1994[1986]) 'Extimité', in M. Bracher *et al.* (eds.) *Lacanian Theory of Discourse*, New York: New York University Press.

Miyoshi, M. (2002) 'The University in the "Global" Economy', in K. Robins and F. Webster (eds) *The Virtual University?*, Oxford: OUP.

Molteno, F. (1984) 'The Historical Foundations of the Schooling for Blacks in South Africa', in P. Kellaway (ed.), *Apartheid and Education*, Johannesburg: Ravan.

Morley, L. (2003) *Quality and Power in Higher Education*, Maidenhead: Open University Press.

Morley, L. (2005) 'The Micropolitics of Quality', *Critical Quarterly*, 47(1/2): 83–95.

Morton, R.B. (1999) *Methods and Models*, Cambridge: CUP.

Mouffe, C. (ed.) (1979) *Gramsci and Marxist Theory*, London: Routledge.

Mouffe, C. (ed.) (1992) *Dimensions of Radical Democracy*, London: Verso.

Mouffe, C. (1993) *The Return of the Political*, London: Verso.

Mouffe, C. (2000) *The Democratic Paradox*, London: Verso.

Mouffe, C. (2005) *On the Political*, London: Routledge.

Mulhall, S. (2001) *Inheritance and Originality*, Oxford: OUP.

Nagel, E. (1961) *The Structure of Science*, New York: Harcourt, Brace & Co.

Nietzsche, F. (1973) *Beyond Good and Evil*, Harmondsworth: Penguin.

Norval, A.J. (1993) 'Social Ambiguity and the Crisis of Apartheid', in E. Laclau (ed.) *The Making of Political Identities*, London: Verso.

Norval, A.J. (1996) *Deconstructing Apartheid Discourse*, London: Verso.

Norval, A.J. (2000) 'The Things we do with Words', *British Journal of Political Science*, 30: 313–46.

Norval, A.J. (2004) 'Hegemony after Deconstruction', *Journal of Political Ideologies*, 9(2): 139–57.

Norval, A.J. (2007) *Aversive Democracy*, Cambridge: CUP.

O'Doherty, D. and Willmott, H. (2001) 'Debating Labour Process Theory', *Sociology*, 35(2): 457–76.

Olson, M. (1965) *The Logic of Collective Action*, Cambridge, Mass.: Harvard University Press.

Olson, M. (1982) *The Rise and Decline of Nations*, New Haven: Yale University Press.

Outhwaite, W. (1987) *New Philosophies of Social Science*, Basingstoke: Macmillan.

Owen, D. (1994) *Maturity and Modernity*, London: Routledge.

Panitch, L. and Leys, C. (2001) *The End of Parliamentary Socialism*, London: Verso.

Panizza, F. (ed.) (2005) *Populism and the Mirror of Democracy*, London: Verso.

Parker, I. (1992) *Discourse Dynamics*, London: Routledge.

Parkin, F. (1982) *Max Weber*, London: Tavistock.

Peirce, C.S. (1934) *Collected Papers of Charles Sanders Peirce*, vol. 5, Cambridge, MA: Harvard University Press.

Peirce, C.S. (1957) *Essays in the Philosophy of Science*, New York: The Liberal Arts Press.

Peirce, C.S. (1960) *Collected Papers*, vols. 1 and 2, Cambridge, MA: The Belknap Press of Harvard University Press.

Petti, P. (2001) *A Theory of Freedom*, Oxford: OUP.

Pettit, P. (1997) *Republicanism*, Oxford: OUP.

Platzky, L. and Walker, C. (1985) *The Surplus People*, Johannesburg: Ravan Press.

Pollitt, C. (1993) *Managerialism and the Public Services*, 2nd edn, Oxford: Blackwell.

Popper, K. (1961) *The Poverty of Historicism*, London: Routledge.

Popper, K. (1966) *The Open Society and Its Enemies*, vol. 2, London: Routledge.

Popper, K. (1972) *Objective Knowledge*, Oxford: OUP.

Popper, K. (1980) *The Logic of Scientific Discovery*, London: Routledge.

Popper, K. (1989) *Conjectures and Refutations*, 5th edn, London: Routledge.

Popper, K. (1999) *All Life is Problem Solving*, London: Routledge.

Potter, J. and Wetherell, M. (1995) 'Discourse Analysis', in J.A. Smith, R. Harre, and L. van Langenhove (eds) *Rethinking Psychology*, London: Sage.

Poulantzas, N. (1969) 'The Problem of the Capitalist State', *New Left Review*, 58: 67–78.

Poulantzas, N. (1973) *Political Power and Social Class*, London: Verso.

Power, M. (1997) *The Audit Society*, Oxford: OUP.

Power, M. (2004) 'Counting, Control and Calculation', *Human Relations*, 57(6): 765–83.

Power, M. (2005) 'Organizations and Auditability', Paper presented at the SCORE Conference 'Organizing the World', 13–15 October.

Prichard, C. (2000) *Making Managers in Universities and Colleges*, Buckingham: Open University Press.

Prichard, C. and Willmott, H. (1997) 'Just How Managed is the McUniversity?', *Organization Studies*, 18(2): 287–316.

Prigogine, I. (1996) *End of Certainty*, New York: Free Press.

Przeworski, A., Alvarez, M.E., Cheibub, J.A., and Limongi, F. (2000) *Democracy and Development*, New York: CUP.

Ranciere, J. (1998) *Disagreement*, Minneapolis, MN: University of Minnesota Press.

Rawls, J. (1971) *A Theory of Justice*, Cambridge, MA: Harvard University Press.

Rawls, J. (1996) *Political Liberalism*, New York: Columbia University Press.

Readings, B. (1996) *The University in Ruins*, Cambridge, MA: Harvard University Press.

Reichenbach, H. (1938) *Experience and Prediction*, Chicago, IL: University of Chicago Press.

Ricoeur, P. (1974) *The Conflict of Interpretations*, Evanston, IL: Northwestern Press.

Riker, W.H. (1962) *The Theory of Political Coalitions*, New Haven, CT: Yale University Press.

Riker, W.H. (1982) 'The Two-Party System and Duverger's Law', in J. Farr and R. Seidelman (eds) (1993) *Discipline and History*, Ann Arbor, MI: University of Michigan Press.

Ringer, F. (1997) *Max Weber's Methodology*, Cambridge. MA: Harvard University Press.

Ringer, F. (2004) *Max Weber*, Chicago, IL: Chicago University Press.

Robbins (1963) The Robbins Report on Higher Education, London: HMSO.

Robins, K. and Webster, F. (eds) (2002) *The Virtual University?*, Oxford: OUP.

Rose, G. (1984) *Dialectic of Nihilism*, Oxford: Basil Blackwell.

Rose, N. (1999) *Powers of Freedom*, Cambridge: CUP.

Rosen, M. (1983) 'Critical Theory', in S. Mitchell and M. Rosen (eds) *Need for Interpretation*, Athlone: Continuum.

Rosen, M. (1996) *On Voluntary Servitude*, Cambridge: Polity Press.

Runciman, W.G. (1970) *Sociology in its Place*, Cambridge: CUP.

Runciman, W.G. (1972) *A Critique of Max Weber's Philosophy of Social Science*, Cambridge: CUP.

Said, E. (1995) *Orientalism*, 2nd edn, Harmondsworth: Penguin Books.

Salecl, R. (1994) *The Spoils of Freedom*, London: Routledge.

Saul, J. and Gelb, S. (1986) *The Crisis in South Africa*, London: Zed Books.

Saussure, F. de (1983) *Course in General Linguistics*, London: Duckworth.

Sayer, D. (1983) *Marx's Method*, Brighton: Harvester.

Sayer, D. (1987) *The Violence of Abstraction*, Oxford: Basil Blackwell.

Schickore, J. and Steinle, F. (eds) (2006) *Revisiting Discovery and Justification*, Dordrecht: Kluwer Academic Publishers.

Schmitt, C. (1996) *The Concept of the Political*, revised edn, Chicago, IL: University of Chicago Press.

Schroeder, M. (1991) *Fractals, Chaos, Power Laws*, New York: W.H. Freeman and Co.

Searle, J. (1969) *Speech Acts*, London: CUP.

Shain, M. (1994) *The Rise of Antisemitism in South Africa*, Charlottesville, VA: University Press of Virginia.

Shapiro, I. (2002) 'Problems, Methods, and Theories in the Study of Politics', *Political Theory*, 30(4): 596–619.

Shapiro, I. (2005) *The Flight from Reality in the Human Sciences*, Princeton, NJ: Princeton University Press.

Shapiro, I. and Wendt, A. (1992) 'The Difference that Realism Makes', *Politics and Society*, 20: 197–223.

Shapiro, I. and Wendt, A. (1997) 'The Misunderstood Promise of Realist Social Theory', in K.R. Monroe (ed.) *Contemporary Empirical Political Theory*, Berkeley and Los Angeles: University of California Press.

Shapiro, M. (2004) *Methods and Nations*, London: Routledge.

Shore, C. and Wright, S. (2000) 'Coercive Accountability', in M. Strathern (ed.) *Audit Cultures*, London: Routledge.

Sim, S. (1998) *Post-marxism: A Reader*, Edinburgh: Edinburgh University Press.

Sim, S. (2000) *Post-marxism: An Intellectual History*, London: Routledge.

Sisk, T. (1995) *Democratization in South Africa*, Princeton, NJ: Princeton University Press.

Skinner, Q. (1991) 'Who are "we"?', *Inquiry*, 34: 133–53.

Skinner, Q. (1994) 'Modernity and Disenchantment', in J. Tully (ed.) *Philosophy in an Age of Pluralism*, Cambridge: CUP.

Skinner, Q. (2002) *Visions of Politics*, vol. 1, Cambridge: Cambridge University Press.

Slaughter, S. (1985) 'From Serving Students to Serving the Economy', *Higher Education*, 14: 41–56.

Sloterdijk, P. (1988) *Critique of Cynical Reason*, London: Verso.

Smith, A.M. (1994) *New Right Discourse on Race and Sexuality: Britain, 1968–1990*, Cambridge: CUP.

Smith, A.M. (1998) *Laclau and Mouffe*, London: Routledge.

Smith, N. (1997) *Strong Hermeneutics*, London and New York: Routledge.

Smith, N. (2002) *Charles Taylor*, Cambridge: Polity Press.

Sono, T. (1975) *South Africa*, MA Dissertation, University of Duquesne.

Sono, T. (1993) *Reflections on the Origins of Black Consciousness in South Africa*, Pretoria: HSRC Publications.

Sorensen, E. and Torfing, J. (eds) (2006) *Theories of Democratic Network Governance*, Basingstoke: Palgrave Macmillan.

Spicer, A. and Fleming, P. (2007) *Contesting the Corporation*, Cambridge: CUP.

Staten, H. (1984) *Wittgenstein and Derrida*, Lincoln, NE: University of Nebraska Press.

Statman, D. (ed.) (1997) *Virtue Ethics*, Edinburgh: Edinburgh University Press.

Stavrakakis, Y. (1999) *Lacan and the Political*, London: Routledge.

Stavrakakis, Y. (2005) 'Passions of Identification', in D. Howarth and J. Torfing (eds) *Discourse Theory in European Politics*, Basingstoke: Palgrave Macmillan.

Stavrakakis, Y. (2007) *The Lacanian Left*, Edinburgh: Edinburgh University Press.

Steinmetz, G. (ed.) (2005) *The Politics of Method in the Human Sciences*, Durham, NC: Duke University Press.

Stengers, I. (1997) *Power and Invention*, Minneapolis, MN: University of Minnesota Press.

Stinchcombe, A.L. (1991) 'The Conditions of Fruitfulness of Theorizing about Mechanisms in Social Science', *Philosophy of the Social Sciences*, 21: 367–88.

Stones, R. (1996) *Sociological Reasoning*, Basingstoke: Macmillan.

Stones, R. (2005) *Structuration Theory*, London: Palgrave Macmillan.

Sturdy, A., Grugulis, I., and Willmott, H. (2001) *Customer Service: Empowerment and Entrapment*, London: Palgrave.

Sturdy, A., Knights, D., and Willmott, H. (eds) (1992) *Skill and Consent*, London: Routledge.

Sunstein, C.R. (1993) 'Commentary on Analogical Reasoning', *Harvard Law Review*, 106: 741–91.

Taylor, C. (1977) 'Human Agency in Action' in C. Taylor (ed.) (1985) *Human Agency and Language, Philosophical Papers*, vol. 1, Cambridge: CUP.

Taylor, C. (1985a) *Philosophical Papers*, vol. 1, Cambridge: CUP.

Taylor, C. (1985b) *Philosophical Papers*, vol. 2, Cambridge: CUP.

Taylor, C. (1985c) 'Connolly, Foucault, and Truth', *Political Theory*, 3: 377–85.

Taylor, C. (1989) *The Sources of the Self*, Cambridge: CUP.

Taylor, C. (1990) 'Comparison, History, Truth', in C. Taylor (ed.) (1995) *Philosophical Arguments*, Cambridge, Mass.: Harvard University Press.

Taylor, C. (1991a) *The Malaise of Modernity*, Concord: Anansi.

Taylor, C. (1991b) 'Comments and Replies', *Inquiry*, 34: 237–54.

Taylor, C. (1994) 'Charles Taylor Replies' in J. Tully (ed.) *Philosophy in an Age of Pluralism*, Cambridge: CUP.

Taylor, C. (1995) *Philosophical Arguments*, Cambridge, MA: Harvard University Press.

Taylor, C. (2004) *Modern Social Imaginaries*, Durham, NC and London: Duke University Press.

Tetlock, P.E. (2005) *Expert Political Judgment*, Princeton, NJ: Princeton University Press.

Tilly, C. (2000) 'Processes and Mechanisms of Democratization', *Sociological Theory*, 18: 1–16.

Tilly, C. (2001) 'Mechanisms in Political Processes', *Annual Review of Political Science*, 4: 21–41.

Tilly, C. and Goodin, R.E. (2006) 'It Depends', in R.E. Goodin and C. Tilly (eds) *The Oxford Handbook of Contextual Political Analysis*, Oxford: OUP.

Topper, K. (2005) *The Disorder of Political Inquiry*, Cambridge, MA: Harvard University Press.

Topper, K., White, S., Moon, D., Farr, J., and Sanders, L. (2006) 'Book Symposium on Political Methodologies', *The Journal of Politics*, 68(3): 733–43.

Torfing, J. (1998) *Politics, Regulation and the Modern Welfare State*, London: Macmillan.

Torfing, J. (1999) *New Theories of Discourse*, Oxford: Blackwell.

Torfing, J. (2005) 'Discourse Theory', in D. Howarth and J. Torfing (eds) *Discourse Theory in European Politics*, London: Palgrave.

Trow, M. (1994) 'Managerialism and the Academic Profession', *Higher Education Policy*, 7(2): 11–18.

Trow, M. (1998) 'American Perspectives on British Higher Education under Thatcher and Major', *Oxford Review of Education*, 24(1): 111–30.

Trowler, P. (1998) *Academics Responding to Change*, Buckingham: Open University Press/SRHE.

Trowler, P. (2001) 'Captured by the Discourse? The Socially Constitutive Power of New Higher Education Discourse in the UK', *Organization*, 8(2): 183–201.

Trowler, P. (ed.) (2002) *Higher Education Policy and Institutional Change*, Buckingham: Open University Press & SRHE.

Tully, J. (ed.) (1994) *Philosophy in an Age of Pluralism*, Cambridge: CUP.

Tully, J. (1995) *Strange Multiplicity*, Cambridge: CUP.

Tully, J. (2002) 'Political Philosophy as a Critical Activity', *Political Theory*, 30(4): 533–55.

Visker, R. (1995) *Michel Foucault*, London: Verso.

Walker, R.J.B. (1992) *Inside/Outside*, Cambridge: CUP.

Weber, M. (1949) *Max Weber on the Methodology of the Social Sciences*, Glencoe, Ill.: Free Press.

Weber, M. (1978) *Economy and Society*, Berkeley, CA: University of California Press.

Weinstock, D.M. (1994) 'The Political Theory of Strong Evaluation' in J. Tully (ed.) *Philosophy in an Age of Pluralism*, Cambridge: CUP.

Weisberg, R. (1993) *Creativity*, New York: W.H. Freeman.

Wendt, A. (1999) *Social Theory of International Politics*, Cambridge: Polity.

Willmott, H. (1993) 'Strength is Ignorance; Slavery is Freedom', *Journal of Management Studies*, 50(4): 515–52.

Willmott, H. (1995) 'Managing the Academics', *Human Relations*, 48(9): 993–1027.

Willmott, H. (2003) 'Commercialising Higher Education in the UK: The State, Industry, and Peer Review', *Studies in Higher Education*, 28(2): 129–41.

Willmott, H. (2005) 'Theorizing Contemporary Control', *Organization*, 12(5): 747–80.

Winch, P. (1974) 'Understanding a Primitive Society', in B. Wilson (ed.) *Rationality*, Oxford: Basil Blackwell.

Winch, P. (1977) 'A Comment', in F. Dallmayr and T. McCarthy (eds) *Understanding and Social Inquiry*, Notre Dame: University of Notre Dame Press.

Winch, P. (1990) *The Idea of a Social Science and Its Relation to Philosophy*, 2nd edn, London: Routledge.

Winch, P. (1997) 'Can we Understand Ourselves?', *Philosophical Investigations*, 20(3): 193–204.

Wittgenstein, L. (1967) *Philosophical Investigations*, Oxford: Blackwell.

Wittgenstein, L. (1979) 'Remarks on Frazer's *Golden Bough*', in C.G. Luckhardt (ed.) *Wittgenstein*, Sussex: Harvester.

Wolpe, H. (1988) *Race, Class, and the Apartheid State*, London: James Curry.

Worthington, F. and Hodgson, J. (2005) 'Academic Labour and the Politics of Quality in Higher Education', *Critical Quarterly*, 47(1/2): 96–110.

Wright, S. (2004) 'Markets, Corporations, Consumers? New Landscapes in Higher Education', *Learning and Teaching in the Social Sciences*, 1(2): 71–93.

Yanow, D. (2003) *Constructing 'Race' and 'Ethnicity' in America*, Armonk, NY: Sharpe.

Yanow, D. and Schwartz-Shea, P. (2006) *Interpretation and Method*, M.E. Sharpe.

Young, H. (1989) *One of Us: A Biography of Margaret Thatcher*, London: Macmillan.

Young, O.R. (1989) *International Cooperation*, Ithaca, NY: Cornell University Press.

Zerilli, L. (2005) *Feminism and the Abyss of Freedom*, Chicago, IL: University of Chicago Press.

Žižek, S. (1989) *The Sublime Object of Ideology*, London: Verso.

Žižek, S. (1991a) *For They Know Not What They Do*, London: Verso.

Žižek, S. (1991b) *Looking Awry*, Cambridge, MA: MIT Press.

Žižek, S. (1993) *Tarrying with the Negative*, Durham, NC: Duke University Press.

Žižek, S. (1994) *The Metastases of Enjoyment*, London: Verso.

Žižek, S. (1997a) 'Multiculturalism, Or, the Cultural Logic of Multinational Capitalism', *New Left Review*, 225: 28–51.

Žižek, S. (1997b) *The Plague of Fantasies*, London: Verso.

Žižek, S. (2000) 'Class Struggle or Postmodernism? Yes, Please!' in J. Butler, E. Laclau, and S. Žižek (eds) *Contingency, Hegemony and Universality: New Discussions on the Left*, London: Verso.

Žižek, S. (2001) *On Belief*, London: Routledge.

Index

abduction 24, 219n12, 219n13, 219n14; *see also* retroduction
absorption 111–12, 124
abstraction 28, 32–4, 96, 125, 133–7, 154, 160–2, 167, 188, 230n6
actions 223n4; beliefs and 56, 58–64, 205; human 61, 225–6, 227n1; interpretation of 57–9; repetitive 104–5; social practices and 104–5; *see also* practices; subjectivity
Adam, H. 150
Adorno, T. 10
affects 57, 98, 217; *see also* emotions
African National Congress 141
agency 30, 55, 74, 78–9, 129, 160–1; *see also* subjectivity
Alchemies of the Mind (Elster) 86
alienation 58–9
Althusser, L. 28, 117–19, 121, 128, 210–11; *see also* ideology; subject
American Political Science Association 2
American politics 54
antagonism 42, 57, 113, 116, 147, 165, 224n6; *see also* conflict; contestation; struggle
apartheid 138–9, 141–2, 143, 149–53, 203, 231–2
application problem 140, 184
applying a rule 52–4, 67–8, 137, 184, 224; *see also* rule-following; rules
Apter, D. 217n6
archaeology 144, 233n2
Archaeology of Knowledge, The (Foucault) 128
Arendt, H.79, 114–15, 235n14; *see also* political; public contestation
Argentina 204
Aristotle 19, 229n1
articulation 16, 47, 161, 165–7, 177–83, 183–91, 207, 232–6

articulatory practice 17, 155–7, 162, 166, 179–80, 183, 188, 196, 214; *see also* practices
associative relations 106, 143–4; *see also* combinatory relations; substitutive relations; syntagmatic relations
atomic mechanisms 232n6; *see also* mechanisms
atomization, logics of 172, 213; *see also* logics
attachment 156, 187
attentiveness 110, 123–4, 131, 147; *see also* ethics
audit regime 233
authenticity 110–11
aviation 122
Azande society 68–70, 205

background conditions 158
Badiou, A. 217n11, 230n5
Bantu Education Act (1953) 232n2
behaviour: mass 61; rule-governed 52
behaviouralism 3
being 30, 71–2, 82, 103, 107–10, 124; *see also* ontical/ontological distinction; ontology
Being and Time (Heidegger) 108
beliefs 51, 213: actions and 56, 58–64, 205; distorted 75–6; false 10; first-order 221n21; interpretation of 59–64, 68–70; societal 68–9; webs of 61–2
Bentham, J. 49, 203
Berlin, I. 50, 218n1
Berlin wall 20
Bernstein, R.J. 1, 2
Bevir, M. 50, 51, 55, 59–64, 74–8, 80–1, 128, 223n3, 225, 226n19; *see also* beliefs; contingency; hermeneutics; individual viewpoints; interpretivism

Bhaskar, R. 10–11, 19, 28, 29–30, 32, 33, 84, 103, 160–1, 211, 220, 228n9; *see also* critical realism; intransitive objects; mechanisms
Billig, M. 98, 98–9
bio-power 45, 46, 47
Birth of the Clinic, The (Foucault) 202–3
Blair, T. 95, 97, 151
Bosnia 167
Bourdieu, P. 104, 137, 216n2
Bradley, F.H. 223n3
breakdown, moments of 158
British civil service 64
British imperialists 149
Burawoy, M. 146, 231n12
Bush, G.W. 151

Campbell, D. 167, 217n8, 223n2
capitalist societies 10, 58–9, 135
case studies 201, 202–4, 208; anomalous 26, 34, 43; vs. comparative method 16, 165, 189, 201–2, 205–7; critical 203; deviant 202–3; extreme 202–3; least likely 203; maximum variation 203; method 201–2, 204; most likely 203; myth of 201, 204; paradigmatic 203; peripheral 203, 205
causal explanation 19, 49–50, 85–6, 223–4, 228–9, 228n6; *see also* causal mechanisms; explanation
causality 85, 91, 101; ideals and language of 89–95; mechanical 236n18; natural science conception of 96–7
causal law paradigm 18–19, 81–2, 213, 218n14
causal laws 3–4, 35, 41, 84, 85, 90–1, 95, 97, 135, 166
causal mechanisms 3–4, 28–9, 32, 41, 83–103, 134, 211, 213, 217n6, 227–9; character and scope of 86–9; idealism and 99–102; intentional mechanisms and 85–6; vs. logics 11, 157–62; problematization of 95–7; psychologism and 97–9; in social science 85–6; subject-independence of 96–7; *see also* Bhaskar; Elster; explanation; mechanisms
Cavell, S. 67, 78, 184, 186
change 2, 14, 21, 62, 77, 145, 170–1, 176, 195, 224n6, 227n20; political 37, 51, 54, 61–2, 77, 106; of practices 39, 64, 122, 145, 152, 187; of regimes 152; social 53, 61–2, 66, 77, 84, 122, 142, 145, 152, 203, 214, 227n3

charity: in interpretation 59, 67, 69; principle of 69
chess, example of 136
civil society vs. state 114, 121
class struggles 181
claims 104, 188
closed systems 30, 31–2, 224n6
closure 118, 120, 124, 146–7, 151, 155–6, 163, 176, 218n16, 232n8
cognitive mechanisms 227n1
Coleridge, S.T. 49
collective action 109
collective actors 61
collective mobilization 122, 141
Collingwood, R.G. 223n3
combinatory relations 106, 144; *see also* associative relations; substitutive relations; syntagmatic relations
common meanings 58, 73
communism 141–2, 151, 203
comparative research 201, 204–7, 208; and case studies 16, 165, 189, 201–2, 205–7
comparing 189, 204–7
competition 177, 178, 185–6, 233n4
complicity 7, 125, 197
concealment 120, 131, 147
conditions 3, 7, 10–11, 22–3, 28, 66, 79, 87–9, 91, 136, 157–8, 161–3, 205–7, 226n14, 227n1, 230n4; of existence 45, 117, 158, 210; of possibility 8, 15, 28–9, 31–2, 58, 82, 103, 154, 159, 163, 180, 192; of impossibility 82, 103, 154
conflict 62, 67, 70, 113–14, 167, 213, 226n15; *see also* antagonism; contestation; struggle
conjectures, informed 3
Connolly, W.E. 16, 154, 155–6, 194, 221n21; *see also* onto-political interpretation
Conservative Party 175
constitution 5, 34, 64, 79, 81–2, 99, 116, 127–8, 142, 152; *see also* construction; institution
constitutive goods 72
constitutive outside 36, 50, 55, 67, 77, 99, 111, 121, 125, 153–4, 158, 197
constitutive rules 230n6
construction 5, 8, 12, 20, 24, 27, 33–4, 38; *see also* constitution; institution; institutionalization
consumerism 169, 174, 177, 196
contestation 14–5, 38, 68, 110–13, 115, 116, 121–3, 145; *see also* antagonism; conflict; struggle

contextualization 95–6, 220n21
contextualized self-interpretation 3–4,
41, 50–1, 83, 102, 134, 211, 213;
epistemological and methodological
aspects 55–64; vs. logics 11, 157–62;
problematization of 64–79, 171;
see also Bevir; hermeneutics; Rhodes;
Taylor; Winch
contingency 74, 78, 82, 84, 104–5,
115, 118–20, 155; empirical
109–10; radical 109–12, 128–9,
197–8, 214
continuity 26, 84, 143
conventionalism 184–5
Coole, D. 110, 218n15
counterfactuals 205–6
counter-hegemonic practices 5
counter logic of radical and plural
democracy 194
counter-logics 194–5, 196, 197, 200, 215;
of democracy and non-domination
196–7; of a plural and democratic
community 194–5, 199
covering law model 21, 86, 93–4, 221–2;
see also Duverger's law; Hempel
covering-over 15
Cox, R. 126, 167
Criminal Justice and Public Order Act
(1994) 148
Critchley, S. 6–7, 121
critical cases 203
critical explanation 8–11, 41–7, 70,
152–3, 211, 213–14; *see also* critique;
explanation
critical realism 1, 2, 10, 30, 31–3, 109,
212, 216n2
critical theorists 9
critical theory 1, 9, 10
critique 8, 155, 191–201, 214–15;
deconstructive 192; ethical 197–9;
explanatory 10; immanent 191;
normative 193–7
Critique of Judgement, The (Kant) 183
cynicism 146

Dasein 232n3
data analysis 62–3
Davidson, D. 50, 61, 223n3
deconstruction 42, 181, 183, 192, 227n20;
see also Derrida
deduction 18–9, 21, 25–6, 35, 221n21
deductive-nomological model 12,
21–3, 35–8, 89, 210–12; *see also*
covering law model

de-institution 142; *see also* contestation;
dislocation; reactivation
demands 115–16; hegemonic
political 115–16; political 104,
107, 115–16, 122–3, 136, 142–5;
simple 8, 115–16; *see also* claims;
grievances
democracy 182, 193, 195, 196, 203
Derrida, J. 76, 128, 155, 165, 192; *see also*
deconstruction
Descartes, R. 9, 227n20
descriptivism 162
desires 59, 61–2, 76–7, 86, 91, 94, 97–9,
152, 213, 224n8, 227n4
determinism 92, 219n11
deviant cases 202–3
Dialectic of Enlightenment (Horkheimer
and Adorno) 10
Diederichs, N. 141, 142
difference, logics of 15, 73, 106, 133,
143–5, 151, 153, 189, 200; *see also*
equivalence; Laclau; Mouffe; logics
dilemma 61, 62
Dilthey, W. 50, 223
dimensions of social reality 14, 112–13,
120–2, 130, 157, 231
disciplinary power 45, 46, 47
discourse 68; analysis 2; apartheid 38–9,
141–3, 149–53, 203, 231–2;
commodification 110, 172; consumer
169, 177, 200; consumption 133, 177,
200; counter- 200; higher education
168–77, 199–201, 208, 222–3;
nationalist 107, 141, 149–50; new
public management 172; as patterns of
sayings and doings 186; populist 46,
186–7; publicly and officially articulated
123; racist 203; of sexuality 42, 44–49,
222–3; Thatcherite 123, 137, 150,
173–4, 177, 193, 233n4, 235n12;
totalitarian 189; unofficial 123;
utopian 189; *see also* Foucault; Laclau;
meaningful behaviour; meanings
discourse theory 4–7, 17, 41, 121,
212, 217n6
discovery, context of 24, 30–3, 36, 38,
40–1, 218n4, 222n24; *see also* Popper;
Reichenbach
discrimination 224n7
discursive articulation 172
discursive entities 109, 127
discursive psychology 98
dislocation 42, 110–11, 112, 121, 157;
dislocatory event 14, 115, 117–19, 129,

dislocation (*Continued*)
143, 200; dislocatory experience 79,
104, 117, 121, 157; dislocatory moment
143, 152; *see also* incomplete; lack;
negativity; void
disruption 158
distorted beliefs 75–6
domination 121, 193, 195, 198, 231
double-hermeneutic 232n3
Dowding, K. 20, 21, 36, 218n1
Dreyfus, H. 21, 46, 50, 236n18
Duverger, M. 18, 37, 108, 135
Duverger's law 2, 22–3, 35, 36–7,
135, 182

Easton, D. 114
ecology 130–1
Education Reform Act (1988) 175
Elster, J. 4, 63, 83–95, 103, 159, 211, 213,
227n1, 228n5, 232n6; *see also* causal
mechanisms; mechanisms
emancipation 9, 10, 42, 71, 150, 210
embodied 10, 43, 56, 120, 216n2
emotions, interpretation of 56–7
empirical analysis 8, 16, 20–1, 30
empirical anomalies 42
empirical contingency 109–10
empirical correlation 19
empirical data 34–5, 43, 48, 63
empirical generalizations 2, 16, 31, 41, 52
empirical research ix, 5–6, 8, 11–12, 34, 39,
43, 63–4, 108
empirical testing 29, 119, 128; *see also*
testing; theory testing
empirical theory 1
empirico-transcendental doublet 163
employee cynicism 146
empty signifiers 122, 130, 184
enjoyment 15, 76, 107, 119–20, 125,
129–32, 147–8, 151–2, 163, 174, 177,
189, 229n3, 236n17; category of 15,
76, 107, 130; of closure 151; fantasmatic
mode of 163; logic of self-transgressive
76, 236n17; mode of 119, 131–2;
non-discursive kernel of 107; ontology
of 107; of openness 151; perverse 107;
vs. pleasure 107, 229n3; subjective
mode of 132, 151, 174; subject of 130,
151, 152, 231n15; theft or stealing of
107, 148, 149; two axes of 163; *see also*
Lacan; Žižek
Enlightenment ideals 10
environment 122
environmental mechanisms 227n1

environmental movement 122
epistemic fallacy 30, 160
epistemic gain 71
epistemological indeterminacy 99–102
epistemology 155
equality 142, 191
equivalence, logics of 15, 106, 133, 143–5,
150–1, 153, 163, 173, 177, 180, 189,
200; *see also* difference; Laclau; logics
essentialism 42, 129, 135, 181
ethical, the 14–15, 82, 119, 124, 192–3;
vs. the ideological 119, 157; vs. the
political 119, 163; and radical
contingency 12, 73, 82, 111, 113, 119,
123, 193, 198; vs. the social 119
ethical critique 16, 197–9; *see also* critique;
normative critique
ethical dimension 111–13, 132, 157, 163
ethico-political interpretation 16, 155–7
ethics 5, 117–20, 123, 151, 163, 198
evaluation, strong 224n7
evidence, generation of 63
evolutionary theory 62
exhaustiveness 21
explanandum 21, 23, 47, 92, 94, 100, 214
explanans 50, 92, 94, 100, 214, 232n6
explanation 8, 11, 15, 84, 222; causal 19,
49–50, 85–6, 223–4, 228–9, 228n6;
through contextualization 95–6; covering
law of 21; critical 41–7, 70, 152–3;
deductive-nomological model of 21–3,
35–8, 210–11; form of 11, 210–11;
functional 228n6; vs. hypothesis 38;
intentional 85–6, 228n5; justification of
34; key approaches to 212; law-like 166,
180, 183, 202; by laws 90–1; logics of
33–4, 63, 217n13; mode of 48, 211;
narrative form of 59–60, 78; positivist
view of 35–6; vs. prediction 22;
retroductive 27–41, 38, 211;
understanding and 223–4
explanatory analysis 55
explanatory concepts 66
explanatory critique 10–11
explicitness 21
Extension of University Education Act
(1957) 232n2
extreme cases 202–3, 204–5

facts 8, 21–2
failure 76, 110, 115, 172; moments of 158;
of fantasmatic objects 150; of normal
ways of going on 158; of signifying
systems 122; of structures 128–9;

see also breakdown; dislocation; disruption; negativity
false beliefs 10
false consciousness 227n1
falsification 31, 202
family resemblance 134, 167, 185, 222n27
fantasmatic logics 15, 107, 130, 134, 145–54, 157, 159–60, 162–3, 173–7, 213
fantasy 15, 106–7, 120, 130, 132, 134, 137–8, 145–7, 149–51, 163, 174–5, 177, 197, 214, 232n3, 232n9; crossing the 163, 232n3; beatific 147, 177; horrific 147, 177
Farr, J. 36, 37, 48, 221–2
feedback effect 221n21
feminism 2, 131
Fink, B. 101
Fleming, P. 146
floating signifiers 152
Flyvberg, B. 201–2, 203, 236n18
formalization 21, 163
formation: social 114, 118, 126, 143, 155; discursive 105, 128, 139, 142; *see also* constitution; construction; institution; state; symbolic order; systems
form of explanation 11, 210–11
Foucault, M. 10, 39, 42, 44–7, 76, 128, 139, 144, 155, 156, 167, 190, 192, 202–3, 204, 207, 210, 223n29; *see also* archaeology; bio-power; disciplinary power; discourse; genealogy; problematization
Frankfurt, H.G. 220
Frankfurt School 191
Frazer, J. 205
Freeden, M. 118, 217n7, 218n16, 231n10
freedom 39, 58, 72, 79, 168, 177, 182, 191
Freud, S. 98, 226n20
Friedman, M. 18
functional explanation 228n6
fundamental norms 230n5
fusion of horizons 232n3

Gadamer, H-G. 50, 51, 57, 232n3
Galison, P. 219n7
game theory 3, 57
genealogy 192, 233n2; *see also* archaeology; Foucault; problematization
generalizations 182, 187–90, 204, 207, 210
general mechanisms 164; *see also* causal mechanisms; mechanisms
Giddens, A. 5, 48, 65, 217n11, 232n3
glasnost-perestroika movement 216n2

Glynos, J. 123, 232n3
God 124
Goodin, R.E. 20, 216n5, 227n1
Gore, A. 219n5
government, problem of 168
Gramsci, A. 114, 121, 122, 203
Green, T.H. 223n3
grievances 104, 121–2; *see also* claims; demands
Griggs, S. 122

Habermas, J. 2, 10, 190, 210
Hacking, I. 8
Hampshire, S. 50
Hanson, N. 19, 24, 25, 26, 27, 47, 92–3, 93–4, 101, 219n9, 228–9; *see also* abduction; Peirce; retroduction
Hegel, G.W.F. 100
hegemonic 5, 18, 24, 54, 59, 92, 105, 125, 126, 130, 142, 193, 196, 197
hegemonic orders and practices 5, 106, 179
hegemonic political demands 115, 116, 175
hegemonic project 173, 179, 197
hegemonic theory 6–7, 42
hegemony 105, 123, 124, 126, 196
Hegemony and Socialist Strategy (Laclau and Mouffe) 179
Heidegger, Martin 50, 51, 79, 103, 108, 158, 160, 232n3; *see also* absorption; being; ontical/ontological distinction; ontology
Hempel, C. 21–2, 93, 177; *see also* covering law model; deductive-nomological model
hermeneutic circle 40, 222n27; vs. retroductive circle 40, 57, 222n27
hermeneutics 50–6, 62–4, 79–82, 103, 158–9, 166, 212; double 48; of recovery 207, *see also* of retrieval 226n20; of suspicion 226n20; *see also* Gadamer; Taylor; Winch
Hesse, M. 9
hierarchy, logics of 172, 195–6
higher education 16–17, 193–4, 199–201, 208, 222–3, 233–5; problematization of 168–71; retroductive explanation of 171–7
historical bloc 125
historical contexts 206–7, 213
History of Sexuality, The (Foucault) 44–7
Hobbes, T. 2
Hodgson, J. 170
Hoggenheimer, figure of 149, 153

Hollis, M. 65
Horkheimer, M. 9–10, 191
Howarth, D. 122, 123
human action 227n1
human emancipation 10
human subjectivity 5; *see also* agency;
    subject; subjectivity
Husserl, E. 2, 116, 181, 210
hypergoods 72, 73
hypotheses 19, 24; vs. explanation 38;
    generation of 26–7; positing and
    accepting 31–2, 33–4, 39–40, 219–20
hypothetico-deductive method 18, 21, 210,
    216n1; *see also* Popper

ideal: causal law 3–4, 13–14, 18–19, 49,
    51–2, 81; Enlightenment 10; of
    explanation by laws 90; law-like 84,
    102; naturalistic 49, 134; positivist 18;
    radical democratic 197, 199; rationalist
    52, 76; republican 199; scientific 21
idealism 99–102, 178, 225n13
ideal theory 21
identification 129, 130, 131
identity 108–9, 128, 130–1, 144–5,
    160, 192
identity-identification dialectic 129–32
ideological dimension 112, 113, 157
ideology 117–20, 198
imaginary 72–3, 117, 147
immanence vs. transcendence 82
immanent critique 191
impossibility 154
incomplete 79, 208; constitutively 14,
    110, 129, 214; essentially 127; order
    130–1; structure 11, 14, 101, 214;
    subject 14; *see also* dislocation; lack; void
incorrigibility thesis 65
indeterminacy 101
indeterminate effects 88–9
individualism 84, 97, 99–100, 227n3
individualization 140
individual viewpoints 74
induction 18–19, 25, 25–6, 221n21
industrialization 122
inequality 195
informed conjectures 3
inner mental processes 98–9
institution 214; vs. de-institution 142; of
    practices and regimes 142–3, 226n14,
    227n3; *see also* constitution; construction
institutionalization 142–3, 147, 174
instrumentalization, logics of 172
instrumental reason 71–2

intellectual honesty 60
intentional explanation 85, 85–6, 228n5
intentional mechanisms 85–6, 95, 96
intentionality 226n15
intermediate cases 205
international regimes 126
interpretation 35, 220n21, 224n6; of
    actions 57–9; of beliefs 59–64, 68–70;
    of emotions 56–7; ethico-political
    155–7; ontopolitical 155; of reality 68;
    of self-interpretations 60, 67, 70–1;
    validity of 71
interpretive approach, marginalization of 1
interpretivism 1, 60, 75
inter-subjective meanings 58–9, 64, 72
intervention 38, 40, 44
intransitive objects 161
intransitivity 33
introjection 130, 135
intuitionism 184–5
iron law of oligarchy 2, 37

Jameson, F. 208
Jarvie, I.C. 65, 68
Jessop, B. 211
jouissance 15, 76, 229n3; *see also* enjoyment
judgement 43, 53, 108, 166, 183–91; acts
    of 186; as situated ability 184;
    characterizing and evaluative 69–70;
    determinative vs. reflective 183; moral
    69; practices of 16, 18, 178, 183;
    situated 185
justification 21, 24, 34, 202; context of 30,
    36, 38, 40–1, 218n4, 222n24; *see also*
    Popper; Reichenbach
justifying 190–1

Kant, I. 8, 10, 183
Kepler, J. 24
knowledge 8, 9, 190
Knowledge and Human Interests (Habermas) 210
Koornhof, P. 149–50
Krasner, S. 126
Kripke, S. 186
Kuhn, T. 44, 220n19
Kunda, G. 146

Lacan, J. 107, 229n3, 232n3; *see also*
    enjoyment; fantasy; lack; master signifier;
    subject; subjectivity; Žižek
Lacanian theory 10
lack/lacking 14, 76, 82, 89, 110, 119, 122,
    127–31, 146–7, 170, 176, 179, 197,
    231n15, 232n4

lack, ontology of 14, 82, 99–102, 129; *see also* dislocation; void
Laclau, E. 6, 42–4, 76, 100, 106, 109, 110, 111, 115, 116–17, 118, 120, 122, 128–9, 130, 133, 135–6, 139, 140, 142, 144, 152, 161, 163, 164, 179–80, 186–7, 193, 204, 231n10; *see also* difference; equivalence; hegemony; logics; political; populism
Lakatos's theory of progressive research programmes 220n19
language 51, 57, 98–9, 224n7; games 75, 134, 140, 184; of logics 152; theory of 74–8
law-like explanation 166, 180, 183, 202; *see also* covering law model; deductive-nomological model; Duverger's law; explanation; Hempel
Lefort, C. 113
Lewis, D. 148
linguistics 66, 74–5, 78–9, 178–9
logics 4, 104–8, 213–14, 231–2; in apartheid discourse 138–9, 141–3, 149–53, 203; of atomization 172, 213; vs. causal mechanism 157–62; of collective action 109; of competition 177, 178, 185–6, 233n4; concept of 11, 134–7; of critical explanation 8–11; critical explanation and 152–3; of difference 143, 144–5; of equivalence 15, 106, 133, 143–5, 150–1, 153, 163, 173, 177, 180, 189, 200; of explanation 63, 217n13; fantasmatic 15, 107, 130, 134, 145–54, 157, 159–60, 162–3, 173–7, 213; of hierarchy 172, 195–6; in higher education 193–4, 199–201, 208, 222–3; of instrumentalization 172; language of 152; of the market 136–7, 139; political 15, 106, 133–4, 141–5, 150–5, 157, 159–60, 162–3, 173–7, 196–7, 213; of refutation 225; relations among 163; vs. contextualized self-interpretations 157–62; social 15, 96, 106, 133, 135–6, 137–40, 143–5, 153, 154, 157, 159–60, 162–3, 171–2, 176–7, 185, 186–7, 195–6, 213; status of 153–4; types of 15; typology of 106–8; of vindication 225
looping effect 221n21
Lukes, S. 198, 231n10

McAnulla, S. 226n19
MacIntyre, A. 65, 71, 206
Making Social Science Matter (Flyvberg) 201–2

Malan, D.F. 149
Marx, K. 28, 133, 135, 181, 226n20, 232–3
Marxism 10, 28, 42, 109, 114, 151, 203
mass behaviour 61
master signifier 130–1
materialism 100–1
materialist ontology 100
materialist theory of ideology 117–18
mathematical methods 18
maximum variation cases 203
meaningful behaviour 51–4; *see also* discourse; practices
meanings 58, 73; *see also* common meanings; discourse; inter-subjective meanings
mechanisms: atomic 159, 232n6; causal *see* causal mechanisms; cognitive 158, 227n1; environmental 88, 227n1; generative 29–30, 32, 160; intentional 85–6, 95–6; type A 87–8, 101; type B 87–8, 101; *see also* Bhaskar; Elster
mechanistic causality 93–4
Mendel, G. 190
metaphysics 179, 192; negative 192; Western 192
methodological atomism 99–100
methodological deficit 6, 7
methodological individualism 84, 97, 99–100, 227n3
methodological pluralism 2
methodology 209–10
Michels, R. 37
Mill, J.S. 49–50
mode of explanation 48, 211
modes of inquiry 63
morality 8
moral progress 71
moral relativism 69
moral theory 71–2
Morley, L. 170, 196
Morton, R. 20
motivation, sources of 74
Mouffe, C. 42–4, 100, 106, 109, 115, 120, 140, 144, 152, 179–80, 193, 231n10; *see also* difference; equivalence; hegemony; political
Mulhall, S. 184, 185–6
myth 10, 107; of the case study 201, 204

Nagel, E. 197
naming 186–7, 194–5, 196
narrative 16, 34, 45, 59–60, 74, 78, 130, 147, 148, 150, 151, 174, 191, 235n11

narrative form of explanation 59–60, 86, 183, 787
national identity 108–9
nationalism 141–2, 144–5
National Party 141–2, 149
naturalism 162–3, 166
naturalist philosophy 28–9
naturalization 141
natural science 2, 220
negative ontology 73, 218n15
negativity 42, 105
negotiation 58
neo-positivism 157, 212, 213
New Age Travellers 148
New Labour 74, 81
new public management 172
New Right 173, 193, 197, 233n4; *see also* Thatcherite politics
Nietzsche, F. 159, 190, 226n20
nihilism 227n20
nomological 28; *see also* deductive-nomological model
normative critique 8, 182, 193–7, 214–15
normative deficit 6–7
normative schema 7–8
normativism 73, 198
norms 5, 7, 10, 14, 63, 105, 111, 115, 119–23, 126–7, 130, 138, 185, 192–3, 198, 205, 215
novel ideas 62

objectivity 10, 116–17
oligarchy 2
Oliver, J. 122
Olson, M. 109, 181–2, 235n14
On Golden Bough (Frazer) 205
On Populist Reason (Laclau) 115
ontical contingency 109–10
ontical/ontological distinction 229–30
onto-ethical critique 155
ontological contingency 109–10
ontological presuppositions 108–13
ontological projection 35
ontology 103–4, 160, 229–31; commitment to 10; concept of 108; of lack 14, 82, 99–102, 129; materialist 100; negative 73, 218n15; of the political 113–17; positivism and 34; poststructuralist 70; signifying 144; of the social 98–9, 113–17; of structures 29
onto-political interpretation 16, 154, 155; *see also* Connolly; onto-ethical critique
open systems 29, 224n6
oppression 8–9, 12, 143, 204

order 46, 130–1
Orientalism 192
organic crisis 42, 151, 193
Other, the 110, 232n3, 232n4; *see also* lack; symbolic order; void
otherness 126, 142, 205; dangerous other 142
Outhwaite, W. 32
outrage 56–7; *see also* affects; emotions
outsider 126
overdetermination of rules 66; vs. underdetermination thesis 66–7

paradiastole 187
paradigmatic cases 203–4, 205
particularity 4, 12, 74, 91, 94, 162, 183, 188, 209, 213, 233n1
Peirce, C. S. 19, 24–5, 26, 47, 219–20; *see also* abduction; Hanson; retroduction
perestroika movement 1
Peron, J. 229n2
Peronism 204, 229n2
persuasion 38, 40, 44, 190–1
philosophy of science 24–7, 30, 218n4
physics 220n19, 236n18
Plato 229n1, 236n18
pluralism 2, 196, 216n2
polarization 57, 59
politeia 229n1
political, the 113–17; vs. ethical 119, 163; vs. ideological 78, 123, 125, 157; vs. social 104–5, 108, 112–17; *see also* political dimension; political logics; political practices; primacy of politics
political analysis i, viii, x, 1–2, 4–5, 8, 10–11, 27, 36, 39, 42, 55, 62, 73–4, 81, 107, 130, 167, 204, 209, 211, 214
political change 62
political demands 115–16
political dimension 112–17, 120, 121–2, 157, 231n9
political logics 15, 106, 133–4, 141–5, 150–4, 157, 159–60, 162–3, 173–7, 196–7, 213; *see also* difference; equivalence; logics; political
political practices 45, 72, 105, 106, 112, 114–15, 117, 119, 121–7, 145–8, 151, 157–8, 192, 198
political science: development of 3; perestroika movement in 1
political-social axis 110–13
political systems 217n6
political theory of politics 217n7
politics, primacy of 5

Politics and Ideology in Marxist Theory (Laclau) 179
Popper, K. 19, 21, 22, 31, 35, 222n23
populism 115
positive theory 2–3
positivism 8, 9, 84, 157, 212, 216n1; challenges to 18; critiques of 51–5; growth of 1, 210; problems with 3, 34; support for 23; transition to post-positivism 33–41
post-analytical philosophy 42
post-behaviouralism 3
post-Marxist theory 42–4
post-positivism 33–41, 220
poststructuralism 76–7, 152, 212, 217n6; criticism of 5–7, 128; dilemmas of 4–8; retroduction and 41
poststructuralist ontology 70
power 190, 231
practical reason 8
practices 14–5, 104–8, 109–10, 116, 120–7, 221n21; articulatory 17, 155–7, 162, 166, 179–80, 183, 188, 196, 214; ideological 157–8, 171; political 45, 72, 105, 106, 112, 114–15, 117, 119, 121–7, 145–8, 151, 157–8, 192, 198; repetitive actions 104–5; reproduction of 16, 104; social 14, 72, 104–10, 117, 119, 121–2, 145–7, 192; *see also* actions; agency; subject; subjectivity
pragmatic 39, 108, 150, 173
pragmatism 216n2
prediction: causal mechanisms for 3–4; concept of 3; deduction and 35–6; vs. explanation 22; vs. interpretation 34–6, 38–9, 51, 55; in political elections 219n5; problem of 20–4, 32–3, 87; vs. prognosis 3; role of 28; understanding 3, 53
predictive power 21
prejudgement 20
presidential election (2000) 219n5
primacy of politics 5
problem of subsumption 16
problematization 10, 11, 35, 38, 44, 64–79, 145, 167–71; *see also* archaeology; Foucault; genealogy; problem-driven research
problem-driven research 11, 20, 84, 167, 207
problem-driven theory 84
prognosis 3; vs. prediction 3
project: apartheid 142; common 129; counter-hegemonic or resistance 5;

Enlightenment 10, 65; European 148; hegemonic 173, 179, 197; Keynesian welfare state 173; Labour Left 193; naturalist 229n9; New Labour 81; New Left 193; New Right 173, 193, 197, 199; one nation 126, 127; political 5, 104, 147, 152; road-building 122; two nation 126–7
proto-explanation 39–40
proto-interpretation 56
Przeworksi, A. 182
psychoanalysis 42, 98–9
psychologism 97–9
public contestation 110, 111–13, 115, 116, 121, 122–3, 145

quasi-transcendental inquiry 153–4

Rabinow, P. 46
racism 153
radical contingency 11–15, 35, 42, 73, 78, 82, 102, 104, 109–10, 112, 128–9, 197–8, 214; vs. empirical contingency 110
Rancière J. 230n5
rational choice theory 3, 63
rationality 68, 71–2
Rawls, J. 40
reactivation 116–17, 183; vs. sedimentation 116
reality 53; dimensions of 116; interpretation of 54–5, 68; social 117, 117–18; socio-political 110–13; structure of 146–7
real, the 11, 28–9, 100–1, 111, 127, 143, 146, 179, 227n20, 231n14; vs. political reality 111; *see also* incomplete; Lacan; lack; negativity; void
real object world 28–9, 30
reasoning: deductive 18–9, 25, 221n21; inductive 19, 25, 221n21; instrumental 71–2; practical 8; retroductive 10; theoretical 8, 9; universal 10
redescription 64, 187
reductionism 94, 99
reference points 58
reflective equilibrium 40
reflexivity 73, 104, 156; first-order vs. second-order 220n21
refutation, logics of 225
regimes 104–8, 109–10, 116, 120; change or transformation of 103–4, 127, 133; reproduction of 16

regularity in dispersion 139, 185; *see also*
    discourse; Foucault
regulative rules 230n6
Reichenbach, H. 19
reification 188
relational contexts 160
relational mechanisms 227n1
relativism 68–9
religious conversions 124
repressive hypothesis 46, 222–3
research strategies 201–7, 208; case studies
    202–4; comparative research 204–7;
    empirical 5
retroduction 19–20, 211, 223n30;
    critical explanation and 41–7; vs.
    deduction 19, 25–6; vs. induction 19,
    25–6; philosophy of science and 24–7;
    post-positivism and 33–41; social
    science explanation and 27–41; theory
    construction and 27, 41–7; *see also*
    Hanson; Peirce; Sayer
retroductive circle 40, 222n27; vs.
    hermeneutic circle 40, 57, 227n27
retroductive explanation 10, 38, 40–1, 44,
    171–7, 211
rhetoric 22, 44, 75, 187
rhetorical redescription 187, 196
Rhodes, R. 50, 51, 55, 59–64, 74–8,
    80–1, 128, 223n3, 225, 226n19; *see also*
    beliefs; hermeneutics; individual
    viewpoints; interpretivism
Ricoeur, P. 50, 226–7
road to Damascus experience 124
Rose, G. 192
Rose, N. 168
rule-following 67
rule-governed behaviour 225–6
rules: applying 52–4, 67–8, 137, 184,
    224n5; constitutive 230n6; following
    52, 226n14; fundamental 115–16;
    overdetermination of 66; regulative
    230n6; underdetermination thesis 66–7;
    see also Winch; Wittgenstein
Runciman, W.G. 5
Russian Revolution 203
Ryan, A. 65

Saddam Hussein 95
Said, E. 192, 235n15
Saussure, F. de 106, 178–9; *see also*
    associative relations; combinatory
    relations; signifiers; substitutive
    relations; syntagmatic relations
Sayer, D. 3, 19, 28

scepticism 227n20
Schleiermacher, F. 50
Schmitt, C. 113–14
science, philosophy of 24–7, 30
scientific knowledge 9
scientific method 18, 21
scientism 2–4, 210
sedimentation 116, 141; vs.
    reactivation 116
segregation 138, 141; vs. apartheid 141;
    see also South Africa
self-defeating prophecies 221n21
self-fulfilling prophecies 221n21
self-interest 181–2
self-interpretations 34–5, 36–7, 41, 91–2,
    224n6; critique of positivism and 51–5;
    inner states and 98; interpretation of 60,
    67, 70–1; vs. logics 157–62; social
    structures and 102; *see also* Bevir;
    Rhodes; Taylor; Winch; Wittgenstein
sexuality 42, 44–7, 222–3
Shapiro, I. 20, 84, 211, 219n6
signifiers 130–1, 143, 152, 184
signifying ontology 144
situated agency 77, 80
situational analysis 37–8, 222n23
Skinner, Q. 187, 192, 207
social, the 104, 108, 113–17; vs. the
    political 104–5, 108, 112–17
social analysis 153
social antagonism 42, 57, 113, 116, 147,
    165, 224n6; *see also* antagonism; conflict;
    contestation; struggle
social change 62, 145
social dimension 112, 121
social identities 5
social logics 15, 96, 106, 133, 135–40,
    143–5, 153, 154, 157, 159–60, 162–3,
    171–2, 176–7, 185–7, 195–6, 213;
    see also fantasmatic logics; logics;
    political logics
social mechanisms 83–4
social movements 56, 74
social objectivity 10
social phenomena, law-like explanations
    of 3
social practices 104–10; dimensions of 14,
    121–2, 130; inertia of 145; relationship
    between fantasmatic logics and 145–7;
    social reality 117; misrecognition of
    117–18; regimes and 120–7; social
    practices and 120–7
social relations 42, 104–5, 109–13, 120,
    143, 225n13

social roles 109

social sciences: crisis in 2; problem of prediction in 20–4

social space 105, 113, 143

social structures 5, 29, 78–9, 102, 121

social systems 105, 114

social theory, value-free 8–9

sociological investigation 53–4

socio-political reality 110–13

Socrates 236n18

South Africa 20, 138–9, 141–3, 149–53, 203, 231–2

South East Asian financial crisis 20

Spicer, A. 146

Stace, W.T. 100

state 10, 61, 114, 121, 125–6, 137, 168, 173–4, 229n1

Staten, H. 67

statistical methods 18

Stavrakakis, Y. 147, 148

Steinmetz, G. 216n1

strong evaluation 224n7

structuralism 5–7, 99, 128

structural linguistics 42

structuration 105, 124

structure 30, 78–9, 129, 160, 160–1; incomplete or lacking 11, 14, 79, 101, 110, 130, 131, 147, 214

struggle: hegemonic 59, 130–1, 195–6; political 5, 130–1; social 5

Study of Politics, The (Duverger) 108

subject 117–19, 124, 128–32, 139, 143, 145–7, 151–4, 159, 163, 183–4; incomplete or lacking 122, 127; *see also* agency; subjectivity

subject-independence 96–7

subjective meanings 58

subjectivity 5, 10, 73, 74–8, 119–20, 127–32, 197, 231

subordination 115, 120, 193, 231n10, 233n1

substitutive relations 106, 144; *see also* associative relations; combinatory relations; syntagmatic relations

subsumption 232n1; vs. articulation 161; formal 232n1; problem of 16, 94, 161, 165–6, 178, 188, 207, 210–11, 232–3; real 232–3n1

subsumptive scope 188

super immanentism 74

symbolic order 11, 14, 82, 119, 127, 130–1, 143, 162; *see also* Lacan; lack; Other; void

symptoms 107

syntagmatic relations 106, 143–4; *see also* associative relations; combinatory relations; substitutive relations

systems: political 217n6; social 105, 114; sub- 114; *see also* Easton; state

systematicity 21

Taylor, C. 50, 52–9, 65, 71–4, 80, 156, 179, 190, 211, 223n3, 224n6, 225n9; *see also* common meanings; evaluation; inter-subjective meanings; hermeneutics; contextualized self-interpretations

temporal asymmetry 92

tendencies 135

testing 3, 12, 14, 19, 21, 24, 27, 28–9, 31–2, 35–6, 38–9, 43, 59, 165, 202, 206, 222; *see also* empirical testing; theory testing

Tetlock, P.E. 20

Thatcherite politics 123, 137, 150, 173–4, 177, 193, 233n4, 235n12

theoretical approaches, integration of 1–2

theoretical reason 8, 9

theory construction 27, 34, 38, 41–7

theory of hegemony 4, 6–7, 42, 121, 126, 152, 203, 236n18

theory testing 28

thick description 63, 166, 201

Tilly, C. 20, 216n5, 227n1

Topper, K. 32, 182, 216n2, 219n7

Torfing, J. 6

tradition 61, 75

traditional theory 9

transcendence 82, 124; vs. immanence 82

transformation 5, 15, 34, 39, 103, 115, 127, 133, 144, 152

transgression 107

transitivity 33

trickle-down policies 218n5

Trowler, P. 170, 195

truth 190

truth value 71

Tully, James 39, 65, 207, 222

two-party system 37

type A mechanisms 87–8, 101; *see also* Elster; mechanisms

type B mechanisms 87–8, 101; *see also* Elster; mechanisms

underdetermination thesis 66–7; vs. overdetermination of rules 66

understanding 132, 139–40, 143, 145, 159–60, 165–8, 172, 188, 191, 194–5, 223–4
United Democratic Front (UDF) 143
universalism 166
universality 21, 90–1, 94, 207, 233n1
universal laws 21–2, 35, 91, 164, 166, 236n18
universal reason 10
universal rights 10
universal subsumption 40–1
university system, UK 168–71, 171–7, 193–4, 199–201, 208, 233–5

validation criteria 65–6, 71
value-free social theory 8–9
values 9, 54, 71–2, 81, 94, 124, 151, 191, 193, 195, 198, 215, 234n10
verification 20, 21, 190, 201, 225n10
vindication, logics of 225
void 129, 199; in the subject 146; in symbolic order 82, 119; *see also* lack; incomplete structure or order
voting 52

Walzer, M. 156
Weber, M. 8–9, 51, 217–18, 223n3
webs of belief 61–2
welfare state 173
White, S. 18
Willmott, H. 195, 233n4
Winch, P. 50–5, 58, 65–71, 80, 81, 137, 205, 207, 223–4, 223n3, 225–6, 225n13; *see also* hermeneutics; meanings; rules
wishful thinking 95–6, 97
Wittgenstein, L. 51, 66–8, 74, 134–5, 139–40, 184–6, 189, 205, 223n3, 226n15; *see also* language games; rules
working class 42, 203, 229n2
world order 126
Worthington, F. 170

Young, O. 126

Zac, L. 111
Žižek, S. 107, 146–7, 152, 186, 208, 231; *see also* enjoyment; subject

Printed in Great Britain
by Amazon